INTERNATIONAL ASSET SECURITISATION

ALSO IN THIS SERIES:

Banks: Fraud and Crime
by Joseph J. Norton and contributors
(1994)

Banks, Liability and Risk
SECOND EDITION
by Ross Cranston and contributors
(1995)

Bills of Exchange and Bankers' Documentary Credits
SECOND EDITION
by William Hedley
(1994)

EC Banking Directives
by Julian Maitland-Walker
(1994)

The Single Market and the Law of Banking
SECOND EDITION
by Ross Cranston and contributors
(1995)

Cross-Border Electronic Banking
by Joseph J. Norton and contributors
(1995)

Environmental Liability for Banks
by Joseph J. Norton and contributors
(1995)

INTERNATIONAL ASSET SECURITISATION

EDITED BY

JOSEPH J. NORTON,
PAUL R. SPELLMAN
AND
MITCHELL S. DUPLER

PUBLISHED JOINTLY WITH
THE INSTITUTE OF INTERNATIONAL BANKING, FINANCE AND DEVELOPMENT LAW AT THE CENTRE FOR COMMERCIAL LAW STUDIES AND IN ASSOCIATION WITH THE SCHOOL OF LAW, S.M.U., DALLAS, TEXAS.

LLP

LONDON NEW YORK HAMBURG HONG KONG
LLOYD'S OF LONDON PRESS LTD
1995

Lloyd's of London Press Ltd
Legal & Business Publishing Division
27 Swinton Street
London WC1X 9NW
Great Britain

USA AND CANADA
Lloyd's of London Press Inc
Suite 308, 611 Broadway
New York, NY 10012, USA

GERMANY
Lloyd's of London Press GmbH
59 Ehrenbergstrasse, 22767 Hamburg
Germany

SOUTH-EAST ASIA
Lloyd's of London Press (Far East) Ltd
Room 1101, Hollywood Centre
233 Hollywood Road
Hong Kong

British Library Cataloguing in Publication Data

A catalogue record
for this book is available
from the British Library

ISBN 1-85044-854-X

Text set 10 on 12 pt Sabon by
Mendip Communications Ltd
Frome, Somerset
Printed in Great Britain by
WBC Print Ltd
Bridgend, Mid-Glamorgan

PREFACE

This volume, a new addition to the Lloyd's of London Press banking and financial law series, concerns the international dimensions of asset securitisation. In a simplistic sense, securitisation is the repackaging of cash flows into securities, finding its genesis in the early repackaging of mortgages in the United States and in various domestic and international loan participation arrangements. However, more significantly, asset securitisation, both in terms of monetary volume and diversity and sophistication of techniques, has become an increasingly important financial technique and risk diversifier for financial institutions on a world-wide basis.

Growing in usage in the United States in the mid-1980s, asset securitisation has now found its way into a number of the European markets (e.g. U.K., France, Germany, Italy, and Switzerland). But, securitisation is now global, covering virtually every continent, and serving as a financial vehicle (and "bridge" between money and capital markets) in both developed and developing economies, as well as in transitioning economies.

This volume addresses various financial, accounting and legal considerations involved with asset securitisation, with primary emphasis on the United States and United Kingdom (as these two jurisdictions currently have the greatest experience with this financial technique). This volume also addresses securitisation in other jurisdictions, that is, in France, Germany, Argentina, Japan and Switzerland. It is hoped that in future editions, this volume will be expanded to cover other jurisdictions utilising securitisation.

Because securitisation was first developed in the United States, offerings in other jurisdictions have incorporated many techniques used there. U.S. structures are expected to continue to provide a preview (albeit an imprecise preview in light of the different legal, accounting, tax and regulatory regimes), of non-U.S. structures. From the U.S. perspective, the globalisation of offerings of securities backed by both U.S. and non-U.S. assets requires an understanding of European, Asian and Latin American markets and the structural differences among the various asset-backed securities traded in such markets.

The editors believe that this volume should be of special value to all major financial institutions, corporations, law firms and accounting firms worldwide.

In putting together this volume, the editors have been privileged to have worked in conjunction with the London Institute of International Banking, Finance and Development Law at the Centre for Commercial Law Studies at Queen Mary and Westfield College, University of London. Under the auspices of the Centre and its Director, Professor Ian Fletcher, the editors have been able to assemble written analyses and views of many of the leading world experts on asset securitisation.

In addition to expressing their sincere thanks to the Centre and to Professor Fletcher, the editors also express thanks to the co-operating institution of the SMU School of Law and its Dean, C. Paul Rogers III. A special thanks is made to the New York law firm of Cleary, Gottlieb, Steen & Hamilton and to the London law firm of Slaughter and May. Further special thanks are expressed to the Dallas law firms of Haynes & Boone, LLP and Jenkens & Gilchrist, P.C., which have provided invaluable support for the production of this volume.

We also express our appreciation to the publishers, Lloyd's of London Press.

The Centre for Commercial Law Studies hopes that this volume (and future editions) will prove to be a quality publication in and meaningful addition to the Lloyd's of London Press distinguished series on banking and finance law.*

March 1, 1995

JOSEPH J. NORTON
MITCHELL S. DUPLER
PAUL R. SPELLMAN

* Messrs Norton and Spellman had published an earlier treatise on *Asset Securitization: International Financial and Legal Perspectives* (London: Blackwell Finance, 1991), which provided a working basis for this expanded, revised and updated "second generation" publication.

PUBLISHER'S STYLE NOTE

The publishers recognised that the preferred English spelling style may vary from country to country. Accordingly, with respect to words that can be spelled with either an "s" or a "z", such as "securitisation", the formal title spelling for this volume is with the "s" (i.e. U.K. preference), though within the various chapters flexibility has been permitted. The publisher and editors recognise that, in the investment and legal fields in the U.S. the "z" version is commonly used.

Also, as the chapter authors come from different jurisdictions, flexibility as to citations has been permitted provided consistency is maintained within each chapter.

The editors and publisher would like to point out that the use of the masculine pronoun "he" is not gender specific.

CONTENTS

CONTRIBUTORS

RUPERT BEAUMONT: Partner, Slaughter and May, London

ROBERT BORDEAUX-GROULT: Partner, Cleary, Gottlieb, Steen & Hamilton, Paris

DIEGO C. BUNGE: Partner, Bunge & Asociados, Buenos Aires

MITCHELL S. DUPLER: Partner, Cleary, Gottlieb, Steen & Hamilton, Washington D.C.

STEPHEN M. EDGE: Partner, Slaughter and May, London

KENNETH N. ELMGREN: Director of Asset Securitisation, NationsBanc Capital Markets, Inc., Dallas, Texas

GRAHAM IVERSEN: Assistant Solicitor, Slaughter and May, London

MARKUS J. KROLL: Partner, Altenburger & Partners, Zürich

HIROSHI MAEDA: Partner, Mitsui, Yasuda, Wani & Maeda, Tokyo

KAYOKO NAITO: Partner, Mitsui, Yasuda, Wani & Maeda, Tokyo

DAVID Z. NIRENBERG: Partner, Orrick, Herrington & Sutcliffe, New York City

JOSEPH J. NORTON: Sir John Lubbock Professor of Banking Law, Centre for Commercial Law Studies, London and School of Law, Southern Methodist University, Dallas, Texas

JAMES M. PEASLEE: Partner, Cleary, Gottlieb, Steen & Hamilton, New York City

JIM ROUNDTREE: Senior Manager, Ernst & Young, Dallas, Texas

PATRICK C. SARGENT: Partner, Andrews & Kurth L.L.P., Dallas, Texas

PAUL R. SPELLMAN: Partner and Head of Asset Securitisation Practice Group, Haynes & Boone, Dallas, Texas

PAUL G. TAYLOR: Managing Director, Duff & Phelps Credit Rating Co., London

CHRISTOF VON DRYANDER: Partner, Cleary, Gottlieb, Steen & Hamilton, Frankfurt

LAWRENCE WILDE : Associate, Stikeman, Elliott, Toronto

TABLE OF CASES

SWITZERLAND

UNITED KINGDOM

UNITED STATES

TABLE OF LEGISLATION

*Page numbers printed in **bold** indicate where text is quoted*

GERMANY

MEXICO

PANAMA

JAPAN

SWITZERLAND

CHAPTER 1

AN OVERVIEW OF SECURITIZATION

1.1 INTRODUCTION

Asset securitization is the process of converting receivables[1] and other assets that are not readily marketable into securities that can be placed and traded in the capital markets. Securitization allows an investor to rely primarily on the creditworthiness and predictability of an issuer's receivable cashflow rather than on the originator's own financial strength.

A securitization relies on collateral and structure to achieve creditworthiness independent of the company originating the receivables. In the U.S. this is accomplished by selling the receivables to a special purpose vehicle ("SPV") or trust that is organized in such a way that the likelihood of its bankruptcy is considered to be remote. The pooling of many individual receivables into a security that has a single aggregate face amount, a single monthly payment date, a single interest rate, and a single monthly principal payment enables investors to take advantage of the yields associated with consumer or corporate lending without the risks and complexities.

Securitization has evolved in three primary investor markets, the public market, the private market and the commercial paper market, each with their own characteristic structures and each focusing initially on specific asset types. Each of these markets have experienced significant levels of growth.

The degree of predictability of cash flow is the key determinant as to which segment of the capital market is more readily accessed by the originator through securitization. Receivables characterized by payment streams with a high degree of predictability are most often securitized in the public or private medium-term debt markets, where investors look for maturities in the three to seven year range. Receivables with payment streams that are less certain as to timing of collections are most often securitized in the commercial paper markets, where it is common to utilize liquidity facilities to absorb some of the payment

1. In the text that follows, the term receivable shall be used to refer to loans and receivables including such things as mortgage loans, auto loans, credit card receivables, lease receivables, corporate trade receivables, and an ever growing list of asset types.

uncertainty. Increasingly, issuers are finding ways to access multiple investor markets with a given pool of assets simultaneously.

Table 1.1 ***New issuance volumes***

($Billions)	*1988*	*1989*	*1990*	*1991*	*1992*	*1993*	*1994*
Public ABS	16.0	25.5	45.0	50.8	50.9	61.7	74.8
Private ABS[1]	23.3	18.6	19.6	29.6	21.8	13.2	12.6
Structured CP[2]	12.0	22.0	40.0	49.0	63.0	65.0	71.0
Total	51.3	66.1	104.6	129.4	135.7	139.9	158.4

1. Includes privately placed mortgage and asset-backed securities (except 1993 and 1994, which is asset-backed only).
2. Includes multi-seller vehicle volumes of $10, $18, $31, $35, $35, $41, and $42 billion, respectively.

1.2 HISTORY OF SECURITIZATION

1.2.1 Origins

The process of isolating the financing of a specific business operation from a larger business operation by having the specific business support itself through internally generated cash flow is a very old concept. Corporations that have financed projects and trade credits (i.e. receivables) independent of their other business operations have not only reduced their own risk against the venture, but have promoted market efficiency by accessing a wider group of investors with cheaper sources of funds. Global exploration in the 1400s was financed as a project, with the investors' returns determined by the success of the venture. Financial institutions have diversified the risk associated with their lending operations through the sale of whole loans and participations for over a century. The financing of credit through factoring arrangements is a well established method of limiting and diversifying risk in some industries. While securitization also serves to isolate cash-producing portions of a business from other perhaps more risky portions of a larger business, it is a much more recent innovation and clearly distinguishable both in purpose and in method.

A project financing generally isolates an entire operating business, whereas in securitization one is concerned only with the isolation of financial assets. In "asset-based financing", the financing obtained is wholly secured by assets, but the collateral is not necessarily structurally isolated from the credit and liquidity of the business of which it forms a part, and the collateral often extends beyond financial assets. In a factoring arrangement, the purchaser of the receivables is usually obligated to collect the receivables, while in a securitization the originator of the receivables generally continues to service the receivables and collect them when they are due.

In a securitization, the originator usually bears the first loss on the receivables through subordination of additional assets and/or future cash flows or the provision of direct recourse. A securitization may involve payment obligations from hundreds of thousands of obligors as opposed to the returns on a single project or a handful of debtors. The yield to the investor in a securitization is set at a rate appropriate to the characteristics and the quality of the asset pool, and to the precision with which the originator is able to quantify the timing and likelihood of payment to the investor. In this sense, unlike its predecessors, securitization is a product of the computer revolution and the growing sophistication in the ability to monitor and track cash flows on highly diversified pools of financial obligations. These improvements in technology and communication have also allowed a broadening of the investor markets through the development of international financial markets, creating greater pricing efficiencies and further diversification of risk.

Securitization began as a result of the housing credit market collapse during the Great Depression, when Congress passed the National Housing Act of 1934. This act was designed in part to create a secondary market in mortgages, thus reducing the reliance of financial institutions on local core deposits. The first public structured financings came in 1970 when the newly created Government National Mortgage Association (Ginnie Mae) began publicly trading "pass-through" securities. In the early 1980s this secondary market for securitized mortgages began to expand significantly and in the mid 1980s the securitization market evolved to include non-mortgage receivables such as auto loans and credit cards. On a parallel track, commercial banks who had been purchasing pools of receivables from corporations on a non-recourse basis and funding them on their balance sheets, began financing these purchases through special purpose entities that access the commercial paper markets so as to reduce the risk-based capital costs associated with funding them.

Securitization transactions have evolved from two different structural and market perspectives. Those assets with highly predictable payment streams from a vast number of diversified obligors (primarily consumer obligations) have generally been securitized in the medium-term public markets. Those assets with very low losses, but often characterized by concentrations among obligors and therefore less predictable payment streams (primarily commercial obligations), have generally accessed the commercial paper market through single-seller or multi-seller special purpose corporations.[2] The lines between these two structures are increasingly converging, though, as technology is developed allowing issuers to access both the medium-term debt and commercial paper market simultaneously with a single pool of receivables.

1.2.2 Reasons for growth

Prior to the advent of securitization, receivable financing was primarily provided by bank funding. Banks funded their own origination of consumer

2. These commercial paper special corporations are often referred to as CP Conduits; they are

receivables through deposit taking, while non-financial corporations funded their commercial receivables through bank loans which in turn were funded by the banks through deposit taking. Securitization has proven to be a more efficient funding source than bank lending for a variety of reasons. Originators are able to access the capital markets directly, with securities which are liquid and tradeable, and whose pricing is determined by market forces, while greatly reducing the intermediary costs imposed by bank lending. Creditworthiness is confirmed by rating agencies who analyze credit risk for institutional and individual investors who have limited ability or appetite for assessing the credit risks associated with lending against receivables, but want to share in the higher credit quality and returns associated with such lending.

Commercial banks incur significant costs to pay shareholders (cost of capital), the Internal Revenue Service, the Federal Reserve System and the Federal Deposit Insurance Corporation, not to mention bank depositors who increasingly demand market rate returns on their deposits. These costs have been increasing with heightened regulatory pressure on financial institutions to maintain or increase capital ratios, in light of greater volatility in interest rates and credit conditions. The fact that consumers have become more sophisticated in requiring market rate returns on their bank deposits has increased banks' cost of funds but has also caused a dramatic growth in the mutual fund industry. The growth of the mutual fund industry has provided a large institutional investor appetite for securitizations, fueling the growth from the investor side.[3]

Securitization provides banks with a means to reduce the costs associated with holding assets on their balance sheet and allows them to generate fee-based income by acting as an intermediary to the capital markets. The savings can be used to reduce costs to borrowers and increase yields to investors.

Three key accounting determinations have been instrumental in the development of securitization: (a) issuance of Financial Accounting Standards Board ("FASB") Statement No. 77, "Reporting by Transferors for Transfers of Receivables With Recourse" in December 1983, (b) issuance of FASB Statement No. 91, "Accounting for non-Refundable Fees and Costs Associated with Originating or Acquiring Loans and Initial Direct Costs of Leases" in December 1986, and (c) issuance of FASB Statement No. 94, "Consolidation of All Majority-owned Subsidiaries" in October 1987.

FASB 77 allows originators to obtain sale treatment for their receivables under GAAP notwithstanding their retention of a recourse obligation. FASB 91, which requires that loan origination fees be deferred and amortized over the life

generally administered by a commercial bank which refers customers to the CP Conduit. The commercial bank administrator generally earns an administrative fee based on the outstandings on the program.

3. The Federal Reserve Board, the Federal Deposit Insurance Corporation, the Office of Thrift Supervision, and the Office of the Comptroller of the Currency have recently published (May 1994) a proposal to reduce the risk-weighting of AAA-rated senior securities purchased by a bank from 100% to 20%. This is likely to further fuel investor demand for securitizations as banks will now find such investments much more attractive.

of the related receivable, is inapplicable upon a securitized sale of receivables allowing more rapid recognition of fees. FASB 94 requires that all finance subsidiaries be fully consolidated for financial reporting purposes,[4] which eliminated this frequently used technique for off-balance-sheet treatment of receivables and related debt, thus increasing the desirability of off-balance-sheet financing via securitization.

Three amendments to the rules promulgated under the Securities Act of 1933 and the Investment Company Act of 1940 recently adopted by the SEC have also had a significant impact on the development of securitization:

(a) in 1992, the SEC allowed investment grade securitizations to qualify for shelf registration under Rule 415 promulgated under the Securities Act of 1933,
(b) also in 1992 the SEC promulgated Rule 3a-7 under the Investment Company Act of 1940 which made the public debt market more accessible to securitization by expanding the definition of eligible assets that may be sold via public offerings without resulting in the issuer being considered to be an investment company,
(c) in June 1991, the SEC adopted amendments to Rule 2(a)7 promulgated under the Investment Company Act of 1940 that essentially require a money market fund to limit its total investment in securities rated A2/P2 or below to 5 per cent of its assets and limit investment in such securities of any one issuer to 1 per cent of its assets.

These amendments increased the ease with which issuers could access the securitization markets, increased the range of assets available to be securitized, and increased investor appetite for the high quality rated securities created through securitization.[5]

1.2.3 Evolution of asset types

The securitization of consumer assets began with, and in sheer volume remains dominated by, residential mortgages[6] which have ideal cash-flow characteristics and benefit from a high degree of contract standardization. The development of the securitization market as a standard funding option across most industries, though, has been the result of a constantly expanding universe of securitizable non-mortgage asset types. The first non-mortgage public securitization occurred

4. Prior to the promulgation of FASB 94, an originator could consolidate a finance subsidiary utilizing the equity method, post FASB 94 the originator must consolidate assets and liabilities of both operations.

5. The U.S. Congress is currently considering two bills to encourage securitization by extending many of the benefits of SMMEA (the Secondary Mortgage Market Enhancement Act of 1984) to securitizations of commercial loans. Independently, the House of Representatives is considering a bill which proposes to extend the tax and legal benefits currently applied to mortgage securitization (i.e. REMIC) to non-mortgage securitizations.

6. The total new issue mortgage securitization market in 1994 was estimated to exceed $750 billion.

in March 1985 with a $192 million offering of lease-backed notes for Sperry Lease Finance. Automobile loans quickly followed with an issue for Home Federal Savings in August 1985 for $103 million. The first credit card securitization occurred about a year and a half later with a $200 million issue for Republic Bank in January 1987. Total new volume of public securitization in 1994 was over $75 billion.

The securitization of commercial receivables began with the establishment of the Commercial Industrial Trade-receivables Company ("CITICO") by Citibank in 1983. These special purpose corporations (often referred to as commercial paper conduits) are designed to purchase a diverse range of receivables from many different originators. At year end 1994, there were over 150 CP Conduits in place with total outstandings in excess of $70 billion.

The evolution of securitizable asset types has been largely dependent on the development of structures which are suitable to protect investors from risks unique to the asset types and to mitigate any impact from idiosyncrasies in the cash flows.

Consumer receivables include receivables with short-term (credit cards and home equity lines) and medium-term (auto, manufactured housing and boat loans) tenors. They are generally characterized by a highly diverse pool of obligors, relatively high but predictable default rates, and relatively slow payment rates which are to a large extent dependent on macro-economic factors. Credit cards receivables, for example, are characterized by relatively short and irregular paydown periods and relatively low individual loan balances. Credit cards are securitized utilizing a revolving purchase structure whereby principal payments are used to purchase new balances, effectively extending the life of the securities issued. At the end of a predetermined period, purchases cease and principal is paid to investors as received. Fluctuations in the aggregate pool balances during the life of the transaction are addressed by the creation of two separate classes of securities. A larger portion in a fixed amount is sold to investors while a smaller portion in a fluctuating amount is kept by the originator. In order to diminish the risks associated with constantly changing characteristics of a pool of credit card receivables, the transaction is subject to early payout events. If any such event were to occur, typically a decline in the credit quality of the assets or default by the pool's servicer, the revolving period would be terminated and principal amortization would begin. Auto loans, on the other hand, exhibit maturities of two to six years, with very stable prepayment patterns. Similar to automobile loans are manufactured housing and boat loans, which usually have 5–15 year terms but display somewhat greater seasonal and interest rate sensitive prepayment patterns. Auto, manufactured housing and boat loans are generally securitized utilizing a pass-through structure under which there is no reinvestment of principal collections; investors receive the cashflow on the receivables as it is received by the SPV.

1994 Issuance of ABS by Asset Type

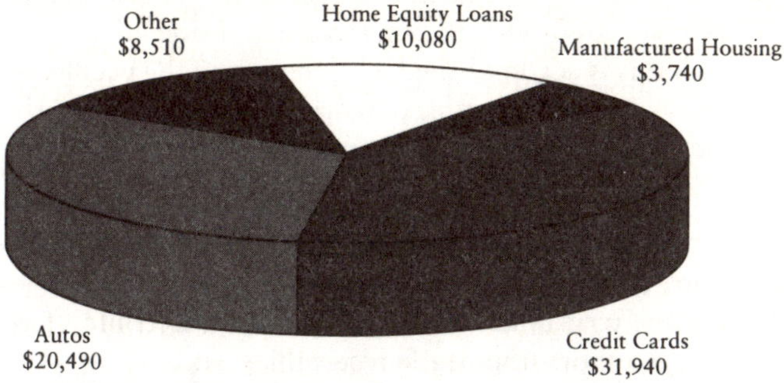

(Dollars in Millions)

1993 Issuance of ABS by Asset Type

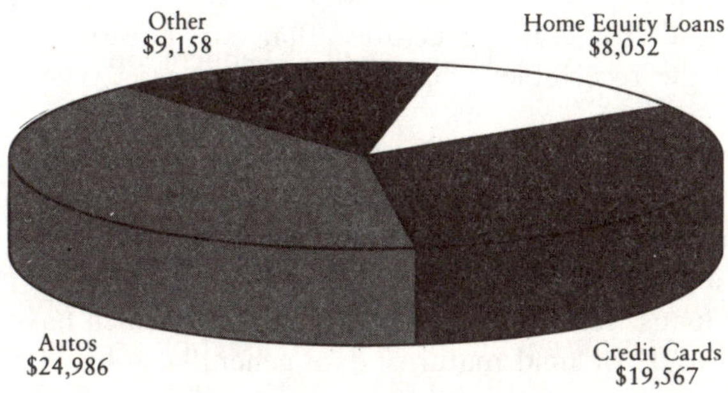

(Dollars in Millions)

Figure 1.1

Commercial receivables, which are generally characterized by 30–90 day trade obligations evidencing a payment obligation between a provider of goods or services and a corporate user of such goods or services, often have greater obligor concentrations, very low default rates and rapid turnover. As a result of the symbiotic relationship between a manufacturer and a user of goods though, credit determination is more focused on the status of the originator of the receivables. While historically these receivables have been securitized utilizing a commercial paper conduit, issuers are increasingly accessing the private and public medium-term markets utilizing structures similar to those developed for credit card receivables.

1.2.4 Structural developments

While the primary goal of any securitization structure is to isolate the receivables from any risks associated with the financial condition of the originator, the method by which this is accomplished is a function of the peculiar nature of the receivables to be securitized, the type of market access desired by the originator, and any specific regulatory issues which must be addressed.

The three key distinctions that dictate structure are:

(a) the type and term of the funding desired to be accessed by the originator,
(b) the type and term of the receivables (installment contract, revolving line of credit, or short-term trade receivable), and
(c) the type of issuer (regulated financial institution or a non-regulated corporation).

As discussed above, the two primary markets to be accessed via securitization are the commercial paper market and the medium-term debt market. That being said, securitization structures have undergone substantial evolution since the inception of securitization. Increasingly, the above distinctions are less important as originators and bankers find ways to access multiple markets simultaneously and to craft structures that so effectively offset any idiosyncrasies of the receivables' characteristics that asset type is much less important.

Basic structures have been developed for specific asset types. Installment contracts, such as automobile, manufactured housing and boat loans, which have defined amortization schedules and fixed final-maturity dates, for example, generally utilize a pass-through structure with certificates sold out of a grantor trust. Revolving loans, such as credit card receivables, which have no specific amortization schedule or final maturity date generally utilize a pay-through structure issued out of an owner trust or a special-purpose corporation, that provides for revolving purchases over a pre-determined period of time. Trade receivables, which are much less homogenous as an asset class, have generally utilized asset-backed commercial paper issued out of a special purpose corporation.

The different structures utilized in securitization can best be described in terms of the type of securities issued. The structure often drives the accounting and regulatory treatment of the transaction for both the issuer and the investor. Securitization can be categorized in the following general structure types:

(1) A pass-through transaction usually refers to the issuance of private or public asset-backed certificates from a trust. The certificates represent an equity-like interest in the trust and thus an undivided fractional interest in the pool of receivables owned by the trust. The trust is usually structured as a non-taxable grantor trust. In order to ensure grantor trust status, the trustee should not have the power to purchase

new receivables or (except for permitted substitution for defective receivables during an initial period) substitute receivables, nor should the trustee have the power to reinvest moneys held by the trust. As a result, in pass-through structures, the distribution of payments to holders of securities issued by the trust will typically correspond to the collection schedule of the receivables. In addition, the trust can issue only one class of beneficial interests without jeopardizing grantor trust status; although two classes are permitted where the sole distinction between the classes is that payments with respect to one class are subordinate to payments with respect to the other.

(2) A pay-through transaction usually refers to the private or public issuance of asset-backed bonds from a special purpose corporation or an owner trust. In a pay-through transaction, the SPV will not qualify as a non-taxable grantor trust, because the SPV is obligated to manage cash flows to assure that its debt securities will be paid at their scheduled maturity. To avoid separate taxation of the SPV in a pay-through transaction, the SPV is usually structured as a single-purpose subsidiary of the originator, so as to qualify as a partnership for tax purposes. If the SPV is a subsidiary with which the originator files consolidated tax returns, any tax liability of the SPV can be offset by losses of the originator or other members of the consolidated group. Similar to collateralized mortgage obligations ("CMOs"), pay-through asset-backed transactions are able to utilize multiple tranches with different maturities.

(3) An asset-backed commercial paper transaction refers to the sale of receivables to a special-purpose corporation which in turn issues commercial paper to finance the purchase. Proceeds from the issuance of the commercial paper finance the purchase of receivables. The commercial paper is supported by the cash flow from the receivables, the issuance of new collateralized commercial paper or from borrowings under a liquidity facility. Asset-backed commercial paper may be issued out of a special-purpose corporation that has been established for a single originator or one that is purchasing receivables from many different originators (i.e. a commercial paper conduit). The market is greatly dominated by the latter.

(4) A master trust transaction generally refers to a transaction where the issuer has sold a pool of receivables to an SPV, usually a trust, that has the capability to access multiple-investor markets simultaneously. Often, the master trust, in separate series, will issue a medium-term pay-through security as well as a pay-through security structured so as to enable it to be purchased by a commercial paper conduit which issues asset-backed commercial paper. The series are all supported by fractional shares in a common pool of receivables. A master trust, by its nature, is obligated to manage cash flows among the various series and

therefore does not qualify as a non-taxable grantor trust but must instead be structured so as to result in the securities issued by the master trust being considered debt of the originator for income tax purposes or must be structured with a partnership fallback. An originator will typically access the public markets for a term issuance and use the commercial paper markets to fund portfolio growth and/or seasonality.

1.2.5 Companies/receivables well suited for securitization

The range of companies and the type of receivables which are good candidates for securitization has expanded dramatically since the inception of securitization.

1994 Top Ten ABS Issuers

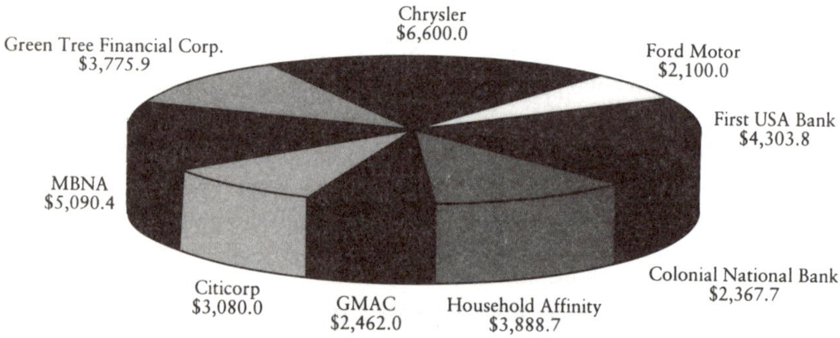

(Dollars in Millions)

1993 Top Ten ABS Issuers

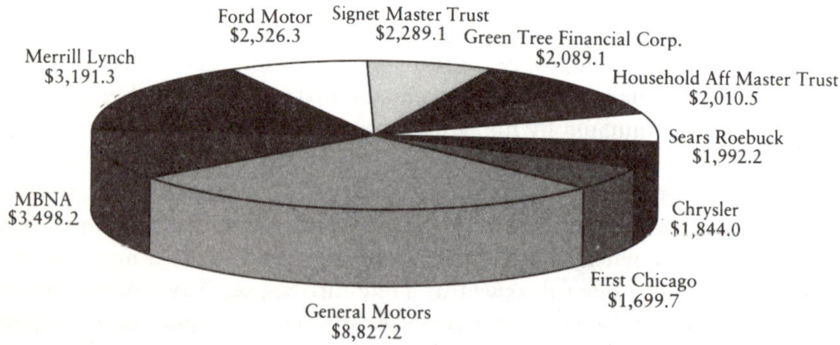

(Dollars in Millions)

Figure 1.2

As a general matter, ideal receivables characteristics for a securitization include:

(i) predictable cash flows,
(ii) predictable and consistently low delinquency, default, and dilution experience,
(iii) credit quality of the receivables that is higher than the originator's own credit quality,
(iv) many demographically and geographically diverse obligors,
(v) ability to perfect a security interest in the receivables cash flows and/or the underlying collateral,
(vi) receivables that represent products or services that have been delivered or performed,
(vii) underlying collateral that has a high liquidation value and utility to the obligors and,
(viii) sale not prohibited by any existing agreements.

A public securitization via a medium-term pass-through or pay-through would also look for asset characteristics such as

(i) total amortization of principal prior to maturity (i.e. no final balloon), and
(ii) an average life of more than one year.

The ideal company characteristics for a securitization include

(i) a financially stable originator and servicer, and
(ii) a company with standardized and centralized servicing.

1.3 ADVANTAGES OF SECURITIZATION

1.3.1 Attractive/reliable funding source

A securitization transaction transforms assets into highly rated securities. As a result it provides companies with an additional, reliable source of funding at a relatively stable cost that is generally attractive to a company when viewed on either a debt or combined debt and equity basis. Securitization allows investors to purchase an issuer's securities based primarily on the credit quality of the underlying assets, when these same investors may not be interested in a conventional debt obligation of the same originator. Since investors are analyzing their credit based primarily on the stength of the receivables, adverse conditions experienced by the originator which do not affect the originator's ability to service the receivables should not affect the program's overall cost or the originator's ability to access investors. This mitigates the impact on the originator's funding costs of market volatility associated with investor perception of industry dynamics or actions of management which have no impact on the pool of receivables.

1.3.2 Ratio improvement

Often, one of the most important objectives of a securitization is to qualify as a sale of assets under the provisions of Generally Accepted Accounting Principles ("GAAP"). As a result, most securitization transactions are structured to qualify as a sale for GAAP under FASB 77 (see section 1.4.5 below). While in most instances a securitization does not change the amount of capital held as reserves by the originator against the expected credit losses on a pool of receivables, the securitization does remove the receivables and their associated liabilities from the originator's balance sheet.

Sale treatment under GAAP may result in several advantages for the originator. First, an originator's financial ratios (such as debt to equity ratio) are likely to be improved; which may allow an originator to satisfy covenants with lenders that otherwise might be under pressure. Even more significantly, removal of the assets and associated debt from an originator's balance sheet raises the possibility that the originator may be able to realize significant equity cost savings equal to the amount of equity that would normally be held against the securitized receivables.[7]

A sale of receivables with recourse also affects the originator's income statement. In the case of receivables which have interest yields in excess of the securitization funding costs, a securitization will accelerate the recognition of income at the time of sale. FASB 77 states that the difference between the sales price (adjusted for expected net credit losses, late payment costs, and the estimated effect of prepayments) and the net receivables amount (which amount is generally referred to as excess servicing) shall be recognized as a gain or loss at the time of sale. In addition, while there is a reduction of receivables interest by the amount of the yield on the sold assets, servicing fee income increases causing an increase in net income. The combination of the increase in net income and the decrease in assets has a dramatic effect on return on assets (ROA). Return on equity is similarly impacted by the increase in net income and has a dramatic effect on ROA in the case where the originator uses the securitization proceeds to reduce debt.

1.3.3 Cost of capital reduction

The technology of securitization is nothing more than the quantification of risk and the maximization of an originator's asset base so as to obtain the lowest

7. Analysts view the impact of securitization on leverage in various ways. The Rating Agencies are formulating criteria that quantifies the amount of risk retained and the amount mitigated or transferred so as to determine the benefit of a securitization transaction on a company's leverage. See "Equity Considerations in Securitizations", *Standard & Poor's Credit Week* (May 22, 1995).

all-in cost of financing. Under FASB 77, a securitization, structured as a sale, requires no allocated equity as support. The loss reserves held by an originator against expected future losses are deemed sufficient to provide for the expected risk of the receivables; catastrophic risks have been transferred to the securitization investor. The amount of equity required by the market to be held against the receivables, pre-securitization, is therefore generally greatly in excess of what would need to be held against the receivables when viewed on a stand-alone basis. As a result, if equity requirements are conventionally viewed as a function of the balance sheet's debt/equity ratio, then no equity or only a fraction (related to the recourse provided) of that required by conventional debt financing is required to fund assets through a securitization. The effect on the all-in cost of capital, assuming any of a range of balance sheet debt/equity ratios and costs of equity can be dramatic.

Assuming that assets are funded by a combination of debt and equity, the true cost of capital is the weighted average cost of these two components: ([percentage of equity × cost of equity] + [percentage debt × cost of debt] = cost of capital). The cost of a securitization transaction with no recourse can be viewed as the cost of the transaction alone (i.e. the funding costs, underwriting costs, etc.), the cost of equity is already loaded in as the cost of enhancement. The break-even cost of equity is the maximum amount of pre-tax equity cost that allows the weighted average cost of capital with conventional funding to break even with a securitization issue.

1.3.4 Asset/liability matching

Securitizations supported by amortizing assets which pay principal to investors as it is received on the underlying assets result in perfect asset/liability matching. Substantial increases or decreases in prepayment behavior will not cause a mismatch with the asset funding. In addition, the ability to pay interest on a monthly basis, not semi-annually or annually as in conventional securities, provides the issuer with additional protection from reinvestment risk. Securitizations characterized by a revolving purchase of assets allow an originator to choose the maturity of the issued liabilities in such a way as to best manage interest rate exposure.

1.3.5 Minimal financial disclosure

Since securitization shifts the investor's credit analysis away from the originator of the receivables to the cashflow emanating from the receivables themselves, the amount of information required to be disclosed with regard to the originator is minimized. In addition to detailed information on the receivables, investors will be interested in information with regard to the originator's underwriting and servicing operations. Information with regard to the originator's broader business operations is generally less important to investors.

1.4 STRUCTURAL CRITERIA

1.4.1 Separating the source of payment from the originator

Securitization transactions commonly utilize a "bankruptcy remote" structure so as to isolate the investors from any financial impairment of the originator of the receivables. This is accomplished by requiring that

(a) the actual transfer of receivables from the originator to the SPV[8] cannot be interfered with (often referred to as creating a "true sale" of the receivables for bankruptcy purposes),
(b) whatever happens to the originator cannot affect the SPV (through assuring non-consolidation of the SPV with the originator), and
(c) the SPV does not itself have any financial obligations that could threaten its solvency (often referred to as making the SPV "bankruptcy remote").

In addition, in almost all securitization transactions, the trustee obtains a perfected security interest in the receivables on behalf of the investors in the event that sale treatment is challenged during bankruptcy of the originator.

There are several considerations in evaluating a true sale for bankruptcy purposes. These include

(a) the amount of recourse,
(b) the tax treatment,
(c) the ability to identify the sold assets, and
(d) the originator's treatment of the transaction as a sale or a loan.

An amount of recourse which is in excess of the amount of losses expected on the receivables pool may cause legal counsel to opine that the transaction constitutes a secured financing rather than a sale. Treatment of the transaction as a non-taxable transfer hinders the argument for a bankruptcy sale, but must be viewed in conjunction with the originator's overall consistent treatment of the transaction. Finally, the ability to identify the sold assets is a practical as well as principled argument for sale treatment.

Isolating the receivables from the risk of an originator's insolvency also requires that the SPV not be subject to consolidation with the originator in the event of the originator's insolvency. An SPV which is owned or controlled by the originator is generally limited in its ability to file a voluntary petition for bankruptcy against the SPV by (a) restrictive provisions in its charter or articles of incorporation, and (b) the requirement for two independent board members each of whom must approve such a filing. In many cases, the SPV is owned by an

8. The term SPV (Special Purpose Vehicle) is used to refer to any bankruptcy remote entity into which receivables are sold. This may include a special purpose corporation, a grantor trust, a Delaware business trust, etc.

independent third party such as a charitable institution which would have no incentive to place the SPV in bankruptcy.

Finally, assuring that investors are subject only to the risk of default on the receivables purchased by the SPV requires a restriction on the SPV incurring any liabilities which could impair its obligation to pay the securitization investors. Providers of services, liquidity or credit are generally required to agree to "no petition" covenants in which they agree to not file a bankruptcy petition against the SPV until one year after final payment of the securitization investors.

1.4.2 The FINCO structure

One of the most significant structural developments in the area of securitization has been the creation of the FINCO structure.[9] In the FINCO structure, the originator transfers receivables to a wholly owned bankruptcy remote subsidiary (SPV1) in part pursuant to a true sale and (to achieve the necessary level of overcollateralization) in part through a capital contribution. The contribution to capital should survive any fraudulent conveyance attack by the originator's trustee in bankruptcy because the subsidiary is wholly owned by the originator. The fact that SPV1 remains part of the originator's consolidated tax group for federal (not necessarily state, as state tax rules vary) tax purposes, the sale of receivables does not result in a taxable transfer. If SPV1 itself were to issue debt securities to investors, the debt would be required to be recorded on its balance sheet, which, pursuant to GAAP, must be consolidated with the originator's balance sheet. The originator could nonetheless achieve "off-balance-sheet" treatment by causing SPV1 to transfer its receivables to a separate and independent bankruptcy remote SPV (SPV2), in a manner structured to constitute a sale of the receivables for accounting purposes, but a loan secured by the receivables for tax purposes. SPV2 which is independent, then could issue debt securities to investors to fund the transfer of such receivables without affecting the liability side of the originator's balance sheet.

The result is effectively to isolate the transferred receivables from the risk of the originator's bankruptcy, thereby permitting the originator to obtain low-cost off-balance-sheet financing without the originator's having to recognize loss or gain for federal tax purposes. Further, any upside from collections of the receivables will be retained by SPV1, a wholly owned subsidiary of the originator.

1.4.3 Servicing requirements

The originator of receivables in a securitization almost always remains as servicer of the pooled receivables on behalf of the investors. The originator services the receivables by sending invoices or coupon books, collecting

9. The FINCO structure derives its name from the Financial Company or "FINCO" utilized to achieve the desired structure.

payments from obligors on the underlying loans, and taking steps as appropriate to enforce delinquencies and defaults. The servicer is paid a market-based fee out of the cash flow on the receivables. In the event of a default by the servicer in its responsibilities, the servicer may be replaced. In those instances where there is a question as to the servicer's ability to adequately service the receivables for the duration of a securitization transaction (as a result of financial weakness or otherwise), the transaction may provide for a back-up servicer who is contractually obligated to step-in should the original servicer need to be replaced.

1.4.4 Credit enhancement

In order to enhance the credit quality of the pool of assets it is usually necessary to provide a buffer against deterioration in portfolio performance. Credit enhancement can be internal to the transaction (cash flow driven) or external (provided by a third party or originator's guarantee). In addition, though not true enhancement, a key component of the credit quality of a securitization is often the structural protections built into a transaction that serve to greatly mitigate the risks to investors.[10]

- *Yield Spread (Excess Servicing)*: The interest rate on the receivables is often greater than the coupon on the securities, particularly in the case of consumer receivables. The difference between the two rates can be allocated to actual servicing costs and provision for losses, with the remainder being considered excess servicing. While this amount would normally revert to the originator as additional profit, it is available to make payments to investors in the event of higher than expected losses on the receivables.
- *Reserve Fund*: A cash reserve fund is created at the time of issuance to reimburse the SPV for losses. It is generally funded out of the yield spread on the receivables. A reserve fund is often used in combination with other methods of credit enhancement.
- *Subordination*: A second class of securities is created which is subordinated in payment of principal and interest to the senior class of securities. This subordinate class may be retained by the originator or sold in the market (with a lower credit rating and/or a higher level of enhancement than the senior class). A key advantage of subordination is that it eliminates the risk of a downgrade of the securitization caused by deterioration of a third-party credit provider such as a letter of credit bank or insurer.
- *Overcollateralization*: The face amount of the portfolio is greater than

10. Note that some of these forms of credit enhancement may be contradictory to the desired objectives of various structures. For example, the ability of banks to provide recourse is constrained by the requirements of sale treatment under Regulatory Accounting Principles.

the securities issued. The securitization will thus amortize more quickly, and a buffer is created against losses. When the security matures, any remaining assets revert to the originator.

- *Recourse*: This could be either an obligation of the issuer to reimburse the SPV for up to a stated maximum of losses or the ability of the trust to put back a certain amount of bad loans to the originator. This method enhances creditworthiness not only through access to the originator's resources, but also by giving the originator a strong incentive to service the portfolio in a diligent manner.
- *Letter of Credit*: A highly rated bank issues a letter of credit equal to a maximum amount of credit support being provided. The letter of credit provider agrees to reimburse the SPV for the amount of receivables charged off up to the amount specified in the letter of credit. Upon usage the liability on the letter of credit decreases unless subsequently reimbursed.
- *Surety Bond*: An insurance company agrees to reimburse the SPV for losses up to a stated amount. The issuer of the bond looks to an initial premium or other support to cover credit losses.
- *Structural Credit Enhancement*: Various features can be created within the structure to raise the credit quality of the securities issued. For example, securitizations of credit card and trade receivables typically contain payout events that cause early amortization if the credit quality of the assets or the performance of the servicer deteriorates significantly.

1.4.5 GAAP accounting treatment

FASB Statement No. 77 allows receivables transferred with recourse to be removed from an originator's balance sheet if the transfer

(a) surrenders control of the future economic benefit of the receivables (which generally means that the originator may not have an option to repurchase the receivables),[11]

(b) where the transferor can reasonably estimate the potential losses associated with any recourse obligations, and

(c) the transferee can only return receivables to the transferor pursuant to the recourse provisions.[12]

If a transfer with recourse meets the FASB 77 requirements and qualifies as a sale, then the originator must account for its recourse obligation in accordance

11. FASB 77 does allow the originator to purchase the receivables when there is a small amount remaining (a clean-up call, generally set at 10% of the original pool amount) so as to assure economies of servicing costs.

12. The International Accounting Standards Committee (IASC) released in January 1994 a revised exposure draft on financial instruments (ED 48) which proposes to allow off-balance sheet treatment for a sale of receivables with recourse as long as recourse can be determined and is considered to be "insubstantial". Insubstantial is generally thought to be less than or equal to 5%.

with FASB Statement No. 5 which essentially requires the originator to reserve against the total amount of the reasonably expected loss resulting from the recourse provision when originally acquiring the receivable and reviewing and adjusting such reserve at the time of sale if appropriate.

While the originator can generally have no options or obligations to repurchase non-delinquent receivables, sale treatment is allowed even though it is probable that the originator will make future payments to the buyer for credit losses, the effects of prepayments, or changes in interest rates, as long as the credit losses and the effects of prepayments can be reasonably estimated. The amount and form of recourse can vary from a small percentage of the receivables balance to, theoretically, 100 per cent and from an agreement to cover defaults on the receivables to guaranteeing a specified return or yield during the term of the securitization.

The present value of the excess servicing (adjusted to reflect any expected prepayments on the receivables) is booked as a gain on sale, where excess servicing is defined as the spread of the implicit rate of return on the collateral net of funding costs and a basic servicing fee. The servicing fee includes the actual cost of staying in the servicing business, plus a fair return over the explicit rate to investors on the securitization. Excess servicing received over the life of the receivable pool is then applied to amortize the gain booked at the point of sale. If the receivables are sold with servicing retained and the stated servicing fee differs from a normal servicing fee, the sales price shall be increased by the present value of excess servicing fees. The estimated recourse obligation is recorded as a direct liability on the transferor's book's and, in the case of banks, attracts risk-based capital treatment accordingly.[13]

1.4.6 RAP accounting treatment

GAAP accounting is relevant to most originators of receivables. Company annual reports and many other financial statements are prepared using GAAP accounting. Most banks, though, are more concerned with Regulatory Accounting Principles ("RAP"). While the sale of receivables through a securitization is often an effective method for a bank to reduce its risk-based capital requirements, banks are subject to more stringent requirements regarding transfers of receivables than non-financial corporations.

RAP accounting, as specified in the instructions for the Commercial Bank Reports of Condition and Income (the Call Report Instructions) published by the Federal Financial Institutions Examination Council (FFIEC), provides that transfers of receivables may be reported as sales only if the transferor (a) retains no risk of loss resulting from any cause from the assets transferred, and (b) has no obligation to any party for the payment of principal or interest for any cause on the receivables transferred. Failure to comply with these provisions result in

13. FASB is widely expected to adopt a new approach to the reporting by originators of retained

the transfer being accounted for as a secured financing which in turn causes the assets to remain on the balance sheet and the securitization to be considered a debt of the selling company.[14] Note that provisions permitting the return of assets to the transferor as a result of a breach in certain basic warranties (i.e. transferor's representations, incomplete documentation, or fraud) would not preclude sale treatment.

A financial institution may subordinate its interest in the excess yield on the receivables by depositing the interest rate or finance charges in excess of the interest rate payable on the securitized debt into a collateral account maintained for the benefit of the investors (this account is commonly referred to as a "spread account").

1.4.7 Regulatory capital treatment

A regulated financial institution that is providing credit enhancement or liquidity to a securitization may also be subject to additional capital requirements. These items, though off-balance sheet, are included in measuring the risk-weighted-asset ratio. The amount of capital required is usually proportional to the face amount of the enhancement or liquidity provided multiplied by a "conversion factor".

Direct credit substitutes are assigned a 100 per cent conversion factor (i.e. maximum risk-based capital must be maintained against them). These include guarantees, letters of credit, and other equivalent irrevocable undertakings that guarantee repayment. Transaction-related contingencies with original maturities exceeding one year are assigned a 50 per cent conversion factor. These include loan commitments, bid bonds, other types of commitments (such as commitments to purchase loans, securities, or other assets or to participate in loans), performance letters of credit, performance bonds, and warranties. Unused portions of such transaction-related contingencies with original maturities of one year or less (or that are unconditionally cancelable at any time, provided a separate credit decision is made before each drawing under the facility) are assigned a zero per cent conversion factor.

1.4.8 Tax treatment

There are three key tax issues in securitization:

(a) whether the transfer of receivables from the originator to the SPV will require the originator to recognize a gain or loss,
(b) the degree to which the SPV will be subject to tax,

---

seller's interests. Under this approach, called the components paradigm, the seller's interest would be treated as a newly acquired financial interest rather than a retained seller's interest.

14. In March of 1995, the Federal Reserve Board amended its risk-based capital guidelines to reduce the amount of capital required to be maintained by a bank in connection with "low-level" recourse to only the amount of recourse retained not the amount of assets sold.

(c) the tax treatment of the securitization investors.[15]

Characterization of a transfer of receivables as a sale or secured loan for tax purposes is determined by whether there has been an effective shift of the benefits and burdens of ownership of the receivables. The tax courts have held both the form and intent of the parties to be important factors in determining sale characteristics. However, the true economic indicators of ownership must complement and not contradict the form. The general principle expressed in the case law is that the originator must transfer to the purchaser the "substantial incidents of ownership" of the assets. This includes the relevant risks and benefits of the ownership of the assets. These risks and benefits fall primarily into four categories: (1) credit risk, (2) risk of changes in value, (3) interest rate risk, and (4) prepayment or reinvestment risk.

First, credit risk is the risk least often transferred to investors, due to investors' concern about the assurance of repayment of their investment. However long standing tax treatment recognizes that receivables are often sold "with recourse" and the IRS agrees that this factor alone will not jeopardize sale treatment.

Second, the risk of changes in the fair market value of the assets can be borne by the investors only if they are given the right to dispose of their beneficial interests. This right is usually granted in the underlying documents. On the other hand, the right of the originator to call the securities and recover the assets when they have paid down to a small fraction (usually 10 per cent) of their size on transfer, has been held not to be inconsistent with sale treatment.

Third, payment characteristics of the security that differ from the characteristics of the underlying assets that cause the originator to be subject to fluctuations in market rates of interest indicate a debt, rather than a sale. This can occur, for example, when the assets bear a fixed rate of interest but a floating rate measured by an independent index is "passed through" to investors.

In the absence of the third factor, the fourth is most often looked to for a determination of pass-through status. As owners, the investors should bear the risk of reinvesting principal cash flows (prepayment or reinvestment risk) through the matching of the assets' payment characteristics to those of the pass-through security. In theory, purchasers in the aggregate should step into the shoes of the originator with respect to the originator's rights under the assets.

An originator of assets recognizes a taxable gain or loss at the time of sale equal to the difference between the amount realized (the sale price) and the originator's adjusted basis in the assets. When the originator retains the servicing responsibilities on the receivables, it will receive monthly servicing compensation out of the receivable cash flows. In general, this servicing income

15. The Department of Treasury is currently reviewing proposed tax legislation that would facilitate securitization (referred to as FASIT or Financial Asset Securitization Investment Trust). This legislation would facilitate a variety of securitization transactions by eliminating tax law considerations, such as distinctions between debt and equity and between borrowings and dispositions.

is all ordinary income to the originator as it is received over time. If the servicing fee is determined to exceed "reasonable" compensation for the services rendered, though, the originator will be treated as having retained the "unreasonable" portion of the spread as a beneficial ownership interest in that portion of the interest payments.

1.4.9 Ratings agency perspective

Asset-backed securities virtually always incorporate some form of credit enhancement in order to raise the creditworthiness of the assets to an investment grade credit quality. To obtain a particular rating, both the quantity and the quality of any credit enhancement must be consistent with the sought-after rating category. To establish the quantity of credit enhancement, a rating agency examines the originator's underwriting standards, the concentration and creditworthiness of the underlying obligors, and the portfolio delinquency and net loss history. The rating agency also examines the transaction documents to determine the integrity of the structure. The originator typically prepares a presentation for the rating agencies describing the loan operation and the portfolio. The rating agencies generally seek historical data for five full years.

1.5 THE FUTURE

The securitization market has shown tremendous growth over the last decade. This growth has been characterized by a broadening of asset types and the development of an increasingly committed investor base. Whereas securitization was once viewed as an arcane funding source driven by accounting and tax considerations that had relevance only for originators with certain special funding requirements, it has evolved into a core funding source for many corporations and financial institutions. The size of the market has led to a high degree of scrutiny from bank and security market regulators, most of which are in the process of developing or modifying current laws so as to promote securitization. Securitization is developing in overseas markets as structures become more standardized and thus more easily exportable to other jurisdictions.

KENNETH N. ELMGREN

CHAPTER 2

U.S. STRUCTURING AND LEGAL ISSUES

2.1 INTRODUCTION

A "structured" financing connotes the issuance of securities backed by mortgages or other receivables, such as automobile loans, credit card receivables and equipment leases, where investors look to the assets themselves (and, often, to arrangements designed to ensure or enhance the performance of those assets) as the principal source of payment of the securities rather than to the credit of the securities issuer or the entity benefiting from the securitization of the assets. Mortgage-backed securities and other receivable-backed securities (collectively in this outline, "asset-backed securities") are structured either as equity-like instruments or as debt securities. The precise structure selected will depend on tax, accounting, regulatory, marketing and other considerations not within the scope of this outline. Pass-through and participation interests are the most common examples of the former. Pass-through certificates, which evidence undivided ownership interests in the underlying assets, are typically issued by a trust to which the entity that originated or acquired the assets (often referred to as the sponsor or depositor) conveys those assets. Asset-backed securities structured as debt instruments rely either on the cash flow generated by the collateral to meet periodic debt service payments (e.g., collateralized mortgage obligations) or on the market value of the assets serving as collateral to ensure that principal and accrued interest can be paid in full in the event of a default by the issuer (e.g., mortgage-backed bonds and credit card receivables-backed notes).

To protect investors against defaults by the obligors on the underlying mortgages or other receivables, additional credit support is often provided as part of the securities' structure. Credit support may take the form of overcollateralization of assets, creation of senior and subordinated interests in the assets, reserve funds, repurchase agreements, guaranties, letters of credit or various types of insurance.

Many of the legal and economic concepts discussed in this chapter relate broadly to asset-backed securities, but we will focus on the residential mortgage market. Because of its depth and relative uniformity, this was the first asset type successfully securitized in the United States.

2.2 WHY SECURITIZE?

To understand the present place of mortgage-backed securities in the United States we must return briefly to the system of mortgage finance that prevailed in the United States up until the mid-1970s. Mortgage finance in this period was in large part the result of a national policy to promote single-family home-ownership. The centrepiece of this policy was the 30-year, fixed-rate, level-payment mortgage, which enabled first-time homeowners to purchase a stand-alone home with a modest down payment.

The development of the 30-year mortgage was facilitated by a broad monetary, fiscal and tax policy, centered around American savings banks and savings and loan associations (commonly known as thrifts and akin to U.K. building societies). This policy attempted to promote both the supply of and demand for 30-year, fixed-rate mortgages. On the supply side, Federal regulations imposed a limit on the interest payable by financial institutions on their deposits. In return for freeing the lenders' cost of funds from market influence, Federal (and state) regulations limited the investment activities of thrift institutions—the key mortgage lender of that day—to the making of residential mortgages. The origination of home mortgages was further subsidized by Federal tax policy, which granted favorable tax treatment to thrifts based on the percentage of their assets invested in qualifying home mortgages. Thrifts were thus in part encouraged and in part required to reinvest their deposits in residential mortgages. On the demand side, homeowners were likewise encouraged to purchase single-family housing by tax laws that permitted the deduction of amounts paid as interest.

In practice, individual savings were invested with thrifts limited by lay to paying three to four per cent on their deposits. Thrifts in turn lent out their deposits in the form of mortgages bearing interest at rates of seven or eight per cent per annum. The spread between the amounts received on the thrifts' assets (the mortgages) and the amounts paid on its liabilities (its deposits), together with the favorable tax treatment afforded mortgage income, assured a constant supply of cheap mortgage capital.

The continued stability of this system depended on the regulatory limit imposed on the maximum rate of interest payable by thrifts, coupled with long-term anti-inflationary policies that made it possible for thrifts to attract sufficient deposits at rates less than the maximum rates permitted by law. This situation changed dramatically in the mid-1970s, when inflation and interest rates rose significantly and savings rushed from the thrift system's limit yields into newly-created money-market funds, which (unlike the thrifts) were not restricted by law as to the rate of interest they could offer their investors.

The withdrawal of thrift deposits led in the first instance to a liquidity crunch in the thrift industry and a corresponding increase in mortgage interest rates, as the deposit-based supply of mortgage capital shrank. In an attempt to restore balance to the system, Congress removed the restrictions on the maximum rate of interest that thrifts could pay on their deposits. Solving one problem created another. As a result of the mismatch between their assets and liabilities, thrifts were now required to pay money-market interest rates of, say, 12 per cent in order to attract additional deposits, while they continued to receive only six per cent on the mortgages they had originated in previous years. At the same time, homeowner demand slipped sharply as the cost of mortgage financing skyrocketed.

There were two principal responses to this crisis. The first was the development of adjustable-rate mortgages with interest rates linked to published indices, such as yields on U.S. Treasury Securities, which permitted thrifts to better match amounts received on newly originated mortgages with amounts then required to attract new depositors. The adjustable-rate mortgage has, however, never been fully accepted by American homeowners, especially in times of low interest rates, when homeowners prefer the protection fixed-rate mortgages provide against a possible interest rate upturn. The second response was the development in late 1983 of a new type of mortgage-backed security, the collateralized mortgage obligation (or CMO). The enormous success of the CMO—hundreds of billions of dollars of CMOs have been issued—is attributable to the fact that the CMO permitted lenders to continue to originate traditional 30-year, fixed rate mortgages, while at the same time locking in a positive spread, regardless of subsequent changes in interest rates.

More generally, the task was to develop a security backed by fixed-rate mortgages that could be priced at a profit based on the thrift's own cost of funds, which, by virtue of deregulation, were now determined by the capital markets. This security would, through private means, reestablish economic stability for both lenders and homeowners.

The industry had long sought to develop a security that could be sold in the capital markets at a positive spread over the thrift's capital-market-determined cost of funds. Traditional capital market investors—pension funds, insurance companies, commercial banks—had, however, never purchased mortgages in large volume; and for good reason. Raw mortgages suffer in a number of significant respects in comparison to traditional "bullet" maturity U.S. government bonds, which provide for periodic fixed instalments of interest and a lump sum payment of principal at stated maturity.

(a) *Credit Quality*: the first capital-market objection to investing in mortgages is the problem of credit quality. An investor who purchases a traditional corporate bond has available to him a wide variety of published materials analyzing the issuer's credit. A purchaser of raw mortgages would presumably want similar information as to the financial condition of the various mortgagors and the location and quality of the mortgaged properties. Capital-market investors were, and are, unwilling to undertake the expensive and time-consuming task of understanding the investment value of a pool of raw mortgage loans.

(b) *Servicing*: a second problem with owning a raw mortgage loan is the problem of servicing the loan. Every month, payments must be collected, deposited and transferred and delinquent payments must be pursued. At times, foreclosure is necessary. These burdens were a significant disincentive to direct investment in mortgages.

(c) *Transfer Costs*: a third barrier lies in the fact that mortgages and transfers of mortgages are subject to recordation, which often involves significant government fees and requires preparation of exacting documents at more than trivial cost.

(d) *Prepayment Risk*: the most important objection, however, to owning a pool of mortgage loans is the problem of prepayment risk. Almost all residential mortgages in the United States may be prepaid at the option of the home owner without penalty. In many States, consumer laws prohibit the origination of residential mortgage loans that require the payment of prepayment penalties. Unfortunately, from the perspective of the potential mortgage investor, home owners tend to prepay their mortgages at precisely the time the investor least wants to receive additional funds. Imagine the case of an investor faced with the choice of purchasing a 30-year Treasury bond bearing interest at 12 per cent or a pool of 14 per cent mortgages. If the investor had purchased the U.S. Treasury bond seven years ago, he would today still be receiving 12 per cent on the amount of his investment. If the investor had instead chosen to purchase the pool of 14 per cent mortgages, it is likely that the underlying home owners would have long since prepaid their mortgages at par. Our hypothetical mortgage investor would then have been faced with the unfortunate task of reinvesting those prepayments at today's much lower interest rates. The homeowner's prepayment option, and the mortgagee's corresponding lack of call protection, are probably sufficient, standing alone, to explain the relatively modest investment in mortgages made by traditional corporate-market investors.

The most basic mortgage backed security—a simple pass-through instrument representing ownership of a pool of mortgages—addressed the first three problems—credit quality, servicing and transfers. By pooling hundreds or thousands of loans, credit quality became a question of actuarial analysis. So long as the disclosure documents address the characteristics of the mortgages and the criteria under which they were made, i.e., underwriting standards, their credit quality can be effectively analyzed. Once loans are pooled, servicing can be handled economically by employing a servicer. Transfer costs are minimized because mortgage recordation fees and procedures do not apply to transfers of a mere certificate representing a fractional undivided interest in a pool of mortgages.

Yet prepayment risk remained. The CMO addressed that issue by permitting the risk of prepayment to be allocated among classes of securities. It is worth noting that the structure of securitization does nothing to change the underlying assets or their tendency to prepay—or not prepay. The risk is allocated.

This point leads to two "rules" of securitization—conservation of cash flow and conservation of risk. In every transaction, the cash flow coming into the deal structure (from all sources) must equal the cash flow coming out. Cash flow may come from credit supports or temporarily be set aside in reserve accounts, but every deal must be structured—and diligence should confirm—that "money in" equals "money out".

Similarly, risk is conserved—it is never created or destroyed in securitization. Risk can be allocated—to credit supports, to junior securities, to classes of securities that take on prepayment risk—but the risk embodied in the assets is unchanged. The allocation of risk is central to disclosure and diligence.

2.3 SECURITIES ACT OF 1933

2.3.1 Registration requirement

The 1933 Act is designed to protect investors by requiring that they be provided with "full and fair disclosure of the character of the securities sold". This goal is accomplished by requiring that a registration statement be filed with and declared effective by the Securities and Exchange Commission (the SEC) before offers and sales of securities are made. Registration is not required if the security is an "exempt security" or is sold in an "exempt transaction".

Definition of a "security"

While the asset underlying an asset-backed security may or may not ordinarily be thought of as a "security" itself, for purposes of the 1933 Act the inquiry will focus on whether the asset-backed instrument, taking into account all of the related arrangements, constitutes an investment contract. Among the factors identified by the SEC in its Release No. 33–3892 (Jan. 31, 1958) as giving rise to such a finding in the context of mortgages are the following:

(i) the selection of the mortgages to be pooled by the seller;
(ii) reliance by investors on the seller's investigation concerning the mortgaged properties;
(iii) the presence of a servicer to make collections and undertake foreclosures on behalf of investors;
(iv) incorporation of a mechanism by which funds are advanced to protect the security of the investment;
(v) the existence of an implied or express guarantee against loss or a guarantee of a specified yield or return.

Credit support as a separate "security"

If payments to holders of asset-backed securities are the subject of additional credit support, such as a guaranty, the credit support itself may be viewed by the SEC as a separate security required to be registered unless an exemption is available.

2.3.2 Exempt securities

Section 3 of the 1933 Act identifies particular classes of securities which enjoy a continuous exemption from the registration requirement (i.e., both on initial issuance and subsequent resale).

Section 3(a)(2)

This exemption includes any security issued or guaranteed by the U.S. or any of its instrumentalities, any security issued or guaranteed by a bank, any security which is an industrial development bond and certain other types of securities. See, e.g., *Republic of Tunisia* (pub. avail. Dec. 29, 1988): notes issues by Tunisia with a U.S. government guarantee of 90 per cent of principal and interest and collateralized as to the remaining 10 per cent by U.S. treasury securities were exempt under Section 3(a)(2). On a limited number of occasions, the SEC staff has taken the position that securities representing interests in securities that are themselves exempted under Section 3(a)(2) need not be registered. See, e.g., *Newman and Associates, Inc.* (pub. avail. Nov. 9, 1987): notes secured by U.S. Department of Defense's obligation to make lease payments in connection with a multi-family housing development for military personnel deemed "for all practical purposes" to be government guaranteed and exempt under Section 3(a)(2); and *Gem Savings Association* (pub. avail. Aug. 12, 1983): participation interests in *individual* industrial development bonds exempt under Section 3(a)(2) where, among other things, holders had direct recourse to the underlying obligor.

In order for securities to be exempt as "issued or guaranteed by a bank" they must be recourse obligations of the bank. Pass-through certificates sold by a bank that is responsible for pooling the underlying assets will not be deemed "issued" by the bank for purposes of Section 3(a)(2). See *Bank of America National Trust and Savings Association* (pub. avail. Apr. 19, 1977).

Section 3(a)(5)

This provision exempts any security issued by a state or federally chartered thrift institution, including savings and loan associations and savings banks. It does *not* exempt securities guaranteed by such institutions (although the guarantee, if a separate security, would itself be exempt under Section 3(a)(5)). Securities offered by federally chartered or insured thrift institutions, are, however, subject to their own offering circular requirements which are modelled on the 1933 Act disclosure requirements.

Section 3(a)(8)

This section exempts insurance policies but, unlike Section 3(a)(2), does not afford an exemption for securities issued or guaranteed by insurance companies. It is typically relied on to exempt credit support devices (e.g., mortgage pool insurance, financial guaranty insurance, surety bonds and the like) rather than asset-backed securities themselves.

2.3.3 Exempt transactions

Section 4 of the 1933 Act identifies particular transactions which are exempt from registration. Unlike exempt securities, resales of securities sold in an exempt transaction must find their own exemption or meet the registration requirements of the 1933 Act at the time of resale.

Section 4(2) and Regulation D

Section 4(2) exempts transactions by an issuer not involving any public offering. Traditionally the SEC and the courts have focused on a number of factors in determining whether a private offering has occurred, including the nature of the information to which investors are given access, the sophistication and number of offerees and purchasers and the manner in which solicitations are made. In an effort to provide more guidance for issuers of securities, the SEC promulgated Regulation D, a non-exclusive "safe harbor" provision which consists of Rules 501 through 506. ("Non-exclusive" means that a failure to satisfy all the conditions of the safe harbor will not preclude an issuer from relying on Section 4(2) as a basis for exemption.) Rules 504 and 505 exempt certain relatively small offerings while Rule 506, assuming its specified conditions are met, exempts limited offers and sales without regard to the dollar amount of the offering.

Under Rule 506 there is no restriction on the number of offerees but there can be no more than 35 purchasers who are not "accredited investors". Accredited investors include specified institutional investors (including, as a result of a recent change, federal or state chartered thrift institutions) and certain wealthy individuals. A non-accredited investor must, in the issuer's reasonable belief, have sufficient knowledge and experience in financial and business matters, either individually or together with his adviser, to be able to evaluate the merits and risks of the proposed investment.

An issuer relying on the exemption from registration afforded by Section 4(2) or Regulation D remains obligated to furnish investors with all material information concerning the securities. Certain specified information must be furnished to non-accredited investors if an issuer relies on Rule 506.

Neither Section 4(2) nor Regulation D provide an exemption for resales of privately placed (or "restricted") securities. Applicable exemptions for such resales may be found in Section 4(1) (transactions by any person other than "an issuer, underwriter or dealer"), Rule 144 (which requires that restricted securities have been held for a specified period of time and imposes certain other conditions on a resale of such securities) or so-called "Section 4(1-1/2)" (a doctrine that has evolved from SEC staff positions permitting private resales of restricted securities to a limited number of purchasers by sellers who, by reason of the breadth of the definition of "underwriter" under the 1933 Act, are precluded from relying on section 4(1)). Rule 144A, which is discussed below, provides a non-exclusive safe harbor for certain resale transactions to qualified institutional buyers with large securities investment portfolios.

Section 4(5)

This exemption, enacted in 1975 in an effort to promote the development of a nationwide mortgage loan trading network, relates exclusively to mortgages and mortgage-backed securities. The statutory conditions that must be satisfied have limited the utility of this exemption. Section 4(5) exempts transactions involving offers and sales of mortgage notes, and participation interests in mortgage notes, secured by a first lien on residential or commercial real estate if the purchaser buys a minimum of £250,000 for his own account and pays cash no later than 60 days after the sale. In addition, the mortgage loans must have been originated either by a commercial bank, a thrift institution or a HUD-approved mortgagee. If originated by a HUD-approved mortgagee, the notes or participations may be sold by it only to banks, thrift institutions or insurance companies or to GNMA, FNMA or FHLMC. Mortgage bankers are thus unable to avail themselves of the exemption for sales to an important segment of the institutional investor community, namely pension funds. Section 4(5) is available for resales of securities provided that all of its conditions are met at the time of resale, including the $250,000 minimum sales price.

2.3.4 Rule 144A

Rule 144A provides a non-exclusive safe harbor from the registration requirements of the 1933 Act for transactions in which eligible securities are resold to "qualified institutional buyers". 17 CFR §230.144A.

Who is a QIB?

A qualified institutional buyer ("QIB") is one which owns or invests at least $100 million in securities not issued by affiliates of the buyer. In addition to this requirement, banks and savings and loan associations must also have a net worth of at least $25 million. Registered broker-dealers will be considered QIBs if they own or invest at least $10 million in securities or if they are acting as riskless principals on behalf of a QIB. Virtually all participants in the primary and secondary markets for asset-backed securities should qualify as QIBs.

Eligible securities

In order to be eligible for the rule, securities must be non-fungible, that is, they may not be of the same class as securities listed on a national securities exchange in the United States, such as the New York Stock Exchange, or quoted on NASDAQ. Asset-backed securities should satisfy this requirement.

Disclosure requirements

Upon request by the holder or prospective buyer, the issuer must disclose certain information about its business. The rule specifies such items as a brief statement of the nature of the issuer's business, its most recent balance sheet, and its profit and loss and retained earnings statement. In the case of asset-backed securities, the information to be provided would include "basic material information concerning the structure of the securities and distributions thereon, the nature, performance and servicing of the assets supporting the securities, and any credit enhancement mechanism associated with the securities". Either the servicer or the trustee may act as the issuer. A private placement memorandum in typical form will usually contain most of the information required under the rule. Further, pooling and servicing agreements generally require periodic reports relating both to performance of the underlying pool.

Procedural requirements

The only procedural requirement is that the seller notify the purchaser that the sale is being made on the basis of the rule; this will probably be done in the confirmation.

PORTAL

PORTAL, which stands for "Private Offerings, Resales and Trading Through Automated Linkages", is a closed screen-based trading and clearance system which has been set up by NASD to facilitate the trading of Rule 144A eligible securities.

Net capital rule

Issuers' equity and investment-grade debt securities eligible for Rule 144A resales will be treated as liquid for purposes of the net capital rule.

Investment Company Act

Resales of privately placed investment company securities pursuant to Rule 144A will not cause the issuing investment company to lose the private placement exemption provided by Section 3(c)(1) of the Investment Company Act. As long as the Rule 144A resale does not cause there to be more than 100 beneficial owners, the issuing investment company will still qualify under Section 3(c)(1); i.e., the Rule 144A sale will not constitute a public offering for Section 3(c)(1).

2.3.5 Registration process

If registration is required, a registration statement must be filed with the SEC before securities may be publicly offered and declared effective before they may be sold. During the "waiting period" between filing and effectiveness, offers may be made either orally or through the use of a preliminary prospectus. The registration process will obviously affect the timing of an offering although shelf registration procedures and/or reliance on Rule 430A (see the discussion below) can accelerate the proces. In addition, there are costs associated with registration, not the least of which is the fee payable to the SEC upon filing of the registration statement.

Form S-11

This form is available to register securities issued by real estate investment trusts and securities of issuers whose primary business is acquiring and holding for investment (i) real estate, (ii) interests in real estate or (iii) interests in other issuers primarily engaged in real estate investment. Investment companies registered (or required to register) under the Investment Company Act of 1940 may not use this form. While not particularly well suited for the purpose, this form is typically used for registration of mortgage-backed securities. In the case of mortgage pass-through certificates, for example, much of the information technically required by the form with respect to the registrant, such as financial data and a discussion and analysis by management of the registrant's financial condition and operating results, is inapposite. Instead, registrants supply information about the composition of the mortgage loan pool, the underwriting standards applied in the origination process and historical loan loss and delinquency experience of the seller/servicer as well as a description of the possible effects on investors of mortgage loan prepayments and other economic factors. Although Form S-11, unlike Form S-3, does not technically permit incorporation by reference into the registration statement of subsequent reports filed under the 1934 Act (discussed below), the SEC has permitted general mortgage loan information to be included in a report on Form 8-K filed promptly after the sale of mortgage pass-through certificates, at least where such securities are rated in one of the two highest rating categories by a nationally recognized rating agency. The SEC permits the use of this device in recognition of the fact that final formation of a mortgage pool may occur contemporaneously with the pricing and sale of the securities backed by the loans in the pool. See e.g., SEC Release No. 33–6499, Nov. 17, 1983.

Form S-3

This form is generally available only for specified offerings by established companies that are obligated to file periodic reports under the Securities Exchange Act of 1934. However, a majority-owned subsidiary of such a company may also use Form S-3 to register investment grade debt securities, such as collateralized mortgage obligations or other collateralized debt.

The SEC will often expedite its review of a registration statement on Form S-3 (as compared to a Form S-11 or Form S-1) and in many cases will inform a registrant that it is making no review. Because Form S-3 incorporates by reference subsequent reports of the registrant under the 1934 Act, updating the prospectus for material developments can occur automatically without the need to resort to the more time-consuming process of filing and having declared effective a post-effective amendment to the registration statement.

Form S-1

This is the form to be used for the registration of securities when no other form is available. It has been used, for example, to register pass-through interests in automobile loans and credit card receivables. This form requires the most extensive disclosure; as is the case with Form S-11, certain of its disclosure requirements must be adapted to reflect the nature of structured financings.

Shelf registration

Under Rule 415 of the 1933 Act, an issuer can register on a single occasion an offering that will be made on a delayed or continuous basis periodically in the future. Once the registration statement containing basic information applicable to all of the securities to be offered has been declared effective, a "takedown" can be timed to take advantage of a window in the market. This is accomplished through the preparation of a supplement to the prospectus which details the structure and terms selected for the particular offering. The prospectus and related supplement are subsequently filed with the SEC under Rule 424 but they need not be reviewed or declared effective prior to their use. In most cases the prospectus and the supplement for a "takedown" must be filed with the SEC by the close of business on the second business day after the earlier of (i) the date of determination of the public offering price and (ii) the date on which the prospectus and supplement are first used. Because of the practical difficulties associated with finalizing the information to be included in a prospectus supplement following the pricing of "mortgage related securities" (defined and discussed immediately below), the prospectus and supplement for an offering of such securities need not be filed within two days after pricing but rather may be filed within two business days after first use.

Availability of the shelf registration procedure is limited to certain specified types of securities. These include "asset-backed securities" rated in one of the four highest rating categories by at least one nationally recognized rating agency.

Rule 415 limits the amount of securities eligible to use Form S-3 that may be registered on a shelf registration statement to an amount reasonably expected to be offered and sold within two years from initial effectiveness. (This does not mean that the registration statement ceases to be effective after two years.) There is no limit, however, on the amount of "mortgage related securities" that may be registered on a shelf registration statement. In order to avail itself of Rule 415, an issuer must undertake, among other things, to file a post-effective amendment to the registration statement whenever there is a fundamental change in the information contained therein. As mentioned earlier, such updating may occur automatically in the case of securities registered on the shelf on Form S-3.

Rule 430A

Prior to the adoption of Rule 430A in May 1987, an issuer in a traditional non-shelf offering was required to file a pricing amendment containing pricing and underwriting syndicate information before the registration statement would be declared effective (and before sales could be made). Unless a registration statement were declared effective by the SEC prior to the opening of the market on the desired sale date, the underwriters would be at risk for adverse movements in the market. Under Rule 430A, a registration statement may be declared effective even though it omits so-called "Rule 430A information", such as the public offering price, underwriting discounts and syndicate data as well as interest rates, payment dates and other terms of the securities dependent on pricing. There is then a five business-day window for pricing. If a final prospectus containing the Rule 430A information is not filed with the SEC by the end of the fifth business day, the issuer must then file (and have declared effective) a post-effective pricing amendment, unless the reduction in volume or change in price involved fall within a materiality standard. Note that Rule 430A is not automatically applicable. In order to rely on the rule, an issuer must include a special undertaking in its registration statement (designed to ensure that, for liability purposes, Rule 430A information will be treated as if included in the registration statement at effectiveness).

The following items are *not* Rule 430A information and must therefore be contained in the registration statement prior to effectiveness: the aggregate amount of securities to be offered; if multiple series of securities are being offered, the aggregate principal amount of each series; for asset-backed securities benefiting from credit support, the percentage of the asset pool to be covered by such credit support; and, for asset-backed securities where the cut-off date for the formation of the underlying pool of assets is prior to effectiveness, the percentage of any interest in the assets to be retained by the seller. If a registrant is uncertain at the time a registration statement is filed whether or not the securities will be offered promptly after effectiveness or on a delayed basis under Rule 415 or if a registrant intends to offer a tranche of securities promptly after effectiveness and the remainder on a delayed basis, both the Rule 415 and 430A undertakings should be included in its filing. The registrant will be presumed to be relying on Rule 430A at the time of effectiveness unless an affirmative statement is made in the registrant's request for acceleration that all or a specified portion of the offering will be made on a delayed basis under rule 415.

2.4 SECURITIES EXCHANGE ACT OF 1934

2.4.1 Registration and periodic reporting requirements

The 1934 Act requires registration on specified forms (e.g., Form 8-A or Form 10) of (i) any security listed on a national securities exchange or (ii) any class of equity securities held by at least 500 persons where the issuer of such securities has total assets of a specified amount. Issuers of securities so registered and issuers of securities that are the subject of an effective registration statement under the 1933 Act also become subject to the periodic reporting requirements of the 1934 Act. These requirements are designed to ensure continuous disclosure of material information to the marketplace about issuers whose securities are being actively traded. Annual, quarterly and other reports containing information about the issuer, including its financial condition, are ordinarily required. The SEC has authority, however, under Section 12(h) of the 1934 Act to exempt an issuer from some or all of the periodic reporting requirements. It has exercised this authority in the context of mortgage pass-through securities to permit the filing of reports containing information appropriate to the nature of the securities. The SEC staff has also responded favorably to no-action requests seeking confirmation that abbreviated reporting will be acceptable. See, e.g., *Sears Receivables Financing Group* (pub. avail. June 22, 1988).

2.4.2 Broker/dealer registration

Section 15(a) of the 1934 Act makes it unlawful for a broker or dealer, unless registered in accordance with the statute, to effect any transaction in, or to induce or attempt to induce the purchase or sale of, any security (other than certain exempted securities). Registration subjects brokers and dealers to extensive regulation regarding the conduct of their operations, including financial responsibility requirements and book-keeping and reporting rules. A "broker" is defined as any person engaged in the business of buying and selling securities for the account of others. A "dealer" includes any person engaged in the business of buying and selling securities for his own account. Banks are expressly excluded from these definitions and therefore need not register with the SEC notwithstanding the nature of their securities activities. The SEC staff has taken the position that a person or organization which buys and sells for his or its own account in the capacity of a "trader" is generally not a statutory dealer but the line between the two can be difficult to draw. See e.g., *National Council of Savings Institutions* (pub. avail. July 27, 1986).

Rule 3a12–4

Since mortgages may be considered "securities" for purposes of the 1934 Act (see, e.g., *Dell Investment Company* (pub. avail. Dec. 15, 1971)), a mortgage banker who buys and sells mortgages (or sponsors the creation of a mortgage pass-through trust) should consider the possible applicability of Section 15(a). Certain mortgage loan trading activities are expressly exempt by virtue of Rule 3a12–4. This rule provides that a "mortgage security" shall be deemed exempt from the broker/dealer registration (and net capital) requirements of the 1934 Act if at the time of sale the security is not in default and has an unpaid principal amount of at least $50,000. The term "mortgage security" means a whole loan mortgage, an aggregated whole loan mortgage (i.e., two or more whole loans grouped together and sold to one person in one transaction), a participation interest or a commitment to purchase any of the foregoing. A "participation interest" is defined quite narrowly to mean an undivided interest representing one of only two such interests in a whole loan mortgage or aggregated whole loan mortgage where the second interest is retained by the originator of the participation. Rule 3a12–4 is not available for transactions involving a sale of mortgages coupled with services or other features which, taken together, constitute an investment contract (discussed above under 2.3.1).

Rule 3a4–1

Subject to meeting the specific requirements of rule 3a4–1, the securities of an issuer may be distributed through the issuer's own officers, directors or employees (or certain other associated persons) without such persons be deemed to be brokers subject to Section 15(a). The rule provides a safe harbor for any such person if, among other things, he (i) is not subject to a statutory disqualification at the time of his participation in the distribution, (ii) is not compensated for his participation by the payment of commissions or other remuneration based on transactions in securities and (iii) is not at the time of his participation associated with a broker or dealer. Notwithstanding rule 3a4–1, employees of an issuer may have to comply with applicable state securities laws concerning broker/dealer registration.

2.4.3 Margin Rules

The margin rules are designed to prevent the excessive use of credit in the purchase or carrying of securities. Section 7 of the 1934 Act empowers the Federal Reserve Board (the FRB) to set margin requirements; enforcement authority rests with the SEC.

Regulation T

The FRB's Regulation T governs the extension of credit by broker/dealers (whether or not registered under the 1934 Act and whether or not members of an exchange) to customers for the purpose of purchasing or carrying securities. In addition to traditional lending arrangements, a sale of securities with delayed delivery is generally deemed to involve an extension of credit. Regulation T provides that credit used to purchase or carry a security must be secured by collateral consisting of cash or securities, having a loan value, at the time the credit is extended, at least equal to the amount of the credit. Acceptable collateral includes "exempted securities" (e.g., securities issued or guaranteed by the U.S. government) and "margin securities". Of the types of securities that fall within the latter category both "OTC margin bonds" and exchange-listed non-convertible debt securities have "good faith" loan value, meaning that a broker/dealer may lend against those securities the amount (not more than the market value) that he would customarily lend in the exercise of his "sound credit judgment . . . without regard to the customer's other assets or securities positions held in connection with unrelated transactions".

An "OTC margin bond" is defined to include any "mortgage related security" (see above) and any private-label mortgage pass-through security meeting all of the following requirements:

(i) the security has been registered under the 1933 Act,
(ii) not less than $25,000,000 aggregate principal amount was issued (for this purpose all of the series of an issuer may be aggregated),
(iii) current reports relating to the securities have been filed with the SEC, and
(iv) the broker/dealer reasonably believes that distributions are being passed through as required and the servicer is meeting its material obligations.

Other asset-backed securities may qualify for good faith loan value under a third branch of the "OTC margin bond" definition if they have the following characteristics:

(i) at the time of original issue not less than $25,000,000 was outstanding,
(ii) the issue of securities was registered under the 1933 Act and periodic reports under the 1934 Act have been filed, and
(iii) the broker/dealer reasonably believes that the issuer is not in default on interest or principal payments.

While the sale of a security subject to delayed delivery is ordinarily considered an extension of credit, "mortgage related securities" are given special treatment in recognition of the fact that the secondary mortgage market depends upon forward trading and delivery mechanisms. Section 7(g) of the 1934 Act, added by SMMEA, provides that credit will not be deemed to have been extended by reason of a bona fide agreement for delayed delivery of a mortgage related security where full payment of the purchase price is to occur within 180 days of purchase.

Regulation T also prohibits a broker/dealer from arranging for another person to extend credit which it would be impermissible for the broker/dealer to extend itself. Private placements of securities which do not qualify as margin securities are exempt from the arranging prohibition.

New York Stock Exchange Rule 431

A broker/dealer who is a member of the New York Stock Exchange will be subject not only to Regulation T at the time it extends credit but also to the Exchange's Rule 431. The minimum margin requirement specified by Rule 431 for a particular category of securities applies not only at the time credit is initially extended but also (unlike Regulation T) as long as the credit is outstanding. Rule 431 imposes special margin requirements for "restricted securities"; such requirements would evidently apply to "mortgage related securities" which are restricted because they are held by an affiliate of the issuer.

Section 11(d) of the 1934 Act

Section 11(d)(1) imposes limits on the ability of a broker/dealer to extend credit during or within 30 days after a distribution of securities. Specifically, a broker/dealer who has participated in a new issue of securities as a member of the selling group is generally prohibited from extending, maintaining or arranging for the extension or maintenance of credit to or for a customer against such securities (unless they are exempted securities) within 30 days after the conclusion of its participation in the distribution. Credit is not deemed extended for this purpose by reason of a bona fide arrangement for delayed delivery (i) of any such security against full payment of the purchase price within 35 days after purchase or (ii) of any "mortgage related security" against full payment of the purchase price within 180 days after purchase. This latter exception was added by SMMEA.

2.5 TRUST INDENTURE ACT OF 1939

The 1939 Act applies to the public issuance of debt securities, regulating the relationships between investors, the issuer of the securities and the indenture trustee. It does *not* apply to securities that are exempt from the registration requirements of the 1933 Act or to equity securities. Asset-backed securities issued in pass-through form are considered by the SEC to be equity securities for this purpose; thus the pooling and servicing agreements under which they are typically issued need not comply with 1939 Act requirements. In practice, however, these agreements often incorporate many of the procedures of the 1939 Act that are designed to safeguard the interests of investors.

If the 1939 Act is applicable, an indenture complying with the statute's requirements must be filed and qualified with the SEC. This occurs simultaneously with the filing and effectiveness of the registration statement for the relates securities under the 1933 Act. Currently, a qualified indenture must include specified provisions regarding, among other things, minimum qualifications for and duties and responsibilities of the trustee (including detailed provisions identifying trustee conflicts of interest), reports that must be submitted by the issuer and by the trustee, communications among bondholders and procedures for valuation, substitution and release of any collateral for the securities.

2.6 INVESTMENT COMPANY ACT OF 1940

See Chapter 4, section 4.

2.7 SMMEA AND LEGAL INVESTMENT CONSIDERATIONS

SMMEA was enacted in 1984 to facilitate the development of the private sector of the secondary mortgage market by removing or liberalizing a variety of restrictions on the issuance, distribution and trading of mortgage-backed securities. Legislation adopted in 1994 will broaden the reach of SMMEA, subject to some limits and conditions, to securities backed by commercial mortgages and small business loans. Among the most important provisions of SMMEA were the statute's preemption of state securities registration (or "blue sky") requirements and state legal investment restrictions for "mortgage related securities" and securities exempt from registration under Section 4(5) of the 1933 Act. The legal investment preemption allows various state chartered and regulated institutions, such as banks, pension funds, insurance companies and savings and loan associations, to invest in such securities to the same extent as they are permitted to invest in U.S. government securities. It should be noted that, pursuant to authority granted in SMMEA, a number of states have overridden these preemption provisions to various degrees by legislation enacted prior to October 4, 1991. SMMEA did not affect state broker/dealer registration requirements or state antifraud statutes.

MITCHELL S. DUPLER

CHAPTER 3

SECURITISATION IN THE UNITED KINGDOM: STRUCTURES, REGULATORY CONTROLS AND SECURITIES REGULATION (WITH EMPHASIS ON MORTGAGE-BACKED SECURITIES)

3.1 INTRODUCTION

By comparison with the United States, securitisation is a relatively recent phenomenon in the international debt market. The first securitisation issue arranged in London for the international market was MINI, a £50 million refinancing of certain BankAmerica Finance Limited UK residential property mortgages, which was launched in January 1985. Since then there has been quite a large volume of rated UK mortgage-backed issues, principally tapping the sterling FRN market.

Since 1990 there has been some activity in the securitisation of UK car loans, consumer and credit card debt, corporate or wholesale finance such as commercial mortgages, leases and swap receivables, and government debt. Overall, the UK asset-backed securities market has grown to become the second largest in the world after that of the United States. Mortgage-backed securities still constitute the largest part of the market.

The commercial considerations which underlie the securitisation market are more fully discussed elsewhere. From the perspective of a consideration of legal issues, the key commercial factor is often the originator's desire to remove the assets from its balance sheet or at least to achieve what is now described as a "linked presentation" (see 3.3). Related to this objective is the question of credit risk, since the retention of any such risk will inhibit the basic objective. Furthermore, where the originator is subject to capital adequacy requirements, the regulatory authorities insist that the credit risk must be removed as one of the conditions for accepting that the assets should be excluded from the originator's own accounts and consolidated accounts for regulatory purposes (see 3.3).

In view of the predominance of mortgage-backed issues, this chapter focuses primarily on the structure of such issues but highlights particular alternative structures which have been developed in relation to other types of asset-backed issues. The discussion of regulatory controls and securities regulation (see 3.3–3.4) is relevant to all types of asset-backed securities.

3.2 OVERVIEW OF MORTGAGE-BACKED STRUCTURES

3.2.1 Rating

The commercial considerations briefly mentioned above all point to a special-purpose issuing vehicle ("SPV") interposed between the investor and the mortgage originator. Concern arising from securities regulation provisions governing collective investment schemes (3.4) is another compelling reason for the use of an SPV.

Reduced to its most basic level, the typical securitisation structure revolves round the SPV and the different methods of making it sufficiently creditworthy for an issue.

The question of creditworthiness raises the issue of rating. The commercial desirability of obtaining a rating from one or both of Standard & Poor's and Moody's also has a very strong influence on the securitisation structure.

The highest rating, and the one which has generally been aimed for in order to raise funds at an acceptable cost, is triple A. A triple A rating is a message to the market that the ability of the issuer to repay the notes and to pay interest in full and on time is extremely strong. The rating agency will only award a triple A rating if it is convinced that the integrity of the issuer and its cash flow is virtually assured, come what may. As part of the agency's assessment of the issuer's resilience, it will determine a "worst-case" scenario, in which the issuer will still be expected to perform its obligations under the notes. For this purpose, particularly in the case of tiered (senior/junior) notes, the agency will require from the issuer and its advisers detailed cash flow projections drawn up on a so-called "stressed" basis, to reflect the worst-case assumptions. For example, despite the fact that UK building society loan loss experience from 1970 to 1987 (inclusive) showed that losses each year on total building society loans outstanding were less than 0.01 per cent and in 1991 and 1992, years of severe recession in the UK housing market, the annual percentage of properties taken into possession by mortgage lenders was still less than 1 per cent, the Standard & Poor's stress criteria can involve an enforcement assumption of 15 per cent, depending on average LTV (and even more where the pool includes mortgages that are assessed to be of lower quality), and a house price decline of up to 47 per cent. The assumptions used by Moody's also include severe house-price declines, as well as high interest rates and lengthy periods between default and sale of mortgaged properties. Another example of the severity of the Standard & Poor's criteria is the assumed rate of return on cash held by the issuer: LIBOR less 5 per cent per annum, unless a rate source of interest at an assured rate can be demonstrated. At the time of writing, Standard & Poor's is to review its criteria to ensure that they reflect the experience in the housing markets in the 1990s.

In the case of arrears pool securitisations, the stressing required by the rating agencies includes, of course, very conservative assumptions about the losses which might be suffered on the pool. Whilst in fact not all mortgages will be enforced—or, as the rating agencies, with their US culture, call it (rather confusingly for an English lawyer), "foreclosed"—the assumption generally is that they will all be enforced; and that, although again this is not realistic in practice, they will each suffer a relatively high rate of loss (called the "loss severity" factor). The capital and liquidity enhancement which this analysis leads to results in an extremely robust structure; as a result arrears deals in the market have been able to achieve triple A ratings. (However, they are more expensive, in terms of interest rate, than pools of performing mortgages, partly because under Bank of England capital adequacy rules (see 3.3) they attract a risk asset weighting of 100 per cent rather than the usual 50 per cent and are thus unattractive to bank investors without an increased coupon.)

"Stressing" enables the rating agency to quantify the amount of capital and liquidity cover it will require to ensure that in the worst-case situations the issuer will still be able to pay its way. It follows that whatever capital and other support the issuer may have must be copper-bottomed in legal terms, not so much in a liquidation of the issuer (since that is reckoned to be a remote eventuality) but in a liquidation of the provider of the capital or other support. Thus, the issuer's lawyer is required to show the relevant rating agency a legal opinion of considerable detail, typically running to 25 or 30 pages.

Securing a triple A rating at the closing of the issue is not, of course, the end of the story. The creditworthiness of the issuer will be kept under constant review by the relevant agency(ies) during the life of the issue. The issuer's credit rating is vulnerable to events affecting third parties, especially where it relies on the credit standing of a third party (such as the provider of pool insurance or a committed provider of credit). This point was illustrated by the highly-leveraged bid by Hoylake for BAT Industries in 1989 which caused doubts to be raised over the credit rating of BAT's insurance subsidiary, Eagle Star. Such doubt in turn impacted on those issues for which Eagle Star had provided pool insurance. To date, in fact, no issue of mortgage-backed securities has been downgraded because of poor asset performance, but some downgrading has resulted from the lowering of ratings on third parties which have provided financial support.

More general developments—concerning the economy as a whole, or a particular sector of it—could also adversely affect the rating of an issue. For example, the difficulties faced in recent years by UK insurance companies generally, and their behaviour in relation to mortgage indemnity insurance, has in turn caused problems for rated securitisation issues—indeed has caused some originators to shift away from credit support in the form of insurance.

The convention in the UK mortgage-backed market is that the investor, not the issuer, takes the downrating risk. The investor may buy a triple A-rated issue, but the downrating of the issue will not cause either an increase in the interest rate or an event of default. This is in contrast to some "event risk" provisions in corporate bond issues, where there is sometimes an event of default if, say, the issuer is subject to a takeover bid which leads to a downrating of its long-term debt. On the other hand, since a downrating without a consequential adjustment to the interest rate may well have an adverse effect on the secondary market price of the notes, this is likely to be of concern to the originator as it will adversely affect the pricing of subsequent issues of notes to securitise that originator's mortgages. Accordingly, an originator does in practice maintain a close and co-operative relationship with its chosen rating agency(ies)—though not, or often not, with any other agency which of its own volition chooses to rate an issue without the issuer's blessing (a so-called "shadow" rating).

3.2.2 Loss and liquidity risks: implications for mortgage-backed structures

(a) Issuer's basic assets

What assets will the issuer have? In the case of a mortgage securitisation, the principal assets will be the initial portfolio of mortgages which will be acquired by the issuer with most of the net proceeds of the note issue. Alternative structures developed in relation to car loan securitisations have involved the transfer of the assets to a separate trust rather than to the issuer itself. This structure can facilitate profit extraction but restrictions arising from the procedures governing the granting of tax relief to mortgage borrowers preclude its use in mortgage-backed issues involving residential mortgages.

The issuer's other assets will include whatever cash it has at the outset, for example through the issue of its share capital and the borrowing of any subordinated debt finance that it needs. Some of this cash will immediately be spent on initial expenses and will thus be replaced by an intangible asset—issue expenses—which is of no use to the noteholders and will be written off over the expected average life of the issue. The balance of such cash will be invested in qualifying short-dated investments or placed on deposit with qualifying institutions and/or be used to purchase additional mortgages (thus "over-collateralising" the rated notes). As the issuer's income comes in—principally interest and, in the case of mortgage-backed issues, MIRAS payments (payments from the UK Inland Revenue representing the amount of mortgage interest relief to which the borrowers, if UK taxpayers, are normally entitled and which they obtain at source by way of withholding from the interest payments they make to the lender)—the cash will either be placed on deposit or invested in qualifying investments. Cash representing principal receipts—mainly on redemption of the securitised assets—will also be so deposited or invested pending its use in making further advances or purchasing substitute loans, if those options are available, or in purchasing or redeeming notes or, perhaps, in meeting revenue or other expenses not covered by income.

The issuer's assets will, therefore, from time to time include cash (i.e. debts owing by banks) or perhaps marketable securities such as gilts.

This basic picture—i.e. asset pool plus qualifying liquid assets—would be the simplest structure. However, it would only be acceptable to the relevant rating agency as providing both the necessary loss protection (both in respect of the asset pool and in respect of any income shortfalls resulting from certain risks enlarged upon below) and the necessary liquidity (i.e. ready cash) to meet the rating agency's various worst case assumptions, if the amount of capital (including subordinated debt finance) paid into the issuer, or unconditionally available to it from an appropriately rated source, was of such a size as, as a practical matter, to be uneconomically large and therefore unacceptable to the originator.

Consequently, a number of alternative techniques have been developed over the years—originating particularly in the US—for enhancing the issuer's basic asset pool and such liquid assets as it may have from time to time, so as to reduce the need for capital.

(b) Credit risk

This is the obvious risk of the issuer suffering a loss because of some weakness in the assets it owns. It potentially applies to both the main assets forming the backing for the issue and also liquid assets and indeed to any other assets such as the benefit of contracts. It applies to both income and principal; if, for example, a mortgage borrower goes into default and a loss is realised on enforcing the security, there is obviously both a loss of principal (and therefore a prospective inability to repay the notes in full) and a loss of interest income in the meantime, leading to a prospective or potential shortfall in funds required by the issuer to pay its note interest and other expenses. A similar risk applies if a bank with which funds are deposited becomes insolvent; this risk is generally thought to be adequately covered by limiting the investment of liquid funds to deposits with banks with the top short-term credit ratings (A1+ or P1) and to certain rated or government money-market instruments, or (sometimes) to the notes themselves, subject in all cases to safeguards.

As regards the credit risk on the assets, there are at present three principal ways of dealing with this in a rated issue—tiered issues (or other forms of "over-collateralisation"), pool policies and the use of "spread accounts".

(i) Tiered (senior/junior) issues (and other "over-collateralisation") This structure is now fairly well-known in the UK market. Normally there are two classes of notes (usually called Class A and Class B (or "mezzanine") notes) but there have been a number of issues with more than two classes.

The principle is a variation on the basic theme that the simplest way of covering the credit risk, and also the various other risks which are mentioned below, is by having a large enough capital. In a two-tier issue, the (much smaller) junior class of notes is effectively another layer of capital for the senior (rated) notes. The proceeds of the capital—whether in the form of junior notes or of subordinated funding and/or share capital provided by (say) the originator—are used either to purchase mortgages (over and above those funded by the (senior) rated notes) or to provide a fund of cash or a combination of the two. In any event, the rated notes are over-collateralised or, put another way, have a margin of security.

In the simpler structures, the junior notes simply defer repaying until after the senior tranche has been repaid in full; and on an enforcement of the security for the notes, they rank junior to the senior notes.

In the more complex cases, started by Household Mortgage Corporation in early 1988, there is a system for redeeming the junior notes, after an initial period where only the senior notes redeem, pro rata and concurrently with the senior notes but only so long as at the relevant time there is no outstanding principal deficiency—i.e. a prospective shortfall in principal caused generally by a mortgage loss—which has not been made good by subsequent surplus income earned by the issuer. In these issues, there is a strict order of payments at and between interest-resetting dates for the notes, designed to ensure that the interest on the senior notes, as well as all other issuer expenses except interest on the junior notes and on any subordinated funding, are paid when they fall due so as to keep the issuer solvent. If necessary, these payments are made at the cost of deferring, at least in the short term but possibly for ever, the relevant interest payment on the junior notes. However, if income and any capital receipts are adequate, such interest as accrues currently is paid and only then is an assessment made as to whether and to what extent the senior and, if appropriate, the junior notes can or must be repaid to reflect receipts of principal moneys by the issuer, mainly from mortgage redemptions. The order of payments is also designed to ensure that the full amount potentially repayable on the senior notes is provided for (if not actually repaid) in calculating what can be repaid on the junior notes.

The deferral of interest and/or principal on the junior notes is not an event of default; these events are limited to the usual events in relation to the senior notes and to insolvency, etc. On enforcement of the security, the junior notes rank in point of security beneath the senior notes.

A novel structure was created in the HMC Financing 9 PLC arrears deal, lead managed by Barings in December 1991. Although, as with most other HMC deals, there were three layers of debt—senior notes, mezzanine notes and HMC-provided subordinated debt—in the Financing 9 deal there was a formal structure for the proportionate repayment, out of the proceeds of mortgage redemptions etc, of the subordinated loan (as well as the mezzanine notes) alongside the senior notes, depending on the extent, if any, to which the mortgage portfolio deteriorated.

(ii) Pool policies Under this structure the issuer is issued with a pool insurance policy by an insurance company with, or backed by, the requisite long-term credit rating. This must be a long-term policy, covering the issuer (normally subject to a cumulative maximum of, say, 8 per cent to 10 per cent of the initial asset pool) against any loss of principal, interest (including interest on interest) and costs suffered in the asset pool to the extent not covered by any other applicable loss insurance (such as a mortgage indemnity policy applicable to the relevant mortgage). If it only pays that share of principal which is not, under the

relevant lending criteria, required to be covered by an applicable mortgage indemnity policy, the insurance company issuing the latter policy must also have—or its payment obligations must be guaranteed or reinsured by an institution which has—the requisite credit rating since its failure to pay will result in a credit loss which is not covered by the pool policy.

The pool insurer normally requires the assets to conform to certain minimum lending criteria, failing which the relevant assets may not be insured, though sometimes cover remains available within a smaller cumulative limit. This risk is passed back to the originator, via warranties to the issuer and a put option in favour of the latter onto the former where there is a breach of warranty. Since the originator may well not be rated to triple A standard (or at all), there is a theoretical risk on a sub-standard credit; thus, the rating agency will, if only for this reason, wish to be satisfied with the consistency of quality and accuracy in the originator's lending procedures. One of the pre-issue procedures which is required by the agency is an audit to a high level of confidence on the securitised pool.

If any excess or deductible is applicable to claims by the issuer under the pool policy, the rating agency will want the full amount of the excess to be funded in cash or by means of a committed facility granted to the issuer by an adequately rated institution. Alternatively, the pool insurer may be prepared to dispense with an excess on claims by the issuer (i.e. provide insurance from the floor up) and instead to rely upon some form of reimbursement obligation on the part of, say, the originator.

All of these differing pool policy structures for the principal loss risk—and there are other permutations which have not been mentioned—will, of course, give rise to different documentation requirements. Pool policy structures are currently out of favour because of the bad payment records of certain insurance companies.

(iii) Spread account In some cases, the rating agency allows the issuer time to build up capital in the form of a cash fund, or allows the cash fund as it builds up to replace some other form of capital initially provided. This build-up is by means of the allocation, according to a strict order of priority of the issuer's cash flow quarter by quarter, of part of the cash flow (if adequate) into a reserve account called the "spread account". This is sometimes on a cash-segregated basis, by requiring a separate bank account representing the reserve account. The funds thus locked into the issuer are permitted to be used for limited purposes, not including the repayment of subordinated loans (or the payment of interest thereon) or the payment of dividends.

(c) Income risks

Under this heading come risks of permanent depletion or loss of income rather than simply the risk of delayed receipt of income; the latter—which is a liquidity risk—is dealt with in (d) below.

(i) Interest mis-match and exceptional expense The most important risk is the possibility of the interest rate payable on the securitised assets by borrowers being less than that required—or deemed by the rating agency to be required—to cover the issuer's quarterly note interest expense plus its other expenses such as agency fees, trustee fees, ordinary management expenses, note purchase or redemption expenses, tax (if any) etc. This risk, sometimes called a "basis risk", is most likely to occur through an increase in LIBOR (and thus the interest rate on the notes) at the rate fixing date, which is not immediately—or is perhaps never—covered by an increase in the borrowing rate payable on the securitised assets. However, the gap could also occur through an unexpectedly high level of other expenditure, such as expected expenses exceeding budgeted levels (a risk Moody's are particularly concerned about), or the occurrence of unexpected liabilities, such as a new form of taxation of the issuer or the costs of convening a meeting of noteholders or litigation.

Interest shortfall risk is generally covered by a requirement on the issuer, through the agency of the administrator, to reset the borrowing rate payable on the securitised assets at a level sufficient to cover the shortfall in cash no later than the ensuing interest payment date for the notes. But this may be commercially unacceptable to the originator/administrator, and thus it is normally provided that funds may instead be paid to the issuer to bridge the gap. The risk might instead be covered by a third party (rated) credit facility. In either case, the documents will have to deal with the terms and conditions relating to the repayment of such funding and the payment of any interest thereon; the degree of subordination tends to vary but the funds should at least be locked into the issuer until the shortfall they were covering has been made good by an increase in the borrowing rate over and above that required to cover a shortfall in subsequent interest periods. Traditionally mortgage lending was done on terms which gave the lender very considerable freedom to adjust the interest rate but there are now in place regulations which render "unfair" terms not binding on consumers and for this reason mortgages which are now securitised may contain restrictions on the lender's discretion. Any such restrictions will need to be reflected in the terms and conditions on which funds are made available to cover interest rate shortfalls. The regulations are discussed further in this section under the heading "Administration".

Fixed rate mortgages, collars, caps and similar products usually give rise to the need for a swap from a rated source for the duration of the fixed rate feature in order to avoid a potential loss caused by the interest note mismatch.

Conversely, if the notes themselves are payable at a fixed rate but are backed in whole or in part by variable rate assets, it is likely that some form of swap or floor will be required (in conjunction with the basis risk protection referred to above to compensate for a shortfall caused by the mortgage rate being less than a notional market rate such as LIBOR).

(ii) Re-investment rate Another income risk applies where cash is held instead

of the normal assets, for example, cash arising from the redemption of mortgages. Such cash will earn interest at less than the mortgage rate previously payable. This will obviously result in a lower income to the issuer and, if the redemption moneys so invested are large enough and are not invested in the notes themselves, could actually result in an income shortfall after taking account of expenditure. This risk is often mitigated by the issuer entering into a deposit agreement with a (rated) bank in which the latter assures to the issuer a fixed rate of return, expressed as a margin by reference to LIBOR, on any liquid funds deposited with it. Although this rate will obviously not be as high as the mortgage rate or even the note rate—it is likely to be around LIBID—it does, if the bank has an adequate credit rating, at least enable the rating agency to allow a more lenient cash re-investment rate assumption for the purposes of the stressed cash flow projections than its normal criterion demands. This arrangement, often called a "guaranteed investment contract", tends to be based on merely an A1+ or P1 credit rating for the relevant bank, i.e. a short-term rating. This means that the issuer needs some form of long-term AAA back-up facility; alternatively, the rating agency is likely to stick to its stringent investment rate assumption for the stressed cash flows after the first year (which is the horizon for a short-term credit rating). Another method of covering the re-investment rate risk, even where a guaranteed investment contract is used, is to have a cash fund available for the purpose.

(d) Liquidity risk

We now move on to the general liquidity risk—i.e. the risk of the issuer having inadequate ready cash or credit lines to pay its debts as they fall due. This is likely to be mainly of relevance to the interest on the notes and the issuer's other revenue expenses, but there is also a liquidity risk on principal—of particular importance on short-dated issues, which are referred to below.

Whether affecting income or principal, the cause of the delay—for example, borrowers changing their bank accounts and failing to complete new direct debit forms—may not necessarily mean that losses will ensue. But the liquidity risk needs to be covered both to avoid insolvency in the issuer and to achieve a rating, which generally implies punctuality in the making of interest and principal payments on the notes.

To the extent that the issuer does not—or is deemed by the rating agency not to—have adequate free cash representing its locked-in capital funds, it will need access to an appropriately rated committed loan or standby letter of credit facility or to a separate fund held in readiness. There have been cases of such a facility being effected in the form of an interim claims facility under a pool policy where, unlike most interim claims provisions in such policies, drawings can be made immediately rather than only when an actual net loss can be estimated after exercise of the power of sale. However, this is most unlikely to be available under current conditions.

Again, the repayment and interest terms under such a facility will require careful documentation; normally the lender would expect, as to both interest on and principal of drawings under the facility, to rank ahead of the notes on an enforcement of the security on the basis that the facility is in the nature of an overdraft, intended only for temporary use. Prior to enforcement, it is common for the liquidity provider to receive repayment of its drawings only as and when the defaulted interest payments giving rise to them are recovered, but to receive interest currently, perhaps funded by drawings under the liquidity facility.

In a senior/junior note structure, the need for an outside facility for liquidity purposes will normally be unnecessary as the deferral of interest on the junior tranche will fulfil that rôle so far as interest on the senior notes (and any other revenue expenses of the issuer) are concerned. Obviously, the "sizing" of the junior tranche will be done having regard not only to the rating agency's assumed worst-case credit loss exposure, but also to the ability of the junior note interest to bear the assumed interest delays on the underlying mortgages. Deferred junior note interest does not itself bear interest.

A common method of minimising the risk of illiquidity for the repayment of note principal in mortgage-backed issues is to structure the issue so that its final maturity occurs after (normally two years after) the final possible mortgage redemption date. However, this is not an invariable practice. For example, there have been a number of five-year fixed-rate note issues on the back of 25-year underlying mortgages. These issues have involved an obvious principal liquidity problem in the absence of some means for the fixed rate note issuer to obtain the requisite funds at year 5. This has in effect been provided by a triple A-rated institution granting to the issuer a put option at par exercisable for value on the maturity date of the notes. But instead of the option being over the then outstanding mortgage portfolio, it has been over a marketable security held by the fixed rate note issuer, namely an equivalent principal amount of conventional underlying long-term FRNs issued by the company holding the mortgage portfolio and secured on the portfolio.

Low-start, stabilised, deferred interest and similar mortgages give rise to a gap in current cash flow (compared with full-payment mortgages). Such products *accrue* interest at a certain rate (usually the normal variable mortgage rate) but for a limited period—say two or three years—only oblige the mortgagor to *pay* interest at a lower rate, the difference being capitalised and added to principal. Thus the deferred interest is eventually recovered on redemption of the mortgage and bears interest in the meantime.

This cash shortfall risk is controlled in a securitisation—first, by there being a limit on the total amount of mortgages of this type and, secondly, by the shortfall itself being covered either by overfunding through the notes (the overfunding being set aside into a fund which is periodically released to supplement cash flow) or by a cash fund being provided by the originator or building up from surplus cash flow or from some other (rated) source on subordinated repayment terms.

(e) Summary of loss and liquidity: support documents

The documents which may typically be required to ensure that the issuer is adequately equipped, in terms of assets and rights over and above its agreed paid up share capital, are:

(i) if the issuer has any form of capital funds by way of loan, including those funds which are used to pay initial expenses, a loan agreement containing suitable subordination conditions and probably including as a party the trustee for the noteholders;

(ii) to meet the credit risk:
- (in the case of a mortgage-backed issue) mortgage indemnity policies, or at least an interest in the originator's existing policies; plus either
- a senior/junior note structure; or
- a pool insurance policy and, possibly, an excess reimbursement undertaking between the pool insurer and, for example, the originator or administrator or alternatively extra capital or unconditional access to a separate fund or a committed facility;

(iii) to meet the interest basis risk and the exceptional liabilities risk, an obligation on the administrator to set the borrowing rate adequately, in the absence of *ad hoc* funding, the terms of which need at least to some extent to be subordinated;

(iv) to meet the reinvestment rate risk, a guaranteed investment contract, with or without enhancement of the counterparty credit risk (e.g. by way of guarantee), and/or a cash fund of some kind;

(v) to deal with the liquidity risk (except in a senior/junior note structure), a facility agreement from an external source of funds, with or without counterparty credit risk enhancement.

3.2.3 Administration

Provision requires to be made for the administration of the issuer's assets and liabilities. This often involves the appointment of the originator as the issuer's and the trustee's agent for that purpose, since the originator is frequently the lender and therefore the institution with the continuing relationship with the borrowers. However, there are issuers and lenders which retain professional third-party administrators. The rating agencies are naturally concerned to ensure that the administrator is properly experienced and has the necessary systems in place. An audit on the initial asset pool to a high degree of confidence is required at the outset and this will be an important part of the rating agency's process of reviewing the administrator's capabilities.

Continuity of administration is obviously of the utmost importance. The administrator may not resign unless a successor is in place. It has been common practice (though now less so), under pressure from the rating agencies, for there to be from the outset an agreement with the issuer from a suitable organisation (such as a clearing bank) to undertake the administration role if the need arises during the life of the notes; this potential successor administrator will require some form of commitment fee from the issuer. Whether or not there is a successor agency agreement, access by the trustee to software and files on termination of the agency is important. Sometimes duplicate disks are held in escrow for release to the issuer/trustee if the administrator's role is terminated.

Other issues which need to be addressed are the level and ranking of administration fees; liability for acts or omissions; and insurance against error and employee fraud.

The custody and storage of deeds are of major importance in mortgage-backed issues, giving rise to provisions governing identification, access and inspection, insurance, and the monitoring and control of removal, whether on redemptions or for other reasons.

The administration of the asset pool includes dealing with the important areas of interest-rate setting and arrears management. Where residential mortgages are involved, regard must be had to the Department of the Environment's and HM Treasury's November 1989 Statement of Practice. Under the Statement of Practice, unless the administrator is also the original lender, or the issuer is a member of the original lender's group of companies, these two discretions will have to be exercised in accordance with the original lender's policies on these matters in relation to its own business.

The Statement of Practice is not legally binding but it has been voluntarily adopted by many mortgage lenders. Although the point is not free from doubt, there is an uneasy acceptance that "adoption" does not incorporate the Statement of Practice into the lender's mortgage terms.

Wide-ranging proposals put forward by the Law Commission in 1991 would, if implemented, have a significant impact on the relationship between mortgage borrowers and lenders and, in turn, on the practice in relation to issues of mortgage-backed securities. The proposals made by the Law Commission include giving mortgagors a statutory right to challenge alterations to the mortgage rate on the grounds of unreasonableness, restrictions on the powers of mortgage lenders to enforce their security and limitations on their rights to sell or otherwise transfer the mortgages.

A significant development after the Law Commission published its proposals was the enactment of the Unfair Terms in Consumer Contracts Regulations 1994. These regulations came into force on 1 July 1995. Under the regulations, "unfair" contractual terms are not binding on "consumers", a category of persons which would include residential mortgage borrowers. Broadly speaking, it is not possible to use the regulations to set aside the core commercial deal between the parties but lenders intending to securitise mortgages do now have to conduct a detailed scrutiny of their standard terms and conditions to ensure that they comply with the regulations and, if necessary, make appropriate amendments. Amendments made by a mortgage lender to ensure compliance may result in the terms and conditions of its mortgages becoming less favourable to the lender than those which have traditionally applied to securitised mortgages. For example, its power to change the interest rate and to collect certain fees from the borrower may be more restricted. Balanced against this, however, the potentially disastrous consequences of a failure of a mortgage to comply with the regulations will mean that the rating agencies will need to be satisfied that there is full compliance.

3.2.4 Structure protection provisions

Various matters need to be the subject of covenants and remedies in favour of the issuer and the noteholders' trustee. Some are also included to protect the originator.

(a) Asset pool

Provisions must be made for the protection of, and future developments relating to, the securitised pool and other assets, which may also, subject to suitable safeguards, give the originator a reasonable degree of flexibility in changing markets. For example:

(i) warranties will be required to be given by the originator at the outset, e.g. as to the pool's compliance with the lending criteria described in the offering circular and as to the originator's title;
(ii) the consequence of a breach of warranty should be provided for;
(iii) there may be a substitution right, involving the need for warranties in respect of the new loans and an increasing array of conditions laid down by the rating agencies, generally to prevent substitution if there is (or is deemed by their criteria to be) a deterioration in the quality of the pool;
(iv) the types of assets which may be substituted may be fairly broadly defined, but different products bring different risks and problems;
(v) further advances may be permitted, subject to appropriate warranties, suitable procedures to avoid legal difficulties related to "tacking" and again various conditions precedent;
(vi) changes in lending and other terms may be permitted, subject to appropriate warranties;
(vii) perfection and/or enforcement of the issuer's and the trustee's titles should be covered (although perfection would not generally be contemplated so long as the security was not in jeopardy).

(b) Corporate constraints

The second main function of these contractual provisions is to lay down certain constraints and corporate disciplines, to the extent not covered by negative pledge and other restrictive covenants in the terms and conditions of the notes (e.g. as to borrowings, disposal of assets and mergers). For example, there will be limits on the use of principal moneys in the issuer's hands, on the types of marketable securities or deposits which are available to the issuer in investing its cash resources, in the use and repayment of loan facilities, and on the use of surplus income to repay subordinated debt or to pay dividends.

3.2.5 Issuer's and trustee's interests in assets

So far as mortgages are concerned, practice has differed as to the type of interest therein that is vested in the issuer. It is now common practice for the issuer's interest in registered land not to be the subject of any form of registration at HM Land Registry or to be notified to borrowers, life companies, etc, but for this step to be reserved in case the trustee becomes concerned that the security is in jeopardy or in case it becomes enforceable. The initial transfer therefore only confers an equitable title on the issuer. A full legal title to mortgages over unregistered land can be taken, though this leads to some complication in the context of further advances and it is now common for only equitable title to mortgages over unregistered land, as well as to mortgages over registered land, to be taken.

(The position with Scottish mortgages—where mere equitable titles are not recognised—is more complicated, but a workable procedure has been adopted for many issues.)

The Unfair Terms in Consumer Contracts Regulations now pose a greater problem to the transferability of mortgages (and therefore their ability to be securitised) than was previously the case. At the time of writing, the way in which securitisations will be accomplished without specific borrower consents has not yet developed.

The trustee's security over the mortgages, which is a sub-charge and neither registered nor notified, takes effect in equity only, both for registered and unregistered land, but is buttressed by further assurance provisions and irrevocable powers of attorney. This involves obvious legal risks, which should be pointed out in the offering circular. (Again, the position in Scotland is different.)

The trustee will, however, require instant access to the title deeds, which should be held to its order in a manner permitting immediate identification and access. Sometimes the position is complicated by the deeds being held by a third-party depositary rather than the originator itself and in these cases the depository should enter into direct undertakings with the issuer and the trustee.

Assignments of insurances (whether by the originator to the issuer and/or by the issuer as security to the note trustee) can be of limited value (and the former can give rise to a stamp duty charge). Normal practice is to have, in addition to such assignments, both the issuer and the trustee named (or identified) on the policy as co-insureds.

So far as consumer and corporate or trade debts are concerned, a full legal transfer requires notice to be given to the relevant borrowers. An equitable transfer can be effected without notice to the borrowers.

3.2.6 Notes and security documents

The notes themselves must (if issued by a UK-resident company, as has normally been the case hitherto) be in bearer form (as well as listed) in order to ensure that the interest can be paid gross. Sometimes a registered option is built in to cater for US investors, but they have to accept that this interest will be paid net of UK basic rate tax unless treaty relief is available. There is no gross-up obligation even for bearer notes. Permanent (in the absence of certain events affecting the clearing systems) global bearer notes, traded only by book-entry at the clearing systems, are commonplace, but give rise to questions as to who exactly the noteholders are *vis-à-vis* the issuer and the trustee.

Practice has varied on whether redemptions of notes are by drawings or pro rata, but the latter is now normal. Pro rata redemption is (in addition to expense and market convenience) a reason for keeping the notes in global form. Where there is a junior tranche of notes, which is designed to absorb losses at the end of the day, the only fair method for them to be redeemed is pro rata, so that all of the holders of that class of notes share pro rata in any losses.

The security provisions include appropriate charges over or assignments (subject to a proviso for re-assignment) of all of the issuer's assets, together with a general floating charge. Certain of the charges expressed as fixed charges may in fact be floating charges, e.g. over liquid assets managed by or on behalf of the issuer and capable of being sold without the trustee's consent each time. In many cases, notices of assignment will be required. Powers of attorney are also executed.

3.3 REGULATORY CONTROLS

3.3.1 Introduction

In any type of securitisation, whether of mortgages or otherwise, one of the fundamental commercial objectives of the securitisation may be to remove the assets and their financing from, or to show only a net "right-hand column" figure in the balance sheet of the originator and the consolidated balance sheet of the group of companies of which it forms part. In the mortgage field, there are some funding organisations which have been set up to make and finance mortgage advances introduced to it by other organisations in exchange for a broking fee with the intention that the relevant mortgages and their funding should never form part of the balance sheet of the broker.

In any of these cases, English (or Scottish or Northern Irish) law and UK accounting practices will be applicable if the originator (the person who wishes to avoid having the assets and its financing on its balance sheet) or any of its parent companies is registered in the United Kingdom.

3.3.2 The Companies Acts

The accounting requirements of the Companies Act 1985 were extensively amended and restated as from 1 April 1990 when amending provisions contained in the Companies Act 1989 were brought into force. Financial Reporting Standard 2 ("FRS2") amplifies the statutory requirements.

A duty now falls on a parent company to prepare group accounts in respect of itself and its "subsidiary undertakings". This expression is defined in Section 258 of the 1985 Act. It is necessary to ensure that neither the issuing vehicle for the purposes of the securitisation nor its parent company, if any, is a "subsidiary undertaking" of either the originator or the originator's own parent company. On the assumption that neither the originator nor any parent company of the originator (referred to below collectively as the originator) seeks to hold or control a majority of the voting rights in the issuer or its parent company (referred to below collectively as the issuer) or to control board meetings of the issuer, the only two situations which are likely to be of concern in the context of securitisations are the following:

(a) if the originator has "the right to exercise a dominant influence" over the issuer, either by virtue of provisions contained in the issuer's memorandum or articles of association or by virtue of a "control contract"; or
(b) if the originator has a "participating interest" in the issuer and either it actually exercises a dominant influence over it or it and the issuer are managed on a unified basis.

It will be noted that where the originator has the right to exercise a dominant influence over the issuer as described above, this alone is enough to make the issuer its "subsidiary undertaking" without the need for any shareholding. The "right to exercise a dominant influence" is amplified in paragraph 4 of Schedule 9 to the 1989 Act as being a "right to give directions with respect to the operating and financial policies of [the issuer] which its directors are obliged to comply with whether or not they are for the benefit of [the issuer]". But, as mentioned above, this right must arise either by virtue of provisions contained in the issuer's memorandum or articles or by virtue of a control contract, i.e. a contract in writing conferring the right, being a right which is of a kind authorised by the memorandum or articles and is permitted by the issuer's law of establishment. In the context of English companies, a control contract may not be compatible with the duty of directors to act in the interests of their company since it contemplates in effect the abdication by the company concerned of its basic business decisions to someone other than its directors, whether or not those decisions are for the benefit of the company.

Item (b) above is concerned with the *de facto* exercise of a dominant influence (rather than the right to exercise a dominant influence) or the management of the two entities on a unified basis, but only in either case where the originator has a "participating interest". This is defined in Section 260 as meaning shares which are held on a long-term basis for the purpose of securing a contribution to the activities of the company in question, by the exercise of control or influence arising from or related to that interest. "Shares" are defined in Sections 259 and 260(3) and so long as there is no shareholding link between the originator and the issuer, nor any deferred shareholding by means of a convertible loan or an option, neither *de facto* dominant influence nor management on a unified basis should cause the issuer to be a subsidiary undertaking of the originator.

3.3.3 FRS5

Following a long period of gestation, in 1994 the Accounting Standards Board finally published Financial Reporting Standard 5 on "Reporting the Substance of Transactions" (FRS5). FRS5 applies in respect of financial statements relating to accounting periods ending on or after 22 September 1994.

Under FRS5, the appropriate accounting treatment in respect of securitisation depends on whether the originator has retained significant benefits and risks relating to the securitised assets and on whether the issuer, if not a subsidiary undertaking, is nevertheless to be regarded as a "quasi-subsidiary" of the originator. A securitisation is normally structured so as to allow the originator to extract profits from the issuer and such arrangements would amount to the retention of significant benefits under FRS5. An originator which retains significant benefits (or risks) is not permitted to cease to recognise in their entirety securitised assets in its individual accounts but, provided it is certain that its downside exposure to loss is limited, it can adopt a "linked presentation" whereby on the face of its balance sheet the finance raised through the securitisation is deducted from the gross amount of the assets resulting in a net figure in the right-hand column (and therefore the footings) of the balance sheet.

A quasi-subsidiary is a company, trust or other vehicle which, though not fulfilling the definition of a subsidiary undertaking, is directly or indirectly controlled by the reporting entity and gives rise to benefits for that entity that are in substance no different from those that would arise were the vehicle a subsidiary undertaking. Where (as would usually be the case in a securitisation) the issuer is a quasi-subsidiary of the originator, its assets, liabilities, profits, losses and cash flows should be included in the originator's consolidated financial statements. It is possible to use a linked presentation.

The true and fair view override contained in Section 227 of the 1985 Act is treated as justification for consolidating quasi-subsidiaries. The true and fair view override requires additional information, over and above that required to comply with specific provisions of the Act, to be included in group accounts where that is necessary in order to provide a true and fair view of the profit or loss and state of affairs of the group.

3.3.4 Capital adequacy

Capital adequacy regulation requires that credit institutions maintain adequate "core capital" to cover their risk-weighted assets such as mortgage, credit card and other loan portfolios. Securitisation has developed as a technique to help institutions reduce the core capital coverage needed by enabling assets to be taken outside the regulatory accounts.

Where the originator is a bank, one of the objectives is likely to be to ensure that the mortgages and their funding are disregarded for banking supervisory purposes as well as for accounting purposes. Thus, in addition to ensuring that the issuer is not a "subsidiary undertaking" of the bank or its parent company and that the structure qualifies for linked presentation under FRS5, the Bank of England's conditions on mortgage transfers as contained in its Notice dated February 1989 (and amended in April 1992, principally in order to set out the Bank of England's policy regarding securitisation of revolving credit) will also have to be satisfied. Equivalent capital adequacy requirements applicable to building societies have also been formulated by the Building Societies Commission, and its views are presently set out in a draft Prudential Note on Securitisation published in June 1994.

Banks and other financial institutions which are subject to capital adequacy requirements are known to be investors in asset-backed securities. The implications of investing in asset-backed securities for capital adequacy purposes have to be considered against the background of the European Community Solvency Ratio Directive and the Capital Adequacy Directive. The Solvency Ratio Directive is implemented in the UK with regard to banks by Notices issued by the Banking Supervision Division of the Bank of England. Under a Notice issued in November 1992, mortgage-backed securities qualify to be classed as 50 per cent risk assets provided certain conditions are satisfied. The conditions are:

(i) The notes embody an express promise to repay the bearer.

(ii) The issue documentation contains provisions which would ultimately enable noteholders to initiate legal proceedings directly against the issuer of the mortgage-backed securities. As an example such provisions would allow noteholders to proceed against the issuer where the trustee, having become bound to take steps and/or to proceed against the issuer, fails to do so within a reasonable time and such failure is continuing.

(iii) The documentation contains provisions which would ultimately enable noteholders to acquire the legal title to the security (i.e. the mortgagee's interest in it) and to realise the security in the event of a default by the mortgagor.

(iv) The issue meets the conditions set out in the reporting instructions to the Bank's Capital Adequacy Return, BSD1.

(v) The mortgage loans must not be in default at the time at which they are transferred to the vehicle.

Mortgage-backed securities which do not satisfy these conditions must be weighted for capital adequacy purposes at 100 per cent.

The Solvency Ratio Directive is implemented in the UK for building societies by Prudential Notes issued by the Building Societies Commission.

Mortgage-backed securities held for trading purposes are within the scope of the Capital Adequacy Directive which is implemented with effect from 1 January 1996 by a Bank of England Notice. Banks which hold mortgage-backed securities as part of a trading book will enjoy more favourable capital adequacy treatment under this Directive than under the Solvency Ratio Directive (a treatment similar to that currently enjoyed by securities firms) because the measurement of risk is done on a more sophisticated basis. The present view of the Building Societies Commission is that building societies are not permitted to operate a trading book.

3.3.5 Profit extraction

Given that taking profit out by way of a continuing fee is likely to run into VAT and/or tax deductibility problems, there are now broadly speaking three ways which may be available to achieve the extraction from the securitisation vehicle of most of its profit for the benefit of the originator, without the latter holding any form of share in the former and ignoring the use of offshore vehicles:

(i) splitting the cash flows receivable by the vehicle by, in effect, partially assigning the assets concerned so that only part of the cash flow is beneficially owned by the vehicle; however, this gives rise to problems in the case of mortgages because of the MIRAS system;

(ii) providing a deferred consideration to the originator where the assets are sold by the originator to the vehicle or brokerage to the originator where they are created by the vehicle at the introduction of the originator; this can only work if the vehicle is a trading, rather than investment, company for tax purposes and is in any case subject to other conditions to achieve tax neutrality in the vehicle;

(iii) establishing a swap or parallel loan between the originator and the vehicle; again tax neutrality is essential but is not always easily achievable.

In all cases the shares in the vehicle must be held otherwise than by or for the originator, and charitable or heritage trusts are common. However, difficult liability questions arise for the directors, and an unlimited indemnity in their favour by the originator could prejudice linked-presentation balance sheet status.

3.4 SECURITIES REGULATION

3.4.1 Investment business

The Financial Services Act 1986 (the FSA) prohibits the unauthorised carrying on of investment business in the United Kingdom. Although "investment business" is widely defined, various exemptions are in place and in most cases one (or more) of these exemptions will apply so that the transfer of assets from the originator to the issuer will not require authorisation even if those assets are investments for the purposes of the FSA.

3.4.2 Collective investment schemes

The securitisation of a mortgage pool or, indeed, any other asset pool has prima facie attributes of a collective investment scheme for the purposes of the FSA. The FSA provisions relating to collective investment schemes are designed to regulate collective participation (for investment purposes) in any kind of assets. Stringent marketing restrictions apply; and the "manager" of the underlying assets needs to be a person authorised to carry on investment business in the United Kingdom. Compliance with the regulations governing collective investment schemes involves substantial time and cost. However, there is an exception from the collective investment scheme requirements (granted partly as a result of representations from those involved in the securitisation markets) where the "rights or interests of the participants [i.e. the investors] are represented by [debt instruments] issued by a single body corporate . . .". An SPV may take advantage of this exception (as may the originator or whoever it is who is to service the mortgage pool). On the other hand, US-style "pass-through" arrangements would almost certainly constitute a collective investment scheme, as would arrangements which interposed a trust structure between the investors and the mortgage pool.

3.4.3 Listing

If asset-backed securities are to be listed on the London Stock exchange, Part IV of the FSA must be complied with. Part IV was amended by the Public Offers of Securities Regulations 1995 in order to implement into English law a European Union directive relating to public offers. One of the main effects of the amendments is to require an issuer to issue a prospectus in many of the circumstances where it would previously have issued listing particulars. Whilst this means that there is an important terminological change, it should be noted that the information required to be included in a prospectus is in substance identical to that required in listing particulars. There are various exemptions from the requirement to produce a prospectus as opposed to listing particulars including the "professionals" exemption (i.e. an offer to persons whose ordinary activities involve them in acquiring, holding, managing or disposing of investments (as principal or agent) for the purposes of their business or to persons who it is reasonable to expect will acquire, hold, manage or dispose of investments (as principal or agent) for the purposes of their business). This exemption is considered to be sufficiently wide for the purpose of most euromarket (including asset-backed) issues. There is also an exemption relating to "euro-securities" but this exemption is subject to conditions which significantly limit the extent to which it can be relied upon in practice.

Listing particulars must be drawn up and published in accordance with the Exchange's Listing Rules. The information that must be included in listing particulars relating to specialist debt securities, including asset-backed securities, is, for the most part, less extensive than that normally required for domestic issues but there are special rules for asset-backed securities under which details of the securitised assets, the structure of the transaction, risks, parties involved and financial enhancements must be disclosed. These special rules are consistent with best practice in issues of asset-backed securities and they do not represent an obstacle to transactions.

The listing particulars must also comply with the general duty of disclosure imposed by Section 146 of the FSA. Listing particulars must contain all such information as investors and their professional advisers would reasonably require and reasonably expect to find there, for the purpose of making an informed assessment of:

(a) the assets and liabilities, financial position, profits and losses, and prospects of the issuer; and
(b) the rights attaching to the securities.

This general duty of disclosure is, in a sense, qualified because in determining what information is required regard is to be had to the nature of the securities and of the issuer, and to the nature of the persons likely to consider acquiring the securities. Asset-backed securities tend only to be brought and traded by professional, experienced investors.

The other market on which asset-backed securities are commonly listed is the Luxembourg Stock Exchange. Under the Public Offers of Securities Regulations 1995 a prospectus must be produced when securities which are not admitted to, nor the subject of an application for, listing in the UK are offered to the public in the UK for the first time. However, this requirement to produce a prospectus is subject to various exemptions which are identical to those which apply to London-listed issues. Accordingly, reliance may be placed on the professionals exemption to the extent that the securities are offered in the UK so as to avoid the requirement to produce a prospectus.

3.4.4 Miscellaneous marketing restrictions

Section 57 of the FSA restricts the issue of investment advertisements in the United Kingdom. This provision is potentially applicable to the various documents which accompany an issue of asset-backed securities such as the invitation telex and allotment telex. Exemption orders can usually be taken advantage of to avoid the application of Section 57 but care must be taken to ensure that any conditions to which an exemption is subject are complied with.

Another marketing restriction is Section 56 of the FSA which regulates the practice of "cold calling". There are wide exemptions covering the operation of the international capital markets so that, in practice, Section 56 is not a significant concern.

3.4.5. Liability

The FSA imposes civil liability on those responsible for listing particulars which contain false or misleading statements or which omit information which should have been disclosed. The directors of an issuer of asset-backed securities are not, merely by virtue of their office, subject to this liability because of a special exemption for debt securities provided by the FSA.

An aggrieved investor could also seek to bring an action at common law for deceit or negligence or for misrepresentation under the Misrepresentation Act 1967.

The subscription agreement between the originator, issuer and managers of the issue will usually contain detailed warranties about the assets being securitised and the parties involved. If any of the warranties proves to be untrue, the managers may pursue their contractual remedies and may, under the terms of the subscription agreement, be entitled to claim an indemnity from the originator and/or issuer.

Criminal liability can arise under the Theft Act 1986, the Companies Act 1985 and, most importantly, under Section 47 of the FSA. Section 47 imposes criminal penalties on the making of misleading, false or deceptive investment-related statements or the concealment of material facts. Section 47 also makes it an offence to do acts or engage in conduct which create a false or misleading impression as to markets or as to the price or value of investments. The offences under Section 47 require intention, purpose or, at least, recklessness and they cannot be committed accidentally or through mere carelessness. Nevertheless, they are an important safeguard against abuse.

3.5 CONCLUSION

The market is developing rapidly and by the time this book is published, certain of the techniques addressed in this chapter may well have been overtaken by innovations. A single chapter covering the whole spectrum of UK legal implications of securitisations can only deal with some of the many legal issues, and even then not in depth; each new product which is sought to be securitised brings with it new legal problems and adds several further pages to the formal opinions delivered by the lawyers.*

RUPERT BEAUMONT

* The author would like to acknowledge with gratitude the considerable help he has received from his colleague, Eilís Ferran, who is also a Lecturer at Cambridge University.

CHAPTER 4

SELECTED LEGAL ASPECTS OF STRUCTURED US MORTGAGE FINANCING

4.1 INTRODUCTION

4.1.1 Nature of structured mortgage financings

Mortgages have both market value and borrowing value. Mortgage-backed securities are securities structured on the basis of the market value or borrowing value of identified mortgages determined, in principle, without regard to the creditworthiness of the seller or borrower.

4.1.2 Types of mortgage-backed securities

Mortgage-backed securities typically take the form, for tax, accounting and other purposes, of a sale or secured financing of a pool of identified mortgages. In the case of mortgage-backed securities structured as financings, the borrowing value of the underlying mortgages may be based on either their market value ("market-value securities") or their anticipated cash flows ("cash-flow securities"). Because mortgages are subject to acceleration and prepayment, referred to generally as early payment, cash-flow securities may be further divided into securities as to which the investor bears the risk of early payment ("pay-through securities") and securities as to which the issuer bears that risk ("fixed-payment securities").

4.1.3 Issuers

In order to maximize the separation between the creditworthiness of the ultimate beneficiary of a mortgage-backed financing and the credit of the mortgage-backed security, it is sometimes necessary, for rating agency and marketing purposes, for the mortgage-backed security to be issued by a trust or a finance subsidiary limited in purpose to the issuance of such securities and activities incidental thereto.

4.1.4 Credit support

Although mortgage-backed securities are structured, in principle, solely on the basis of the market value or borrowing value of the underlying mortgages, it is often necessary, again for rating-agency and marketing purposes, to provide supplemental credit support to protect against the underlying obligors' payment default. This credit support may take the form of an insurance policy, a guarantee, a repurchase obligation or arrangements under which credit risk is allocated among classes of securities—senior and subordinated—to enhance the credit of the senior class or classes.

4.1.5 Servicing

Mortgages must be "serviced" on behalf of their owner either by the originator of the mortgages, by an affiliate of the originator, or by an independent, third-party servicer. The servicer typically collects payments on the mortgages and remits those payments, net of the servicer's fee, to the owner/investor. In the event the obligor fails to make a required payment, the servicer is also typically required to pursue payment and, if necessary, foreclose (or otherwise liquidate) the pledged collateral.

4.1.6 Examples

Mortgage-backed securities generally take the form of instruments that purport to be either a sale or a financing of the underlying mortgages.

Securities evidencing the sale of mortgages

Mortgage-backed securities evidencing the sale of mortgages ("pass-through securities") generally take the form of an undivided fractional ownership interest in the corpus of a passive trust consisting of mortgages (a "pass-through certificate") or the form of an assignment of a participation interest in specified financial instruments (a "participation certificate"). The GNMA's "fully modified pass-through" mortgage-backed certificates and the FNMA's mortgage-backed securities are examples of pass-through certificates. "Stripped" pass-through certificates represent a further evolution. In the typical "strip" transaction, a trust issues two classes of pass-through certificates, each representing a different ownership (or participation) interest in the principal and interest payments on the underlying mortgages. For example, one class of pass-through certificates might represent the right to receive all principal, with the other class representing the right to receive all interest payments. Pass-through securities may also provide for senior and junior ownership interests in the trust's assets, in which event the right of the junior certificate-holders to receive periodic distributions is subordinate to the right of the senior certificate-holders. Since the adoption of the REMIC tax legislation, discussed in Chapter 8, it has been possible to issue securities in multiple classes or tranches, with a wide variety of interest rates or formulas, and with specified priorities as to the sequence of distribution of principal payments. Hundreds of billions of dollars of such securities have been issued in the last few years.

Debt securities

The prevalence of REMIC structures has made debt issues less common in recent years, but debt offerings can be divided into three types.

(1) Market-value securities An example of a market-value security is a bond secured by mortgages having at all times a market value at least equal to a specified multiple of either (a) the bond's outstanding principal balance plus accrued interest or (b) a portfolio of US government securities having future cash flows at least equal to the future debt service on the bonds. In the event the market value of the collateral falls below the specified level, the issuer may be required to pledge additional collateral, to pay off a principal amount of bonds such that the remaining collateral satisfies the market value test, or to purchase a portfolio of US government securities sufficient to "defease" the bonds.

(2) Cash-flow securities The most common examples of pay-through securities are so-called fast-pay/slow-pay collateralized mortgage obligations (CMOs), which are typically structured as multiple-class financings secured by a pledge of a single pool of mortgages. Principal payments on each class of bonds are made in the order of their stated maturity, such that no principal payment is made on any class of bonds until each earlier class of bonds has been paid in full, or in another designated sequence. Prepayments on the underlying mortgages are "paid through" to bondholders such that the remaining principal amount of bonds can be supported by the minimum future payments on the remaining mortgages. As a result, the amount and timing of principal payments on a CMO are determined by reference to the amount and timing of principal payments on the underlying mortgages.

(3) Fixed payment securities A fixed-payment security is a bond having a fixed stated instalment of principal and interest due on each payment date. The aggregate amount of the instalment may not exceed the minimum scheduled cash flow on the mortgages pledged as collateral. The issuer of a fixed-payment security is typically required to invest any early payments at a rate at least equal to the rate initially used in determining the future debt service requirement on the bonds. Early payments on the underlying mortgages thus do not affect the amount or timing of principal payments on a fixed-payment security.

4.1.7 Sale versus financing

The use of thinly capitalized limited-purpose finance subsidiaries and, in the case of cash-flow securities, the close connection between the payment terms of the security and the payments received on the issuer's assets may call into question the proper characterization, for tax, accounting and other purposes, of mortgage-backed securities. This issue is discussed in section 4.2 below.

4.1.8 Bankruptcy

The legal issues relevant to the insulation of the financial performance of a mortgage-backed security from the bankruptcy or insolvency of the issuer and its affiliates are discussed in section 4.3 below.

4.1.9 Investment Company Act

The assets of an issuer of mortgage-backed securities typically consist primarily of mortgages and instruments backed by mortgages (such as pass-through securities), some of which may be considered "securities" within the meaning of the Investment Company Act of 1940. Section 4.4 below discusses the application of the Investment Company Act to mortgage-backed securities.

4.2 SALE VERSUS FINANCING

A mortgage-backed security may purport to be either a sale of mortgages or a financing secured by a pledge of the underlying mortgages. The intended characterization, as a sale or financing, of the transfer of mortgages to a limited-purpose finance subsidiary and their subsequent transfer in favour of security-holders (or a trustee acting on behalf of security-holders) are each subject to recharacterization for bankruptcy, tax and accounting purposes. The issues relevant to the recharacterization of a transfer for bankruptcy purposes, although less well developed, generally look to the same factors considered relevant for tax and accounting purposes. The existence of other creditors having equitable claims on a bankrupt's estate may, however, result in a bankruptcy court recharacterizing a purported sale as a secured financing, without a corresponding recharacterization for other purposes.

4.2.1 "True sales"

The independence of the market or borrowing value of a pool of mortgages may be affected by the recharacterization (as a secured financing) of their purported sale to a limited-purpose finance subsidiary, or by the recharacterization (as a secured financing) of the subsidiary's subsequent purported sale of the mortgages to investors (or to a trustee acting on their behalf). If the parent company is subsequently declared bankrupt and the purported sale to its limited-purpose finance subsidiary is recharacterized as a secured financing, the transferred assets will remain the property of the parent's estate, subject to the automatic stay and other provisions of the Bankruptcy Code discussed in section 4.3 below. A similar result will follow if the purported sale to investors by the subsidiary is later recharacterized as a secured financing in the subsidiary's bankruptcy. By contrast, if the initial transfer to the limited-purpose finance subsidiary and the subsequent transfer to investors are "true sales", the subsequent bankruptcy of the parent company or the limited-purpose subsidiary would not affect the market or borrowing value of the transferred assets (absent a "substantive consolidation" of the parent's and the subsidiary's assets of the type described in section 4.3 below).

Recourse and control

A variety of factors may affect the characterization of a transfer as a "true sale" or a financing. The principal factor is the transferee's direct or indirect recourse against the purported seller in the event of non-payment by the underlying obligor, in an amount in excess of historical default rates. Having invested on the basis of the seller's credit, the purported purchaser is likely to be treated in bankruptcy together with the seller's other creditors. Recourse to the seller has traditionally taken the form of a direct call on all of the seller's assets. In the case of junior/senior pass-through securities where the junior interest is retained by the seller, it can be argued that similar recourse is indirectly provided in the form of the seller's guarantee of the senior interest, albeit limited to amounts that would otherwise be received by the seller as the holder of the junior interest. The likelihood that the retention of the junior interest will be treated as a guarantee by the seller obviously increases to the extent the amount of the subordinated interest effectively protects the senior certificate-holders against the risk of defaults on the underlying mortgages.

A second important factor in characterizing a transfer is the purported seller's right, as servicer of the mortgages, to control payments received from the underlying obligors and to commingle those payments with its own funds pending their remittance to investors. Amounts on deposit in a bankrupt's general account, invested for the benefit of the bankrupt and not otherwise identified or segregated, may be made available to the bankrupt's creditors in preference to the ownership claims of investors who failed to insist that payments purportedly purchased by them be at all times invested for their benefit and be identifiable as such.

Other factors

Other considerations relevant to the characterization of a transfer include:

- whether the seller/servicer remits a fixed amount to the buyer each month, regardless of the amount actually collected on the underlying mortgages;
- whether the seller/servicer has the right to repurchase the underlying mortgages;
- whether the buyer retains the right unilaterally to alter the terms of the transfer;
- whether the buyer makes an independent evaluation of the creditworthiness of the obligors;
- whether the buyer notifies the obligors of the sale; and
- whether the seller/servicer is entitled to payments in excess of the "purchase price" and reasonable servicing compensation.

Application to pass-through securities

The "true sale" issue is perhaps of greatest relevance in the case of pass-through securities that are intended to be purchased and/or rated without regard to the subsequent creditworthiness of the seller/servicer. Steps that can be taken to reduce the likelihood of recharacterization of pass-through securities include delivery of the mortgage notes and related mortgages to an independent custodian or trustee, recordation of assignments of mortgage in the name of the independent trustee, and segregation of mortgage payments pending their remittance to investors. The decision to take one or more of these steps, all of which involve administrative and other costs, should reflect the intended use of the pass-through securities. For example, participation certificates intended to be used to facilitate whole-loan trading among sophisticated institutions have not traditionally been documented with the same concern for the recharacterization issue as has been the case with pass-through securities intended to be rated and sold to the public or to be used as collateral for other rated mortgage-backed securities.

Guaranteed pass-through securities

A pass-through security guaranteed by the seller or one of its affiliates generally precludes the rendering of a "true sale" opinion of the type required to obtain a rating without regard to the creditworthiness of the seller/servicer, but also renders such an opinion unnecessary in that the rating of a 100 per cent guaranteed pass-through security should be based on the creditworthiness of the guarantor, rather than that of the underlying mortgages.

Treatment of thrift-sponsored pass-through securities

Prior to the enactment of the Financial Institutions Reform, Recovery and Enforcement Act of 1989 (FIRREA) rating agencies and counsel drew comfort in transactions involving thrift-sponsored pass-through securities intended to be treated as sales from a letter released by the Office of General Counsel of the Federal Home Loan Bank Board stating that, in its opinion, a typical transaction involving a junior/senior pass-through security in which a thrift sells mortgages to a trust and retains the junior interest in the mortgages would be treated as a sale in the event of the insolvency of the thrift in which the Federal Savings and Loan Insurance Corporation (FSLIC) acted as receiver. Under FIRREA, the FSLIC was dissolved and the Federal Deposit Insurance Corporation (FDIC) (or the Resolution Trust Corporation acting under FDIC management) was designated as the primary receiver for insolvent thrifts. The FDIC subsequently indicated that it concurs with the views expressed in the letter of the Federal Home Loan Bank Board's General Counsel.

4.2.2 Accounting considerations

Statement of Financial Accounting Standards (FAS) No. 77, "Reporting by Transferors for Transfers of Receivables with Recourse", together with FASB Technical Bulletin No. 85–2, specify circumstances under which transactions that "purport to be" sales of mortgages with recourse to the seller should be accounted for as sales, rather than as financings. Three conditions must be satisfied in order to obtain sale treatment:

- the transferor must surrender its control of the "future economic benefits" relating to the mortgages;
- the transferor must be able to make a reasonable estimation of its obligations under the recourse provisions; and
- the transferee must not be able to "put" the mortgages sold to the transferor except pursuant to the recourse provisions.

Sale treatment is unlikely if a seller of mortgages is able, at its option, to repurchase the mortgages at a later date, and thereby retain their future economic benefit. This situation may be distinguished from "clean-up calls", often granted to seller/servicers of pass-through securities, which permit the seller to repurchase transferred mortgages when their aggregate outstanding balance is minor and "not significant to the transferor". FAS No. 77 acknowledges that such "clean-up calls" should not alone preclude a transfer from being recognized as a sale. Sale treatment is also less likely if the seller is unable to estimate the amount of its contingent obligation pursuant to the recourse provisions. According to the Financial Accounting Standards Board, the liability to estimate reasonably the amount of a contingent recourse obligation results in the postponement of sale recognition not because risk has been retained *per se*, but because of the significant uncertainty associated with the amount of retained risk.

Special application to CMOs

FAS No. 77 does not by its terms apply to CMOs, since CMOs do not "purport to be sales" and are not structured as sale agreements but rather as collateralized borrowings. As a result of the uncertain application of FAS No. 77 to CMOs, in March 1985 the Financial Accounting Standards Board issued FASB Technical Bulletin (TB) No. 85–2, which establishes a presumption that CMOs are to be accounted for as secured financings. TB No. 85–2 does, however, contemplate that a CMO could be recognized as a sale transaction if all but a nominal portion of the future economic benefits inherent in the collateral have been irrevocably transferred to the investor and no affiliate of the issuer can be required to make future payments on the CMOs. Any CMO structured to qualify as a sale under TB No. 85–2 is, absent a REMIC election, unlikely to qualify as a financing for federal income tax purposes, with the adverse tax consequences discussed above.

4.3 BANKRUPTCY AND SECURITY INTERESTS

4.3.1 Bankruptcy Code and non-Bankruptcy Code debtors

Limited-purpose finance subsidiaries of thrifts and other issuers of mortgage-backed securities are subject to the Federal Bankruptcy Code of 1978, as amended (the "Bankruptcy Code"). Insolvent thrifts, by contrast, are subject to conservatorships or receivership proceedings. A conservatorship or receivership will generally be conducted by the FDIC (or the Resolution Trust Corporation (RTC) acting under FDIC management) under FIRREA but in some cases may depend on the thrift's insurer, the thrift's chartering authority (state or federal) and the circumstances under which the receiver was appointed. A thrift may be insured by either the FDIC or a state insurance agency. Since the vast majority of thrifts are FDIC insured, this outline focuses on FDIC (or RTC) conservatorships and receiverships under FIRREA.

4.3.2 Issuer bankruptcy

Sales

In the event of the bankruptcy of a seller/servicer of a mortgage-backed security not recharacterized as a financing, the underlying mortgages would not become property of the issuer's estate under section 541(d) of the Bankruptcy Code. In the case of direct offerings by thrift institutions, regulations proposed by the Federal Home Loan Bank Board prior to the enactment of FIRREA made clear that the same result would obtain in the event of the receivership of a thrift. While these regulations might not bind the FDIC (or the RTC) as conservator or receiver of a thrift, it is not likely that a conservator or receiver would attempt to include purportedly sold mortgages in an insolvent thrift's estate without attempting to recharacterize the transaction as a financing.

Financings

In the case of a mortgage-backed security characterized as a financing (either explicitly or by recharacterization) and issued by a Bankruptcy Code debtor, the collateral securing the mortgage-backed security would remain the property of the debtor's estate and foreclosure would be prohibited by operation of the automatic stay provision contained in section 362 of the Bankruptcy Code. The debtor would also have the right to use the collateral so long as the secured party is afforded "adequate protection".

If the issuer is a thrift institution, there is no explicit provision similar to the Bankruptcy Code's automatic stay. Under FIRREA, the FDIC is granted a substantial amount of discretion in conducting a conservatorship or receivership of an insolvent thrift. One option available to the FDIC is to organize a new thrift to take over the insolvent thrift's assets and to assume some of its liabilities. Prior to the enactment of FIRREA, such a "purchase and assumption" transaction was the most common method of dealing with thrift insolvency. In such a transaction, secured creditors are generally not entitled to accelerate their claims and proceed against the collateral if the secured obligation is assumed, which is usually the case. In addition, a secured creditor presumably would not be able to liquidate collateral pending a decision by the FDIC as to whether the new thrift will assume the obligation. It is not yet clear whether the FDIC will continue the practice of structuring "purchase and assumption" transactions under FIRREA.

Regardless of the method of resolution of an insolvency, FIRREA gives the FDIC (or the RTC), as conservator or receiver of an insolvent thrift, the power to determine claims, including claims of "security, preference or priority" under routine claims procedures. It is generally thought that these procedures will not be applicable to the liquidation of collateral in the possession of a secured creditor. In addition, FIRREA would generally prohibit the exercise of any rights by a secured creditor without the FDIC's consent if those rights arise "upon, or solely by reason of", insolvency or appointment of a conservator or receiver. Thus a trustee for mortgage-backed bonds issued by a thrift would not be entitled to accelerate the bonds or liquidate the collateral upon the insolvency of the thrift absent the occurrence of an event of default other than the insolvency event. Assuming no default exists prior to the insolvency, the trustee may be required to wait until the next payment is missed before it can exercise any rights against the collateral.

4.3.3 Parent bankruptcy

The issuance of mortgage-backed securities through a finance subsidiary does not necessarily insulate investors from the subsequent bankruptcy or insolvency of the issuer's parent. In addition to the consequences of a bankruptcy court recharacterizing the parent's transfer of assets to its finance subsidiary as a secured financing, discussed above, under certain circumstances a bankruptcy court may order the "substantive consolidation" of the assets and liabilities of the subsidiary with those of its parent. Substantive consolidation may occur without regard to the solvency of the subsidiary.

Strictly speaking, substantive consolidation may be ordered only when both parent and subsidiary are in bankruptcy proceedings. The term, however, has come to be used more generally to refer to any court order that disregards the separate legal identity of a subsidiary, whether by "piercing the corporate veil" or by finding that the subsidiary is a "mere instrumentality" or "alter ego" of the parent. The following factors support recognition of the "separateness" of the issuing subsidiary:

- the presence of independent officers and directors; a separate business office, even if space is subleased from the parent;
- separate books and records and no commingling of assets; and
- the "holding out" of the subsidiary as a separate entity and not as a division or branch of the parent.

The consequences of substantive consolidation will differ dramatically depending on whether the securities issued constitute secured debt or equity. In the case of secured debt, the security interest should remain effective as against the parent even though the collateral would remain subject to the automatic stay provisions in the case of a Bankruptcy Code debtor. In the case of an equity security, a securityholder would be a stockholder whose claims might be subordinate to those of all the creditors of the consolidated entity.

4.3.4 Fraudulent conveyance

A trustee in bankruptcy may recover, as a "fraudulent conveyance", any amount transferred for less than a "reasonably equivalent value" if the debtor was insolvent or rendered insolvent at the time of transfer.[1] A bankruptcy trustee may also recover any amount transferred in violation of state fraudulent conveyance laws.[2] The various state fraudulent conveyance statutes differ in

1. Bankruptcy Code section 548.
2. Bankruptcy Code section 544(b).

language, but generally are to the same effect as the Bankruptcy Code provision. A "transfer" for such purposes includes the sale or a pledge of assets. The concern that a transfer will subsequently be found to have been a fraudulent conveyance is greatest in the case of market-value securities, where the market value of the mortgages transferred to a finance subsidiary and pledged in favour of investors may be of the order of 180 per cent of the proceeds realized on issuance and remitted to the parent company. The issuer's subsequent obligation to "top up", by transferring additional collateral sufficient to satisfy the specified market-value test, raises the same issue. Under the Bankruptcy Code, the satisfaction of antecedent debt would (and under state fraudulent conveyance laws should) constitute value given for the newly transferred assets.

4.3.5 Preferences

A trustee in bankruptcy may recover from a transferee any amount "transferred" on account of an "antecedent debt" within one year prior to the filing of a bankruptcy petition in the case of a transfer in favour of any "insider", and within 90 days in all other cases.[3] Corporate affiliates will generally be "insiders". Preference problems typically arise in connection with the pledge of additional collateral ("topping up") or the pledge of substitute collateral having a value in excess of the released collateral. The use of an unsecured demand note as a credit-support mechanism also raises preference problems, if payment is made during the preference period. The pledge of collateral simultaneously with the making of the demand note and the issuance of the mortgage-backed security would, however, be for "new value", and not on account of an "antecedent debt". To the extent that the demand note is not under-collateralized, a subsequent payment thereunder in an amount not in excess of the market value of the collateral securing the demand note should therefore not be deemed to be a transfer on account of an "antecedent debt".

4.3.6 Right of purchase

Under a former FSLIC regulation, a FSLIC-insured thrift was required to grant the FSLIC a 30-day right of first refusal in the event of a foreclosure following an event of default (whether or not insolvency-related) involving "illiquid" collateral. "Illiquid" collateral included whole mortgage loans and most privately placed mortgage-backed securities. This right of first refusal could both delay foreclosure and reduce foreclosure proceeds.[4] The continuing applicability of this rule is unclear.

3. Bankruptcy Code section 547.
4. 12 C.F.R. section 563-8.2 (1984).

4.3.7 Security interests

In the case of mortgage-backed securities characterized as secured financings, appropriate steps must be taken to create and perfect the investors' security interest in the underlying mortgages. Otherwise, in the event of the issuer's bankruptcy, investors would have only an unsecured claim against the bankrupt's estate.

Even in the case of transactions that purport to be sales, it is prudent to take the same steps to protect the interests of investors in the event the transaction is recharacterized as a financing. These precautionary steps, generally of little economic or administrative cost, are not likely to be given great weight by a court in determining whether to recharacterize a purported sale transaction as a secured financing.

Perfecting security interests in instruments and chattel paper

A security interest in an obligation constituting an "instrument" within the meaning of Article 9 of the Uniform Commercial Code (UCC) (for example, a mortgage note, any other negotiable instrument and any certificated security) may be perfected by possession. Because there is some judicial authority that certain proceeds of a GNMA certificate (that is, a "certificated security") are "general intangibles" for purposes of the UCC, it may be prudent to file a UC financing statement in the appropriate jurisdiction to ensure perfection of an investor's security interest in the distributions on certificated securities. If the obligation instead constitutes "chattel paper" within the meaning of Article 9 (for example, a lease or an instalment sales contract relating to equipment or other personal property used as additional collateral for a mortgage loan), the secured party must either file a UCC–1 financing statement against the debtor or take possession of the chattel paper. If possession is not practicable, the chattel paper should be stamped to note that it has been sold or pledged. Absent such notation, a purchaser for value who takes possession, in the ordinary course of business, without knowledge of the security interest, in a subsequent sale or financing involving the same chattel paper, may have priority over the interest of the secured party.

Perfecting security interests in mortgages

Although mortgage notes constitute instruments for purposes of Article 9, there is no uniform rule as to whether the provisions of Article 9 are applicable to the related mortgage. The source of this confusion is a conflict between UCC sections 9-102(3) and 9-104(j). Section 9-104(j) excludes from the coverage of Article 9 "the creation or transfer of an interest in or lien on real estate", implying that mortgages would not be covered by Article 9. Section 9-102(3), however, states that Article 9 is applicable to obligations secured by transactions or interests outside the scope of Article 9.[5] Based on Comment 4 to section 9-102(3), the safer answer appears to be that perfection of an interest in a mortgage note is accomplished by possession, while perfection of an interest in the related mortgage is governed by local real property law and may require the filing of an assignment of mortgage executed by the debtor. Because various jurisdictions have adopted different interpretations of sections 9-104(j) and 9-102(3), local case law should be consulted. Unlike most other steps required to perfect a security interest, recordation of an assignment of a mortgage may involve considerable expense and administrative inconvenience.

Perfecting security interests in book-entry securities

The issuance of FNMA and FHLMC (Federal Home Loan Mortgage Corporation) securities in book-entry form raises complicated perfection issues. Transfer of these securities is governed by federal regulation. Effective transfer of book-entry securities to a purchaser or pledgee will, in most cases, require at least two transfers: a transfer on the books and records of an eligible Federal Reserve Bank to a depository bank maintaining an account with such Federal Reserve Bank, and a transfer on the books and records of such depository bank in favour of the purchaser or pledgee. The interplay of the federal regulations that expressly govern such transfers and the provisions of the UCC that are invoked by the federal regulations may raise questions with respect to, among other things, the bona-fide purchaser status of a transferee and the correct method of transfer.

Perfecting security interests in securities held through a clearing corporation

Virtually all GNMA certificates have been deposited with Participants Trust Company (PTC) which transfers the interests of its members in the GNMA certificates only on PTC's books and records. PTC's agent bank retains physical possession of the certificates. Transfer of interests in GNMA certificates will therefore be governed by the UCC provisions governing the transfer of "certificated securities" by clearing corporations.[6]

4.4 THE INVESTMENT COMPANY ACT OF 1940

4.4.1 General application

The Investment Company Act of 1940 (the "1940 Act") was originally intended to prevent abuses by investment managers in the administration and investment

5. See also Comment 4, as amended, to section 9-102(3).
6. UCC section 8-320.

of large liquid pools of funds, typically mutual funds. The 1940 Act regulates any entity that is an "investment company", defined as any entity that

(1) engages primarily in investing, reinvesting or trading in securities (or holds itself out as doing so);
(2) issues face-amount certificates of the instalment type; or
(3) engages in investing, reinvesting, owning, holding or trading in securities and owns (or proposes to acquire) investment securities whose value exceeds 40 per cent of the value of the issuer's assets.

4.4.2 Application to structured mortgage financing

It can be argued that the protections of the 1940 Act are not required in the case of CMOs (and certain other mortgage-backed securities), since first, the underlying financial instruments are pledged in favour of a trustee under a Trust Indenture Act qualifying indenture, and thereafter no mortgage is added to or substituted for those initially pledged, and second, the payment terms of the CMO are fixed on the date of issuance. Nevertheless, structured financings will generally involve an "investment company", since the SEC staff has ruled that notes (or other instruments) are "securities" within the meaning of section 3(a) of the 1940 Act.[7] As a result of the costs and administrative inconvenience of registering under the 1940 Act, most issuers of mortgage-backed securities have structured their operations so as to fall within one of the statutory exceptions to the definition of an investment company or have sought individual exemptive orders pursuant to section 6(c) of the 1940 Act.

4.4.3 Structured financing exemption: Rule 3a-7

In response to the extremely rapid growth of structured financing in the United States and the increasingly evident constraints that the Act was imposing on the development of innovative structures for the securitization of new classes of assets, the Commission proposed Rule 3a-7 in May 1992. On November 19, 1992, the Securities and Exchange Commission (the "Commission") adopted Rule 3a-7 ("Rule 3a-7") under the 1940 Act. Rule 3a-7 exempts certain structured financings from regulation under the 1940 Act by excluding from the definition of "investment company" certain issuers engaged in acquiring and holding eligible financial assets. Payments on such an issuer's securities must depend primarily on the cash flow generated by such eligible assets. An entity exempt under Rule 3a-7 may publicly issue investment-grade fixed-income securities, may sell unrated on non-investment-trade fixed-income securities to institutional accredited investors and may sell any type of securities to qualified institutional buyers (as defined in Rule 144A under the Securities Act of 1933) or to persons involved in its organization or operation.

7. See, for example, *Mortgage Backed Income Fund* (pub. avail. 31 July 1979).

Subject to some restrictions, Rule 3a-7 exempts "any issuer who is engaged in the business of purchasing, or otherwise acquiring, and holding eligible assets (and in activities related or incidental thereto)". Eligible assets consist of *any* financial assets, either fixed or revolving, that by their terms convert into cash within a finite period of time. Although the Commission did not include in the final rule an illustrative list of eligible assets as it did in its original proposal, it noted that all the assets enumerated in the proposing release and the additional assets specified in subsequent comment letters would be considered eligible assets.[8] Noting that "it is impossible to devise a definition of eligible assets that will include *all* types of assets that can be securitized", the Commission invited no-action requests with respect to specific assets that may not meet the rule's definition of "eligible assets" but meet the rule's intent.

Rule 3a-7 defines "eligible assets" in a manner that includes credit and liquidity arrangements supporting payment of the securities or the underlying assets, such as mortgage insurance and title insurance, and ancillary or incidental assets such as short-term reinvestments, proceeds received in respect of eligible assets and collateral securing an eligible asset. In addition, Rule 3a-7 allows issuers to engage in activities that are related or incidental to the business of acquiring and holding eligible assets, such as filing registration statements and servicing assets.

While permitting a broad range of assets to be securitized, Rule 3a-7 imposes several conditions that the Commission found to be consistent with current practice in the structured finance market. The rule imposes restrictions on the types of securities that may be sold to the public, places limits on the management of securitized assets and requires the use of an independent trustee in structured financings other than certain commercial paper programs.

Rule 3a-7 requires that an issuer's securities "entitle their holders to receive payments that depend primarily on the cash flow from eligible assets". The Commission made clear that the requirement is exclusive—that is, the issuer may issue *only* such securities. The Commission noted that the "cash flow" requirement is intended to preclude reliance on the rule by "market value" structures that rely on the sale of assets to repay investors. However, because the rule requires only that the securities depend *primarily* on cash flows for payments, some sales of assets are permitted, as discussed more fully below. The Commission's emphasis on cash-flow structures also underlies the rule's prohibition of the issuance of redeemable securities.

The rule defines "fixed-income securities" as any securities entitling the holder to receive:

8. These include notes, bonds, debentures, evidences of indebtedness, certificates of deposit, leases, instalment contracts, interest rate swaps, repurchase agreements, guaranteed investment contracts, accounts receivable (including credit card accounts and dealer warehouse receivables), chattel paper, cumulative preferred stock, guarantees, annuities, revolving home equity loans, mortgage pass-through certificates and franchise fees.

"(i) a stated principal amount; or
(ii) interest on a principal amount (which may be a notional principal amount) calculated by reference to a fixed rate or to a standard or formula which does not reference any change in the market value or fair value of eligible assets; or
(iii) interest on a principal amount (which may be a notional principal amount) calculated by reference to auctions among holders and prospective holders, or through remarketing...; or
(iv) an amount equal to specified fixed or variable portions of the interest received on the assets held by the issuer; or
(v) any combination of [the foregoing amounts]."

"Substantially all" of the payments to which the holders of fixed-income securities are entitled must be of the types enumerated above. In adopting this definition of "fixed-income securities", the Commission explicitly stated that interest-only and principal-only securities would be eligible for public sale under Rule 3a-7.

- Fixed-income securities that are rated investment grade at the time of initial sale may be sold to the general public.
- Fixed-income securities not rated investment grade may be sold to certain institutional accredited investors.
- Other securities may be sold only to qualified institutional buyers as defined in rule 144A under the Securities Act of 1933 or to persons (or affiliates) involved in the organization or operation of the issuer.

Rule 3a-7 also restricts the management of securitized assets—in a manner consistent with the structures addressed in this chapter—and requires use of an independent trustee.

4.4.4 Mortgage exemption: Section 3(c)(5)(C)

The legislative history of the 1940 Act indicates that Congress was concerned that traditional investment companies were susceptible to insider abuse.[9] Companies whose business is primarily holding mortgages and other interests in real estate were excluded from the definition of investment company under the 1940 Act "because they do not come within the generally understood concept of a conventional investment company investing in stocks and bonds of corporate issuers".[10] Section 3(c)(5)(C) specifically exempts from the definition of an investment company (and, consequently, from the operation of the 1940 Act) entities that do not issue "redeemable securities" and are primarily engaged in... purchasing or otherwise acquiring mortgages and other liens on and interests in real estate". The section 3(c)(5)(C) exemption is available only if an issuer is "primarily engaged" in acquiring or holding "interests in real estate" within the meaning of section 3(c)(5)(C).

With the adoption of Rule 3a-7 the mortgage exemption has become less significant. Where it is necessary to rely on the mortgage exemption in

9. Sen. Rep. No. 1775, 76th Cong., 3rd Sess. (1940).
10. Sen. Rep. No. 184, 91st Cong., 2nd Sess. 37 (1970).

transactions in which the underlying assets are not wholly or primarily whole mortgages, issues arise as to whether pass-through certificates (representing a "whole pool" or a "partial pool") and participation certificates satisfy the exemption.[11] Issues can also arise as to the portion of the issuer's assets that must consist of mortgages or other qualifying real estate investments.[12]

4.4.5 SEC exemptive orders

Section 6(c) of the 1940 Act authorizes the SEC to exempt any person, transaction or security (or class thereof) from any of the 1940 Act's provisions to the extent that such exemption "is necessary or appropriate in the public interest and consistent with the protection of investors and the purposes [of the 1940 Act]". Although section 6(c) orders have been issued, generally in the context of CMO conduit programmes and in relaxation of the whole-pool requirement, the process involves delay and uncertainty of result, as well as a public review process. The need to obtain a section 6(c) exemptive order may cause an issuer to miss a favourable market opportunity, and can also force disclosure of innovative financing structures prior to their use. Since section 6(c) allows the SEC to grant an exemption conditionally, the SEC's imposition of conditions on an exemption may cause expense and delay.

4.4.6 Banks and thrifts

Banks, thrifts and insurance companies are exempted from the definition of an investment company. Mortgage-backed securities issued directly by any of such institutions (as opposed to their subsidiaries) are thus exempt from the 1940 Act, provided that the securities are issued "with recourse" to the issuing institution. This caveat, however, makes the exemption of little use, since such recourse is rarely attractive for the issuer, and a pass-through security not otherwise exempt under the 1940 Act would not be exempt solely because it was nominally issued by a bank or thrift, if the bank or thrift is not obligated on the security. Indeed, a security issued by an exempt institution, but which is likely to be of limited recourse as an economic matter, may also need to be analysed as a separate entity for the purposes of the 1940 Act.[13]

MITCHELL S. DUPLER

11. See, *US Home Mortgage Credit Corporation* (pub. avail. 22 June 1983); *Landmark Funding Corp.* (pub. avail. 20 September 1984); *Premier Mortgage Corporation* (pub. avail. 14 March 1983); *Baton Rouge Building and Construction Industry Foundation* (pub. avail. 1 August 1984; *Arlington Investment Company* (pub. avail. 31 August 1974); and *Federal Home Loan Mortgage Corp.* (pub. avail. 14 June 1985).

12. See, *Salomon Brothers Mortgage Securities, Inc* (pub. avail. 8 November 1983); *Landmark Funding Corp.* (pub. avail. 20 September 1984); *CMO Mortgage Corp.* (pub. avail. 22 July 1985); and *Salomon Brothers Inc* (pub. avail. 22 July 1985).

13. See, *Prudential Insurance Co.* v. *SEC*, 326 F.2d 383 (3rd Cir. 1964), *cert. den.*, 377 U.S. 953 (1964).

CHAPTER 5

SECURITIZATION OF US NON-MORTGAGE RECEIVABLES

5.1 INTRODUCTION

As discussed in Chapter 1, entities holding or acquiring portfolios of receivables or other financial assets (referred to in this chapter as "sponsors") can access capital markets by pooling the assets and issuing securities backed by payments on the pools. If the credit strength of an asset pool (including any supplemental credit support) is sufficiently strong, the asset-backed securities so issued may qualify for an investment-grade debt rating from a nationally recognized rating agency. Further, if the securities are structured so that the asset pool is inaccessible to creditors of the sponsor and of other participants in the transaction (other than participants whose own debt is rated as high as the asset pool and participants that are "bankruptcy-remote" as discussed in Chapter 1), then the securities may be rated higher than the sponsor's own debt.

In the US, the growth of securitization has been driven primarily by (1) the ability to remove securitized assets from sponsors' balance sheets and (2) the ability to obtain high debt ratings and, thus, an attractive funding cost. As discussed in Chapter 1, securitization has other benefits than these and many securities have been issued in the US that were either on-balance sheet or unrated. However, because these two elements are so important, the term "securitization" is normally not applied to a transaction that is *both* on-balance sheet to the sponsor and unrated. In order to obtain the types of ratings normally sought by investors, the asset-backed securities must be "debt-like", i.e., represent obligations to pay principal at a specified (not necessarily fixed) maturity and to pay interest, if any, on the unpaid principal balance at a specified (again, not necessarily fixed) rate at a specified time or times.

This chapter will apply the foregoing considerations to the securitization of various types of US assets.

5.2 FACTORS FAVORING OR DISFAVORING SECURITIZATION FOR PARTICULAR ASSET POOLS

The following factors are among those that govern the degree of difficulty and expense that may be encountered in attempting to securitize a particular pool of assets.

5.2.1 Uniformity of documentation

The use of uniform documents by the originator of the assets facilitates due diligence document review by the parties and enables the issuer to disclose to investors the terms of the documents governing their rights within a reasonable space. Uniform documentation also facilitates the process of transfer of servicing of the obligations, if necessary. The use of non-standard documents increases the risk that the terms of the obligations may not conform to the disclosure document or to the assumptions used in structuring the transaction.

5.2.2 Seasoning and payment history

The level of credit enhancement required is generally based on an estimation of the frequency, severity and timing of future losses on the underlying receivables.[1] Portfolios that can withstand potential adverse circumstances receive the highest ratings for a given level of credit enhancement.[2] Experience has shown that, with respect to a variety of receivables, delinquency and loss levels are highest during the early years.[3] Thus, the greater the "seasoning", or average age, of the receivables, the lower the delinquency rate. Similarly, pools of receivables with established and stable payment histories are superior for this purpose than pools with little or no payment history.

5.2.3 Interest rates

Assets with a constant yield are generally easier to securitize than long-term variable-rate obligations. Investors tend to favor securities bearing a fixed rate of interest or a variable rate that fluctuates in tandem with a well recognized index such as LIBOR, prime lending rates, and so on. If the underlying asset is variable-rate and the security is fixed-rate, then credit enhancement, interest rate floors or other structural features must be implemented to assure that the cash flow from the underlying assets will be sufficient to service the securities. If both the underlying assets and the security bear interest at a variable rate, but the indices are different, the "basis risk" of non-parallel index changes must be

1. Moody's Investors Service, Inc., "A Framework for the Analysis of the Default Risk of Securitized Assets", *Moody's Structured Finance* 1 (April 1993).

2. Standard & Poor's Corporation, *S&P's Structured Finance Criteria* 25–26 (1988).

3. *Id.*, at 72, 73, 89.

addressed. Even if the same index is used for the assets and the securities, basis risk will nevertheless exist unless the interest rates on all of the underlying assets as well as on the securities are reset at the same periodic times according to a common index.

Wide variations in interest rates (whether fixed or variable) within a pool are undesirable. If the obligors on the assets have the right to prepay the obligations, consideration must be given to the effect on pool performance if the higher yielding obligations are prepaid and the lower yielding obligations are not. As a general rule, prepayment rates are higher for higher yielding assets.

5.2.4 Payment terms

Short-term obligations and fully amortizing level payment obligations are the most easily securitized. Balloon payments and other non-level payment terms lead to non-uniform cash flows available to investors. Furthermore, obligations with balloon payments may carry a higher default risk.

Fully amortizing level payment obligations in the US generally fall within one of three categories: “actuarial”, “simple interest” or “rule of 78s”.

(1) *Actuarial loans*

Each scheduled periodic payment on an actuarial loan consists of an amount of interest equal to the remaining principal balance multiplied by the per-annum stated interest rate divided by the number of scheduled payment periods within each year. The remaining portion of each payment is applied to reduction of the principal balance. With certain exceptions, payments that are made early or late by a few days do not alter the allocation of a payment between principal and interest. Actuarial loans resemble most US home mortgage loans and present the fewest problems in securitization.

(2) *Simple-interest loans*

Each payment on a simple-interest loan consists of an amount of interest equal to the remaining principal balance multiplied by the per-annum stated interest rate multiplied by the fraction of a year that has elapsed since the prior payment. The remaining portion of each payment is applied to reduction of the principal balance. The amount of each scheduled payment is the amount that would retire the loan on its stated maturity if each schedule payment were made on its due date. Early payments reduce the principal by more than the scheduled amount and vice versa. Therefore, early payments will result in a reduction of the final payment at maturity or an acceleration of maturity while late payments will result in a balloon payment at maturity. Because payments on securities are generally made on fixed payment dates regardless of when payments occur on the underlying obligations, early payments on simple-interest loans result in a potential yield loss to investors that must be covered by credit enhancement or otherwise.

(3) *Rule of 78s loans*

Rule of 78s loans are non-level yield instruments. The portion of each payment that is allocated to earned interest is computed based on the "rule of 78s". The yield during the beginning period of such a loan is greater than the actuarial yield and the yield at the end of the loan is lower than the actuarial yield. At any time after the first periodic payment, the amount of principal that must be paid to prepay a rule of 78s loan in full is greater than the amount that would be required to prepay in full an actuarial loan with the same initial principal amount and the same periodic payments. Publicly offered securities backed by rule of 78s loans have generally been structured by converting the payments to an actuarial basis using an imputed principal balance. Because the imputed principal balance of a seasoned loan is less than the rule of 78s balance, securitization of such a loan may result in a slight loss, depending on the accounting treatment of future excess yield.

5.2.5 Quality of servicing

Servicing of assets includes making collections from obligors, record-keeping, reporting and enforcement of the terms of the obligation, including, for example, policing insurance of the collateral. Investors have a greater level of security if the servicer is financially strong and is experienced in servicing similar assets for its own account. The servicing agreements with investors generally require that the same policies and procedures be applied with respect to the securitized obligations as those applied to the servicer's own portfolio.

5.2.6 Other factors

Other factors that may impede securitization include

(1) contractual rights of the obligors to vary the payment terms,
(2) a small number of assets in the pool,
(3) a high ratio of the largest asset in the pool to the average asset size, and
(4) infrequent payment dates.[4]

5.3 SECURITIZATION STRUCTURES

Securitization structures in the US generally fall within one of three broad categories. The first category consists of securities whose aggregate principal

4. Prior to adoption in 1992 of Rule 3a-7 by the Securities and Exchange Commission under the

payments during any payment period are generally designed to track the aggregate principal payments on a fixed pool of amortizing receivables. This category will be referred to as "term liquidating structures". The second category consists of long-term or intermediate term securities backed by a revolving pool of short-term or revolving credit receivables, referred to herein as "term reinvestment structures". The third category consists of commercial paper backed by a pool of short-term or revolving credit receivables, referred to herein as "commercial paper structures".

5.3.1 Term liquidating structures

5.3.1.1 Pass-through structure

Most of the early securitization transactions involving mortgage loans, automobile loans and other types of installment loan obligations were structured as "pass-through" transactions. In a pass-through securitization of installment obligations, investors purchase certificates representing fractional undivided beneficial ownership of the underlying receivables. In public offerings, the receivables, together with any related security interests in collateral securing the receivables, are normally transferred to a trust and investors purchase fractional interests in the trust. The trustee of the trust acts on behalf of investors in dealing with other parties to the transaction, including the seller, the servicer and credit enhancers. In private offerings to a limited number of sophisticated investors, the investors may have the capability to deal directly with other parties and to enforce their rights, in which case the intermediate trust can be eliminated and the securities issued in the form of participation certificates representing direct ownership of fractional undivided interests in the underlying assets.

Payments on a traditional pass-through security on each periodic payment date consist of

(1) scheduled principal payments due during the related collection period (for example, a pass-through on the fifteenth day of each month and the "collection periods" are the respective preceding calendar months),
(2) unscheduled principal payments received during the related collection period, and
(3) interest at a stated rate (the "pass-through rate") on the remaining principal balance of the pass-through securities.[5]

Investment Company Act of 1940, 15 U.S.C. section 80a *et seq.*, another significant obstacle to securitization was the fact that the availability of an exemption from the registration requirements of that Act often depended on the type of asset being securitized. Rule 3a-7 has greatly reduced this dependency.

5. US mortgage-backed securities have been issued in pass-through formats that vary from the "traditional structure" described in the text, for example, interest-only and principal-only "strips" and multiple-class sequential payment structures. To date, such pass-through structures have not been extended to non-mortgage assets. Such structures are facilitated by the REMIC provisions of Internal Revenue Code of 1986 sections 860A–G, which are currently applicable only to mortgage assets.

Shortfalls in collections of interest and scheduled principal are covered by credit enhancement. The "remaining principal balance" of the pass-through security is the initial face amount reduced by all amounts passed through with respect to principal, whether from collections on the underlying obligations, payment from credit enhancement or otherwise. Thus, if defaults occur on the underlying obligations that are covered by credit enhancement, the remaining principal balance of the underlying obligations will exceed the remaining principal balance of the securities.

In a traditional pass-through structure, the aggregate interest payable on the underlying obligations exceeds the aggregate interest at the pass-through rate on the securities during each collection period. The excess is available to pay servicing fees, amounts due to credit enhancers and other parties. Amounts remaining after such payments may be retained by the seller.

Pass-through structures offer the opportunity to qualify for sale treatment for accounting purposes provided that the appropriate limitations on recourse and control are respected. One significant limitation is that the right of the sponsor to redeem or repurchase the underlying obligations is severely limited.

Pass-through transactions may qualify as "grantor trusts" for US federal income tax purposes.[6] If the arrangement qualifies for this treatment then, provided that the transfer of the receivables qualifies as a sale rather than a financing (see the later discussion of some of the relevant factors), the trust will not be taxed and the investors will be taxed as if they directly owned their pro rata shares of the underlying receivables. If, however, the transfer is treated as a sale for tax purposes but the arrangement fails to qualify as a grantor trust, the pass-through trust may be treated as an association taxable as a corporation. In the latter event, the trust itself would be taxed on its income, without any deduction for distributions to investors, and payments to investors would be treated as taxable dividends.

5.3.1.2 US federal income tax treatment of pass-through structure

In order to qualify as a grantor trust, the arrangement must satisfy, among others, the following conditions[7]:

(1) the trust must not engage in the conduct of a business for profit,
(2) the trust must be a "fixed investment trust" with no ability to vary the terms of the investments, and
(3) the trust must have a single class of ownership interests.

Fixed investment Asset-backed securities structures typically include represen-

6. But see, for example, Chrysler Auto Receivables Company, $250,000,000 Certificates for Automobile Receivables CARCO Series 1986–1, Preliminary Prospectus dated 17 July 1986, at p. 30 (debt treatment for US federal income tax purposes).

7. US Dept of Treasury Regulations section 301.7701–4.

tations and warranties as to factual matters regarding each receivable. Upon discovery of a breach of a warranty concerning a receivable that cannot be cured, the sponsor is required to repurchase the receivable. In other asset-backed structures, such as the revolving credit delayed pass-through trust structure, the sponsor may be given an additional option to substitute a new receivable for the defective receivable. However, with certain exceptions, a general right to substitute receivables would violate the fixed investment requirement for grantor trusts and, therefore, is not seen (except under narrow restrictions) in pass-through arrangements classified as grantor trusts.[8]

Custom and practice in certain installment lending businesses include periodic granting, on a discretionary basis, of "skip a payment" offerings whereby the borrower is allowed to omit one or more periodic payments and to accrue interest during the interim. It is feared that the granting of such options by the sponsor with respect to obligations that are securitized in a pass-through structure would violate the fixed-investment requirement. However, prohibitions against such programs need not apply to extensions that are granted for credit-related reasons to enhance, in the servicer's judgment, probability of ultimate payment.

No trade or business If grantor-trust treatment is sought, the servicer must not be given unfettered discretion with respect to the servicing of the receivables. For example, the disposition of collateral following foreclosure should be based on standard procedures that do not involve protracted intentional delays based on speculation in the markets for such goods. Otherwise the trust might be viewed as carrying on the business of dealing in such goods.

Single class of ownership interests US Department of Treasury regulations[9] preclude grantor-trust treatment for trusts with multiple classes of ownership interest. The regulations allow for exceptions wherein the existence of multiple classes is incidental to the purpose of facilitating direct investment.[10]

5.3.1.3 Pay-through structures

For many transactions, the grantor-trust tax rules may be too restrictive. In some cases, the transaction may be more efficient if principal and interest payments

8. US Dept of Treasury Regulations section 301.7701–4(c)(1). The Internal Revenue Service has ruled that, under certain circumstances, the right to transfer assets to a trust for a period of 90 days after its creation does not constitute a power to vary the investment, Rev. Rul. 86–92, 1986–2 C.B. 214, and the right to substitute a new mortgage for a mortgage that has been found to be defective within the first two years of the pool is consistent with grantor-trust treatment, Rev. Rul. 71–399, 1971–2 C.B. 433.

9. US Dept of Treasury Regulations section 301.7701–4(c)(1).

10. The regulations, at section 301.7701–4(c)(2), provide examples of multiple-class structures that qualify for trust treatment including (1) a two-class senior/subordinated structure in which the subordinate piece is retained by the sponsor as credit enhancement and (2) a stripped coupon structure in which each certificate represents the right to receive a particular payment with respect to a specific bond.

are divided among multiple classes of securities having different interest rates and different timing of principal payments, in a manner similar to the collateralized mortgage obligations and REMIC securities discussed in Chapter 10. In other cases, it may be desirable for the servicer to have more flexibility in modifying receivables or for the trustee to hold funds for reinvestment for longer periods. Such transactions may be effected without incurring double taxation by use of an issuer that is not subject to taxation at the entity level. Instead of placing the receivables in a grantor trust, the receivables are transferred to the issuer, who issues debt or equity securities having the desired payment characteristics. If the aggregate principal payments on the securities track the aggregate principal payments on the receivables, the transaction is referred to as a "pay-through" transaction.

One form of pay-through transaction is the use of an issuer that is consolidated for US federal income taxation with the transferor of the receivables, or the transferor itself. This structure is seldom used because it generally does not constitute a sale for accounting purposes. A preferred method is to use an issuer whose financial statements are not consolidated with the transferor and who is treated as partnership for US federal income tax purposes. The most common form of entity selected for this purpose is a trust formed under common law or under the business trust laws, if any, of the applicable state. Such trusts are commonly referred to as "owner trusts" to distinguish them from grantor trusts.

In order to qualify for taxation as a partnership rather than as a corporation, an entity must lack at least two of the following characteristics:

(1) continuity of life;
(2) centralized management;
(3) limited liability; and
(4) free transferability of interests in the entity.[11]

A variety of structural elements are incorporated into an owner trust to ensure that it satisfies this test. In most cases, use of these elements involves an incremental administrative burden above that of the grantor trust.

5.3.2 Term reinvestment structures

The term liquidation structures discussed above function most effectively when investor demand exists for securities having maturities and payment characteristics roughly equivalent to those of the underlying asset pool. Examples include mortgage loans, automobile and other vehicle loans and various types of leases. In contrast, the term liquidation structures do not work well for assets with very short average life, such as trade receivables, or revolving credit assets, such as credit card receivables. For the latter types of assets, two basic approaches have

11. US Dept of Treasury Regulations section 301.7701–2(a).

been taken. One approach is to issue commercial paper periodically in amounts that fluctuate with the aggregate balance of the asset pool. The other approach, the term reinvestment structure, is based on reinvestment of collections on the receivables for a predetermined period of time.

5.3.2.1 Description of typical term reinvestment structure

While the ingenuity of capital markets participants has generated a wide variety of structural features, most term reinvestment structures have the following basic characteristics.

- The sponsor transfers, as settlor of a trust (the "trust"), all of its interest in all accounts receivable, whether then existing or thereafter created, in specified accounts. The trust issues certificates ("investor certificates") representing ownership of undivided interests in the trust in an aggregate amount (the "investor interest") equal to the aggregate face amount of the investor certificates, which is less than the aggregate outstanding balance of the receivables. Other interests in the trust may also be sold. The investor certificates are sold to the public. In exchange for the receivables, the sponsor receives (1) the net proceeds of the offering of the investor certificates and other sold interests and (2) an ownership interest in the trust representing the remaining undivided interest in excess of the investor interest.
- Interest payments are made on the investor certificates in arrears with respect to the outstanding investor amount at the rate and frequency specified in the investor certificates. In the absence of specified unexpected events (sometimes referred to as "payout events", "amortization events" or "liquidation events" and referred to herein as "early principal payment events"), no principal payments are made on the investor certificates during a preset "interest-only period". Early principal payment events may include, among other things, high portfolio loss rates, yield reduction and other events that may indicate an impaired ability to service principal and interest on the securities. If the investor certificates are supported by a third-party facility to guarantee payment of the outstanding investor interest (a "maturity facility"), the interest-only period may continue until final maturity of the investor certificates. Otherwise, principal payments are made in installments, based on collections on the receivables.
- During the interest-only period, amounts allocable to the investors' share of collections of principal receivables are paid to the sponsor in exchange for a corresponding amount of principal receivables that would otherwise be allocated to the sponsor, thus maintaining the investor amount at its original level, less any write-offs of principal receivables that are not covered by credit enhancement. It should be noted that this "reinvestment" may be either in new receivables or simply an increased

interest in existing receivables. Thus, if the transaction was over-collateralized, the principal amount of the investor interest may remain constant for a period of time as some receivables pay down, even if the retired receivables are not replaced with new receivables.

- Collections with respect to the sponsor's share of the receivables are paid to the sponsor. No recourse may be had to such collections to cover shortfalls in payments on the investor certificates.

A popular variant of the structure described above is the "master trust", wherein multiple series of securities are issued backed by the same pool of receivables. When a master trust is used, the securities issued in a single transaction are backed by a fractional interest in the pool based on the ratio of the principal amount of such securities to the aggregate balances of the pool. Securities issued in one transaction may have completely different payment and maturity terms than those of other series.

5.3.2.2 US federal income tax treatment of term reinvestment structure

Although the issuance of asset-backed securities through a term reinvestment trust structure is normally treated as a sale in form and for accounting purposes, the form of the transaction, although an important factor, is not conclusive of its classification for US federal income tax purposes.[12] A transfer of property constitutes, for such purposes, a sale of the property when the owner has relinquished substantial incidents of ownership, especially when the transferee has assumed the burdens of ownership by bearing the risk of loss of the property, and has acquired the benefits of ownership by having the opportunity to realize gain on the property.[13] If, however, holders of the investor certificates bear no significant risk of economic loss and the sponsor retains the opportunity to realize gain on the credit card accounts, the form of the transaction is not dispositive.

Economic risk As discussed below, highly rated securities are required to include credit enhancement sufficient to protect investors against any shortfall of principal or interest payments under stressful economic conditions. Unless actual conditions are worse than the worst-case scenarios or the stressful economic environments, it is expected that investors will suffer no loss. Instead, the risk of loss from defaults on the investor interest receivables will be borne by the sponsor or the credit enhancer.

Opportunity for gain The interest payable on the investor certificates is in the

12. See *Helvering* v. *Lazarus & Co.*, 308 U.S. 252 (1939); *Stein* v. *Director of Internal Revenue*, 135 F.Supp. 356 (E.D.N.Y. 1955).

13. See, for example, *United Surgical Steel Co.* v. *Commissioner*, 54 T.C. 1215 (1970), *acq.* 1971–2 C.B. 3; *Town & Country Food Co.* v. *Commissioner*, 51 T.C. 1049 (1969), *acq.* 1969–2 C.B. xxv.

nature of compensation for the time value of the funds that investors have advanced to the sponsor, that is, interest. Thus, such interest is not in the nature of profit from the difference in market interest rates and the rate of finance charges on the accounts.[14] Gain on the receivables resulting from appreciation in their fair market value (for example, as a result of declining market interest rates) is not available to investors. Because the terms of the investor certificates and the underlying receivables differ so significantly, any gain that could be realized by an investor with respect to its ownership interest in the receivables is gain from the investor certificate as a separate instrument and not from the underlying receivables. Further, because the sponsor generally retains entitlement to all amounts payable with respect to the investor interest in excess of amounts payable to investors, amounts payable to the credit enhancer and other fees and expenses, the sponsor, in effect, retains the opportunity for gain resulting from decreases in defaults or increases in yield on the receivables.

Other factors Other factors to be addressed in determining whether a term reinvestment trust transaction may be treated as a debt for US federal income tax purposes include the following:

(1) *Control and possession*: retention of possession and control of the property by the transferor is more consistent with a loan than with a sale.[15]

(2) *Differences in terms of obligations*: when receivables are assigned to an assignee, if the terms of the instrument under which the assignee is paid, including the interest rate, amount due, dates of payment and maturity date, are not related to the terms of the payment on the underlying receivables, the transaction is more likely to be viewed as a mere pledge of the receivables and not a sale.[16] Conversely, the greater the similarity in terms of the underlying receivables and the instrument under which the assignee is paid, the greater the likelihood of the characterization of the assignment as a sale of the receivables.[17]

(3) *Other incidents of ownership*: giving notice to the obligors on the receivables or otherwise making them aware of the transfer of the receivables suggests a sale characterization. Typically, such notice is not given. Placement of responsibility for collection of the accounts and for expenses thereof on the transferee of the receivables suggests a sale characterization of the transaction. Typically, the transferer retains servicing responsibilities. Placement of liability for all property,

14. Cf. G.C.M. 39584.

15. *United Surgical Steel Co.* v. *Commissioner*, 54 T.C. 1215, 1229–30 (1970), *acq.* 1971–2 C.B. 3; *Town & Country Food Co.* v. *Commissioner*, 51 T.C. 1049, 1057 (1969), *acq.* 1969–2 C.B. xxv; *Mathers* v. *Commissioner*, 57 T.C. 666 (1972), *acq.* 1973–1 C.B. 1.

16. *Town & Country Food Co.*, at 1057; *United Surgical Steel Co.*, at 1228; *Schaeffer* v. *Commissioner*, 41 T.C.M. (CCH) 752, 756 (1981).

17. *Bogatin* v. *United States*, 79–2 U.S.T.C. para. 9733 (W.D. Tenn. 1978); Rev. Rul. 65–185, 1965–2 C.B. 153.

excise, sales or similar taxes that may arise with respect to the receivables on a transferee suggests sale characterization.[18] An agreement that provides for the transferor to hold the transferee harmless from any action brought against the transferee arising out of the transferor's continued responsibility to make collections will suggest a characterization of the transaction as a loan.[19]

5.3.3 Commercial paper structures

Revolving credit receivables and short-term assets such as trade receivables have been securitized through "special purpose vehicles" (SPVs), that is, corporations not formally affiliated with sponsors whose business is limited to acquisition of assets to be securitized and the issuance of commercial paper or other debt instruments backed by such assets.[20] The normal expectation is that maturing commercial paper will be retired through the issuance of new commercial paper. In order to assure that sufficient funds will be available to retire maturing commercial paper in the event of disruption in the commercial paper market, the commercial paper is supported by a maturity facility, generally a refunding loan commitment from a bank consortium. In addition, credit enhancement must be provided to cover defaults.

The SPV commercial paper structure enables the sponsor to obtain a funding source that may be funded from time to time in varying amounts according to the outstanding balances of the underlying receivables. The overall financing cost may be attractive, depending on commercial paper rates and other factors.

5.3.4 Other structures

In lieu of the term reinvestment structure described above, credit card receivables have been securitized through the issuance of debt instruments secured by a pledge of the receivables. In this structure, the securities are secured by a pledge of all balances, including after-acquired balances, arising from time to time in specified revolving credit accounts. As in the term reinvestment structure, the securities have an initial interest-only period that may be terminated by an early principal payment event. During the interest-only period, all collections on the receivables in excess of the debt service requirement and

18. See *Illinois Power Co.* v. *Commissioner*, 87 T.C. 1417, 1439 (1986) (burden of paying taxes and other governmental charges weighed in balancing burdens and benefits of ownership for federal income tax purposes). See also *Yancey Bros.*, 319 F.Supp. at 445–6 (taxpayer's treatment of intangibles tax on transferred notes was evidence of taxpayer's ownership of such notes), and *Schaeffer*, 41 T.C.M. (CCH) at 757 (taxpayer's payment of state income tax on interest received on a transferred note was evidence of pledge of the note, not a sale).

19. G.C.M. 39584.

20. The term "commercial paper", as used in US parlance, is normally confined to instruments satisfying the exemption from registration pursuant to section 3(a)(3) of the Securities Act of 1933, as amended, 15 U.S.C. section 77c(a)(3)(1982), which, among other things, must have maturities of not more than nine months at the time of issuance.

servicing fees, if any, are retained by the sponsor. Thereafter, all collections on the receivables in excess of any servicing fees are available for debt service. It is generally unnecessary to provide for any allocation between principal receivables and finance charge receivables when this structure is used. Protection against net reduction in outstanding balances, as well as credit support, may be provided by simply over-collateralizing or by third-party support.

In some cases, the secured debt structure offers advantages over the term reinvestment trust structure. Because no allocations are made between principal receivables and finance charge receivables or between the sponsor's interest and the investors' interest, more cash flow may be available for debt service in a secured debt offering than in a term reinvestment structure offering backed by the same pool of accounts. Because the security is classified as a "debt instrument" and not an "equity security", qualification of the instrument as a legal investment for certain classes of institutional investors, including pension funds subject to the Employee Retirement Income Security Act of 1974, as amended (ERISA),[21] is less difficult than is the case with the delayed pass-through security. However, use of the secured debt structure precludes sale treatment for accounting purposes. For this reason, the structure has not been widely employed.

5.4 CREDIT SUPPORT AND OTHER THIRD-PARTY SUPPORT

Credit enhancement consists of support mechanisms that cause the risk of default on an asset-backed security to be lower than the risk of default on the underlying assets.[22] Credit enhancement may consist of supplemental assets such as a cash reserve fund, third-party enhancement such as a guarantee or letter of credit, or "self-enhancement" which is essentially over-collateralization. Securities issued in multiple classes may provide for subordination among the classes, in which case the subordinate classes serve as credit enhancement for the senior classes. The amount of required enhancement depends on an estimation of the frequency, severity and timing of future losses on the underlying receivables.[23]

Third-party support is necessary in some structures in order to protect against mismatches in timing between due dates on the asset-backed securities and due dates on the underlying receivables. In a commercial paper transaction, liquidity support is generally necessary to ensure that sufficient funds are available to retire the commercial paper at maturity in the event that funds available from

21. 29 U.S.C. sections 1001 *et seq.* (1982).

22. See generally, Kravitt (ed.), *Securitization of Financial Assets*, Chapter 8 (New York: Prentice Hall, 1994 ed.).

23. Moody's Investors Service, Inc., "A Framework for the Analysis of the Default Risk of Securitized Assets", *Moody's Structured Finance* 1 (April 1993).

newly issued commercial paper together with funds from receivables payments are insufficient. Certain term reinvestment securities include a promise to retire the oustanding principal balance of the securities in a single "bullet" payment or a series of fixed installments. In such case, third-party support is generally necessary to protect against shortfalls in available funds from receivables payments.

Swap agreements are used to provide third-party support to asset-backed securities in circumstances where the receivables pool, together with other third-party support, is considered sufficiently strong to support payment in a particular currency or at a particular yield that differs from the currency or yield, respectively, of the securities. The most common examples in the US include floating-rate securities and US dollar-denominated securities backed by foreign assets.

5.5 COLLATERAL PROTECTION

One of the essential elements of a securitization transaction is the creation of a security whose credit quality is based on the performance of the underlying pool of receivables and related credit enhancement and whose credit quality is independent of the financial strength or weakness of the sponsor (or any other third-party other than credit enhancers). The cash flow from the securitized assets must not be subject to interruption from adverse claims against the securitized assets or from the insolvency of the sponsor.

5.5.1 Perfection of the asset transfer

In many securitization transactions, the sale or pledge or the transfer of assets to investors or their trustee is subject to Article 9 of the Uniform Commercial Code (UCC). Table 5.1 indicates generally the classification of various commonly securitized assets under the UCC. Variances from the table may occur, depending on specific circumstances.

Pledges of accounts and general intangibles are perfected under the UCC by filing a financing statement in a central office in the appropriate jurisdiction that, among other things, "contains a statement indicating the types, or describing the items, of collateral".[24] Sales of accounts are treated, for such purpose, in the same way as a pledge of accounts.[25] However, a sale of general intangibles is not currently subject to Article 9 of the UCC[26] and perfection is governed by applicable local law. Because credit card portfolios generally include both accounts and general intangibles, the delayed pass-through trust structure

24. UCC section 9–402(1).
25. UCC sections 1–201(37), 9–102(1)(b).
26. Proposals have been made to expand the scope of UCC Article 9 to include sales of general intangibles. See Weise, "Refurbishing Article 9", 3 *Business Today* 58 (July–August 1994).

requires both UCC filing and compliance with the perfection requirements of applicable local law. By contrast, a credit-card-backed debt offering generally requires only a UCC filing.

Table 5.1

Type of asset	*UCC classification*
Credit card receivables arising from purchase of goods or services	Accounts
Credit card receivables arising from cash advances	General intangibles
Vehicle loans, leases, or installment sales contracts	Chattel paper
Trade receivables	Accounts
Unsecured consumer loans	Instruments

Both pledges and sales of chattel paper may be perfected either by a UCC filing or by delivery of possession of the documents constituting the chattel paper to the transferee or its bailee.[27] If perfection is solely by filing, the transferee's interest is subordinate to rights of a purchaser for value without notice[28] who takes possession of the chattel paper in the ordinary course of business. With respect to securitization of automobile loans, the standard practice has evolved of perfecting only by filing and disclosing to investors the risk that, through fraud or negligence of the servicer, their rights in the collateral could become subordinate to third parties.

Although the transferee of chattel paper acquires a perfected interest in the chattel paper, the transfer does not in all cases automatically perfect a security interest in the underlying goods in favor of the transferee. For example, in many states, perfection of a security interest in a motor vehicle is effected by notation of the lien on a certificate of title. In some states, a transfer of the lien may be ineffective unless the transferee's name is noted on the certificate of title. Perfection of a security interest in an instrument can, with certain limited exceptions, be effected only by delivery of possession of the instrument.[29]

Article 9 of the UCC provides that an unperfected security interest (including an unperfected sale of accounts or chattel paper) is subordinate to the rights of, among others, lien creditors, certain innocent purchasers, bankruptcy trustees and receivers in equity.[30] In addition, non-UCC law may impose significant restrictions on transfer or may alter priority of the transferee's interest.[31]

27. UCC sections 9–304(1), 9–305.
28. UCC section 9–308(1).
29. UCC section 9–304(1).
30. UCC section 9–301.
31. For example, US federal income tax law provides for a lien in favor of the US government that, with certain exceptions, has priority over other property rights. Internal Revenue Code of 1986, as amended, sections 6321 *et seq*. The assignability of certain health care receivables under federal programs is limited. 42 U.S.C. section 1396g(c)(1982), 42 U.S.C.A. section 1396a(a)(32)(West Supp. 1989).

A concern exists that a partial assignment of a receivable may compromise its enforceability on behalf of investors. At common law, a partial assignee cannot enforce a debt without the debtor's consent.[32] In equity, at the discretion of the court, a partial assignment is enforceable without the debtor's consent if all parties can be joined in one suit,[33] but in some jurisdictions a partial assignment without the debtor's consent may be invalid even in equity.[34] Even if the equitable doctrine applies, additional delays in collection may occur in the event of the transferor's insolvency because of the necessity of joining the receiver, or the entity to whom the receiver has distributed the unassigned interest, as a party in any suit to enforce a claim. As a general rule, the assignment of receivables by the sponsor should be free of participations and other fractional interests.

5.5.2 Insolvency considerations

If the timely payment of principal or interest on an asset-backed security could be interrupted by the insolvency of the sponsor, then the security cannot be rated materially higher than the credit rating of the sponsor. If the sponsor is an entity subject to the US Bankruptcy Code,[35] certain procedural elements of that Code create a significant risk of impairment of timely payment in the event that the securitized assets are included in an estate subject to a proceeding under that Code.[36] In such offerings, assurance is needed that ownership of the assets has been completely disposed of by the sponsor and that such dispositions not subject to avoidance by the bankruptcy court through characterization of the transfer as a preference,[37] a fraudulent conveyance[38] or a pledge rather than a sale[39] or by "substantive consolidation" of the assets of the sponsor and the assets of the transferee.[40]

Banks, thrifts and certain other institutions are ineligible to be debtors under

32. *First National Bank of Wayne* v. *Gross Real Estate Co.*, 162 Neb. 343, 75 N.W.2d 704 (1956); 6 Am.Jur.2d "Assignments" section 76 (1963).

33. See generally, 80 A.L.R. 413; 6 Am. Jur.2d "Assignments" section 77 (1963); *Restatement (Second) of Contracts* section 326, Comments b and c and Reporter's Note; 3 *Williston on Contracts* section 441–44 (3rd ed. 1960).

34. See *Burnett* v. *Crandall*, 63 Mo. 410 (1876); *Citizens & Southern National Bank* v. *Bruce*, 420 F.Supp. 795, 798 (E.D.Mo.—E.Div. 1976), *affirmed* 562 F.2d 590 (8th Cir. 1977); *Skobis* v. *Ferge*, 102 Wis. 122, 78 N.W. 426 (1899); 80 A.L.R. 428–30; 6 Am. Jur. 2d "Assignments" section 77, n. 1135. 11 U.S.C.A. sections 101 *et seq.* (1979 and 1989 West Supp.).

36. Such procedural elements include the automatic stay (section 362), the ability of the trustee to use, sell or lease property of the estate (section 363), the ability of the trustee to obtain credit secured by a junior lien on the property of the estate (section 364), the requirement to turn over property of the estate (section 542), the avoidance of preferential transfers (section 547), and limits on the post-petition effect of security interests (section 552).

37. 11 U.S.C.A. section 547 (1979 and 1989 West Supp.).

38. 11 U.S.C.A. section 548 (1979 and 1989 West Supp.).

39. See, for example, *Major's Furniture Mart, Inc.* v. *Castle Credit Corporation, Inc.*, 602 F.2d 538 (3rd Cir. 1979).

40. See, for example, *In re 1438 Meridian Place, N.W., Inc.*, 15 B.R. 89 (Bankr. D.D.C. 1981); 5 *Collier on Bankruptcy*, para. 1100.06 (1988).

the US Bankruptcy Code.[41] If the sponsor is such an institution, the sponsor may retain an ownership interest in the securitized assets, provided that the transfer of the investors' interest is properly perfected and is not subject to avoidance (for example, as a fraudulent conveyance) by a receiver of the institution in a potential insolvency proceeding.

For further discussion of insolvency risks, see Chapter 4.

5.6 US SECURITIES LAW CONSIDERATIONS

Many aspects of US securities laws regarding asset securitization are covered in Chapter 2. This section will address certain aspects that relate specifically to non-mortgage assets.

5.6.1 Shelf registration

Prior to 1992, most public offerings of non-mortgage asset-backed securities were ineligible for "shelf" registration under Rule 415 of the Securities and Exchange Commission ("SEC"), which permits offerings of securities on a delayed or continuous basis.[42] Accordingly, for each offering, a separate registration statement had to be filed with the SEC and no sales could be effected until the registration statement was declared effective by the SEC. In contrast, Rule 415 permitted shelf registration of "mortgage-related securities, including such securities as mortgage backed debt and mortgage participation or pass through certificates".[43]

In 1992, the SEC amended its regulations "in order to eliminate this anomaly".[44] The method chosen by the SEC was to amend Form S–3 to make offerings of investment grade asset-backed securities eligible for registration on such form.[45] For purposes of Form S–3, the term "asset-backed security" means "a security that is primarily serviced by the cashflows of a discrete pool of receivables or other financial assets, either fixed or revolving, that by their terms convert into cash within a finite time period plus any rights or other assets designed to assure the servicing or timely distribution of proceeds to the security holders".[46] The "anomaly" was not completely eliminated, however. The amount of securities that may be registered for the shelf in reliance on this provision is limited to the amount reasonably expected to be offered and sold within two years from the initial effective date of the registration,[47] a restriction

41. 11 U.S.C.A. para 109 (1979 and 1989 West Supp.).
42. 17 C.F.R. §230.415.
43. 17 C.F.R. §230.415(a)(1)(vii).
44. "Simplification of Registration Procedures for Primary Securities Offerings", SEC Release No. 33–6964, 34–31345, [1992 Transfer Binder] Fed. Sec. L. Rep. (CCH) ¶85,053 at. 83,387 (Oct. 22, 1992).
45. 17 C.F.R. §239.13 General Instruction I.B.5.
46. *Id.*
47. 17 C.F.R. §230.415(a)(2).

not applicable to securities that fall within the mortgage-related securities provision cited above.[48]

5.6.2 Investment Company Act of 1940

Prior to 1992, an even more serious impediment to the public offering of certain types of asset-backed securities was the potential regulation of issuers as "investment companies" under the Investment Company Act of 1940 (the "1940 Act").[49] Regulation of investment companies under this statute is so restrictive that it would be impracticable for an issuer in a typical securitization transaction to comply with it.[50] In a 1992 release (the "40 Act Release"),[51] the SEC recognized that the growth and development of the structured finance market had been constrained in some degree by the 1940 Act[52] and adopted Rule 3a-7[53] with the intent of excluding virtually all structured financings from the definition of investment company, subject to certain conditions.[54] The principal conditions that must be met in order to qualify for the exclusion include:

(1) the issuer must be engaged in the business of purchasing, or otherwise acquiring and holding eligible assets (defined similar to those described in Section 5.6.1. above for eligibility for Form S–3) and in related activities;
(2) the issuer must not issue "redeemable securities", as defined in the 1940 Act[55];
(3) the issuer must issue debt-like "fixed-income securities" rated in an investment-grade debt category by a nationally recognized rating agency;
(4) the issuer must comply with certain limitations applicable to sales by the issuer of unrated or less than investment-grade securities and securities that do not qualify as "fixed income";
(5) the issuer must comply with certain limitations applicable to modification of the initial asset pool; and

48. *Id.*; see note 43, *supra*.
49. Investment Company Act of 1940, as amended, 15 U.S.C. §80a–1 *et seq.*
50. Kravitt, note 22, *supra*, 11-3–11-4.
51. "Exclusion From the Definition of Investment Company for Structured Financings", SEC Release No. IC–19105, [1992 Transfer Binder] Fed. Sec. L. Rep. (CCH) ¶85,062 (Nov. 19, 1992).
52. *Id.*, at 83,500.
53. 17 C.F.R. §270.3a–7.
54. 40 Act Release, note 51, *supra*, at 83,500.
55. "Redeemable Security" is defined in Section 2(32) of the 1940 Act, 15 U.S.C. §80a–2(32), as any security, other than short-term paper, under the terms of which the holder, upon its presentation to the issuer or to a person designated by the issuer, is entitled (whether absolutely or only out of surplus) to receive approximately his proportionate share of the issuer's current net assets, or the cash equivalent thereof.

(6) if the issuer issues any securities other than commercial paper exempt from registration under the Securities Act of 1933,[56] the assets backing the securities must be assigned or pledged to an independent trustee.

Most asset-backed securities that have been publicly offered in the US, would qualify for this exception. If Rule 3a-7 is not available, other possible exemptions under the 40 Act include the following:

(1) Section 3(c)(1).[57] This provision exempts issuers not involved in public offerings of securities whose outstanding securities (other than certain short-term paper) are beneficially owned by not more than 100 persons. The provision contains an attribution rule whereby, for purposes of the 100 person limitation, if a company owns 10 per cent or more of the outstanding voting securities of the issuer, beneficial ownership is deemed to be that of the holders of such company's outstanding securities unless certain conditions are met.
(2) Section 3(c)(5).[58] Prior to enactment of Rule 3a-7, this exception provided the exemption most frequently relied on for public asset securitization transactions. The exception is available for issuers not in the business of issuing "redeemable securities", "face amount certificates of the installment type" or "periodic payment plan certificates", as such terms are defined in the 40 Act, and who are primarily engaged in one or more of the following businesses:

    (A) Purchasing or otherwise acquiring notes, drafts, acceptances, open accounts receivable, and other obligations representing part or all of the sales price of merchandise, insurance and services;
    (B) Making loans to manufacturers, wholesalers, and retailers of, and to prospective purchasers of, specified merchandise, insurance and services; and
    (C) Purchasing or otherwise acquiring mortgages and other liens on and interests in real estate.

Because of the limitation in §3(c)(5)(A) to "obligations representing part or all of the sales price of merchandise, insurance and services", it was generally believed that securitization of certain types of non-mortgage assets including student loans, credit card cash advance receivables and operating leases created exposure to the requirement to register under the 40 Act, whereas securitization of many other types of receivables qualified for the exception. One of the primary benefits of Rule 3a-7 was the near-elimination of this anomaly.

PAUL R. SPELLMAN

56. 15 U.S.C. §77c(a)(3).
57. 15 U.S.C. §80a–3(c)(1).
58. 15 U.S.C. §80a–3(c)(5).

CHAPTER 6

COMMERCIAL MORTGAGE SECURITIZATION

6.1 INTRODUCTION

The securitization of commercial mortgages has grown substantially in the last four years. While the Resolution Trust Corporation (RTC) was not the first securitizer of commercial mortgage loans, its entry into the market place in 1991 served as a springboard for others to follow. Previously, commercial mortgage securitization was not thought to be viable, due in part to the lack of uniformity in the loan documents that exists within the residential market and has fostered its growth. Moreover, the secondary market for commercial mortgages had not advanced to the stage where the capital markets could efficiently and effectively compete with other more traditional lenders such as insurance companies and banks. Finally, the subordinated or first loss securities often involved in a commercial mortgage transaction were not well understood and consequently difficult to sell.[1] The fall of the real estate markets in the mid-eighties and the resultant problems experienced by the banking and savings and loan industry ironically have also fostered the acceptability and viability of securitization for commercial mortgages.

Initially, the RTC dominated the market with issuances of nearly $14 billion in commercial mortgage-backed securities (CMBS), including multi-family issues (the M-Series), 12 commercial issues (the C-Series) and three mobile home park issues (the MH-Series). Currently, the RTC is winding down its securitization activity as the pool of assets it is disposing has dwindled, but still is working on a non-performing (N-Series) and sub performing (S-Series) pool of loans. As the RTC participation dwindles, the rest of the market has picked up the slack. As of first quarter 1994, nearly one trillion dollars of mortgage debt was outstanding on commercial properties, including multi-family. Of this amount, approximately 60 billion dollars has been securitized.[2] The CMBS market is therefore far from saturated.

For purposes of this article, CMBS will include the following property types:

1. R. Ellson and J. Mulligan, "Developments in Commercial Mortgage Securitization", *Capital Sources for Real Estate* (Vol. 1, No. 2, February 1994).

2. *Mortgage-Backed Securities Letter*, at p. 4 (September 26, 1994).

(1) Multi family residential;
(2) Office;
(3) Retail;
(4) Congregate care/nursing home;
(5) Mobile home parks;
(6) Warehouse;
(7) Regional shopping malls; and
(8) Hotels.

To date, each of these properties types has been the subject of securitization. One of the complexities associated with CMBS is the differing issues that arise in each property type. These will be explored briefly in Section 6.6 below.

As with any structured financing or securitization, the primary structural goal is to isolate the assets or collateral that will generate the cash flow to investors. This hallmark of structured finance allows investors and rating agencies to analyze the assets alone to determine the risks and exposure associated with the investment. Outside credit risks should be eliminated to the greatest extent possible. Consequently, it is extremely important to create a bankruptcy remote special purpose vehicle (SPV) in connection with a CMBS transaction. While the SPV is discussed in a number of other chapters in this book, CMBS transactions include variations and other associated problems that merit special attention. These are discussed in Section 6.5 below.

6.2 TRANSACTION TYPES

In the CMBS market, the transaction types fall into four principal groups:

1. Multiborrower;
2. Single asset;
3. Single borrower, multiple asset; and
4. Credit lease

While credit lease transactions are not viewed by some as securitizations in the traditional sense, in that the outside credit of another entity is relied upon in the rating, many recent credit-lease transactions contain structural characteristics similar to securitizations.

A. Multiborrower

The multiborrower programs contain a pool of loans originated to various unrelated borrowers. The RTC transactions are examples of multiborrower programs to one extreme, in that these huge pools may have over a thousand different loans to different borrowers. These large pools enjoy borrower and geographic diversity, seasoning and in many instances property type diversity. However, with the RTC programs, negative factors include lack of uniformity in underwriting and due diligence, as well as insufficient information concerning environmental and engineering issues and operating history. Recently, the Federal Deposit Insurance Corporation (FDIC) entered the CMBS market for the first time with a pool of 1,800 loans offered through a real estate mortgage investment conduit (REMIC) aggregating approximately $759 million, which carried a partial FDIC guaranty.[3] The move to securitization was a departure from its typical whole loan sale for disposition.

Multiborrower programs also spawned the relatively recent emergence of commercial mortgage conduits. These conduits typically involve an alliance between a lender entity (either an investment bank or other financial institution) with a commercial mortgage originator. The growth of these conduit alliances has surged in the last two years to 21 funding sources for 75 originators.[4] Principally, these alliances are effected by investment banks that provide warehouse financing for commercial mortgage originators, who do the primary due diligence and origination of loans. The conduit programs allow access to the capital markets for small commercial property owners seeking loans ranging in size from one million to 15 million dollars, which have been unavailable as banks, insurance companies and other traditional lenders retreated from the market after the real estate and banking crises. When these mortgages are pooled together in sufficient critical size, such as 100 million dollar pools, securitization of the pool can occur.[5]

In addition to the conduit alliances, certain multiborrower transactions may involve loans to a small group of large property owners/developers that have been funded by investment banks and warehoused pending securitization. These transactions frequently involve substantially larger individual loans resulting in less borrower diversity and possibly less geographic diversity.[6] Nonetheless, in general the benefits of newly originated commercial loans for securitization include more uniformity of documentation, recent MAI appraisals and engineering reports, recent environmental testing, typically at least a Phase 1 environmental report, uniformity in underwriting standards, and the ability to coordinate mortgage loan terms, such as fixed and variable interest rates as well as maturity (balloon risks).

While the multiborrower programs facilitate capital access and financing for commercial real estate owners, it is important for investors and participants in

3. "FDIC Launches its First CMBS Deal", *Mortgage-Backed Securities Letter*, at p. 8 (August 15, 1994).

4. "Conduits Set Ambitious Goals for 1995", *Commercial Mortgage Alert*, at p. 1 (February 6, 1995).

5. See, for example, DLJ Mortgage Acceptance Corp. Multifamily Mortgage Pass-Through Certificates, Series 1994-MF11, Prospectus Supplement dated June 29, 1994, a transaction involving the securitization of 78 mortgage loans secured by multi-family complexes.

6. See, for example, Nomura Assets Securities Corporation Commercial Mortgage Pass-Through Certificates, Series 1994-MDII, Prospectus Supplement dated July 25, 1994. This transaction involved six mortgage loans on a diverse group of commercial and multi-family residential properties. While the properties had geographic dispersion, the six borrowers included several newly organized real estate investment trusts (REITs).

CMBS transactions to recognize the potential risks associated with the relatively new entry of commercial real estate in the capital markets. Purchasers of commercial loans from originators for ultimate securitization must take particular care to assure that sufficient due diligence and underwriting have been carried out. Ultimately, the sponsors of CMBS bear liability under securities laws for the adequacy and accuracy of disclosure relating to pools of mortgage loans on commercial properties.

B. Single asset transactions

Another type of securitization that has enjoyed strong growth in the past year is the single asset transaction, which typically involves a refinancing on a seasoned trophy property. Due to the costs and complexities of securitization, a single multi-family complex or retail strip center generally would not be economical to effect as a single asset securitization. Accordingly, most transactions have been in a minimum amount of approximately $50 million, and the prime candidates are super-regional malls and office buildings. While these transactions are most often sold in the private placement market, the securitization of the mortgage underlying the Sawgrass Mills Regional Mall in Sunrise, Florida, was recently effected as a public registration. A $160,000,000 eight-year balloon loan was secured by the mall and conveyed into a real estate mortgage investment conduit (REMIC) trust. Certificates evidencing beneficial interest in the trust were issued in four tranches rated from AAA to BB.[7]

Single asset transactions clearly have the negative attributes of borrower concentration, geographic concentration and, in most cases, balloon risk. The negative aspects frequently are offset by other credit considerations such as high debt service coverage ratios (DSCR) and low loan to value ratios (LTV). In addition, significant due diligence is conducted in connection with these transactions, including engineering reports, appraisals, environmental assessments, and evaluation of lease roll over exposure and insurance coverage.

C. Single borrower/multiple property

In some instances, securitization transactions will involve a pool of properties that is owned by one borrower or group of affiliated borrowers. For example, large developers may attempt to refinance their properties and consolidate debt as well as secure favorable financing terms, particularly with cross collateralization. In addition, single borrower transactions may be effected in tandem with or immediately following an equity inflow pursuant to creation of a real estate investment trust (REIT) or a so-called "Umbrella Partnership REIT" transaction wherein an existing REIT is admitted as a partner to the developer's partnership which owns all of the properties to be securitized. These are

7. Sawgrass Finance REMIC Trust Commercial Mortgage Pass-Through Certificates, Prospectus dated December 15, 1993.

complex transactions and involve substantial planning and tax issues and considerations, which are beyond the scope of this chapter.[8]

As in single asset transactions, one negative implication is borrower concentration, but substantial geographic diversity may be obtained, and in some instances, property type diversity. In the single borrower as well as single asset cases, the competency and experience of the property manager are important factors. As stated above, there may be credit benefit by cross collateralization, and these transactions also benefit from recent appraisals, engineering and other similar reports.

One recent example of a single borrower multiple property securitization is the $455,000,000 private placement of DeBartolo Capital Partnership Commercial Mortgage Pass-Through Certificates, which was effected in conjunction with a $560,000,000 initial public offering REIT transaction. The borrower was a newly organized SPV partnership that was wholly owned by the newly formed REIT. A mortgage loan in the amount of $455,000,000 was secured by 17 properties, including 15 regional shopping malls, one community shopping center and one mixed use (retail/office) property, which was conveyed into a trust issuing six classes of certificates rated from AAA to BBB.[9] Another example is the $100,000,000 Tucker financing transaction, which was registered with the Securities and Exchange Commission (SEC). This transaction consisted of a mortgage note secured by six properties, five community shopping centers and one mixed use property, which note was conveyed into a trust constituting a REMIC.[10]

D. Credit lease transactions

Credit lease transactions do not neatly fit into the securitization mold, inasmuch as securitizations typically rely on an evaluation of the particular assets that are pooled together. Thus, for example, the cash flow, LTV and DSCR of a pool of multi-family properties are evaluated as a whole to determine ratings and investor risk and expectations from that pool. Credit lease transactions, on the other hand, are reliant on the credit rating of a single tenant. The best example of this is a sale leaseback transaction where a large user of properties, such as KMart, will sell the fee interest in its stores and lease the property back from the fee purchaser. These corporations typically have tax, accounting or balance sheet reasons for not wanting to carry the fee ownership of buildings on their books and the transactions therefore provide attractive investment opportunities for purchasers of the fee interest and for investors who buy CMBS backed by an assignment of such leases. Thus, the property is owned by an SPV which

8. See Chapter 11 in this book for a more detailed discussion of tax consequences for mortgage-backed securities in general.

9. "DeBartolo's Long Wait Pays Off", *Commercial Mortgage Alert* (April 18, 1994).

10. Kidder, Peabody Acceptance Corporation I Commercial Mortgage Pass-Through Certificates, Series 1994-C2, Prospectus dated May 11, 1994.

then grants a mortgage secured by an assignments of leases and rents to the lender. The loan and assignment then serve as the collateral for the notes issued to investors. Careful attention must be paid to the terms and provisions of the lease that serves as credit, particularly with respect to termination rights, and allocation of property maintenance expenses to the tenant.[11]

6.3 STRUCTURES

CMBS transactions typically take one of two forms, either pass through certificates or debt instruments such as notes or bonds.

A. Pass-through certificates

Probably the most frequently utilized form of CMBS is the pass-through certificate. A trust is created, generally pursuant to a pooling and servicing agreement, into which the mortgage assets are conveyed. Beneficial interests in this trust are then issued to investors. These interests may be in the form of a single class, or multiple classes which are then carved up to meet investor demands relating to yield, maturity, and risk. With the advent of REMIC legislation,[12] investors may choose from multiple classes of certificates with varying characteristics, secured by the same pool of assets. For example, these pass-through certificates may be structured as interest-only strips (IO), principal-only strips (PO), planned amortization classes (PACs) and various senior/subordinated classes. The pass-through payments may be made serially, or ratably but in the indicated priority. The extensive flexibility afforded by the pass-through certificates is one of the principal attractions. Since the pass-through certificates typically represent the investors' right to receive all payments passed through the trust from payments made on the underlying mortgages, they frequently do not have a maturity date that would subject them to default proceedings if payment is not made. In many instances a scheduled maturity date may be set based on the structurer's estimation from the assets in the underlying pool, but the debt instruments themselves are the mortgages contained in the pool owned by the trust.

Pass-through certificates nonetheless are frequently priced based on a specified spread over U.S. Treasury securities with an assumed comparable maturity. For example, a pool of seven-year interest-only mortgages typically would be priced on a spread over the related seven year U.S. Treasury securities. In this situation, the investors must carefully assess the balloon risk in the event refinancing of the underlying balloon mortgage is not secured at the end of the

11. See, for example, KMart Funding Corporation Secured Lease Bonds, Series A, B, C, D, E, F and G, $175,500,000, Prospectus dated August 22, 1994. This transaction involved a substantially more complex ownership arrangement of the fee interest as well as some reverting interests that are not typical in sale leaseback obligation bond transactions.

12. Tax Reform Act of 1986, Pub. L. No. 99–514, 100 Stat. 2085. For an in-depth discussion of the tax aspects and consequences of the REMIC legislation, see Chapter 11.

seven-year term. While the servicer under the pooling and servicing agreement will pursue its remedies under the mortgage after such a default, a realization on such property to pay off the mortgage could take up to a year or more before liquidation proceeds are received. This example also illustrates the tension between the underwriter's desire to price securities based on the shortest term maturity possible and the rating agency's view that ultimate payment could be a one-to-five year period in excess of the original seven-year maturity. This timing tension along with other rating issues are discussed in Section 6.7 below.

B. Notes/bonds

A CMBS transaction also may take the form of notes or bonds, that is, debt that is secured either by a mortgage on the underlying property or a pool of mortgage loans that is collateral for such debt. While the pass-through certificates and the debt structures differ in form, in many respects the economic substance is virtually the same. It is less common to see a note or bond structure for multiple classes of CMBS, but single class transactions may use this structure. As indicated, this structure provides less flexibility but may be more suitable for investors who are unaccustomed to pass-through certificates or simply require a debt instrument for their investment portfolio.

In some transactions, where the rating agencies or other transaction participants do not want a default on an underlying mortgage necessarily to result in a default on the issued CMBS, the structure may be put together as a "back-to-back" debt offering. In this case, a mortgage and related note are created and issued by the borrower owning the fee interest in the property and held by the lender. The lender, which may be an affiliate of the SPV borrower, is also an SPV and immediately thereafter issues notes or bonds that are collateralized by an assignment of the mortgage note and related mortgage and assignment of leases and rents. In this transaction, a default in the underlying mortgage would not necessarily result in a default on the issued CMBS, particularly where an advancing facility was in place and payments were not disrupted to investors. These structures may be used, for example, where the rating agencies assume the possibility of ultimate foreclosure and build in a period of time (tail period) to effect the liquidation and disposition during which a liquidity facility is in place so that investors ultimately receive all payments of principal and interest.

C. Credit enhancement

As stated above, structured financings in general rely on the credit worthiness of the assets underlying the CMBS. In some instances, however, some form of credit enhancement may be necessary in order to achieve the desired rating on all or a portion of the CMBS and, consequently, a lower cost of funds. Several credit enhancement alternatives are available in CMBS transactions as discussed below.

1. Senior/subordinate structure

A senior/subordinate structure provides internal credit enhancement for a CMBS issuance by establishing payment priority among the several classes of securities issued. The most senior class would be entitled to payments of principal and interest prior to all lower classes, which thereby suffer the losses, if any, and provide a credit cushion to the senior class. The priority may be tailored to the specific needs of the investors. For example, the principal payment priority may be set as to each monthly distribution thereby allowing subordinate class amortization, or it may apply serially so that the senior class receives all principal payments first, thereby resulting in rapid amortization. In a $100,000,000 offering, the Class A certificates may represent 70 per cent of the transaction and bear an AAA rating with a resulting lower coupon, the next three classes, each at 10 per cent, may have ratings of AA, A, and BBB, respectively. This is purely hypothetical and the actual tranching and ratings will differ significantly depending on the assets and cash flows. Nonetheless, it illustrates how internal credit enhancement may be utilized to achieve a lower overall cost of funds. This also enables sales of CMBS to a broader group of investors.

2. Letter of credit

A letter of credit may be issued in partial support of a CMBS offering. For example, the amount may be tied to an estimated minimum percentage of the pool which would allow the entire pool to achieve a higher rating and therefore a lower cost of funds. Letters of credit must be structured so that draws thereon would not be deemed part of the borrower's bankruptcy estate in the event of a bankruptcy or insolvency proceeding. Moreover, letters of credit must be issued by financial institutions with a credit rating that satisfies rating agency criteria. This is typically an ongoing requirement for the life of the transaction. Additionally, letter of credit fees must be paid either in advance or a satisfactory provision for payment must be built into the transaction.

3. Surety bonds

In some instances, a surety or other similar bond may be issued for the benefit of one or more classes of investors. Once again, the credit of the institution issuing the bond will be an important factor during the life of the issue.

4. Overcollateralization

While overcollateralization may not be the most efficient use of funds, a CMBS transaction collateralized by 110 per cent or more in value of mortgage assets would certainly merit a higher rating. Typically, the unused excess would either be retained by the issuer after payment in full of the securities, or passed through to the residual holder.

5. *Reserve funds*

A transaction may incorporate one of more reserve funds as credit enhancement. The RTC transactions, for example, included a substantial reserve fund provided by the RTC to support losses from the underlying mortgages. The reserve fund typically is owned by the borrower and pledged to the trustee on behalf of the CMBS holders. One disadvantage of a reserve fund is the risk of a bankruptcy or other insolvency proceedings concerning the borrower in which case the reserve fund likely would be caught up in the borrower's bankruptcy estate. While the trustee would have a security interest therein, delays and expenses may be incurred. Reserve funds may also be used as a means of liquidity that is not necessarily tied to a credit enhancement. Liquidity issues are addressed in Section 6.7 below.

6. *Interest rate caps and swaps*

With the varying investor demands for fixed and variable rate securities, some transactions may involve an interest rate cap or swap. Generally, the SPV borrower's obligation should be a fixed or capped interest rate in order to assure the borrower's ability to make determinable debt service payments from cash flow. Investors desiring floating rate securities may require the borrower/issuer to enter into an interest swap agreement where the fixed rate is swapped with a floating rate payment or to purchase an interest cap. Any such agreement must be with a cap provider or swap counterparty that has a rating at least equal to that of the rated securities.

6.4 TRANSACTION PARTICIPANTS

CMBS transactions involve a number of different participants. It is critical that each participant understands the structuring process, the related legal, accounting and tax issues and the role of the other parties to the transaction.

A. Owner/seller

The owner/seller is the entity providing the assets subject to the securitization. In a multiborrower program the owner/seller frequently is the originator of the mortgage loans, or may be a purchaser of mortgage loans in the open market from the initial originators for subsequent resale into a securitization. Sellers frequently include insurance companies, investment bankers purchasing for their own account or for ultimate securitization, and other banks, mortgage companies and financial institutions. Owners may include REITs, or other large property owners and developers seeking attractive financing from the capital markets. Other sellers have included the RTC, more recently the FDIC, and the commercial mortgage conduit alliances.

B. Investment banker

The investment bankers are clearly an integral participant in the structured financing since they raise the capital through the sale of the CMBS. More importantly, they also are responsible for the complex structuring of the classes and terms of each CMBS, which is a function of the terms and provisions of the mortgage assets on the one hand, and the various yield, maturity and risk requirements of the investors on the other hand. Their ability to create an efficient CMBS structure that meets investor needs and demands in the market is the key to success. In addition, investment bankers must coordinate the real estate loan with the difficult timing and pricing challenges presented by the capital markets. The real estate borrower is sometimes an unwary victim of capital market fluctuations. In some instances it is difficult for a real estate borrower to determine his cost of funds until pricing in the capital markets has been completed. This has been particularly troublesome for the small real estate owners unaccustomed to capital markets and their norms. They frequently get their first taste of capital market criteria and short fuse timing on mortgage pricing in lending transactions through the commercial mortgage conduits. Many investment bankers have assumed the interest rate risk by warehousing the loans until a sufficiently large pool has been amassed. A negative move in the markets during this period could ruin the economics of the securitization. Coordinating the real estate side of the transaction with the capital market sale and execution is a complex science, but eminently critical for the successful investment banker.

C. Trustee

The trustee's role in a structured finance transaction is a crucial one that requires skilled and experienced personnel. The trustees are in effect the guardian of the rights of the investors in CMBS, and there is a growing demand that trustees take a more active role in overseeing the performance of CMBS. In fact, the trustee's role has become considerably more complex in structured finance transactions than in typical corporate debt issuances. Trustees are called upon to monitor certain borrower calculations, the provision of quarterly and annual financial statements and other reports, and certain events constituting a default under the transaction documents.[13] Frequently, in rating a transaction, the rating agencies will specifically approve or disapprove of the initial trustee and may set minimum criteria for any successor or transferee trustees.

13. See, for example, *In Trustees We Trust, Strengthening the Role of Trustees in Asset Backed Transactions*, Duff & Phelps Credit Rating Co. (1993). For a listing of the top 10 trustees involved in CMBS transactions in 1994, see "State Street, La Salle Top Trustee Ranking", *Commercial Mortgage Alert*, at p. 1 (February 20, 1995).

D. Master servicer/special servicer

More frequently the servicer has become a significant participant in CMBS transactions, particularly those involving large pools of mortgage loans. The servicer, rather than the trustee, directly handles the day-to-day dealings with the mortgagor and has substantial oversight responsibility concerning the properties. The enumerated duties, include

(i) the receipt of payments of principal and interest and remittance to the trustee,
(ii) the receipt and monitoring of tax and insurance escrows,
(iii) preparation of statements to investors concerning mortgage loan disbursements, defaults and dispositions,
(iv) conducting inspections of the properties,
(v) overseeing permitted mortgagor transfers and lien releases, and
(vi) realizing upon the property in the event of default requiring foreclosure or liquidation.

In fact, the servicer section of a typical pooling and servicing agreement is substantial in length and detailed in scope. The servicer's duties may also include advancing for property protection expenses such as taxes, insurance, and critical maintenance expenses.

Increasingly, servicers are viewed as liquidity providers and are called upon to advance principal and interest payments not made by the borrower. The servicer must be repaid all such advances (including property protection expenses) plus interest from liquidation or other proceeds received on such loan prior to making any payments to investors. Consequently, the servicers must have substantial financial wherewithal and skilled personnal adept at managing large commercial mortgage portfolios.

Similar to trustees, the servicers will undergo close scrutiny by the rating agencies prior to assigning a rating to a particular transaction. Most rating agencies have a specific commercial servicer approval process and publish or maintain an approved commercial servicer list.[14] While servicers may allow sub-servicers to perform certain assigned tasks, they remain ultimately responsible and liable for the enumerated duties.

In addition to master servicers, a separate entity is frequently called upon to serve in a special servicer capacity. This special servicer may be found more commonly in transactions with seasoned and distressed properties that require closer management in non-performing or default scenarios. For example, the RTC transactions included a separate special servicer who is assigned to handle properties after defaults. Special servicers are frequently given latitude in modifying and amending mortgage loans within specified parameters with a view to the maximization of timely recovery of principal and interest on the

14. See, for example, "Approved Commercial Servicer List", *Standard & Poor's Structured Finance*, at p. 28 (February 1995).

mortgage loans. The real estate crisis of the 1980s spawned a number of professionals skilled in workout situations.

E. Rating agencies

Rating agencies perform a critical role in CMBS transactions for a number of reasons. First, investors increasingly rely on the due diligence, analysis and stress tests provided by agencies in determining the rating of the securities. Secondly, a satisfactory rating may be important to meet a particular institution's investment guidelines, capital adequacy requirements or other risk-related capital and portfolio criteria. Thus, from an investor's perspective, the rating agencies perform an important role in assessing credit risks. From the issuer/borrower perspective, the higher the rating, obviously, the lower the cost of funds.

Rating agencies are also taking on an increasing role in various rules and regulations issued by the Securities and Exchange Commission (SEC). For example, in order to qualify as a "mortgage related security" pursuant to Section 3(a)(41) of the Securities Exchange Act of 1934 (the "1934 Act"), the security must be, among other things, rated in one of the two highest rating categories by at least one nationally recognized statistical rating organization (NRSRO).[15] Additionally, NRSROs also play a large role in the recently adopted Rule 3a-7 under the Investment Company Act, which exempts certain structured financings from registering under the Investment Company Act.[16] The role of the NRSROs has become so significant in the eyes of the SEC that it recently issued a request for comment on

(i) whether the SEC should continue to employ the NRSRO concept;
(ii) a uniform definition of the term NRSRO for purposes of all of its rules;
(iii) the procedures utilized by the SEC for designating NRSROs;
(iv) the practice of NRSROs charging fees on rated transactions;
(v) the use of limited scope ratings that may not denote an assessment solely of the credit risk of an instrument; and
(vi) whether the SEC should take further steps to increase its regulatory oversight over NRSROs.[17]

In a companion release, the SEC also issued proposed rules to require disclosure with respect to securities ratings in prospectuses under the Securities Act of 1933 and material changes in security ratings in Form 8-K under the 1934 Act.[18]

15. 15 U.S.C. §78c(a)(41). This definition was added by the Secondary Mortgage Market Enhancement Act of 1984 (SMMEA), Pub. L. No. 98–440, 98 Stat. 1689 (1984). SMMEA, as well as the recently adopted Community Development Act, are discussed in Section 6.8 below.

16. See Investment Company Act Release No. 19,105 [1992 Transfer Binder] Fed. Sec. L. Rep. (CCH) ¶85,062 at p. 83,505 (November 19, 1992).

17. SEC Release No. 33–7085; 34–34616; IC-20508, 59 Fed. Reg. 46314 (September 7, 1994). The comment period under this release terminated December 6, 1994.

18. SEC Release Nos. 33–7086; 34–34617; IC-20509, 59 Fed. Reg. 46304 (September 7, 1994).

Clearly, the rating agencies play a significant role in securitization transactions, from the perspective of issuers in achieving lower costs of funds, from the perspective of the investors in securing comfort regarding credit risks and from the SEC in its oversight of the securities markets.

The principal rating agencies involved in securitization transactions are Standard & Poor's Ratings Group, Moody's Investor Service, Inc., Duff & Phelps Credit Rating Co. and Fitch Investors Service, Inc. These entities are NRSROs as defined by the SEC.[19] In general, the rating agencies in a CMBS transaction will analyze the individual properties and pools of properties, including quantitative and qualitative characteristics of the real estate, credit enhancement, security structure, and legal documentation.[20] The ratings address the assessment of the risk of timely payment of interest and, unless otherwise stated, ultimate payment of principal. Not only do the rating agencies rate the initial issuance of the securities, but frequently are called upon to monitor the securities and will issue upgrades or downgrades on their rating as the performance of the securities merits. Although the rating agencies do not participate in or perform the structuring of CMBS transactions, transaction participants would be wise to discuss various legal, structural and credit issues with the rating agencies in contemplation of a CMBS transaction.

F. Other professionals: attorneys, accountants, engineers, environmental specialists

CMBS transactions also involve a host of other important professionals. At the risk of overplaying the importance of the role of this author's profession in these types of transactions, it is true that they involve many complex legal issues, including those arising under real estate law, tax law, the Uniform Commercial Code, bankruptcy law, environmental law, securities laws at the state and federal levels, and banking or other similar regulatory laws when federally or state chartered financial institutions are involved in the transaction. Accountants also play a significant role in structuring the transactions, certifying as to certain calculations and providing financial statements with respect to property operations. The due diligence involved with property evaluations includes a satisfactory engineering report with respect to the property which includes not only structural matters, but also addresses needed reserves for capital improvements and on-going maintenance. Finally, due to the substantial risks associated with violation of federal and state environmental protection laws, it is extremely important that a review of the properties be conducted by a qualified environmental engineer.[21] For new loan origination, it is commonly required

19. Release No. 33–7085, 59 Fed. Reg. at 46315. In all, six rating organizations currently are designated as NRSROs, at least for purposes of the net capital rules under the 1934 Act. See 17 C.F.R. §240.15c3–1.

20. See, for example, *The Rating of Commercial Real Estate Securities*, Duff & Phelps Credit Rating Co. (1994); *Standard & Poor's Structured Finance Criteria* (1988).

21. Unlike the real estate industry of 20 years ago, participants now face substantial federal and

that at a minimum a "Phase 1" environmental site assessment report accompany each mortgage loan. For mortgage pools containing substantially seasoned loans originated when conducting such an environmental assessment was not common practice, substantial reserves or subordination within the transaction likely will be required. Alternatively, borrowers could purchase environmental insurance which only recently has been utilized in securitization transactions.

6.5 CREATING THE BANKRUPTCY REMOTE SPECIAL PURPOSE VEHICLE (SPV) AND OTHER BANKRUPTCY ISSUES

A. General overview and criteria for SPV

The creation of a bankruptcy remote SPV is a critical part of the overall goal to isolate the assets that are the basis of the securitization. The first stage of the process is to limit the entity's ability to engage in any business other than that related to acquisition, financing and disposition of the assets that will be the subject of the securitization. Consequently, this restriction should be incorporated into the organizational documents. Secondly, the entity should be expressly prohibited from incurring any indebtedness or other obligations other than the rated debt and indebtedness permitted thereunder. The clear intent of this structure is to reduce the likelihood that any creditor of the SPV, other than the holders of the rated securities, would be able to place the SPV into bankruptcy. By reducing the scope of operations and the potential pool of creditors, this goal can be more easily accomplished.

In CMBS transactions, the SPV issue frequently arises at two levels of the transaction. The first level is the issuer of the securities or the sponsor of the trust into which a pool of mortgages is conveyed. That entity typically is not the ultimate obligor under one or more of the mortgages and instead is solely in the business of acquiring mortgages and securitizing them. Consequently, there likely is no other creditor of the SPV except possibly in connection with the initial acquisition or warehousing of the commercial mortgage loans.

The second level of concern for creation of an SPV is at the property owner level. The owner of the property, whether a multi-family apartment complex, a retail shopping center, a regional shopping mall, or a large office building, must also be formed as an SPV. The goal is to isolate the operation and economics of a particular property from possible credit exposure of the owner of that property

---

state laws governing various aspects of environmental protection. Federal laws, which carry substantial liability and exposure for owners and operators of contaminated properties include the Comprehensive Environmental Response, Compensation and Liability Act of 1980 ("CERCLA"), 42 U.S.C. §9601 *et seq.*, as amended by Superfund Amendments and Reauthorization Act of 1986 ("SARA"), Pub. L. No. 99–499, 99 Stat. 1613; the Resource Conservation and Recovery Act of 1976, 42 U.S.C. §6901 *et seq.*; The Federal Water Pollution Control Act, 33 U.S.C. §1251 *et seq.*; the Hazardous Materials Transportation Act, 49 U.S.C. §1801 *et seq.*; and the regulations thereunder, including those promulgated by the Environmental Protection Agency (EPA) (see, e.g., 33 C.F.R. and 40 C.F.R).

and its other business ventures. Accordingly, when investors and rating agencies conduct due diligence and review the property and its operations, they are better able to rely principally on the economics of that property and avoid factoring in unquantifiable outside credit exposures.

In a single asset transaction, the entity that owns the property may also directly issue rated debt secured by a mortgage on the property, and therefore only one SPV is required. However, the terms of the mortgage may impact the structure. For example, a short-term balloon obligation (five to seven years) with minimal amortization may present a refinancing risk that rating agencies determine is so great that a period of time to foreclose and liquidate must be built into the transaction. Consequently, a "back-to-back" structure may be implemented. In a "back-to-back" transaction, a second SPV may be set up to act as the originator of the mortgage loan to the fee owner SPV, and immediately use that loan to collateralize the issuance of mortgage-backed bonds or convey the mortgage loan into a trust which would then issue certificates of interests.

Multiborrower transactions typically involve the most frequent use of two levels of SPVs, with the first level being the SPV issuer/depositor and the second level being the SPV required for each property owner whose mortgages are contributed into the securitization pool. The flurry of activity by commercial mortgage conduit alliances has highlighted one of the difficulties of accessing the capital markets by real estate owners and developers; that is, compliance with the somewhat complex and difficult criteria for creating an SPV and furnishing the accompanying non-consolidation opinion. This section discusses creation of the SPV, while subsection F below addresses the non-consolidation opinion requirement.

Notwithstanding the care and detail with which SPVs are created, it is important to note that these entities are bankruptcy *remote* and not bankruptcy *proof*. As discussed above, the exposure to an involuntary bankruptcy by creditors of the SPV is limited by the restrictions concerning business operations and the incurrence of other indebtedness. The SPV may not be restricted from voluntary bankruptcy since it is against public policy for an entity to agree not to file or avail itself of rights under the United States Bankruptcy Code (the "Bankruptcy Code").[22] To reduce the risk of a voluntary bankruptcy, other procedures are incorporated into the structure. Consequently, one provision thought to reduce the likelihood of an SPV bankruptcy and to provide other safeguards is the requirement that the SPV specifically provide for one member of the board of directors to be an "independent director". The definition of independent director typically would require him or her to be a person who is not and has not been during the two years preceding the individual's appointment

(i) a stockholder, director, officer or employee of the SPV or its parent or other affiliates,

22. 11 U.S.C. §101 *et. seq.*; see, e.g., *In re Tru Block Concrete*, 27 B.R. 486 (Bankr. S.D. Cal. 1983); *In re Adana Mortgage Bankers, Inc.*, 12 B.R. 989 (N.D. Ga. 1980); and *Fallick* v. *Kehr*, 369 F.2d 899, 906 (2d Cir. 1966).

(ii) affiliated with a significant customer or supplier of the SPV or its affiliates, or
(iii) a spouse, parent, sibling or child of any such person.

The concurring vote of the independent director is required in any action relating to

(a) amendment of the SPV provisions in the organization documents,
(b) voluntarily placing the SPV into bankruptcy or other insolvency proceedings,
(c) selling or otherwise transferring SPV property or
(d) dissolving or liquidating, or merging or consolidating with any other entity.

While the independent director will not guarantee that none of these events would occur against the wishes of the holders of the securities, it does provide some level of comfort that an objective, independent person would exercise prudence and business judgment in his or her capacity as director without undue influence from the equity owner.

The comfort stems in part from a board of directors member's duty of care, including fiduciary duties to the corporation. In order to bolster the idea of independence and duty to the corporation, some SPV articles expressly state that the independent director shall not have a fiduciary duty or obligation to the stockholder (except as may specifically be required by statutory law of the applicable jurisdiction), and instead the director's fiduciary duty is owed to the corporation, including its creditors. While this concept of fiduciary obligation may raise issues within standard corporate jurisprudence, the Delaware Court of Chancery has held that directors of corporations approaching insolvency have a fiduciary duty both to creditors and shareholders.[23] By imposing the requirement that each SPV have an independent director, it is hoped, though not guaranteed, that the SPV will not voluntarily be placed in a bankruptcy proceeding without a thoughtful and independent analysis by a board member with no direct economic stake in the transaction. Thus, the SPV structure with an independent director has called upon a growing number of "independent" directors to deal in the evolving and somewhat nebulous area of corporate directors' fiduciary duties.

Apart from the internal structuring of the SPV to minimize the SPV's ability to incur indebtedness or obligations unrelated to the assets being securitized, the process also seeks to limit the potential adverse consequences of credit problems associated with the SPV's parent or other affiliates. Typically, this risk manifests

23. See *Geyer* v. *Ingersoll Publications Co.*, 621 A. 2d 784 (Del. Ch. 1982). For a discussion of the evolving scope of the director's duties during the period of time when the debtor corporation is facing bankruptcy but is still solvent, as well as other evolving federal notions of fiduciary duty in comparison to traditional state concepts of fiduciary duty, see Roberts, "The Conundrum of Directors' Duties in Nearly Insolvent Corporations", 23 Memphis St. U.L. Rev. 273 (1993).

itself in the doctrine created by bankruptcy jurisprudence known as substantive consolidation. "Substantive consolidation is the merger of separate entities into one action so that the assets and liabilities of both parties may be aggregated in order to effect a more equitable distribution of property among creditors."[24] While this doctrine is not expressly provided in the Bankruptcy Code or regulations thereunder, it has been exercised with some degree of frequency by bankruptcy judges based on the broad general equity jurisdiction of a court of bankruptcy under Section 105(a) of the Bankruptcy Code.[25] Substantive consolidation is discussed in greater detail below, but is mentioned here briefly in order to understand the origin of many of the criteria for the SPV.

Additional undertakings, restrictions and covenants are secured from the SPV, the substance of which are the factors that courts have viewed as significant, in the aggregate, in determining whether substantive consolidation is appropriate. Accordingly, the following undertakings should be incorporated into CMBS transaction documents and SPV organizational documents (sometimes referred to herein as "separateness covenants"):

(i) The SPV will be adequately capitalized.
(ii) The SPV will maintain its books and records separate and apart from its parent and any affiliates.
(iii) There will be no commingling of the assets, properties, funds or accounts of the SPV with any other entity.
(iv) The SPV will hold itself out to the public as a separate and distinct entity from its parent and other affiliates.
(v) The SPV will prepare its own tax returns, or if part of a consolidated group, it will be shown as a separate member of such group.
(vi) Regular board meetings will be held to approve SPV activities, and transactions with affiliates must be approved by the independent director.
(vii) The ownership of the assets of the SPV will be clearly shown on its financial statements, and the existence of the SPV will be clearly shown on the financial statements of its parent and affiliates as being owned by the SPV.
(viii) The SPV will not guarantee or pay the debts or obligations of its parent or any other entity; similarly, the parent will not guarantee obligations of the SPV (other than certain limited guaranties, such as securities law indemnifications to underwriters in the CMBS transaction).
(ix) All transactions with the parent or any affiliate will be on an arm's-length basis and effected pursuant to enforceable agreements.
(x) Expenses relating to common employees and overhead shared with affiliates will be appropriately allocated and charged.

24. *Matter of Baker & Getty Financial Services, Inc.*, 78 B.R. 139, 141 (N.D. Ohio 1987); see also, Sargent, "Bankruptcy Remote Finance Subsidiaries: The Substantive Consolidation Issue", 44 *Business Lawyer* 1223 (1989).

25. 11 U.S.C. §105(a); see, e.g., *In re Richton International*, 12 B.R. 555, 557 (S.D. N.Y. 1981).

(xi) The SPV will utilize its own letterhead, telephone and accounts and will maintain an office distinct from its parent.

(xii) The SPV will observe all corporate and other legal formalities in the conduct of its operations.

In some instances, the SPV may also be required to secure non-petition agreements from its parent and creditors. These agreements generally provide that the parent and each creditor will not file an involuntary petition in bankruptcy or pursue any other similar insolvency proceeding against the SPV so long as the rated obligations are outstanding and for up to one year and one day after the obligations are paid in full. In contrast to agreements by a debtor not to avail itself voluntarily of the bankruptcy courts, agreements with creditors not to pursue such action do not contravene public policy and should be enforceable.[26]

At least one commentator has suggested the idea of requiring the equity owner of the SPV to provide a "springing guaranty" that would come into effect only in the event the SPV or other securitization vehicle were placed in bankruptcy while the entity was solvent.[27] This tactic presents at least two problems: one legal and the other marketing. First, several bankruptcy decisions list the existence of intercompany guaranties as a factor weighing in favor of substantive consolidation.[28] Although the springing guaranty is contingent in nature, its existence still could adversely affect the attempt to avoid substantive consolidation. Secondly, while the guaranty may be an effective tool to dissuade an equity owner from voluntarily placing the SPV into bankruptcy, many commercial real estate transactions are structured as non-recourse indebtedness. Borrowers and their principals may be required to carve out from the non-recourse nature of the debt actions involving fraud or misapplication of funds, but the insistence of the springing guaranty is not typical and makes the transaction look more like recourse debt. Lenders insisting on this type of guaranty may find themselves at a marketing disadvantage to other real estate lenders that insist on no more than the traditional carve-outs.

As has been discussed, many of the foregoing attributes, covenants and provisions assume that the SPV will be related to the originator of the mortgage or the entity that owns a property. In some instances, however, the SPV will be an orphan corporation, which may be owned by a charitable trust or other entity unaffiliated with the borrower. This extra precaution removes the secur-

26. See Schorer and Rosenberg, "No-Petition Agreements Seem Sound", *The National Law Journal*, at p. 9 (May 2, 1994), including cases cited therein such as *Moulton* v. *Coburn*, 131 F. 201, 203 (1st Cir. 1904), *cert. denied*, 196 U.S. 640 (1905); and *In re MacFarlane Webster Associates*, 121 B.R. 694 (Bankr. S.D.N.Y. 1990).

27. "Days Inn's SPC Filing Spawns Securitization Poison Pill", *Asset Sales Report*, at p. 1 (November 25, 1991) (comments of Steven Schwarcz).

28. See *In re Vecco Construction Industries, Inc.*, 4 B.R. 407, 410 (Bankr. E.D. Va. 1980); *In re Richton*, 12 B.R. at 558; and *In re Stop & Go of America, Inc.*, 49 B.R. 743, 747 (Bankr. D. Mass. 1985). On the other hand, one could argue that the existence of a guaranty by a separate entity shows the recognition of the debtor as a separate entity from the guarantor.

itization entity even further away from the potential credit problems of transaction participants. While the foregoing discussion addressed corporate SPV criteria, several different types of entities may be used and are discussed in more detail below.

B. Corporation as SPV

The corporation is frequently utilized as an SPV. All of the provisions described above, including (1) the limitation in the articles of incorporation to the one type of business in which it may engage, (2) the requirement for an independent director, and (3) limitations on activities such as conveying property, amending the articles, or dissolving or merging without the unanimous approval of the board, including the independent director, should be incorporated into the corporation's organizational documents. The corporation may be a wholly owned subsidiary of the originator or other participant in the securitization transaction. Other factors, however, clearly must be considered in selecting the proper entity. For example, in view of entity level taxation under federal income tax laws, particularly in real estate transactions, a corporation may not be the most attractive vehicle, unless the S corporation election is made to secure pass-through treatment, where all participants meet the requirements thereof.[29] Corporations may, however, be more frequently utilized as the depositor/ sponsor of a pass-through trust into which mortgage assets are conveyed.

C. Limited partnership as SPV

The limited partnership generally is a more attractive vehicle for borrowers in CMBS transactions due to the ability to pass-through items of income, loss and gain for federal income tax purposes. Consequently, a slight modification to the structure described for a corporate SPV is necessary. First, since a partnership does not have a board of directors, and instead is managed by its general partner, the independent director concept does not directly apply to the partnership entity. Rather, the sole general partner should be a corporation that meets all of the criteria for an SPV described above. In addition, the limited partnership agreement should contain similar limitations, including limiting the partnership's business to ownership and operation of the property that is the subject of the securitization, and not amending the partnership agreement, dissolving or conveying assets without general partner consent. The difference is that any such activity requiring the vote of the general partner should require the unanimous vote of the board of directors, including its independent director. Moreover, the provisions stated above for a corporate SPV should be modified slightly to account for this corporation's role as a general partner in the borrower partnership SPV, with the undertakings and limitations applying both

29. See United States Internal Revenue Code §1362. In general, an S corporation may not be owned by another corporation.

to the corporation for its own actions and for the partnership where the corporation acts as the general partner. Finally, the general partner should agree not to withdraw voluntarily as general partner so long as the rated debt is outstanding.

Another concern with a partnership entity is the potential for dissolution of the entity under state law. Unlike corporations, partnerships generally provide for a finite life and may otherwise be dissolved upon the occurrence of events specified in the laws of the jurisdiction of organization. For example, under Delaware law, a limited partnership may be dissolved upon the occurrence of the events specified in the partnership agreement, the consent of all partners, or an event of withdrawal of a general partner unless at the time there is at least one other general partner and the partnership agreements permits the business of the partnership to be carried on by the remaining general partner; or, if within 90 days after withdrawal all partners agree to continue the business of the partnership.[30] Thus, in order to assure the continued existence of the SPV partnership and avoid an untimely dissolution, the partnership agreement should allow as few events as possible to cause a dissolution, and provide further that the minimum number of partners permissible may vote to continue the business of the partnership after an event of dissolution. Moreover, the partnership agreement should provide that at all times when the partnership's indebtedness is outstanding, a corporate general partner containing the SPV criteria discussed herein shall be in place.[31]

D. Limited liability company (LLC) as SPV

Limited liability companies have emerged as a vehicle of choice for many new businesses, including for the ownership and operation of real estate. The attraction stems in part from the ability to organize freely an entity that may be held by a small or large group of persons using a flexible organization structure and management options. At the same time, the LLC carries the equally attractive quality of limited liability enjoyed by corporate shareholders and limited partners. Most importantly, the LLC also enjoys the pass-through treatment of income, loss and gain for federal tax purposes similar to partnerships. However, it is extremely important that the LLC meets Internal Revenue Service criteria for achieving treatment as a partnership for tax purposes.[32]

30. Del. Code Ann. Tit. 6, §17–801.

31. In general, see "Real Estate Finance—Special Purpose Bankruptcy Remote Entities", *Standard & Poor's Corporation* (1993).

32. See, for example, Rev. Rule 93–38, 1993–21 I.R.B. 4, wherein the IRS ruled that a Delaware limited liability company can assume the characteristics of a corporation or a partnership for federal tax purposes depending on the provisions of the LLC agreement. See Smith and Miller, "Limited Liability Companies-Delaware", Vol. 8 *State Limited Partnership Laws—Limited Liability Company Statutes* (M. Bamberger and A. Jacobson, eds.) 1994–3 Supplement (hereinafter referred to as "*State Limited Partnership Laws*").

While the LLC offers many advantages, it is not without problems. First, even though the LLC has recently gained popularity, it is still an entity less familiar to most practitioners than the corporation or limited partnership. Similarly, not all jurisdictions have approved the LLC as an entity that may be formed under that jurisdiction's laws, or that may qualify to do business in that jurisdiction, although as of August 1994, approximately 46 states have one or more variations of the LLC statute in place.[33] This lack of familiarity and the relative newness of these entities in commercial transactions could cause delays in closing transactions and may result in the loss of limited liability status or the inability to achieve either a qualification to do business in certain jurisdictions or the desired pass-through treatment for tax purposes.

Second, from a purely structural standpoint, the LLC suffers the same concerns regarding dissolution that a limited partnership does. Accordingly, one rating agency has issued criteria that call for any LLC in a rated transaction to have at least one member meet its corporate special purpose corporation requirements (i.e., the SPV criteria for a corporation substantially described hereinabove).[34] The requirement for a corporate SPV member parallels the requirement for a corporate general partner in a limited partnership, and addresses the dissolution issue. Apart from addressing the dissolution risk, requiring a corporate SPV as a member seems to be overly cumbersome. Since LLCs may be managed by managers who are not necessarily members, it would seem appropriate to require merely that any LLC maintain an independent manager with duties and criteria similar to the independent director in a corporate SPV.

E. Trust as SPV

A trust is frequently used as the securitization vehicle into which mortgage assets are conveyed and certificates of beneficial interest therein are sold to investors. This structure offers several advantages: first, it achieves the pass-through treatment for federal income tax purposes. However, if the trust is designed as a grantor trust, special attention must be paid to assure compliance with applicable regulations so that it is not treated as a corporation for federal income tax purposes.[35] The issuer may also be an owner trust or a business trust created under the various state laws. A second advantage of the trust format is that in

33. See Donn, "Practical Guide to Limited Liability Companies", Vol. 8, *State Limited Partnership Laws*, footnote 32 *supra*, at p. PGLLC-6.

34. "Legal Criteria for LLCs Established", *Standard & Poor's Structured Finance Quarterly*, at p. 36 (August 1994). This criteria also requires that transaction participants provide an opinion of counsel to the effect that (i) upon the insolvency of a member or any successor member, the LLC or its assets would not be consolidated with that insolvent member, and (ii) that the LLC will be taxed as a partnership and not as a corporation.

35. For a discussion of tax issues involving trusts and other entities in securitization transactions, see Schmalzl, Craven & Levy, "Tax Issues", Vol. I, *Securitization of Financial Assets* (Jason H.P. Kravitt, ed.) 1993–1 Supplement (hereinafter "*Securitization of Financial Assets*").

general, trusts are not eligible debtors under the Bankruptcy Code.[36] One critical limitation is that a trust that qualifies as a "business trust" will be eligible as a debtor under the Bankruptcy Code, with the principal distinction being that business trusts are created for the purpose of carrying on a business or commercial activity for profit while a non-business trust is created to protect and preserve the trust estate.[37]

F. Substantive consolidation

As mentioned above, one of the bankruptcy issues that plays a significant role in structured finance transactions is the risk of the bankruptcy of a parent or affiliate of the SPV adversely affecting the SPV. This could occur, for example, when the creditors of the parent or affiliate desire to cause the court to consolidate the assets of the SPV with those of the bankrupt debtor parent or affiliate. Unfortunately, substantive consolidation has been granted not only where the entity to be consolidated is itself a debtor under the Bankruptcy Code, but also where the subsidiary is not a debtor and remains solvent.

The participants in a securitization transaction, including underwriters, investors and the rating agencies rating the securities, require some level of comfort that the SPV will not be consolidated with the parent or other affiliate in the event of bankruptcy. While most commercial transactions include an obligation on the part of counsel to the borrower to render opinions as to authorization, legality and enforceability of the transaction documents, these opinions typically exclude the effect of bankruptcy, insolvency and other debtor relief laws. Structured finance transactions, on the other hand, specifically require that an opinion be rendered to the effect that in the event of insolvency under the Bankruptcy Code of the parent, partner or certain other affiliates, that the assets and liabilities of the SPV would not be consolidated with those of such parent, partner or affiliate. With the growing number of securitization transactions and acceptance of these requirements by counsel regularly practising in this area, there fortunately has evolved some degree of uniformity into the general format of these opinions and the limited scope and nature of their meaning.[38] These opinions are lengthy, reasoned opinions that discuss case

36. H.R. Rep. No. 595, 95th Cong., First Sess. 311–14 (September 8, 1977), reprinted in 1978 U.S. Code Cong. & Admin. News at 6268–71. Section 109 of the Bankruptcy Code indicates who may be a debtor, specifying the requirements for each chapter of the Bankruptcy Code, and often using the term "person". 11 U.S.C. §109. Section 101(41) defines "person" as an individual, partnership and corporation; and defines a corporation in Section 101(9) as including a business trust. 11 U.S.C. §101(9), (41).

37. *In re Secured Equipment Trust of Eastern Airlines, Inc.*, 153 B.R. 409, 413 (S.D.N.Y. 1993), *affirmed*, *Shawmut Bank Connecticut* v. *First Fidelity Bank* (*In re Secured Equipment Trust of Eastern Airlines, Inc.*), 38 F.3d 86 (2d Cir. 1994). This case involved an equipment trust financing setup for Eastern Airlines and the aftermath of its bankruptcy. The trust, which conveyed proceeds from the sale of its certificates to Eastern Airlines in exchange for Eastern's right, title and interest in a pool of aircraft and aircraft engines, was held not to be an eligible debtor under the Bankruptcy Code.

38. See Special Report by the TriBar Opinion Committee, "Opinions in the Bankruptcy Context:

law and analogous factual settings, none of which exactly mirrors the situation of a structured financing. Since the power to substantively consolidate is within the equitable discretion of the bankruptcy court, the opinions rely heavily upon certain factual circumstances being true at the closing and during the term of the financing and are in all events subject to the discretionary powers of the bankruptcy courts. These factual situations are derived from circumstances in which courts have granted substantive consolidation in the past and consequently have been the basis for the covenants, undertakings and requirements described above for the SPV organizational documents. Consequently, a discussion of the case law development in the area is instructive.

The practice of substantive consolidation is not expressly authorized under the Bankruptcy Code. Rule 1015 under the Bankruptcy Code provides for joint administration of cases; however, the Advisory Committee Notes thereunder state that "[c]onsolidation, as distinguished from joint administration, is neither authorized nor prohibited by this rule since the propriety of consolidation depends on substantive considerations and affects the substantive rights of creditors of the different estates".[39] Accordingly, the power to substantively consolidate derives from the general equity jurisdiction of a court of bankruptcy under Section 105(a) of the Bankruptcy Code.[40] Nonetheless, courts recognize that as a general rule "the power to consolidate should be used sparingly because of the possibility of unfair treatment of creditors of a corporate debtor who have dealt solely with that debtor without knowledge of its interrelationship with others".[41]

In analyzing whether substantive consolidation of a parent and subsidiary is appropriate, courts have utilized a "piercing the corporate veil" or "*alter ego*" approach. The courts have considered the following factors relevant in determining whether the subsidiary is the mere instrumentality of the parent and the two entities should be treated as one:

(i) the parent owns all or a majority of the capital stock of the subsidiary;
(ii) there are common directors and officers;
(iii) the parent corporation finances the subsidiary;
(iv) the parent corporation is responsible for incorporation of the subsidiary;
(v) the subsidiary has grossly inadequate capital;
(vi) the parent company pays the salaries or expenses or losses of the subsidiary;
(vii) the subsidiary has no independent business from the parent;
(viii) the subsidiary is commonly referred to as a subsidiary or as a department or a division of the parent;

Rating Agency, Structured Financing, and Chapter 11 Transactions", 46 *Business Lawyer* 717 (1991) (hereinafter cited as "Special Report by TriBar Opinion Committee").

39. Fed. R. Bankr. P. 1015; and Advisory Committee Note thereunder.

40. *In re Richton International*, 12 B.R. 555, 557 (S.D.N.Y. 1981).

41. *Chemical Bank New York Trust Company* v. *Kheel*, 369 F.2d 845 (2d Cir. 1966).

(ix) directors and executive officers of the subsidiary do not act independently but take direction from the parent; and
(x) the formal legal requirements of the subsidiary as a separate and independent corporation are not observed.[42]

Other courts subsequently produced a separate list of seven elements relevant to determining the appropriateness of consolidation:

(1) the presence or absence of consolidated financial statements;
(2) the unity of interests and ownership between the various corporate entities;
(3) the existence of parent and inter-corporate guarantees on loans;
(4) the degree of difficulty in segregating and ascertaining individual assets and liabilities;
(5) the transfer of assets without formal observance of corporate formalities;
(6) the commingling of assets and business functions; and
(7) the profitability of consolidation at a single physical location.[43]

Although existence of the foregoing elements is instrumental in determining whether the parent and subsidiary should be treated as a single entity, their existence alone does not necessarily mandate substantive consolidation. The courts recognize that these factors should not be mechanically applied and are not alone dispositive, but they must be evaluated in the overall "balancing of equities" favoring consolidation versus those favoring separation.[44] The party proposing consolidation bears the burden of demonstrating that any prejudice resulting therefrom is outweighed by the benefit to be obtained, and this burden is a "substantial" one.[45]

The balancing test also has been stated:

(i) There must be a necessity for substantive consolidation or a harm to be avoided by the use of substantive consolidation; and
(ii) The benefits of substantive consolidation must outweigh the harm to be caused to objecting creditors.[46]

42. See *Fish* v. *East*, 114 F.2d 177 (10th Cir. 1940) (subsidiaries were mere instrumentalities of the parent); *Matter of Gulfco Investment Corporation*, 593 F.2d 921 (10th Cir. 1979) (consolidation not proper; no purpose to hinder or defraud creditors).

43. *Eastgroup Properties* v. *Southern Motel Assoc., Ltd.*, 935 F.2d 245, 249 (11th Cir. 1991); *In re Vecco Construction Industries, Inc.*, 4 B.R. 407, 410 (Bankr. E.D. Va. 1980); *In re Murray Industries, Inc.*, 119 B.R. 820, 830 (Bankr. M.D. Fla. 1990); *In re Richton International*, 12 B.R. at 558; *In re Stop & Go of America, Inc.*, 49 B.R. 743, 747 (Bankr. D. Mass. 1985).

44. See *In re DRW Property Co. 82*, 54 B.R. 489, 495 (Bankr. N.D. Tex. 1985); *In re Doughnut Queen, Ltd.*, 41 B.R. 706, 709 (Bankr. E.D.N.Y. 1984).

45. *In re N.S. Garrott & Sons*, 48 B.R. 13, 18 (Bankr. E.D. Ark. 1984); *In re Snider Bros., Inc.*, 18 B.R. 230, 238 (Bankr. D. Mass. 1982).

46. *In re F.A. Potts & Co., Inc.*, 23 B.R. 569, 572 (Bankr. S.D.N.Y. 1978). This approach is clarified by the court in *In re Snider Bros., Inc.*, 18 B.R. 230, 234 (Bankr. D. Mass. 1982): "While several courts have recently attempted to delineate what might be called the 'elements of

Therefore, even in cases where a significant number of the foregoing factors and elements were present, the courts considered them in the context of specific circumstances that on balance weigh in favor of consolidation. Current case law indicates that the circumstances in which substantive consolidation has been held appropriate may be categorized generally as follows:

1. Fraud or injustice on creditors

Where affiliates of the debtor were organized to hinder and delay judgment for creditors and property transfers were for the sole purpose of placing property beyond the reach of creditors, consolidation is appropriate.[47] Consequently, courts generally will hold that it is proper to disregard a separate legal entity when necessary to avoid fraud or injustice following an *alter ego* or piercing the corporate veil approach. Even if the 10 factors cited above in *Fish* v. *East* were present to a "considerable degree", consolidation may not be appropriate because of the absence of a purpose to organize the corporate subsidiaries to hinder and delay creditors fraudulently.[48] Thus, the mere identity of corporate names, stockholders and officers or the fact of ownership of capital stock in one corporation by another alone are not sufficient to justify disregarding the corporate fiction. The corporation must have been "organized or used to hinder, delay or defraud, the creditors, of the bankrupt, and constitutes mere legal paraphernalia observing form only and not existing in substance or reality as a separate entity".[49] As described below, however, fraud is not the only instance justifying consolidation. The focus of the judiciary has continued to be on the effect of the debtor's action on the creditors, but a showing of fraud, while sufficient, is not the minimum threshold.

Apart from viewing the debtor's action and its direct impact on creditors, courts also will review the circumstances to determine whether the effect of substantive consolidation will work an injustice on one creditor to the benefit of another. For example, consolidation has been denied where it would unjustly benefit creditors of a parent corporation over creditors of the subsidiary proposed to be consolidated.[50]

---

consolidation', [citations omitted] I find that the only real criterion is that which I have referred to, namely the economic prejudice of continued debtor separateness versus the economic prejudice of consolidation. There is no one set of elements which, if established, will mandate consolidation in every instance. Moreover, the fact that corporate formalities may have been ignored, or that different debtors are associated in business in some way, does not by itself lead inevitably to the conclusion that it would be equitable to merge otherwise separate estates."

47. *In re Tureaud*, 45 B.R. 658 (Bankr. N.D. Okla. 1985). *Accord*, *In re Stop & Go of America, Inc.*, 49 B.R. at 748 (shell corporation formed to hold franchise was a "deliberate scheme" to protect franchise seller's interest in a manner likely to result in fraud on creditors; corporation had no telephone, office, bank account, expenses or income).

48. *Matter of Gulfco Investment Corp.*, 593 F.2d 921, 928 (10th Cir. 1979).

49. *Maule Industries, Inc.* v. *Gerstel*, 232 F.2d 294, 297 (5th Cir. 1956).

50. *In re Flora Mir Candy Corporation*, 432 F.2d 1060 (2d Cir. 1970) (subsidiary's debenture holders would be unfairly disadvantaged).

2. *Creditor reliance on enterprise as a group*

Courts also have allowed substantive consolidation in cases where the creditors have relied justifiably on the assets and credit of a group of entities, or the credit of a parent when dealing with its subsidiary.[51] In *Soviero* v. *Franklin National Bank of Long Island*, there were clear findings of commingling of assets and functions of the affiliated entities and flagrant disregard of corporate forms.[52] Moreover, creditors were advised that the bankrupt was a "consolidated enterprise" and were delivered consolidated financial statements listing assets of the affiliated companies as those of the bankrupt without separation.[53] In granting consolidation where creditors relied on the consolidated enterprise, the Second Circuit in the *Soviero* case also made it clear that consolidation should not be limited to cases where the subsidiary was organized for the purpose of hindering or defrauding creditors.[54]

On the other hand, where creditors rely solely on the representations and credit of a parent corporation and additional security from subsidiary corporations is not required, substantive consolidation of a subsidiary into its parent should not be imposed.[55] Similarly, where a creditor extended credit to a debtor based on that debtor's finances alone, without knowledge of the debtor's negotiations to merge with another entity, the Second Circuit in *In re Augie/Restivo Baking Company, Ltd.* held that consolidation would impair the rights of that creditor and unfairly benefit later creditors of the merged entities.[56] The court went on to hold that the considerations enumerated in prior decisions "are merely variants on two critical factors: (i) whether creditors dealt with the entities as a single economic unit and 'did not rely on their separate identity in extending credit' … or (ii) whether the affairs of the debtors are so entangled that consolidation will benefit all creditors".[57]

3. *Intermingling and intertwining of corporate accounts and business*

As indicated by the Second Circuit in the *Augie/Restivo* decision, the second factor meriting consolidation is excessive entanglement of business and operations. The Second Circuit articulated this second factor in an earlier decision saying "where the interrelationships of the group are hopelessly

51. See *Stone* v. *Eacho*, 127 F.2d 284 (4th Cir. 1942) *cert. denied*, 371 U.S. 635 (1942).
52. 328 F.2d 446 (2d Cir. 1964).
53. *Id.* at 447; see also *In re Richton International Corporation*, 12 B.R. 555 (S.D.N.Y. 1981); *In re Food Fair, Inc.*, 10 B.R. 123 (Bankr. S.D.N.Y. 1981); and *In re Murray Industries, Inc.*, 119 B.R. 820 (Bankr. M.D. Fla. 1990).
54. *Soviero* v. *Franklin National Bank*, 328 F.2d at 448.
55. *Anaconda Building Materials Co.* v. *Newland*, 336 F.2d 625 (9th Cir. 1964) (so holding, notwithstanding that the parent held all the outstanding stock of each subsidiary, there were some common officers and directors, and some evidence that the subsidiaries were minimally capitalized). See also *In re Flora Mir Candy Corporation*, 432 F.2d 1060, 1062–63 (2d Cir. 1970).
56. 860 F.2d 515 (2d Cir. 1988).
57. *Id.* at 518.

obscured and the time and expense necessary even to attempt to unscramble them so substantial as to threaten the realization of any net assets for all the creditors, equity is not helpless to reach a rough approximation of justice to some rather than deny any to all".[58] The situation must be extremely egregious, however, and amount to an impossibility of reconstructing financial records to determine intercorporate claims, liabilities and ownership of assets.[59] Although inequities may be involved in the consolidation, they may be outweighed by practical considerations such as accounting difficulties and expense, which may occur where interrelationships of corporate groups are highly complex or untraceable.[60]

4. *Facilitating reorganization plan*

Where consolidation will facilitate or expedite reorganizational proceedings for a number of related debtors, consolidation may be imposed, particularly if separate plans of reorganization would not be feasible.[61] The ability to consummate a plan quickly alone, however, may not justify consolidation, particularly if the rights of creditors of the proposed consolidated entity would thereby be diminished.[62]

Traditionally, substantive consolidation has been granted by the courts "sparingly" due to the extreme impact on substantive rights of creditors. The Eleventh Circuit Federal Court of Appeals, however, in adopting for the first time a standard by which to evaluate motions for substantive consolidation, noted what it termed "a 'modern' or 'liberal' trend toward allowing substantive consolidation, which has its genesis in the increased judicial recognition of the widespread use of interrelated corporate structures by subsidiary corporations operating under a parent entity's corporate umbrella for tax and business purposes".[63]

The Eleventh Circuit requires that the proponent of substantive consolidation show that (i) there is substantial identity between the entities to be consolidated; and (ii) consolidation is necessary to avoid some harm or to realize some benefit. Upon making these two showings, the court held that a presumption arises that creditors have not relied solely upon the credit of one of the entities involved in the consolidation. The burden then shifts to the objecting creditor to show that it (a) has relied on the separate credit of one of the entities being consolidated, and

58. *Chemical Bank* v. *Kheel*, 369 F.2d at 847.

59. See *In re 1438 Meridian Place, N.W., Inc.*, 15 B.R. 89 (Bankr. D.D.C. 1981) (neither the court nor the creditors could intelligently sort out or separate the financial affairs of the corporations).

60. See *In re Continental Vending Machine Corp.*, 517 F.2d 997, 1001 (2d Cir. 1975), *cert. denied sub nom. James Talcott Inc.* v. *Wharton*, 424 U.S. 913 (1976).

61. *In re Interstate Stores, Inc.*, 15 Collier Bankr. Case 634, 640–41 (Bankr. S.D.N.Y. 1978); *In re F.A. Potts & Co., Inc.*, 23 B.R. 569 (Bankr. E.D. Pa. 1982).

62. *In re Flora Mir Candy Corporation*, 432 F.2d 1060, 1063 (2d Cir. 1970); *In re F.W.D.C., Inc.*, 158 B.R. 523 (Bankr. S.D. Fla. 1993).

63. *Eastgroup Properties* v. *Southern Motel Association, Ltd.*, 935 F.2d 245, 248 (11th Cir. 1991) (quoting *In re Murray Industries, Inc.*, 119 B.R. at 828).

(b) will be prejudiced by substantive consolidation. Finally, if the objecting creditor successfully demonstrates the foregoing, then the court nonetheless may order consolidation, but only if it determines that the benefits of consolidation "heavily" outweigh the harm.[64] The decision falls within the "creditor reliance" fact situations discussed above, except that it creates a presumption of creditor non-reliance merely upon a showing of substantial identity and the avoidance of harm or realization of benefit from consolidation. While such a presumption may not necessarily follow from the required showing, creditors of a limited purpose finance subsidiary formed in connection with a structured finance transaction presumably could show both reliance on a separate entity and substantial harm and prejudice from consolidation.

The Eleventh Circuit's decision also demonstrates that consolidation may be granted not only with respect to a parent and its subsidiary, but also to members of a consolidated group, and entities that merely have "common ownership". In this case, one debtor was a limited partnership that had three corporate equity owners, which were also the ultimate owners of the other debtor, a corporation. Other decisions also indicate that the bankruptcy courts will consolidate the estates of a partnership and its general partners, as well as the estates of corporations, partnerships and individual debtors.[65]

Although the foregoing discussion identifies factors that courts consider and certain fact situations that are frequently cited as meriting substantive consolidation, there is no clear litmus test. Courts have focused, however, on the relationship of the entities to be consolidated and the effect of consolidation on their respective creditors, with the result that cases are to a great degree *sui generis*.[66]

It should be noted that limited case law specifically addresses the legality of substantive consolidation of a bankrupt debtor and a non-debtor solvent affiliate. Although a split of authority exists, it has been held that creditors (who did not have a claim against the non-debtor affiliates directly) could bring before the court parties alleged to be the "*alter ego*" of the debtor.[67] Alternatively, the parties may be able to bring a non-debtor affiliate before the court by satisfying the requirements of substantive consolidation in a showing that assets were commingled or creditors relied on the consolidated group or extending credit.[68]

On the other hand, the court in *In re Alpha & Omega Realty, Inc.* held that a solvent affiliate of the debtor would not be consolidated with the debtor's estate

64. *Id.* at 249 (citing *In re Auto-Train Corp.*, 810 F.2d 270, 276 (D.C. Cir. 1987)).

65. See *F.D.I.C.* v. *Colonial Realty Co.*, 966 F.2d 57 (2d Cir. 1992); *In re Nite Lite Inns*, 17 B.R. 367 (Bankr. S.D. Cal 1982).

66. 5 *Collier on Bankruptcy* ¶1100.06[1] at p. 1100–35 (L. King 15th ed. 1994).

67. *In re 1438 Meridian Place N.W., Inc.*, 15 B.R. 89, 95–96 (Bankr. D.D.C. 1981). See *In re Crabtree*, 39 B.R. 718, 722–26 (Bankr. E.D. Tenn. 1984) (the right to bring additional parties before the court who are the *alter ego* of the debtor is independent of the right of creditors to force a person into bankruptcy under Section 303 of the Code).

68. *Matter of Munford, Inc.*, 115 B.R. 390, 398 (Bankr. N.D. Ga. 1990) (consolidation is a complex turnover proceeding where the debtor asserts an inseparable interest in the affiliate's assets).

because the affiliate was not itself a debtor.[69] In support of the position against consolidation of non-debtor parties, the court in *In re DRW Property Co. 82* stated that it was "unaware of any statutory or common law authority to substantively consolidate debtor and *non-debtor* partnerships. The non-debtor partnerships are certainly well-outside of the scope of this Court's jurisdiction".[70]

In the only decision in the United States Supreme Court on the issue, the court held in *Sampsell* v. *Imperial Paper & Color Corporation* that substantive consolidation of a non-debtor corporation into an individual bankrupt's estate was proper where the transfer of property by the individual to the corporation was not in good faith, was made for the purpose of placing it beyond the reach of the individual's creditors, and where the effect of the transfers was to hinder, delay or defraud the individual's creditors.[71] Thus, the decisions in favor of consolidation of a debtor's solvent affiliate at least require some sort of harm or fraud on creditors and typically include a determination that the solvent entity was the *alter ego* of the debtor, although a showing of commingling of assets or creditor reliance on the consolidated group may be sufficient.

The discussion of substantive consolidation cases typically does not include any decision involving an SPV in a structured financing. This is due in part to the efforts made by the parties to isolate the assets of the SPV, but also to the relatively short time during which the SPV structure has been in use. It appears that only one transaction involving an SPV has resulted in consolidation. The Bankruptcy Court in the District of Delaware granted substantive consolidation upon motion by the debtors, which included a limited purpose finance subsidiary created in a structured finance transaction for Days Inn of America, Inc. (now known as Buckhead America Corp.).[72] The bankruptcy court's opinion made many factual findings that are inconsistent with the undertakings, arrangements and representations discussed in this chapter and required for SPVs. Moreover, the nature of the assets conveyed to the SPV is different from those in a typical CMBS transaction: Days Inn had contributed its franchise system, agreements and trade names, trademarks and logos to the SPV, which the court found were essential for an effective reorganization. Finally, the

69. 36 B.R. 416 (Bankr. D. Idaho 1984).

70. 54 B.R. 489, 497 (Bankr. N.D. Tex. 1985) (emphasis in original). See also *In re The Julien Company*, 120 B.R. 930 (Bankr. W.D. Tenn. 1990) (motion to consolidate debtor corporation with non-debtor shareholder violates due process rights of non-debtor and its separate creditors); *In re Lease-A-Fleet, Inc.*, 141 B.R. 869, 872 (Bankr. E.D. Pa. 1992) ("caution must be multiplied exponentially in a situation where a consolidation of a debtor's case with a non-debtor is attempted, by a single party which . . . is a creditor of the debtor only and whose efforts are not joined by any other interested parties").

71. 313 U.S. 215, 217–18 (1941) (so holding despite the Court of Appeal's finding that the non-debtor corporation could not be deemed the *alter ego* of the individual bankrupt under California law).

72. *In re Buckhead America Corp.*, Case Nos. 91–978 through 91–986 (Bankr. D. Del. Aug. 13, 1992).

objecting parties withdrew their objections to the application prior to the bankruptcy court's decision.

The *Buckhead America* decision illustrates, however, the importance of the conduct of the parties in a structured finance transaction and how they interact with creditors and carry on the business operations. Further, it demonstrates that creditors relying on the separate credit of an SPV in a structured financing may need to argue vigorously their case in a bankruptcy proceeding to avoid consolidation. Consequently, even if ultimately successful, investors may suffer the effects of a preliminary injunction or other temporary relief pending a final determination on the merits.

It is important to note that non-consolidation opinions should not be viewed as carrying the same degree of weight as a legality or enforceability opinion. In fact, the primary comfort that is given to the underwriters, investors and rating agencies by these opinions is the knowledge that counsel familiar with the various factors weighing favorably toward substantive consolidation has been closely involved in structuring the transaction, creating the SPV entity and causing the principals, officers and directors of the SPV to make certain undertakings and covenants in regard to the operation and conduct of the affairs of the SPV and its affiliates.

G. True sale

The transaction should be structured to ensure that the SPV has complete and absolute ownership of the assets used to secure the securities issued. Accordingly, the transfer of the assets from the parent/affiliate to the SPV should be treated as a "true sale" or, if made as a capital contribution, an "absolute conveyance". In the case of a pass-through transaction, the seller/depositor must convey all right, title and interest in the assets to the trustee for the benefit of the certificate holders. An opinion of counsel to the issuer generally will be required to the effect that such assets will not be deemed property of the transferor under Section 541 of the Bankruptcy Code.

In the event the parent enters bankruptcy proceedings, a creditor or the trustee in bankruptcy could challenge the transfer of the mortgage assets by the parent or affiliate to the SPV as a direct pledge to secure the bonds or notes backed by the mortgage assets instead of a sale. The result of the transfer being deemed a pledge instead of a sale would be inclusion of the mortgage assets in the bankruptcy estate of the parent or affiliate under applicable provisions of the Bankruptcy Code. The determination of whether or not a bankrupt's estate has an interest in property is made pursuant to state law.[73]

Courts on occasion have recharacterized as a "pledge" a transfer and assignment of assets treated by the parties as a sale or absolute assignment.[74] In

73. *Butner* v. *United States*, 440 U.S. 48 (1979); *In re National Equipment & Mold Corp.*, 64 B.R. 239 (Bankr. N.D. Ohio 1986).

74. See *In re Major Funding Corporation*, 82 B.R. 443 (Bankr. S.D. Tex. 1987); *Fox* v. *Peck Iron*

analyzing whether a transaction is a true sale or merely a financing arrangement with the assets used as security, the courts generally look to the following factors:

(i) whether the transferee exercises the normal benefits and burdens of ownership of the assets;
(ii) the existence and degree of recourse by the transferee against the transferor;
(iii) the allocation of risk relating to ownership of the assets;
(iv) the course of dealings between the parties, including their conduct and relationship;
(v) the consideration granted in exchange for the assets; and
(vi) the overall structure of the transaction, including documentation thereof.[75]

The issue of the parties' intent, though not determinative in all cases, is significant. "If the parties actually intended to effect an absolute transfer of ownership, a court of equity will not ignore that intent and make another contract for them."[76] This is especially true where the parties are sophisticated in the financing transactions and their intent is clear.[77]

With respect to the issue of consideration exchanged for the assets, case law supports the view that any transfer by a parent to a wholly-owned subsidiary is presumed to be for reasonably equivalent value. Since the parent owns all of the common stock of the subsidiary, any transfer to the subsidiary should inure to the benefit of the Parent.[78]

Apart from the objective indications of the intent of the parties, many courts independently assess the legal characteristics of the transaction. Factors that some courts have cited as leading to the conclusion that a sale should be characterized as a loan for purposes of an insolvency or bankruptcy proceeding

---

and Metal Company, Inc., 25 B.R. 674 (Bankr. S.D. Cal. 1982) (sale/leaseback transaction); *In re O.P.M. Leasing Services, Inc.*, 30 B.R. 642 (Bankr. S.D.N.Y. 1983); and *Major's Furniture Mart, Inc.* v. *Castle Credit Corporation, Inc.*, 602 F.2d 538 (3d Cir. 1979).

75. See generally, *Major's Furniture Mart* v. *Castle Credit, supra*, 602 F.2d at 544–46; *In re Major Funding, supra*, 82 B.R. at 448; *Matter of Bevill, Bresler & Shulman Asset Management Corporation*, 67 B.R. 557, 597 (D.N.J. 1986); and *Fox* v. *Peck Iron, supra*, 25 B.R. at 688.

76. *Matters of Kassuba*, 562 F.2d 511, 514 (7th Cir. 1977).

77. *Id.* at 515. While the documents executed by the parties will not alone dictate the characterization of a transaction, the objective manifestation of the parties' intent to consummate a sale rather than a loan as contained in the documents together with testimony at trial has proven significant in finding that a sale transaction occurred. See *In re Lemons & Associates, Inc.*, 67 B.R. 198, 209–10 (Bankr. D. Nev. 1986); *In re National Equipment*, footnote 73 *supra*, 64 B.R. at 245; see also *Matter of Bevill, Bresler*, footnote 75 *supra*, 67 B.R. at 590–94 (extrinsic evidence of intent includes the treatment of the transaction in the books and records of the parties, recognized accounting conventions, regulatory treatment and trade custom and usage).

78. *In re Royal Crown Bottlers of North Alabama, Inc.*, 23 B.R. 28, 30 (Bankr. N.D. Ala. 1982) ("because the subsidiary corporation is an asset of the parent corporation, . . . what benefits the asset will ordinarily accrue to the benefit of its owner.") See also *Johnson* v. *First National Bank*, 81 B.R. 87 (Bankr. N.D. Fla. 1987); *Iannacone* v. *Capital City Bank* (*In re Richards*), 58 B.R. 233 (Bankr. D. Minn. 1986).

include (i) the ability of the seller to substitute new property for the property transferred, (ii) the obligation of the seller to transfer additional property to the buyer without any additional payment from the buyer, (iii) the seller's ability to repurchase the assets, (iv) the seller's right to retain any surplus after payment of the underlying obligation, and (v) a structure providing for level payments by the seller to the buyer regardless of amounts collected on the transferred property.[79]

The characterization of a transaction as a sale or financing for tax purposes follows a review and analysis of similar elements. The relevant factors are:

(1) whether legal title passes;
(2) how the parties treat the transaction;
(3) whether the purported purchaser acquires any equity in the property;
(4) whether the contract creates a present obligation on the purchaser to make payments;
(5) whether the right of possession is vested in the purchaser;
(6) which party bears the risk of loss or damage to the property; and
(7) which party receives the profits from the operation and sale of the property.[80]

Many of the above factors relate to the economic substance of a transaction, the analysis of which is an essential element in the characterization process. The major factor cited by courts in reviewing the economic substance of transactions labeled as sales is the extent to which risks and benefits associated with ownership of the property have been transferred to the purchaser.[81] The risks of ownership are essentially that the property transferred either will decline in value or will experience payment defaults. When the buyer has recourse to the seller to compensate it for losses so occasioned, courts have concluded that the seller has retained the related risk and that the economic substance of the transaction is that of a secured loan by the buyer to the seller.[82]

A relevant case decided by the Ninth Circuit Court of Appeals concerned the rights of investors in mortgages originated by a loan brokerage company that eventually became insolvent. In *Bear* v. *Coben* (*In re Golden Plan of California, Inc.*), the Court of Appeals reversed a lower court holding that certain investors

79. See, e.g., *In re Major Funding*, footnote 74 *supra*, 82 B.R. at 448; *Fireman's Fund Insurance Companies* v. *Grover* (*In re The Woodson Company*), 813 F.2d 266, 272 (9th Cir. 1987); *Major's Furniture Mart*, footnote 74 *supra*, 602 F.2d at 545; *Fox* v. *Peck Iron*, footnote 74 *supra*, 25 B.R. at 689. Characteristics indicating a transfer or assignment for security purposes as interpreted pursuant to the Uniform Commercial Code, include the following: (i) the right to deficiency if the assigned property does not provide sufficient funds to satisfy the debt, (ii) the assignee acknowledges that its rights in the assigned property are extinguished if the debt were paid from another source, (iii) the assignee must account for any surplus received from the assigned property, (iv) the assignor's debt is not reduced on account of the transfer or assignment, and (v) the express language of the contract. *In re Evergreen Valley Resort, Inc.*, 23 B.R. 659 (Bankr. D. Me. 1982).

80. *In re Gran*, 108 B.R. 668, 671 (Bankr. E.D. Ark. 1989).

81. *Fireman's Fund Insurance Companies* (*In re The Woodson Company*), footnote 79 *supra*, 813 F.2d at 271; *In re Nite Lite Inns*, 13 B.R. 900, 908 (Bankr. S.D. Cal. 1981).

82. See, e.g., *Major's Furniture Mart*, footnote 74 *supra*, 602 F.2d at 545.

who did not take possession of the instruments assigned to them had merely an unperfected security interest.[83] Golden Plan, the loan brokerage company, originated loans secured by deeds of trust and assigned them to investors providing the funds. Golden Plan frequently retained possession of the notes, deeds of trust and assignments, acted as loan servicing agent pursuant to a written collection agreement (directly or through an affiliate), and provided certain advancing services in consideration for late payment charges. In holding that the parties intended to effect sales of the notes and deeds of trust, the court looked to the documentation, particularly the assignments "without recourse" and noted that investors received no contractual guarantee of repayment or compensation in case of foreclosure.[84] While the court found that the notes and deeds of trust were "instruments" for purposes of the California UCC, and had held in prior decisions that a secured party's failure to take possession of the instruments caused the security interests therein to become unperfected, the court stated that Division 9 of the UCC does not apply to an assignment intended to be a sale of a note or trust deed. The principal test in determining whether a transaction is subject to Division 9 is whether the transaction is intended to have effect as security.[85]

In order to address many of the concerns and factors cited above, the buyer and seller in a CMBS transaction, among other things, generally make representations and warranties regarding the quality and characteristics of the mortgage assets conveyed. Any obligation of or recourse to the seller should result only from conditions in existence at the time of the sale and should not relate to any decline in value or other credit factor regarding the mortgage assets subsequent to the sale. The representations and warranties should not confer any additional rights on a purchaser or impose any added burdens on a seller beyond those applicable under general contract law and, by analogy, under Section 2–608 of the Uniform Commercial Code in the context of sales of goods, in the rescission of a sale of non-conforming property.

The documents executed between the parties should clearly indicate the seller has sold and transferred all of its right, title and interest in and to the mortgage assets to the buyer, free and clear of all adverse claims, rights and interest therein and passed legal title thereto, and the buyer has the benefits and burdens of ownership thereof.

Even where the seller will act as servicer for the mortgage loans, this role should not adversely affect true sale treatment. In fact, the existence of a servicing agreement weighs favorably to the conclusion of sale treatment, even where the servicer performs an advancing function, so long as the servicer may be removed for breach of its duties under the agreement, and the terms for

83. 829 F.2d 705 (9th Cir. 1986).

84. *Id.* at 709.

85. *Id.* at 708 and n.2. See Note, "Bankruptcy and the UCC as Applied to Securitization: Characterizing a Mortgage Loan Transfer as a Sale or a Secured Loan", 73 Boston U.L. Rev. 873 (1993).

servicing set forth therein are customary and usual in the mortgage lending market.[86]

H. Fraudulent conveyance/transfer

In some instances, it will be necessary to ensure that the transaction will not be deemed a fraudulent conveyance or fraudulent transfer under applicable state law or Section 548 of the Bankruptcy Code. This may occur either in the case of a sale by one affiliate to another, or a capital contribution by a parent to its SPV subsidiary. The need for comfort on this issue increases as the parent/transferor's credit is unrated or potentially unstable. Section 548, which is similar in many respects to the various state fraudulent conveyance or fraudulent transfer codes, provides that the trustee may avoid any transfer made within one year of the date of filing if the debtor: (1) made the transfer with actual intent to hinder, delay or defraud any creditor; or (2) received less than a reasonably equivalent value in exchange for such transfer and either (a) was insolvent at the date of transfer or became insolvent as a result thereof, (b) was engaged in business for which its remaining capital was unreasonably small, or (c) intended to incur debts beyond its ability to pay.[87]

A legal opinion may be required, although as a legal matter it is of little value due to the factual nature of fraudulent conveyance issues and serves mainly to organize and present the relevant factual data. Consequently the opinion giver will rely exclusively on extrinsic evidence (rather than assumptions) as to these highly factual (as opposed to legal) points. Accordingly, underlying certificates or other evidence as to (i) the intent of the parties (i.e., no intent to hinder, delay or defraud creditors), (ii) the solvency of the transferor and (iii) the fair value of the consideration received for the property transferred are most important. The fair value certificate should come from a valuation expert, which may include the underwriter or placement agent involved in the offering. MAI appraisals of the property conducted by licensed independent appraisers are also competent third-party evidence as to value. Evidence of the solvency of the transferor may be secured through audited financial statements. While counsel rendering the opinion justifiably should not opine as to fair value or solvency, mere representations by the transferor may be inadequate.[88]

86. See *Bear* v. *Coben*, footnote 83 *supra*, 829 F.2d at 709 ("the practice of advancing does not alter the nature of the transactions at issue as sales").

87. 11 U.S.C. §548.

88. See generally, Special Report by the TriBar Opinion Committee, footnote 38 *supra*, at pp. 727–29 and "Exhibit A".

6.6 REAL PROPERTY AND STRUCTURE CONSIDERATIONS

Commercial mortgage loan securitizations are actually two distinct financing transactions. The first is a real estate transaction, which frequently is complex and covers a host of issues and considerations in and of itself. The second is a securities transaction, which gives rise to the securitization. Due to the complexity and significance of each type of transaction, it is critical to have competent and skilled professionals involved at each stage. This section will discuss certain aspects of the real estate transaction as well as the securities transaction that may be helpful to highlight, although it is by no means exhaustive.

A. Environmental issues

Few issues concerning real estate have had as vast an impact over the past 15 years as the environmental and hazardous waste laws, including the Comprehensive Environmental Response, Compensation and Liability Act (CERCLA).[89] While these laws have no doubt focused attention on some of the ills we have wrought upon our environment by carelessly disposing of various hazardous substances, they have also spawned a whole industry of professionals engaged in the evaluation and remedying of environmental problems. Moreover, they require substantial expenditures in order to decontaminate properties and thus significantly affect the purchase, sale and financing of real property. Consequently, very few property transfers or financings have occurred in the recent past without the purchaser or lender first conducting an environmental site assessment of the property. The extensive and far reaching liabilities associated with persons who own, operate, or in some instances finance properties, make such assessments and testing a mandatory part of any property transaction.

Lack of information concerning environmental matters is typically not a problem with newly originated mortgage loans, since environmental testing has become common practice. However, pools of seasoned mortgage loans that may not have the benefit of a "Phase 1" environmental report or any other similar comfort as to compliance with environmental laws, will necessitate either (i) conducting an environmental site assessment, adding the cost to the transaction, (ii) setting aside a substantial reserve to cover the possibility of environmental problems in the future, or (iii) otherwise giving allowance to this potential and unknown exposure, for example through larger subordination levels or guaranties or repurchase obligations in the event of subsequently discovered environmental problems.

Most current loan documents address environmental issues by requiring representations and warranties as to past and continued compliance with all

89. For a list of several federal environmental laws impacting real estate transactions, see footnote 21 *supra*.

state, federal and local environmental and hazardous waste laws, notification to the lender of any notices received from approprate authorities regarding non-compliance, and undertakings to cause tenants of the properties to comply within the lease agreements and through reasonable due diligent oversight. Additionally, in many instances a separate environmental guaranty will be required of the parent or other financially sound affiliate of the borrower. Since these types of guaranties relate to the limited instance of environmental exposure, they should not adversely impact the undertakings and assumptions regarding intercorporate guaranties discussed under "Substantive consolidation".[90]

B. Insurance

Various real property risks are addressed by insurance, where the lender is a named beneficiary. One fundamental concern is that title to the property is vested in the borrower and the lender's lien is valid. Thus, the borrower must provide title insurance covering the lender's lien on the property subject only to those exceptions that do not adversely affect the value of the collateral.

Additionally, each property should have insurance coverage for other common risks. First, casualty insurance should cover fire and extended perils within the "all risks of physical loss" category. The amount of insurance should equal the actual replacement cost of the property and should be in an amount sufficient to avoid any co-insurance provisions. The replacement cost provision is necessary to insure that in the event of a casualty, insurance proceeds will not be reduced for wear and tear or depreciation. The property should be restored from insurance proceeds without additional funding, other than the amount of an acceptable deductible.

Second, flood insurance likely will be required in the event the property is located within the 100-year federal flood plain. Similarly, if the property is located in areas prone to earthquake damage, earthquke insurance will be required if available for commercially reasonable amounts. In the alternative, in some instances a satisfactory engineering report, viewed in the context of the area's proneness to earthquake activity, may alleviate the need for earthquake insurance, particularly where it is cost-prohibitive.

Third, business interruption or rental loss insurance for a minimum period, usually at least 12 months, should be obtained. Depending on the type of property, this period may be extended to up to two years, for example with respect to office buildings or certain retail properties. The period is usually a function of the anticipated time required to restore and release the property after a substantial casualty.

Fourth, various other insurance coverage typically called for in commercial lending transactions should be secured, including comprehensive general

90. See discussion in Section 6.5.F, *supra*.

liability insurance, workers' compensation insurance or similar coverage under various state laws, and boiler or other machinery failure insurance, depending on property type.

The policies should have deductibles not in excess of what is common for the type and size of property. In addition, there should be a provision in the transaction documents for periodic updates of coverage levels and provision of annual renewal certificates of insurance and evidence of payments of premiums.

Due to the importance of insurance coverage as a protection of the collateral, the financial strength of the insurance carrier likely will be subject to minimum criteria, which may be imposed by rating agencies. The importance of the insurance carrier increases as the size and diversity of the pool of properties decreases. For example, it is quite common that in a single asset transaction or a small pool of properties, the insurance carrier would be required to have a minimum claims paying ability rating of "A". On the other hand, in a large diverse pool of properties owned by unaffiliated borrowers, the claims-paying ability rating of any single insurance company on a single property would be less significant, although the scope of coverage itself would not change.

The transaction documents also should stipulate how insurance proceeds are to be applied in the event of a casualty to the property. In general, it is preferable to have a property restored to full operations after a casualty, rather than applying proceeds to payment of the mortgage and salvaging a damaged property for an amount that may not be sufficient to pay the balance in full. As in any lending situation, sound business judgment and prudence should prevail. Accordingly, the existence of business interruption or rental insurance is an essential component in order to provide a period of time during which the property can be restored. If the damage is so substantial that restoration time and lease-up would exceed the period of time for which insurance coverage is available, and consequently the amount of damage is a substantial portion of the value of the property, then a payment in reduction of the mortgage likely would be appropriate. In order to provide adequate oversight on this process and the disbursement of funds, the mortgage typically will call for amounts in excess of an immaterial amount, such as 5 per cent of the mortgage balance, to be paid to the lender or servicer for disbursement as restoration is completed and upon the presentation of receipts and architect certificates. On the other hand, insurance proceeds from a casualty in an immaterial amount may be paid directly to the borrower for application to restoration. In the event the borrower is more efficient in restoring the property to its prior condition, excess insurance proceeds may be retained by the borrower. This would be contingent upon the receipt of an architect's certificate indicating the property had been restored to substantially its prior condition. Payment of excess insurance proceeds after proper restoration, however, should not be confused with condemnation proceeds. Condemnation represents a taking of the collateral and therefore such amounts should be distributed to the mortgage holder as a prepayment (without premium or yield maintenance).

C. Engineering report

A recent engineering report should be conducted on the property to identify deferred maintenance, structural integrity concerns and necessary improvements that will be required for the property over the term of the financing. As mentioned above, it may also indicate whether earthquake concerns may be ameliorated due to design benefits. From the engineering report, the lender, uderwriter or rating agencies may determine that certain capital reserves are necessary to be established at closing or built up over time to address these costs.

D. Mortgage file

Each real property transaction involves a number of transaction documents that together must be provided to the purchaser of the mortgage loans, or the trustee, in the event of a securitization. The mortgage file typically includes the following:

(i) mortgage note;
(ii) mortgage or deed of trust;
(iii) assignment of leases and rents (which could be a part of the mortgage);
(iv) title insurance policy, assignable to successor holders of the note;
(v) form UCC financing statements covering personal property subject to the Uniform Commercial Code;
(vi) environmental guaranties;
(vii) assignments of the mortgage in recordable form to the transferee, together with assignments or endorsements of the other security and transaction documents;
(viii) insurance certificates indicating that the holder of the mortgage is a named beneficiary thereunder (other than for business interruption or rental insurance);
(ix) other security documents or certificates that may be necessitated by different property types or transaction terms.

The foregoing documents will constitute the mortgage file and should be conveyed to the trustee in the securitization or its custodian. The trustee, custodian or servicer should be charged with reviewing the mortgage file within a specified period of time to confirm that all of the documents are located therein with respect to each property. The assignments of mortgage should be filed in the appropriate real estate records and certified copies thereof should be maintained with the mortgage file. The indenture or pooling and servicing agreement should provide various triggers to insure that the review has been conducted and that any deficiencies are cured by the seller/depositor or otherwise the mortgage should be repurchased.

E. Specialized properties

Depending on the type of property, a number of other issues could arise that merit special attention. For example, in transactions involving hotel or similar hospitality properties, there has been a significant issue as to the nature of the hotel receipts and how a security interest therein is perfected. The courts have differed as to whether these receipts constitute "rents" for purposes of Section 552 of the Bankruptcy Code permitting continuation of the security interest, or whether they are "accounts" subject to perfection under the Uniform Commercial Code and the security interest which terminates upon commencement of the bankruptcy.[91] Fortunately for lenders, Section 214 of the Bankruptcy Reform Act of 1994 (the "Bankruptcy Reform Act") clarifies this ambiguity by amending Section 552 to provide that a security interest in amounts paid as rents on the property or the fees, charges, accounts or other payments for the use or occupancy of rooms and other public facilities in hotels, motels or other lodging properties granted pursuant to a security agreement prior to commencement of the case is extended to such rents, fees, charges, accounts or other payments after the commencement of the case to the extent provided in the security agreement; an amendment to Section 363(a) clarifies that such rents, fees, charges, accounts or other payments are included in the definition of "cash collateral".[92]

Hotel properties actually incorporate a variety of business operations. First, many involve restaurant operations, and various licenses under local and state law, including food and beverage licenses, are necessary. The hotel may be operating under a franchise agreement, compliance with which is essential in order to assume continued access to trademark rights and hotel reservation systems. Consequently, consents and notice provisions regarding any defaults should be secured on behalf of the lender. Hotel properties involve intensive and specialized management, and the management team and related contract must be viewed carefully as they impact the lender and its right to realize upon the collateral. Convention or other meeting operations also may be an important

91. Some courts have concluded that receipts generated from the use of hotel rooms are not "rents" within the meanings of Sections 552(b) and 363(f) of the Bankruptcy Code and therefore do not constitute "cash collateral". Rather, they are viewed as "accounts", an interest in which is perfected by filing under the Uniform Commercial Code. Thus, a mortgagee's pre-petition interest in such receipts does not continue after the borrower's commencement of a bankruptcy proceeding because of the application of Section 552. See *In re Majestic Motel Associates*, 131 B.R. 523 (Bankr. D. Me. 1991); *In re Shorehave Motor Inn, Inc.*, 124 B.R. 617 (Bankr. S.D. Fla. 1991); *In re Nendells-Medford Joint Venture*, 127 B.R. 658 (Bankr. D. Ore. 1991); *In re Green Corp.*, 154 B.R. 819 (Bankr. D. Me. 1993). However, other courts have held that hotel receipts do constitute "rents". See, e.g., *Financial Security Assurance Inc.* v. *Days California Riverside L.P.* (*In re Days California Riverside L.P.*), 1994 W.L. 259707 (9th Cir. 1994); *In re T-H New Orleans, L.P.*, 10 F.3d 1099 (5th Cir. 1993), *cert. denied*, 114 S.Ct. 1833 (1994) (Nothing in the legislative history indicates that Congress intended to exclude "hotel revenues" from the term "rents" as used in Section 552(b)); *In re S.F. Drake Hotel Associates*, 131 B.R. 156 (Bankr. N.D. Ca. 1991) *affirmed*, 147 B.R. 538 (N.D. Cal. 1992).

92. Bankruptcy Reform Act of 1994, Pub. L. No. 103–394, 108 Stat. 4106 (1994). President Clinton signed the legislation into law on October 22, 1994.

part of the hotel business. The revenue streams and the various components thereof must be evaluated to determine whether additional steps should be taken.

In retail and shopping mall transactions, the various lease terms, including lease rates, maturity and renewal options factor heavily into the financial analysis. Similarly, the rights to terminate or cause a financial obligation on the part of the landlord are equally significant. Leases should be evaluated for any landlord obligations, rights of first refusal or negative covenants that could impact the property's operations and ability to lease to other tenants. In super-regional malls, the operating agreements among the anchor tenants, the owner and other large stores that own their own property are significant in determining the revenue stream to pay common area expenses, utilities and taxes. Additionally, the property must be evaluated to determine easement obligations and any other rights or obligations associated with the property.

Nursing homes and congregate care facilities have recently emerged as popular subjects of mortgage origination for CMBS transactions. Depending on the nature of the residents and the scope of services provided to them, issues such as compliance with federal entitlement programs such as Medicare and Medicaid and the licensing of personnel and facilities may arise. State government agencies may also regulate nursing homes necessitating a review of appropriate licenses and permits. If any other agency or authority provides funding or subsidies to the operations, compliance with applicable requirements and terms should be investigated.

F. Ground leases

While mortgage loan transactions involving loans secured by a fee simple ownership interest in the real estate are most common and certainly preferred, a number of transactions arise where the borrower owns a leasehold estate for a period of years in the underlying real estate and is mortgaging its rights in such leasehold interest and the improvements. These ground lease transactions add a layer of complexity and risk to a CMBS transaction, but they do not necessitate exclusion from a pool.

Because the lender has a lien only on the leasehold interest and its improvements, the lender is at risk to the extent the borrower fails to comply with the ground lease. In order to address this risk, the borrower must provide satisfactory evidence to the effect that the ground lease allows the mortgagee to receive notice of the borrower's default, to cure a borrower default, to be beneficiary under casualty insurance proceeds, to foreclose on the borrower's leasehold interest and to assign the ground lease to a new tenant in connection with a foreclosure sale without the consent of the ground lessor. Lenders must also examine the ground lease for increases in rent over the proposed term of the financing. The term of the ground lease should exceed the fully amortized term of the financing by at least 10 years.

The foregoing concerns deal primarily with the risks associated with the borrower's performance under the ground lease. In addition, ground leases present a concern about the financial health of the ground lessor. For this reason, it is important to determine whether the fee ownership interest is likewise subject to indebtedness and whether that would be a priority over the lender's mortgage on the leasehold improvements. In the event the ground lessor becomes subject to bankruptcy proceedings, Section 365 of the Bankruptcy Code generally allows the trustee in bankruptcy to accept or reject any executory contracts and unexpired leases.[93] Consequently, there is a concern whether the ground lease may be rejected and therefore the borrower/ground lessee would be forced to vacate, or that rents could be raised to a level making the borrower's costs excessive when coupled with the leasehold mortgage. Fortunately, however, Section 365(h), as amended by Section 205 of the Bankruptcy Reform Act, states that if the lessor's trustee in bankruptcy rejects the lease, the lessee may either treat the lease as terminated or, in the alternative, the lessee may retain its rights under the lease for the balance of the term and for renewals or extensions by paying the stated rents.[94] Furthermore, the lessee may offset against the rent any damages occurring after the date of filing that are caused by non-performance of the debtor/landlord, which offset is the only right to damages the lessee has. As one might imagine, this accommodation for lessees has not been free of problems. For example, under the language of the Bankruptcy Code prior to the recent amendments, which stated only that the lessee could "remain in possession of the leasehold", one court viewed the possessory right as a personal property right of the ground lessee and not a continuation of the rejected lease; therefore, a lender foreclosing on a borrower lessee after the ground lessor's bankruptcy and rejection of the ground lease would not be able to assign the foreclosed ground lessee's interest to a new leasehold purchaser.[95] The Bankruptcy Reform Act has addressed concerns and conflicting case law by clarifying the rights of a lessee in the lessor's bankruptcy. Section 365, as amended, now states that the lessee "may retain its rights under such lease (including rights such as those relating to the amount and timing of payment of rent and other amounts payable by the lessee and any right of use, possession, quiet enjoyment, subletting, assignment or hypothecation)" for the balance of

93. 11 U.S.C. §365.

94. 11 U.S.C. §365(h)(1), as amended by Section 205 of the Bankruptcy Reform Act; see footnote 92 *supra*.

95. See *In re Carlton Restaurant, Inc.*, 151 B.R. 353, 356 (Bankr. E.D. Penn. 1993), where the court held, in a case of first impression, that upon the rejection of a lease by a debtor/landlord, the rejection terminates the lease and the tenant has only a personal right to possession which may not be assumed or assigned by a third party. Compare *In re Lee Road Partners, Ltd.*, 169 B.R. 507 (E.D. N.Y. 1994), where the court held that the term "in possession of the leasehold" granted to a tenant under Section 365(h)(1) of the Bankruptcy Code includes a tenant who has sublet the premises to one or more other parties. See also *In re Upland/Euclid, Ltd.*, 56 B.R. 250, 255 (Bankr. App. 9 (Cal.) 1985) (non-debtor lessee has an estate in real property; 365(h) allows lessor/debtor to interfere only by eliminating services to tenant and not by increasing rent).

the term and renewals or extensions.[96] Further, when the debtor/lessor rejects a lease in a shopping center and the lessee elects to retain its rights thereunder, rejection does not affect enforceability of provisions relating to radius, location, use, exclusivity, or tenant mix or balance.[97]

G. Credit lease securitizations

As mentioned above, credit lease transactions differ from traditional securitization in that the credit of a particular tenant provides the basis for a rating on securities backed by the lease to such tenant. A typical transaction would include the sale of the fee ownership of the property to an SPV and the contemporaneous leasing back of the property from the SPV. In order to be rated in a securitization, the leases should be "bondable" leases which require the tenant to pay directly or have passed through as additional rent charges for real estate taxes, insurance, and repairs and maintenance. The obligation to pay rent must continue during any casualty associated with the property. Moreover, the tenant frequently will have an obligation to effect a rebuilding of the property in the event of casualty. In some instances, this obligation may be predicated on a casualty less than the amount required to repay the outstanding amount owed on the bond secured by the lease assignment. The landlord should have few if any responsibilities under the lease, so as to avoid any opportunity for a default by the landlord, which in any event should not terminate the tenant's obligation to pay. Moreover, the term of the lease should exceed the term of the bonds collateralized by such lease. Opportunities for the tenant to terminate the lease without further obligation to pay rent should be eliminated and any other possible expenditures required of the landlord should either be passed through to the tenant or a proper reserve established. One of the benefits of this structure is the additional security provided by the mortgage on the fee ownership interest on the property. This structure has been utilized to provide the acquisition financing for buyers of stores leased by KMart Corporation.[98] If the SPV is owned by the credit tenant, rather than unaffiliated persons, at least one case has collapsed the loan transaction from a lender to a subsidiary and the sub-lease from the subsidiary to the credit parent to find that the sub-lease was not a true lease but rather a secured loan from the creditor directly to the parent corporation.[99] Significantly, the court found that the parties had not adhered to the structure that was put in place.[100] Consequently, the decision illustrates the

96. 11 U.S.C. §365(h)(1)(A)(ii), as amended by Section 205 of the Bankruptcy Reform Act; see footnote 92 *supra*.

97. 11 U.S.C. §365(h)(1)(C), as amended by Section 205 of the Bankruptcy Reform Act; see footnote 92 *supra*.

98. "Merrill Finances Nine KMarts", *Commercial Mortgage Alert*, at p. 3 (January 10, 1994). Commercial Trust I Lease-Backed Certificates, Series 1993-KA, was privately placed in a structure where nine newly created SPV entities purchased the properties and leased them back to KMart Corporation. An assignment of the lease and a mortgage were conveyed to the lender as additional security.

99. *In re Best Products Co., Inc.*, 157 B.R. 222 (Bankr. S.D. N.Y. 1993).

100. *Id.* at 227.

significance of the conduct and operations of the parties involved in assuring the integrity of the transaction structured. It also demonstrates that as the title says, credit lease deals are primarily dependent upon the credit of the tenant regardless of the other structure aspects of the transaction.

H. Trustee and servicer duty of care; limitations on liability

Securitization documents carefully set forth the duties to be performed by each of the participants, particularly the trustee and, if applicable, the servicer. The parties play an extremely important role in the securitization transaction in overseeing the rights of the securities holders and maintaining the collateral. The trustee under an indenture or pooling and servicing agreement has a more limited role and less discretion than a servicer who handles the day-to-day interfacing with the borrower under a mortgage loan. The provisions for a trustee typically involve receipt and distribution of funds and preparation of certain reports to securities holders. Prior to the occurrence of an event of default, the trustee will perform only those duties specified in the documents and any decision authority is governed by a vote of the securities holders. The documents typically provide that upon the occurrence of an event of default, the trustee will use the same degree of care and skill in exercising the rights and powers under the document as a prudent person would exercise or use in the conduct of such person's own affairs. Additionally, the trustee is typically not held liable for any error of judgment made in good faith by a responsible officer, unless it is proved that the trustee was negligent in ascertaining pertinent facts.

With the trustee's duties thus enumerated and the objective standard of care established, it is common and appropriate both to limit the liability for losses, expenses and liabilities arising out of the securitization transaction and to indemnify the trustee for any such losses, expenses and liabilities either out of funds from the transaction or from a third-party guarantor. The limitation of liability and indemnification from costs and expenses is not applicable, however, for any such loss, expense or liability incurred by reason of willful misfeasance, bad faith or negligence in the performance of the trustee's obligations and duties under the documents.

Similarly, pooling and servicing agreements typically establish an objective standard of care in the performance of the servicer's duties by requiring the same care, skill, prudence and diligence with which prudent institutional commercial mortgage lenders and loan servicers service comparable mortgage loans in jurisdictions where the related properties are located, subject to applicable law, and with a view to the maximization of timely recovery of all principal and interest on the mortgage loans. This standard is applicable without regard to

(i) any relation between the servicer and the mortgagor,
(ii) the ownership by the servicer of any of the underlying securities,
(iii) the requirement of the servicer to make principal and interest or property protection advances, or
(iv) the right to receive compensation for services.

The servicers are governed by extensive provisions relating to administration of the mortgage loans, collection of payments, maintenance of insurance, realization upon defaults, property inspections, reports to the trustee and securities holders, management of foreclosed property and the modification or amendment of mortgage loans. Nonetheless, they also exercise somewhat broader discretion than trustees for which they receive a higher fee. In carrying out these extensive duties, the servicer is likewise limited from liability to the trust fund or securities holders for actions taken in good faith pursuant to the agreement or for errors in judgment. The servicer is also afforded indemnification for any losses, expenses or liabilities arising out of performance of duties under the agreements so long as they are not occasioned by wilful misfeasance, bad faith or negligence in the performance of those obligations or duties.

The foregoing standard of care and provision for limitation of liability as well as indemnification are common and appropriate in CMBS transactions. It is important to give the trustee and servicer comfort that they will not be subjected to undue liability or exposure in carrying out their duties under the agreement so long as they act in good faith and are not negligent. These participants cannot be held accountable as guarantors for performance of the underlying mortgage loans and should not be held liable for errors in judgment made in good faith. Nonetheless, investors are entitled to a commercially reasonable standard of care and the performance of such participant's duties in accordance with the terms of the documents. Accordingly, it would seem wholly inappropriate and without foundation to lower the threshold of performance from a simple negligence standard to a gross negligence standard in assessing liability or providing indemnification. Some transaction participants argue that they should not be held liable for losses or liabilities unless it is determined that they were grossly negligent. Thus, they would not be liable for losses incurred by their own negligence. Additionally, they expect indemnification for any losses or expenses suffered unless occasioned by their gross negligence. The result would be that a participant that caused losses for itself and for the trust fund through its own negligence would not be liable to the trust fund, and in fact would be reimbursed by the trust fund for the participant's losses and expenses. In a rated, structured financing where the participants are supposed to be sophisticated, proficient and experienced, it is difficult to understand any justifiable argument for such a low threshold and for saddling investors with the cost of indemnifying participants for their own negligence.

In other areas concerning securities, participants are held to a simple negligence standard. For example, the Trust Indenture Act of 1939 ("Trust Indenture Act")[101] stipulates the trustee's duty of care similar to that recited above. The indenture trustee is to exercise such rights and powers vested in it by the indenture and use the same degree of care and skill as a prudent person

101. 15 U.S.C. §77 aaa *et seq.* (herein cited to the specific section of the Trust Indenture Act).

would exercise under the circumstances in the conduct of his own affairs.[102] Moreover, the indenture

> shall not contain any provisions relieving the indenture trustee from liability for its own negligent action, its own negligent failure to act, or its own willful misconduct, except that... such indenture shall automatically be deemed (unless it is expressly provided therein that any such provision is excluded) to contain provisions protecting the indenture trustee from liability for any error of judgment made in good faith by a responsible officer or officers of such trustee, unless it shall be proved that such trustee was negligent in ascertaining the pertinent facts...[103]

On the servicing side, far from being indemnified for its own negligent actions, a servicer of Federal National Mortgage Association (FNMA) mortgages is required to indemnify FNMA for any losses, damages, judgments or expenses resulting from its failure to perform its services and duties in accordance with FNMA guidelines.[104] Clearly, trustees and servicers in the securities and mortgage industry should be accustomed to a negligence standard. It is certainly not unreasonable where investors rely on their skills and expertise to perform in accordance with the requirements of the agreements. Even trustees in bankruptcy proceedings are held to a simple negligence standard. The courts have held that a trustee in bankruptcy is subject to personal liability for negligence in the performance of his or her duties.[105] It should not even be subject to debate that trustees and servicers must be held to a simple negligence standard of care.

6.7 CERTAIN RATING AGENCY CONSIDERATIONS

Rating agencies conduct substantial review and due diligence on rated commercial mortgage transactions. Each of the four primary rating agencies, Standard & Poor's Ratings Group (S&P), Duff & Phelps Credit Rating Co. (Duff & Phelps), Moody's Investors Service, Inc. (Moody's) and Fitch Investors Service, Inc. (Fitch) publish their own rating criteria which may change from time to time. Additionally, they typically publish monthly or quarterly reports that contain analyses of recent issues as well as updated reports on evolving credit and legal issues affecting rated transactions. Periodic updates or reports on significant issues also are published from time to time. For example, S&P publishes *Standard & Poor's Credit Week* and *Standard & Poor's Credit Review*; Duff & Phelps publishes the *Duff & Phelps Asset-Backed Monitor* and *Duff & Phelps Credit Decisions*; Moody's publishes *Moody's Structured Finance* on a monthly basis; Fitch publishes *Fitch Insights*, *Fitch Rating Register* and *Special Reports* on a periodic basis.

102. Trust Indenture Act §315(c).
103. Trust Indenture Act §315(d).
104. See FNMA Multi-Family Guide, Section 201.02 (August 30, 1991).
105. See *In re Gorski*, 766 F.2d 723 (2d Cir. 1985); *In re Rigden*, 795 F.2d 727 (9th Cir. 1986); *In re Cochise College Park, Inc.*, 703 F.2d 1339 (9th Cir. 1983); and *In re Barrows*, 1994 W.L. 496860 (Bankr. D.N. H. 1994).

Many of the criteria for commercial real estate securitization have been published by each rating agency, but at the time of this writing, several agencies were updating their criteria for new publication. Accordingly, the discussion in this chapter relates to criteria in general based upon past publications, specific transactions and discussions with rating agency personnel. Anyone interested in determining the most current criteria from a particular rating agency should contact that agency directly. The criteria is evolving and will vary within certain parameters depending on the specific structure, properties and payment terms involved in the proposed transaction. For the most part, the rating agencies are eager to discuss prospective transactions and their criteria concerning that transaction. As in any business, some are more responsive than others.

A. Qualitative and quantitative criteria

The qualitative analysis typically incorporates consideration and review of the following:

1. Market and real estate site;
2. Area economy;
3. Leases and tenants;
4. Construction quality;
5. Property management and leasing;
6. The owner/developer;
7. Loan and property seasoning; and
8. Environmental hazards.[106]

The rating agencies conduct extensive analysis of these issues, frequently including review of all or a significant portion of the properties (in large pools). Other factors will be impacted by the property types and size of the pool. The quantitative analysis focuses primarily on the loan to value (LTV) ratio of the properties, based either on recent MAI appraisals or the internal appraisals conducted by the rating agencies. A second focus point is the debt service coverage ratio (DSCR) of the properties. This ratio is calculated based upon the agency's own computation of allowable expenses, and may include provision for a minimum amount of capital expenditure reserves. The cash flows that factor into the DSCR are generally stress tested based upon certain assumptions and economic fluctuations. Thus, properties with certain maximum LTVs and certain minimum DSCRs would slot into the various rating categories within defined parameters. However, they may also be affected by the other qualitative factors described above.

B. Legal, structure and bankruptcy issues

As discussed above, the isolation of the assets to be securitized is the primary structural goal for any securitization. Thus, while the exact SPV criteria may

106. See generally, *The Rating of Commercial Real Estate Securities*, Duff & Phelps Credit Rating Co. (1994).

vary somewhat from agency to agency, the general structures described above generally will be required by the rating agencies. Having thus isolated the assets in creating the related SPV structure, whether on a single-tier or a double-tier basis, a further analysis of possible bankruptcy exposure is evaluated. Consequently, participants in the securitization transaction should expect that at least one or more of the previously discussed bankruptcy opinions will apply.

For example, in a single asset transaction where the owner of the property is also the issuer of the rated securities, a non-consolidation likely will be required for that entity and its parent. In a multiborrower transaction with a pool of mortgages on properties owned by unaffiliated borrowers, a non-consolidation opinion likely would be required by each borrower, or group of affiliated borrowers, whose loan or loans comprised five per cent or more of the pool.[107] In addition, the party accumulating the pool of mortgage loans, that is the depositor in a pass-through transaction, generally must be an SPV and must provide a non-consolidation opinion with respect to itself and its parent. However, the non-consolidation opinion may not be required of the depositor if a true sale opinion can be rendered with respect to the conveyance of the pool of mortgage loans from the depositor to the trust fund created by the pooling and servicing agreement. The true sale opinion generally renders the non-consolidation opinion unnecessary in this structure. If the issuer of the CMBS accumulates mortgage loans but pledges them as collateral for a collateralized mortgage obligation (CMO), then the non-consolidation opinion will be necessary.

Fraudulent conveyance opinions may also be called for where the transferor of the property or the mortgage loans is not financially sound, or where substantially all of the assets are conveyed. Additionally, these opinions may be required where a pool of properties contains cross-default and cross-collateral provisions. As discussed above, the fraudulent conveyance opinion as a legal matter provides very little to the recipient, other than the identification of the purely factual basis upon which the opinion giver relies; that is, the solvency of the transferor and the basis upon which a determination that reasonably equivalent value has been received.[108]

C. Liquidity and credit support

Although credit enhancement in general was discussed above, liquidity is a different issue. Credit enhancement addresses the need for additional collateral to ensure that an investor will be able to realize the return of payments of principal and interest on the obligations. Liquidity, in turn, addresses potential cash flow disruptions, and provides for the timely receipt of those funds, but is not a collateral or credit enhancement. For example, a debt service reserve may

107. See, e.g., *Commercial Real Estate Conduits—Keys to Achieving Lower Subordination Levels*, Duff & Phelps Credit Rating Co. (1993).

108. See Special Report by the TriBar Opinion Committee, footnote 38 *supra*, at pp. 727–29.

be established with the lender or trustee that provides sufficient sums to pay principal and interest for a minimum period of time, such as one month, three months or more. Depending on the credit analysis of a particular transaction, the rating agencies may require a reserve fund in an amount sufficient to pay principal and interest payments during the estimated time necessary to effect foreclosure and liquidation of the property. This period of time may include an estimated time to allow for bankruptcy proceedings. Each state has laws that differ in terms of lender's foreclosure and liquidation rights, which will most certainly impact the period of time necessary to liquidate real property collateral. Additionally, the ability to predict with any accuracy the period of time in which a borrower may be tied up in a bankruptcy proceeding relies more on a crystal ball than any quantifiable criteria. Consequently, the determination of a proper period of time is difficult.

A more common liquidity provider is the requirement that the servicer of the mortgage loans advance principal and interest payments as well as property protection expenses such as taxes and insurance. These advances are payable out of recoveries on the properties and are payable to the servicer prior to any payments to investors. Advancing requirements in pooling and servicing agreements generally call for payments to be made through foreclosure and liquidation. Nonetheless, the servicer need only advance such amounts as the servicer determines in its reasonable business judgment to be recoverable out of ultimate collection of proceeds from the disposition of the property. It is important to note that servicer advancing is a liquidity feature only, since the servicer's determination is based upon the amounts it has advanced, that is, its own exposure, and does not assure that the outstanding amount of the mortgage is also recoverable. However, the servicer is still bound by the standard of care calling for maximization of the realization of amounts owed to investors under the mortgage.

D. Capital expense reserves

In the qualitative analysis, rating agencies will factor in an analysis of the deferred maintenance and necessary upkeep for the properties during the life of the financing. Accordingly, while newly constructed properties may require only minimal reserve allowances, more seasoned properties typically demand a greater reserve. An example for multi-family properties is generally an amount equal to $200 per unit per year for capital expenditures. Office buildings, regional malls and warehouse properties generally have an amount based on square footage. The capital reserve may be funded by a lump-sum amount up front or through periodic deposits from cash flow, to be retained by the servicer or trustee.

E. Representations and warranties as to mortgages

Representations and warranties regarding commercial mortgage loans constitute a significant part of the due diligence and analysis. There are two principal areas of concern in representations and warranties. First, the specific representations and warranties and their content. Second, the party providing the representation and warranty.

Representations and warranties can be broken down into three principal categories. The first relates to the originator/seller of the loans. Representations should address at least the following: the originator's licenses and permits to originate the mortgage loan; origination was effected in compliance with applicable laws and regulations; the specific underwriting criteria used in originating the loans together with a statement that all loans were originated in compliance therewith; there is no right of rescission, offset, abatement or counterclaim against the holder; there have been no amendments, offsets or waivers of the loans by the originator/seller; the originator/seller owns the loans free and clear of all liens, encumbrances, claims and interest and is conveying the loans free and clear. The second area of concern is the property secured by the mortgage. Representations should address at least the following: environmental compliance; that the property is in good repair and condition; there is no proceeding for condemnation; the property complies with all applicable laws and regulations, including zoning, use and occupancy; the property is insured in compliance with applicable criteria by financially suitable insurance carriers; the description of leases is as set forth in attached schedule and the information thereon is true and correct in all material respects; and each property has been inspected by the seller within the last 12 months. Third, representations should address certain aspects of the mortgage loans, including at least the following: each is a legal, valid and binding obligation of the borrower; each loan is covered by satisfactory title insurance assignable to successor purchasers; the loan documents contain customary and enforceable terms; the mortgage has a due-on sale clause and prohibits additional debt without the consent of the holder; the payment terms are as specified on an attached schedule; the borrower is not in material default under any provision thereof and there has been no payment default except as specified on the schedule; the mortgage file contains an assignment of leases or rents, filed in the appropriate real estate records granting a first priority security interest in favor of the lender; each of the assignments of the mortgage loan documents to the purchaser is legal, valid, binding and enforceable; the borrowers are required to provide annual audited financial statements, certificates of insurance and such other reports as are customarily required by financial institutions.

Other representations and warranties may be appropriate depending on the nature and type of the properties involved. In most instances, the seller/originator should be providing the representations and warranties without qualification. However, certain representations may be based upon the title insurance, engineering reports, surveys or other reliable documents provided by independent third parties.

The party providing representations and warranties must meet minimum financial criteria. Because the seller/originator most often has an obligation to repurchase loans with respect to which a material breach of the representations and warranties has occurred, this obligation will not be viewed lightly. For example, in multiborrower transactions, the originators of the mortgage loans may be thinly capitalized conduits who sell to investments banks for securitization. Frequently, the investment banks assign the representations and warranties received from the originators by a mortgage loan purchase agreement into the trust that will issue certificates representing an undivided interest in the loans. Where the conduit originator is not approved as to financial wherewithal by the rating agencies, the investment bank may be required to provide the representations and warranties directly.

F. Property management

Suitable property management is an essential part of underwriting. The property will perform best if it is managed best. Accordingly, at origination of the CMBS transaction as well as during the term of the underlying mortgage loans, many transactions will set forth criteria for property managers. The criteria frequently relate to the number of years the manager has been in business (usually a minimum of five years) and a minimum number of units (in the case of multi-family properties) or square footage of similar properties under management. Frequently, either the borrower or affiliate will be the property manager, subject to termination after a default by the borrower or possibly after the performance of the property falls below certain specified levels. Consideration should be given to whether the exercise of control over the property manager could subject the lender to liability or to be treated as the *de facto* owner of the property.

G. Balloon risk/mortgage extensions

Because of the tension between the investment bankers' desire to price the securities off of the shortest maturity available in order to achieve the lowest coupon, and the concern from the rating agencies about refinancing a balloon mortgage, mortgage extension or "tail" provisions have sometimes been incorporated. For example, a balloon mortgage with a term of seven years may be viewed as too short a period of time to satisfy the refinancing risk assessed by the rating agencies. This risk is addressed either by reducing the loan proceeds, and therefore the LTV, or increasing the amortization during the seven-year life. If neither of these terms is acceptable for the transaction, the rating agencies may require that the mortgage itself contain automatic annual extensions of up to five years. In such instances, these "amortizing tail" extensions are predicated upon a trapping of all cash flow in excess of principal and interest payments and operating expenses. The excess cash flow is then used as a rapid amortization of the mortgage. The trapping of cash, and possibly a higher interest rate during the tail, are additional incentives to the borrower to secure replacement financing. The rapid amortization reduces the balance of the mortgage to an acceptable level within the rating agency criteria for refinancing at the rating category assigned to the CMBS. The tails do not place the borrower immediately into default, and therefore may avert an untimely and undesired bankruptcy proceeding (notwithstanding the SPV criteria).

The extension or tail requirements may be especially useful where the mortgage directly secures the rated debt instrument. Thus, during the extension/tail term, the debt obligation is not in technical default, and is instead being closely managed with more stringent paydown provisions in order to facilitate a quick refinancing. In a pass-through transaction, whether or not the mortgage itself is in default may be less important, because by definition pass-through transactions pass through the payments as received. If the servicer is providing liquidity by advancing, the ultimate payment of principal should be received in due course after a foreclosure and liquidation, unless the value of the collateral has deteriorated to below the debt. If however, the pass-through certificates have a stated or final maturity date that falls on a date before the maturity of the mortgage loan plus the term of the extension/tail, the rating may be impacted.

H. Lockbox collections

In transactions where the LTV is high and the DSCR is low, or where there is a perceived weakness in the collection process, the transaction may need to be structured with a lockbox. Essentially, a lockbox structure reduces the cash flow control risk by giving the secured lender direct access to and oversight of the rents to the property. Accordingly, payments of principal and interest may be set aside first, and operating expenses may be closely monitored. In order to effect the lockbox, payments by the underlying tenants are made in the name of the trustee and sent directly to the trustee (or servicer, as the case may be), without being collected by the borrower or its property manager. Detailed information is then provided by the servicer or trustee to the property manager and the borrower regarding collections. This is the most stringent of lockbox arrangements, sometimes referred to as a "hard lockbox". The hard lockbox may not be favored by borrowers principally because they must instruct tenants to make out and send rent checks to the servicer or trustee directly. This removes the borrower from the collection process and from dealing directly with the tenants. It also slows down slightly the time period during which they accumulate information on payments and the like. The collection of payments is thus secured, and after sufficient amounts for principal, interest, taxes, insurance, capital reserves and other setasides are collected, the remainder may be distributed either to the property manager or the borrower directly. The borrower or property manager generally will pay operating expenses directly, but some lockbox arrangements allow payment only upon presentation of invoices.

A more lenient form of lockbox allows the borrower or property manager to collect the payments directly and deposit them immediately into an account for the benefit of the trustee for the benefit of the certificate-holders. Payments accumulate in this account until principal and interest payments for the succeeding month have been met, and then may be released to the borrower or property manager.

Several variations of the lockbox may be incorporated into a given transaction, depending on the perceived need to maintain control over the flow of funds, either at the outset of the transaction, or to impose these controls immediately upon a default.

I. Subordinate debt

The general guideline for each property owner is to prohibit any other financing that is secured by the property. In addition, indebtedness by the SPV borrower in general is prohibited other than the mortgage, trade accounts payable and certain purchase financing acquisitions, such as equipment.

Super-regional mall or office building transactions that have acceptable LTV levels may allow a minimum percentage of subodinate indebtedness either secured or unsecured by the property. The use of this indebtedness must be strictly for additions to the property and may require that satisfactory subordination agreements be executed.

Occasionally, subordinate debt either unsecured or secured by the property may be permitted. In these instances, a satisfactory intercreditor subordination agreement would be necessary to minimize any possible interference with the senior rated debt. The agreement should contain terms whereby the junior creditor agrees:

(i) to subordinate its right to receive payments to the prior receipt by the senior creditor of its payment in full (although payments of excess cash flow to the junior creditor may be allowed so long as the borrower is not in default),
(ii) to refrain from accelerating the debt, pursuing any remedies for default or commencing any bankruptcy, insolvency or similar proceeding against the borrower until the senior creditor has been paid in full, plus applicable preference periods,
(iii) to assign to the senior creditor all of its rights in a bankruptcy proceeding involving the borrower, including voting rights and rights to distributions (until the senior creditor is paid in full),
(iv) to waive any rights against the senior creditor to contest its lien or demand specific action or remedies, and
(v) to execute a similar agreement, if requested, in connection with the refinancing of the senior debt.

Unlike agreements by borrowers to waive rights in bankruptcy, a subordination agreement among creditors is generally regarded as enforceable and is specifically contemplated by the Bankruptcy Code.[109]

J. Trustee and servicer eligibility

Due to the importance of the trustee and servicer in rated CMBS transactions, rating agencies frequently will establish minimum eligibility criteria. In many transactions, the trustees have a minimum capital surplus requirement of $50 million or more and a minimum long-term debt rating of at least investment grade. Where the trustee is acting as an advancer on the principal and interest payments, the long-term rating may be increased to "A" or better. Rating agencies may also review the trustee's internal procedures and policies for handling matters that may arise in the course of the transaction.

In the case of servicers, an approved servicer list may be either published or internally maintained by the rating agencies.[110] The servicer eligibility is frequently a function of the rating agency's review of its internal procedures and history of managing and servicing other similar mortgage portfolios. Where the servicer is required to advance, financial criteria will also be imposed. For example, many servicers are required to maintain a long-term debt rating of single "A" or better.

The servicer role may frequently be segregated into a master servicer and a special servicer. The special servicer is selected to handle troubled properties, particularly where the borrower has defaulted and failed to make debt payments for two months or more. More recently, some of these transactions include special servicers that also purchase the most subordinate or first-loss class of the CMBS issue. A situation where the first-loss investor is also the special servicer of the defaulted mortgage loan presents both a benefit and a concern. First, there is a perceived benefit to the senior class of securities in that the servicer will have an incentive to maximize recovery on the defaulted loan. Rather than earning only the established servicing fee, the servicer will use its best efforts to make sure losses are minimized. However, on the other hand, a servicer that has a financial stake in the property may go to unreasonable lengths to try and salvage some recovery from the mortgage loan. This may occur, for example, when the servicer delays foreclosure proceedings with the hope that real estate prices will recover. The downside to investors is a delay in recovery of funds beyond a

109. 11 U.S.C. §510(a). See, e.g., *In re Credit Industrial Corporation*, 366 F.2d 402, 410 (2d Cir. 1966) ("A bankruptcy court, in order to effectuate its duty to do equity, must enforce lawful subordination agreements according to their terms and prevent junior creditors from receiving funds where they have explicitly agreed not to accept them"); *In re Kors, Inc.*, 819 F.2d 19 (2d Cir. 1987); *In re Leasing Consultants, Inc.*, 2 B.R. 165 (Bankr. E.D.N.Y. 1980) (right to participate in bankruptcy assets governed by subordination contract); *In re Ionosphere Clubs, Inc. et al.* v. *Midlantic National Bank et al.*, 134 B.R. 528, 532 (Bankr. S.D.N.Y. 1991) ("Under 11 U.S.C. §510(a), full effect must be given to pre-bankruptcy subordination agreements"). See also discussion at footnote 26 *supra*, and accompanying text.

110. See footnotes 13 and 14 *supra* and accompanying text.

reasonable period, and possibly losses exceeding those that would have been incurred had foreclosure been more timely.

The rating agencies have responded to the desire by servicers to invest in the subordinate tranches by considering certain parameters within which such purchases might be acceptable. Some of the proposals include appointing an independent party or a representative of the senior certificates to monitor the servicing procedures utilized and rule on any conflicts of interest; establishing a minimum period of time, such as two years, during which a restructure or write-off of the loan must occur; prohibiting payments on the subordinate pieces until the senior securityholders are paid in full; and limiting the special servicer's discretion on certain amendments to the loan terms, requiring a demonstration that the modifications are in the best interest of the trust fund on a net present value basis.[111]

K. Transfers and releases of property

Properties securing mortgages in a CMBS transaction generally may not be conveyed to any other entity so long as the indebtedness is outstanding. Certain exceptions may be provided where the transferee is an SPV that meets the same criteria of the original borrower at the outset of the transaction. In connection with the proposed transfer, the rating agencies likely will require that the transferor not be in default and that a satisfactory non-consolidation opinion be rendered as to the transferee and its owners. In addition, other typical matters such as bring down of insurance and the provision of standard legal opinions and documentation should be provided.

In large, single asset transactions or in small pools of large asset transactions, the owners may want additional flexibility in their ultimate disposition of the property. The properties may be conveyed, subject to the mortgage backing the rated security, to a subsidiary of a financially strong purchaser utilizing the SPV criteria above, or may be conveyed outright to an entity whose long-term debt rating (covering at least the term of the mortgages) by the same rating agency that rated the CMBS is equal to or greater than the rating ascribed to the securities. The transfer provisions recently have evolved to take into account various transfer opportunities so long as credit and bankruptcy protections are incorporated into these provisions.

Partial or total releases of property from the lien of the mortgage may arise in several instances. For example, in a super-regional mall, outparcels will secure the mortgage but may be released in connection with a purchase by a suitable prospective user or a beneficial lease arrangement. Frequently, the property owner will be required to utilize proceeds received from the sale of the outparcel to pay down the mortgage indebtedness, after payment of any necessary

111. See "Special Servicers Face Tighter Controls", *Commercial Mortgage Alert*, at p. 1 (July 25, 1994).

infrastructure or buildout that is required. In some cases, the property owner may retain a specified portion of the proceeds. The terms of the mortgage paydown or retention of proceeds by the owner will depend in part upon the value of the parcel released as determined by the rating agency.

Second, a release of property may be requested in connection with cross-collateralized properties from a single borrower pool. For example, in a pool of multi-family loans owned by a single developer, the developer may want to take advantage of the opportunity to sell one or more properties from time to time. In such instances, the rating agencies typically will require a paydown of the indebtedness equal to the allocated mortgage amount for that property plus an additional amount, usually up to 25 per cent of the allocated mortgage amount. There may also be criteria relating to the impact on debt service coverage ratios for the remaining properties.

L. Additional amounts/gross-up

The availability of capital for real estate investment from the European markets has occasioned the provision in securitization documents of so-called "gross-up" or "additional amount" provisions. Euromarket investors often are promised a "gross up" of the interest rate on their investment in the event their return is reduced by the action of the government where the borrower is located, for example the imposition of a withholding tax. Thus, if the government imposes a 20 per cent withholding tax on interest payments to foreign investors, the borrower is obligated to gross up the interest payment to foreign investors to an amount that will yield the same rate of return as the investor had prior to the imposition of the withholding tax. In the alternative, the borrower is generally afforded the right to redeem the bonds immediately, since the effective interest rate would no longer be attractive or competitive with financing that could be obtained elsewhere.

The rating agencies must evaluate whether this unquantifiable risk is one that could be covered by high levels of debt service coverage and cash flow from the properties, or whether the relatively low margin over debt service and operating costs would overly strap the borrower. In the latter case, the gross-up provision either should be deleted (resulting in a marketing problem) or a satisfactory form of credit provider should be secured up front to cover the possible obligation. Additionally, the rating agencies must take into account the ability of the borrower to refinance the property in the event it takes the likely course of redeeming the bonds. In several transactions that have been sold in the European markets to date, the rating agencies have become comfortable with the level of financing and the debt service coverage ratios so that no additional steps or precautions were necessary.[112]

112. Several privately placed super regional mall financings have included gross-up terms. See, e.g., "Investors Gobble Up Mall Notes", *Commercial Mortgage Alert*, at p. 2 (October 17, 1994) (discussing Twelve Oaks Mall transaction offered pursuant to Rule 144A).

6.8 SECURITIES LAWS ISSUES

A. General overview

As a general rule, federal and state securities laws will apply to a typical CMBS transaction. This chapter will not discuss in detail the specifics of securities laws and their various applications and consequences, since this topic is discussed in more detail elsewhere in this book. Nonetheless, certain aspects of the securities laws are peculiar to CMBS transactions and have been impacted by recent legislation. These will be discussed only briefly herein.

B. Public registration vs. private placement

Since CMBS transactions are generally treated as constituting "securities" for purposes of federal and state securities laws, the issuer must determine whether to register the securities with the Securities and Exchange Commission (SEC) pursuant to the Securities Act of 1933 ("1933 Act"). Filing with the SEC for a public registration generally requires more time, for the SEC to review and comment, and expense. The ease of transferability and the resulting lower coupon rates on securities sometimes make this alternative nonetheless desirable.

Alternatively, many issuers have opted to sell their securities in the private market, thereby foregoing the time and expense of public registration with the SEC. Since these private transactions are still subject to securities laws, they typically are structured to meet the available safe harbor exemptions under applicable state and federal laws. For example, transactions are typically structured as private placements not constituting a public offering as contemplated by Section 4(2) of the 1933 Act. Frequently, issuers will use Rule 506 of Regulation D promulgated under the 1933 Act for sales only to "accredited investors".[113] In the CMBS market, however, more and more issuers are relying on the resale exemption afforded by Rule 144A promulgated under the 1933 Act, which allows the resale of securities to "qualified institutional buyers".[114] The rule does not require any filing with the SEC, but merely requires the seller to reasonably believe that purchasers are qualified institutional buyers (QIBs), that the seller take reasonable steps to notify the purchaser that it may be relying on Rule 144A, and that the issuer undertake to provide certain information so long as the security is restricted. The sale of securities pursuant to Rule 144A is facilitated by the ease with which issuers may access the institutional capital markets and the lack of formal criteria for offering circulars. Rule 144A transactions are increasing, both in terms of number and aggregate dollar amount, in comparison to publicly registered transactions with the SEC.[115] For

113. 17 C.F.R. §230.501 to .508 (1993).

114. 17 C.F.R. §230.144A (1993).

115. "144A Deals Account for Growing Share of New Issues", *Commercial Mortgage Alert*, at p. 5 (May 9, 1994); "Commercial MBS Issuance: Steady Patterns Emerge", *Commercial Mortgage Alert*, at p. 2 (November 14, 1994).

example, Rule 144A transactions in the commercial and multi-family market accounted for 26 per cent of the transactions by principal amount issued through the third quarter of 1994, compared to 25 per cent issued pursuant to public registration. This compares to 26 per cent for rule 144A transactions and 43 per cent for public SEC registration in the full year of 1993.[116] Interestingly, private issues not utilizing Rule 144A declined from 38 deals for 1993 to only 11 deals through the third quarter of 1994 and issues by the Federal National Mortgage Association and the Federal Home Loan Mortgage Corporation increased substantially from four deals in 1993 to 12 deals through the third quarter of 1994.[117]

C. Rule 3a-7; exemption from Investment Company Act of 1940

For years, participants in the securitization market toiled feverishly to avoid the securitization transaction being subject to the Investment Company Act of 1940 (the "1940 Act"). The extensive reporting and other regulatory restrictions imposed on "investment companies" make this a very unattractive law for CMBS issuers. Certain exemptions available to issuers from the 1940 Act, prior to 1992, were stringently followed in order to avoid issuers becoming investment companies. However, in November of 1992, the SEC adopted Rule 3a-7 which excludes most structured financings from the definition of "investment company", provided certain minimum criteria are met, including:

(i) the issuance of fixed income securities or other securities entitling holders to receive payments depending primarily on the cash flow of eligible assets;
(ii) the securities must be rated in one of the four highest rating categories by one NRSRO;
(iii) the issuer may acquire or dispose of eligible assets only in compliance with the rule; and
(iv) the trustee acting on behalf of the security-holders must meet certain eligibility criteria.[118]

D. Form S-3 and Rule 415 shelf registration

Rule 415 under the 1933 Act permits the offer and sale of securities on a delayed or continuous basis, commonly referred to as a "shelf registration".[119] Shelf registration has been available for "mortgage-related securities" as defined under the Rule, but amendments to the Form S-3 eligibility requirements expanded the availability of Form S-3, and therefore Rule 415, to issuers of asset-backed securities. Although CMBS transactions could fall within the prior

116. *Id.*
117. *Id.*
118. 17 C.F.R. §270.3a-7 (1993). See Investment Company Act Release No. 19105, *supra* footnote 16.
119. 17 C.F.R. §230.415 (1993).

wording of Rule 415, the use of the more favorable disclosure format in Form S-3 is an additional attractive feature. The amendment allows any offering of investment-grade asset-backed securities as an additional category of transaction that may utilize Form S-3.[120]

While shelf registration may be an attractive means of accessing the capital markets, several positions by the SEC staff are important to bear in mind. First, Rule 140 has been interpreted to require that any party that receives a substantial benefit or has a substantial interest in the underlying properties (45 per cent or more) is deemed a co-registrant for purposes of the 1933 Act registration provisions.[121] Accordingly, if an investment bank has a shelf registration and it wants to issue CMBS collateralized by properties owned by one borrower representing 45 per cent or more of the pool, that borrower would be deemed a co-registrant. Consequently, investment bankers and borrowers should be mindful of the diversification requirements in order to avoid becoming co-registrants.

Additionally, the SEC has indicated that if a property (or mortgage secured by such property) represents 20 per cent or more of the pool, or if several properties owned by the same borrower are cross-collateralized and relate to 20 per cent or more of the mortgage-backed securities, then audited financial statements will be required; if such property or properties represent 10 per cent or more (but less than 20 per cent) of the pool, then significant information will still need to be provided.[122] Since the evolution of the CMBS market is relatively recent and the types of securitization transactions do not fit neatly into prior securities law regulation formats, the rules also evolve and at least currently are more a function of SEC practice rather than actual rulemaking.

E. SMMEA and the Community Development Banking Act of 1994

The foregoing discussion has related primarily to securities regulation under federal law. In addition, each state has its own laws concerning registration and exemption therefrom for issuance of securities, frequently called "blue sky" laws. Accordingly, in connection with any offering, the issuer must be sure that it is aware of and in compliance with applicable state securities laws.

In an effort to facilitate the development of the mortgage-backed securities market, Congress in 1984 passed the Secondary Mortgage Market Enhancement Act of 1984 (SMMEA), which among other things provided an exemption from any state law requiring registration or qualification of securities that are "mortgage-related securities" as defined therein.[123] SMMEA allowed for states

120. SEC Release Nos. 33–6964, and 34–31345, 57 Fed. Reg. 48970 (1992).

121. 17 C.F.R. §230.140 (1993); see FBC Conduit Trust I, SEC No-Action Letter [1987–1988 Transfer Binder] Fed. Sec. L. Rep. (CCH) ¶78,662 (Oct. 6, 1987).

122. These positions are based substantially on requirements and positions as to materiality taken by the SEC in Staff Accounting Bulletin Nos. 71 and 71A, and Regulation S-X Rules 3–10, 3–14 and 1.02.

123. Secondary Mortgage Market Enhancement Act of 1984, Pub. L. No. 98–440, 98 Stat. 1689 (1984); see §3(a)(41) of the Securities Exchange Act of 1934.

to opt out of its preemption, which 10 states did prior to the deadline. More recently, however, Congress passed the Community Development Banking Act of 1994, which extends the treatment afforded by SMMEA to the securitization of commercial mortgages by amending the definition of "mortgage related security".[124] This Act will also be subject to opting out by states, similar to the original SMMEA. Nonetheless, it evidences a willingness on the part of Congress to facilitate the growth and development of commercial mortgage securitization.

6.9 CONCLUSION

The growth of commercial mortgage securitization in recent years demonstrates that the capital markets have an appetite for this type of financing and that structures of these transactions have overcome difficulties and complexities associated with commercial real estate that initially made it a difficult candidate for securitization. Additionally, in view of the substantial amount of indebtedness currently outstanding that is secured by commercial real estate and has not yet been securitized, the future prospects for continued commercial mortgage securitization look bright.

Notwithstanding the bright prospects for this market, CMBS transactions involve complex commercial real estate transactions as well as the complex and extensive aspects of the capital markets securitization. Consequently, it is extremely important to have competent professionals involved at each stage of the transaction in order to assure that the transactions are structured properly and all areas of interest have been covered. The complexity of the transactions and the continued viability of CMBS as an attractive investment in the capital markets highlight the need for skilled and experienced trustees and servicers acting on behalf of investors. Additionally, the role of the rating agencies is extremely significant in addressing problem areas in advance and providing information and guidelines to transaction structurers concerning criteria necessary for securing various rating levels.

Although a number of legal, structural, real estate and rating agency issues have been discussed in this chapter, the CMBS market is relatively new and continues to evolve. New structures and criteria will continue to develop in response to investor demands as well as risks associated with real estate investment.

PATRICK C. SARGENT

124. Community Development Banking Act of 1994, Pub. L. No. 103–325, 108 Stat. 1689 (1994).

CHAPTER 7

CREDIT RATINGS ON INTERNATIONAL ASSET-BACKED SECURITIES

7.1 INTRODUCTION

This chapter aims to provide an overview of uses of credit ratings in international markets and of how the process of assigning a rating works for asset-backed securities. The obvious starting point is the role of credit ratings, their definition and uses. This is followed by an explanation of how credit ratings attempt to evaluate comparable levels of risk between differing markets, entities and structures. Examples of rating criteria for asset-backed securities in different markets and for varying asset types are then discussed.

The terms "asset-backed" and "structured finance" are used interchangeably, and both include the entire spectrum of collateralised transactions.

7.2 THE ROLE OF RATINGS IN FINANCIAL MARKETS

There is an increasingly wide spectrum of issuers in the international capital markets, and an increasing number of investors looking for investment opportunities beyond their traditional home markets. Credit ratings help bring these two groups together. Most investors do not have the specialised credit analysis capabilities required to look at all markets they may be interested in, particularly in the field of structured finance. Even those that do often wish to have access to other opinions. With such a plethora of names, countries and structures to look at, it is no wonder that investors are increasingly seeking third-party opinions on the credit quality of particular securities. A rating also provides a readily understandable, quick and reliable indication of credit quality, thus saving time in the investment decision.

Theories of financial markets suggest that greater information leads to better-informed investment decisions and greater financial market efficiency. The reality is that investors generally do not want to read all the documents to which they are entitled. Many will not even read the prospectus from cover to cover.

The use of ratings on asset-backed securities, or any securities, aims to take the complex and simplify it in a way the investor can readily grasp, at the same time giving him adequate information to make an informed investment decision. An investor takes comfort from a rating for many reasons. The foremost among these are:

— it simplifies his investment decisions,
— it means an investor knows an objective third party has examined the transaction, and
— it gives him a benchmark from which to determine an acceptable level of yield for his portfolio.

An issuer has different concerns, but may also find a rating useful:

— it allows balance-sheet management, for example obtaining off-balance-sheet treatment upon the sale of assets,
— it helps an issuer to know where his debt should be priced,
— it may help him decrease his cost of funds,
— it may help access a new investor base,
— it may enhance the liquidity of his securities in the secondary market, and
— it helps to get his story across to potential investors.

Regulatory agencies in a growing number of markets also look to ratings, on structured financings in particular, for example, to determine required capital levels for such investments.

It is important to emphasise that rating agencies are not parties to any documentation for a particular issue. The role is to assess what is presented, rather than have input into how a transaction is structured—although particularly for structured finance issues, rating agency criteria often play an important part in how certain points are treated. A rating will always represent an impartial, objective view. The relationship with other parties to the transaction will be on an arm's-length basis. Since the whole business of a rating agency is based upon its credibility and the accuracy of its ratings over time, there is no place for any other approach.

It should also be stressed that a rating is not a buy or sell recommendation. It does not say whether a particular security is appropriate for a particular investor. Neither does a rating talk about the price of a security at any point in time. What is addressed is the credit quality of that security.

7.3 WHAT DOES A CREDIT RATING ADDRESS?

D&P's [Duff & Phelps Credit Rating Co.] intention is to tell investors the likelihood with which they will be repaid principal and interest on time and in full in accordance with the terms of an issue. As stated above, the rating says nothing about the appropriateness of a security for any investor's portfolio, and in particular it is *not* a buy or sell recommendation. For example, an investor who buys a highly rated floating-rate, sterling-denominated asset-backed security can be confident that he will receive the promised amount of floating-rate sterling in a timely manner, even if the underlying collateral consists of fixed rate, French franc assets. That is, the rating addresses any structural mechanisms required to generate the promised returns from the underlying assets. The rating says nothing about the suitability of floating-rate sterling for that investor's portfolio.

Given the volume of securities on offer, the need for concise information is the key. Hence rating symbols. D&P uses the symbols shown to differentiate among securities according to their credit quality. Those securities rated BBB– and above are considered investment grade, that is, an investor's principal is not considered to be at risk, while those below BBB– are considered speculative grade, implying that a higher return should be anticipated since principal may be at risk. Table 1 lists these rating symbols.

Table 1. Duff & Phelps Rating Symbols for investment grade issuers

Long-term	*Short-term*
AAA	
AA+	
AA	D-1+
AA–	
A+	D-1
A	
A–	D-1–
BBB+	
BBB	D-2
BBB–	D-3

Once upon a time most rated debt in the Euromarket was AAA or AA, and investors here were considered extremely "risk averse". Over time, interest has grown in the whole array of rated debt. Generally speaking, the ratings on asset-backed securities have not followed this trend, with senior tranches invariably still requiring a AAA or AA rating. However, a development has been the growth of lower investment grade ratings on junior or subordinated debt tranches of an asset-backed issue. As the markets have grown and the need for investors in subordinated debt has increased, so a growing number of investors have devoted the time and effort in understanding the risk and return profile of junior debt.

Future developments will likely involve further expansion of investor appetite for lower-rated debt, albeit the main body of investors will continue to require high investment grade ratings.

Ratings should give the investor a basis for comparison among instruments in the market—a yardstick for comparing credit quality among debt instruments. In a world where credit quality was the only risk-return measure, all AAA bonds or all AA bonds or all BBB bonds would trade at the same price.

From the above, it follows in principle that a AAA rating implies debt of the highest quality, with negligible risk factors, whether one buys UK government securities, World Bank securities, or AAA-rated UK mortgage-backed bonds.

There are differences between transaction types not addressed by a rating that investors should be aware of. For example, unsecured debt is based purely on the issuer's promise to pay. An evaluation of the likelihood of payment hinges on past performance, management, vulnerability to cyclical market forces and strategy. Management can adapt strategy to respond to market developments.

Management can also be bought out or make damaging acquisitions, potentially changing a company's rating overnight. Issuers of asset-backed transactions generally have no ability to go in and alter, for good or for ill, the rated transaction. This means that it is less adaptable to changing circumstances, and protections to cope with all conceivable problems must be in place from the outset. Therefore, in principle, asset-backed ratings are less volatile or susceptible to what is called "event risk" than unsecured ratings.

However, asset-backed ratings can rely on a variety of third parties who play a role in the transaction. These ratings are called supporting ratings. Changes in the unsecured rating of a supporting party in an asset-backed transaction can affect the rating on that issue's rating. This relationship was clearly seen in the early 1990s in the UK mortgage-backed securities market, where a high proportion of issues were downgraded following the downgrade of a small number of insurance companies that provided credit enhancement to these issues.

The other key difference is that a structured transaction is secured by the assets in the vehicle company set up to issue the debt. In this way an investor knows exactly what is available to him to reimburse his debt. In the UK, the investors' interest in the collateral is overseen by the trustee. In other countries, such as the US and France, the investor may actually have a direct ownership interest in the vehicle, and hence the collateral, if trust certificates are issued instead of debt instruments.

7.4 COMPARABILITY OF RATINGS ACROSS MARKETS

Is it possible to say that a pool of French mortgages is as sound as a pool of English mortgages, or Swedish credit cards, or Japanese consumer loans? How does this risk compare to a Danish corporate credit, or a Hong Kong bank? A rating represents a benchmark by which an investor should be able to compare the *credit risks* of instruments available in different markets. Ratings must therefore be comparable across borders and debt type. It is relatively easy to compare General Motors with Toyota or BP and Shell with Exxon, but how can one compare the relative performance of heterogeneous markets such as mortgages or credit cards or automobile loans in different countries? Here, many factors including lending conditions, national practices, levels of consumer indebtedness, accounting and regulatory treatment, and legal procedures vary tremendously from country to country.

D&P's ability to say that ratings are comparable is based upon the consistency of analytical approach used. Remember also that a rating is actually defined as a measure of relative or comparative risk. This means that while conditions and criteria may differ from country to country, D&P should be saying with its rating that an investor is buying comparable credit risk—but not identical securities.

This consistency of analytical approach in rating asset-backed securities is illustrated below. The intention is to give an indication of how credit risk varies among countries, and how the rating approach can adjust for such variations.

7.5 RATING ASSET-BACKED SECURITIES

Duff & Phelps rates transactions only with the co-operation of the originator. This is important, since the nature of asset-backed transactions requires full access to the appropriate information for a complete and accurate analysis to be performed.

A good starting point for any analysis is an assessment of the collateral itself. The assets (or asset) involved can take many forms, ranging from very short-term, low-denomination trade receivables to 25-year mortgage loans, aircraft leases or commercial property. Each asset category requires a specific form of analysis. The details of this analysis are available in separate D&P publications that go into far more detail than is appropriate here. However, a number of common questions and areas of analysis are applicable whatever the asset type, or the jurisdiction involved. I will discuss some of these below.

With any asset, a good starting point is an analysis of historic performance. D&P would normally look for around five years of historic performance data. However, there are no hard and fast rules. The quality of data is often more important than the quantity. Thus for example, UK mortgage performance data for the period 1988 to 1991 represents extremely good quality data, given the severe recession in this market during this period. The UK mortgage market is also a good example of why historic performance data alone is not the only factor in the analysis. Anyone looking at UK mortgages in 1987, based on the previous 30 or 40 years of data, would not have been able to predict the severity of the downturn in the late 1980s. The removal of high inflation from the equation fundamentally altered the performance of these assets. A second example is the severe downturn in the Swedish and Japanese commercial property markets in the late 1980s. While commercial property markets invariably demonstrate a cyclical pattern, the severity of these particular downturns was generally quite unexpected.

Possible market changes, like the ones illustrated above, must be factored into the analysis. The resulting credit and liquidity cover numbers are often hard for originators to take on board, but, as stated above, structured finance transactions are not capable of adapting to meet market changes. The rating analysis is not saying what is likely to happen in the future, but rather what is possible in adverse economic scenarios. The severity of any downturn and resulting performance assumptions will be greater the higher the rating desired.

It is also essential to retain a flexible approach when assessing asset data. Practices vary between markets, resulting in the need to avoid applying the exact same approach across borders. For example, contrast the French and UK residential mortgage market. In France, the concept of a "loan-to-value" ratio is not widely used. Rather, the value of a property is the purchase price. However much greater emphasis is placed on an assessment of a borrower's ability to repay the debt. UK lenders, until recently, often took a more collateral-based approach to lending.

A wide variety of other factors can affect the expected performance of an asset. These factors vary depending on the characteristics of the asset in question. For auto loans, whether the vehicle is new or old, how much against vehicle purchase price was borrowed and term of the loan need to be analysed. For commercial property transactions, they include quality of the tenant(s), location, property type and maintenance costs. Trade receivable analysis will include a review of dilution levels. For transactions involving asset pools, geographic concentrations need to be taken into account. A pool that has a heavy concentration of assets in one location could suffer undue problems if that local economy encountered severe problems due, for example, to a downturn in a particular industry upon which that locality relied heavily. Problems in Texas following the oil price decline in mid-1980s illustrate this point. Loan seasoning can have a positive impact on the analysis. Generally speaking, older loans will be less likely to default than newly originated loans. Obligor concentration may be an issue with any asset type.

Much time is spent discussing the quality of the collateral in these transactions. While the quality of the collateral backing the transaction is key to the quality of the bond issue and its safety, there are other factors that must be assessed to determine the overall quality of a security. For example, no matter how good the quality of the cash flow is, if the issuing vehicle cannot gain access to it in all scenarios, it is worth nothing. Also, once the cash from the assets has been received, there are a number of factors that may need addressing before payment is made to the security holders and thus the desired rating can be achieved. Grouped together, these points, which I would call cash flow mechanics, are just as vital to the transaction's integrity as the underlying assets.

If the problem is one of timing only, and assuming the length of time for which cash will be withheld (or possibly lost in some cases) can be sized, additional liquidity (or credit) cover can be used.

A common cause of cash-flow timing concerns is commingling of funds at the originator, who is also usually the asset administrator. If it is assumed that the originator of the assets becomes insolvent, it could take many months, or even longer, to ascertain what cash is due to whom. Since the rating addresses timely as well as ultimate payment of principal and interest, a structured transaction must be able to continue to perform during such a scenario. Other possible cash-flow timing concerns could involve the ability of third-party credit enhancement providers to pay on time—both from an ability and willingness perspective, and the bank account mechanisms via which cash moves.

Another example of cash-flow mechanics playing a vital role in the overall rating is the ability to convert cash flow from the assets, which could be for example in Swedish krona, and convert this cash flow to the currency required to pay principal and interest on the debt, which could be in US dollars. The role of any swap counterparty or foreign exchange provider is crucial. The terms upon which the counterparty agrees to perform are also of great importance. It is no good having a counterparty who can terminate the agreement if, for example, the asset originator becomes insolvent or a withholding tax upon payments is made, unless the effect of such an ability has been fully analysed and any impact on the rated securities assessed and discounted or covered somehow.

Prepayments from the assets (including assumed levels), if applicable, will also need to be dealt with in the transaction's cash-flow mechanics. These funds may need to be reinvested between security payment dates, resulting in possible shortfalls between interest earned on these prepaid funds and that earnt on the assets and payable on the debt. The availability to the issuer of contracts with guaranteed rates of return can help in this situation.

Many of the above cash-flow issues revolve around the need for transaction documentation to be clear, concise and accurate in covering these situations. All documentation to a transaction is reviewed by D&P prior to assigning a rating. This invariably involves analysing a large number of individual documents. It is obviously essential too for any analysis to recognise local laws and regulations. Table 2 gives an example of typical documents seen in an asset-backed transaction.

The legal regulations governing asset-backed transactions around the world are often open to interpretation. Outside expert legal advice is always obtained prior to assigning a rating and a legal opinion is provided for each transaction. Where uncertainties exist, D&P exercises extreme caution. Each possible scenario is analysed. Where the possibility of cash-flow delay or loss exists, additional enhancements will be required.

An example that illustrates many aspects of the legal analysis to a transaction is the possible scenario of a transfer of administration of the assets following insolvency of the original administrator and originator. A number of concerns can arise here. These include the legal ability of the issuer (via a trustee in most jurisdictions) to gain access to the assets and the related cash flow, the ability of any receiver of the failed originator to capture and/or delay payments, the ability of any third-party creditors to interrupt cash flow, as well as the practicalities and costs of physically moving asset administration if required (bank account arrangements, personnel, systems, files etc.).

Table 2. Sample documents seen in an asset-backed transaction

Offering circular/prospectus
Indenture or trust deed
Deed of charge and assignment of the assets
Sale agreement for the assets
Administration or servicing agreement
Credit support agreement
Liquidity support agreement
Issuing and paying agency agreement
Swap agreements
Legal opinions

There will also be a host of other documents including audit letters, issuer memorandum and articles of association, fee letters and various insurance contracts.

In addition to a detailed legal analysis to ensure cash-flow integrity and the inability of any third party to access the transaction's collateral, a full analysis of the tax position of the issuer will be undertaken. Generally, structures aim to be tax neutral. Any transaction that takes an aggressive stance on tax, with a view to avoiding tax that may otherwise have been payable on the assets, will be treated cautiously, and an opinion from the relevant tax authorities may well be required (if applicable). Problems with structural and/or legal issues may result in a lower than desired rating being assigned to a transaction. If the problems are fundamental to the integrity of the transaction, it may not be possible to assign any rating.

Finally, it is essential to ensure that all parts of the transaction proposal agree. For example, any cash-flow model must reflect the terms of the documentation that governs the issue. The on-going administration of the assets must also reflect the terms of the documentation, in particular how funds are identified and managed. This last point leads in to another important part of the overall rating—surveillance.

Once a rating has been assigned to a public debt issue, the process does not end there. The rating remains outstanding on that security until its scheduled maturity, or earlier redemption. The surveillance process involves regular receipt and review of asset-performance data, notification, and action if appropriate, of any changes to transaction documentation, and periodic review meetings with the transaction administrator. The administrator review meetings are designed to ascertain that the administrator continues to demonstrate the ability to manage the assets effectively in accordance with the transaction documentation. If any problems are evident, be it asset performance or administrative concerns, negative rating action will be considered. Any resulting change to the rating will be fully explained to investors at the time of the change.

7.6 CONCLUSIONS

Ratings are designed to aid investors in making their investment decisions. They represent an independent, expert opinion of the credit quality of a particular security. For asset-backed transactions they can make complex instruments and structures appear more straightforward. The investor can take comfort that many hours work have gone into analysing a particular structure and ensuring, not only that credit and liquidity enhancement levels are satisfactory, but also that all aspects of that structure work together to ensure the final result of payments as promised to the security holders. D&P always explains the rating rationale for a transaction in published material. If more information is required regarding how a particular rating decision has been reached, investors, and other interested parties, are encouraged to contact the relevant analyst, who will always be willing to explain the analysis in more detail.

PAUL G. TAYLOR

CHAPTER 8

UK TAX CONSIDERATIONS

8.1 INTRODUCTION

The principal tax issues that arise in relation to an asset securitisation are as follows:

- the need to avoid withholding tax on the various flows of income;
- the need to obtain relief for funding costs and front-end costs;
- the need to extract the profit element implicit in the true value of the assets in a tax-efficient manner; and
- the need to minimise the impact of irrecoverable value added tax (VAT).

This chapter will consider the above issues as they apply to securitisations involving mortgages and HP receivables and also sub-participation in debt receivables, which in many respects is very similar to securitisation. The various issues that arise will, at least in the case of mortgages and HP receivables, be considered within the basic framework of a sale of assets to a special-purpose vehicle which finances the purchase by issuing bonds secured on those assets.

It is important to avoid any tax leakage in securitisation structures. Cashflows have to be calculated at the inception of the transaction so as to ensure that the securitisation vehicle will have sufficient funds to meet all of its liabilities, including tax liabilities. If any unanticipated tax liabilities arise in the vehicle, or any tax liabilities arise in the vehicle earlier than anticipated, the vehicle will not generally have sufficient funds to meet those liabilities, and this may lead to the vehicle becoming insolvent. The Inland Revenue have generally been helpful in discussing some of the issues that may arise on particular transactions in advance, so as to avoid such problems.

8.2 MORTGAGES

An initial point to note is that it is preferable to use a corporate vehicle rather than a trust in a securitisation; where a trust is used, difficulties may be encountered regarding tax relief for interest paid. The tax regime in the UK differs in this respect from the regime in the USA, where trusts have often been used as securitisation vehicles.

8.2.1 Withholding tax

The income flow from the borrower will be affected by whether the mortgages have been taken out for domestic purposes, in which case the MIRAS scheme will apply, or whether they are commercial, including those which have been taken out by companies, and are thus outside the scope of the MIRAS scheme. MIRAS, which stands for mortgage interest relief at source, is the statutory mechanism for enabling individual borrowers to obtain tax relief at source (generally at the rate of 15 per cent for the tax year 1995/6) up to a specified borrowings limit, on their interest payments.[1] The borrower pays over to the mortgagee the interest net of tax and thereby obtains tax relief on that amount. The mortgagee then recovers its shortfall in interest by claiming the tax which has been withheld directly from the Inland Revenue. Claims may be made on a monthly or quarterly basis in advance and so can be done with little or no cash-flow disadvantage, provided that interest payments on the securities issued to fund the purchase or the mortgage portfolio are timed accordingly. On the other hand, if the mortgage advances are made to commercial borrowers, the MIRAS scheme will not apply and the more serious withholding tax issues discussed below will need to be considered. The recovery of tax withheld under the MIRAS scheme can only be made by MIRAS registered vehicles. However, the Inland Revenue have been co-operative in allowing vehicles to be registered well in advance of any securitisation.

Interest on loans which have been taken out by borrowers which are companies, or partnerships of which a company is a member, and which thus fall outside the scope of the MIRAS scheme, must be paid net of tax at the basic rate unless the lender is a bank recognised as such by the UK Inland Revenue.[2] Where corporate borrowers are involved, the assignment of the loans by a UK bank to a special-purpose vehicle (SPV) may give rise to a further withholding obligation where, because of the banking exemption, none existed before (although the Inland Revenue have, in some recent cases, confirmed that the banking exemption will continue to apply following assignment to a non-bank). Therefore, portfolios of commercial mortgages will often not be attractive assets for securitisation purposes as UK tax law currently stands. This is discussed further in section 8.4 on debt participation.

The payments of interest by the issuing vehicle on the mortgage-backed securities will also need to be made without any requirement to withhold tax. This can be done by structuring the instruments as "quoted Eurobonds", which means securities in bearer form, carrying a right to interest and listed on a recognised stock exchange (which includes London and Luxembourg). If

1. Ss.369 to 379 of the Income and Corporation Taxes Act 1988.
2. S.349 *ibid.*

interest is paid on a quoted Eurobond through a non-UK paying agent, the interest can be paid free of UK withholding tax. If such interest is paid through a UK paying agent, however, the paying agent must withhold UK tax at the basic rate unless the interest is paid on a quoted Eurobond held within a recognised clearing system or the person beneficially entitled to the interest produces evidence, in the approved form, that he is not UK resident.[3] An alternative approach would be to pay the return on the notes as original-issue discount, which does not attract any UK withholding tax.

8.2.2 Relief for funding and front-end costs

Different considerations will be relevant depending on whether the SPV is a trading company or an investment company for UK tax purposes. A trading company, as the name implies, must carry on some kind of dynamic ongoing trading activity. Thus a company which originates mortgages on its own behalf as well as purchasing them is more likely to be given trading status. It will often be possible to set up arrangements under which the originator will write new business as agent for the securitisation vehicle, so that the vehicle (as principal) is carrying on an active business. On the other hand, a company which buys a pool of mortgages and then issues securities on the strength of them without doing anything further is likely to be an investment company.

A "two pool" structure has sometimes been used. In such cases, the securitisation vehicle acquires mortgages written by the originator and issues bonds to fund that acquisition. The vehicle also originates new mortgages funded by separate bonds or loans made by the originator. The purpose of this second pool is to create an active business so that the vehicle may be regarded as trading. When the mortgages in the second pool become "seasoned" (i.e. suitable, from a credit risk point of view, for securitisation), they are passed across to the securitised pool and re-financed with mortgage-backed securities.

The above distinction between trading and investment company status should not be material in determining whether interest paid on the mortgage-backed bonds is deductible, provided that the bonds have a maturity of more than a year. However, the distinction does matter so far as the timing of deductions is concerned. A trading company is taxed on an accruals basis, whereas an investment company is taxed on a cash basis. This means that a payment of interest by an investment company should be made to coincide as closely as possible with (but before) the end of the company's accounting period for tax purposes so as to avoid deferring the tax relief until the following accounting period. If the SPV issues short-dated securities (i.e. with a maturity of less than one year) then the interest payable on them would be short interest for UK tax purposes. A trading company may deduct short interest if it is paid wholly and exclusively for the purposes of its trade or to a UK recognised bank, a recognised

3. Ss.124 and 349(3)(c) *ibid.*

member of the Stock Exchange or a recognised discount house. On the other hand, an investment company can only obtain a deduction for short interest if it is paid to a recognised bank, a recognised member of the Stock Exchange or a recognised discount house.[4] In practice, short-dated securities can be issued at an original-issue discount, in which case the difficulties mentioned above do not arise. The discount will then generally be deductible by either a trading company or an investment company.

Consideration needs to be given to the question of where the front-end costs should be borne. One problem may arise where front-end costs are borne in the SPV from the fact that those costs must be amortised for accounting purposes. This amortisation may give rise to a different level of profit for accounting and tax purposes. If the profit is to be extracted from the SPV by way of dividend, then a reduced accounting profit would mean that less profit can be paid by way of dividend to the parent and then ultimately to the originators by way of a broking fee. This would partly frustrate the objective of obtaining a deduction for the fee in the parent company which can be used by way of group relief to offset the taxable profits in the vehicle.[5] In other words, there may be a mismatch between profits for tax purposes on the one hand and accounting purposes on the other which leads to an insufficiency of group relief.

It should also be remembered that group relief can only be utilised on a current-year basis.[6] This can give rise to locked-in losses in the parent company which, although available for use by the SPV in earlier years, are not used, because the vehicle itself has carried forward losses owing to the fact that the front-end costs are borne in the SPV.

Where the assets which are the subject of the securitisation are property mortgages then the credit-rating agency requirements may stipulate that they are supported by insurance policies to deal with defaulting borrowers. There is some doubt as to whether a premium paid under such a policy is deductible by an investment company, and so if possible it should be borne by a trading company within the group. The premium might be borne by the originator; the originator, if it is a trading company, will then claim a deduction for the payment. In such a case, it will be necessary for the originator to establish that the premium was incurred for the purposes of the originator's own trade. This will often be difficult, although it will be helpful to show that the originator has incurred the obligation to pay the premium as one of the terms of the transfer of the mortgages to the vehicle.

Other front-end costs, such as legal and accounting fees, rating agency fees, printing expenses and the remuneration of the trustees are deductible by virtue of a specific statutory provision[7] as the incidental costs of obtaining loan finance.

Some FRN (floating rate note) issues have featured two classes of notes,

4. S.338(3) *ibid.*
5. S.402 *ibid.*
6. S.408 *ibid.*
7. S.77 *ibid.*

namely senior and junior notes. The senior notes will have a lower rate of return but have preferred security. The junior notes on the other hand will have a higher rate of return but will be the first to bear any losses incurred. This structure may mean that the return payable on the junior notes is dependent in some way on the results of the vehicle company's business. The notes should be carefully structured to ensure that the return on the junior notes cannot be held to be a deemed distribution, which would not be tax deductible and would give rise to an obligation to account for advance corporation tax.[8] If the junior notes are held by a UK corporate (for example, where the originator buys the junior notes itself), the problem will be avoided by virtue of a specific exemption.[9] If the junior notes are instead to be issued to third parties, and it is impossible to be certain that the notes will be held by UK corporates, it is particularly important that the notes should be structured so that the obligation to pay interest on them is never abated. Payments of interest should merely be deferred where the vehicle does not have sufficient funds to make those payments. It is thought that where interest is merely rolled-up in this way, the return on the notes should not be regarded as results-dependent.

In May 1995, the Inland Revenue published a Consultative Document proposing certain radical changes to the taxation of bonds in the UK. If implemented, the effect of the changes in relation to UK issuers of bonds will be that tax relief for payments of interest will be given on an accruals basis, regardless of whether the issuer is a trading or an investment company. At the time of writing, the Inland Revenue were engaged in a process of consultation on the proposals, with an announcement expected in July 1995.

8.2.3 Profit extraction

The extraction of the profit element implicit in the true value of the mortgages being securitised represents the most difficult area from a tax viewpoint. A securitisation vehicle will generally realise profits, because the interest payable on the bonds issued by it will usually be lower than the interest received by it on the mortgages. The originator will want to extract those profits for its own benefit (after leaving a small amount of income in the vehicle, ultimately for the benefit of the charity or other entity which beneficially owns the shares of the vehicle). There are a number of ways in which the profit might be extracted.

One seemingly straightforward method would be for the vehicle to pay dividends to the originator. However, it seems that for accounting and Bank of England purposes the originator may not own shares in the vehicle. This method is not, therefore, usually practicable.

Another seemingly straightforward solution would be partial assignment of the receipts from the mortgages to the vehicle company whereby only so much as is required to service the debt on the bonds together with running costs is

8. S.209(2)(e)(iii) *ibid.*
9. S.212 *ibid.*

assigned to the vehicle company. Thus the profit element would simply remain in the hands of the originator. A problem arises with this route where domestic mortgages subject to the MIRAS system are being securitised. In this situation, the Inland Revenue take the view that if both the originator and the vehicle company were to be qualifying lenders for MIRAS purposes, this would lead to excessive difficulties in administering the MIRAS system, and therefore they will not permit both companies to be registered. It is not clear that this view is technically correct, but in practice it means that other methods of profit extraction must be considered.

A further problem may arise if the profit is to be paid out by way of a broking fee, which might on the face of it be considered a suitable method of profit extraction because such a fee should not attract a liability to VAT (see below). The problem will arise where the paying company is an investment company, because there is some doubt about whether such a company is entitled to a tax deduction for such a fee.[10] It may be possible for the vehicle company to pay the profit to its trading parent company by way of dividend, which would be tax neutral between the two companies, and then for the parent company to pay the broking fee to the originator by way of a trading expense which would be deductible. The parent would then use the loss it has incurred to relieve the profit in the vehicle company by way of group relief, thus leading to tax neutrality. As mentioned in section 8.2.2 above, careful consideration must be given to the question of front-end costs and the problem which arises where the amortisation of front-end costs leads to a mismatch between group relief and taxable profits in the vehicle company. This problem will not arise if the vehicle company itself has trading status.

Where the vehicle company has trading status then the profit can be extracted by way of deferred consideration. The mortgages would be purchased at par and then further payments of deferred purchase consideration linked to the funding margin on the mortgages and bonds would be made. If the paying vehicle company and the originator have trading status then the tax treatment will be symmetrical. As in the previous case, problems arise, however, where the vehicle is an investment company. This is because the further payments will be in consideration for the acquisition of a capital asset for investment purposes and, therefore, the vehicle will not be entitled to a tax deduction when it makes the payments. The payments will still be taxable, however, in the hands of the recipient. This could lead to the profit element being taxed twice. A vehicle with investment company status will be entitled to treat such deferred payments as increasing its base cost in the mortgages for capital gains tax purposes. However, the mortgages will not be redeemed at more than par; therefore, the effect of such an increase in the vehicle's base cost will generally be to create a capital loss on redemption, which the vehicle is unlikely to be able to utilise.

Alternatively, the profit can be paid out by way of a management or

10. See *Capital and National Trust Ltd.* v. *Colder* (1949) 31 T.C. 265.

administration fee in respect of the originator's ongoing functions of managing and administering the mortgages. Once again, the fee could be calculated by reference to the interest rate margin realised by the vehicle on the mortgages and bonds. Since the originator will effectively extract all (or almost all) of the profits of the vehicle by means of such a fee, there may be some concern that the amount of the fee will be regarded as higher than an arm's-length amount and will not be deductible. In practice, it appears that so long as a small margin is retained by the vehicle, the arrangement will generally be regarded as commercially justifiable. Such a fee would therefore be deductible by an investment company vehicle. However, the fee would generally bear VAT at the rate of 17½ per cent; and, because the originator would usually be fully exempt for VAT purposes, that VAT would not be recoverable and would therefore represent a direct cost to the transaction. For a fuller discussion of the mechanics of VAT, see section 8.2.4 below.

A further option would be for the vehicle company and the originator to write an interest rate swap between themselves. Thus the originator would agree to pay to the vehicle company an amount equivalent to the interest rate on the bonds, while the vehicle would pay to the originator an amount equal to the interest received on the mortgage assets from the borrowers. The running expenses incurred by the vehicle company would need to be considered and usually factored into the swap. The law regarding the tax treatment of swaps is currently somewhat unsatisfactory. Payments made under a swap are calculated by reference to interest rates, but there is no underlying principal indebtedness. Thus doubt arises as to whether those payments are actually payments of interest and therefore as to their deductibility, although in practice the Inland Revenue regard the payments as annual payments which are deductible for tax purposes. Payments under interest rate swaps are subject to withholding tax (in practice this only applies to the net differential actually paid), unless one party is a bank, in which case payments can be made gross.[11] It may therefore be necessary to use a UK bank as an intermediary. Concerns may again arise about whether the concessionary practice of the Inland Revenue will be applied and a deduction allowed for swap payments where it is highly likely, when the parties enter into the swap, that all of the net differential payments will be made by the vehicle. This may be of particular concern where the originator is entitled, under an administration or similar agreement, to set the interest rate on the mortgages, so that it is in a position to ensure that the interest rate on the mortgages will always exceed the interest rate payable on the bonds and the vehicle's running expenses (and hence that any net differential payment under the swap is payable by the vehicle). Because of the various uncertainties in this area, parties often approach the Inland Revenue in advance with a view to obtaining confirmation that the swap payments will be deductible.

A new tax regime in relation to financial instruments was enacted in the

11. Extra-Statutory Concession C17.

Finance Act 1994 and takes effect in relation to accounting periods beginning on or after 23 March, 1995. The broad effect of the new regime in relation to interest rate swaps will be that profits and losses will be taxed or relieved as income on an accruals basis (at least where payments are made to UK residents). Withholding tax will not apply to those payments. However, the new legislation contains a number of anti-avoidance provisions. In particular, deductions may be denied or restricted where transactions are entered into otherwise than on arm's-length terms.[12] It may be, therefore, that interest rate swaps will become a less attractive method of profit extraction following the introduction of this new tax regime.

8.2.4 Value added tax and stamp duty

Value added tax is levied on supplies of most goods and services at the rate of 17½ per cent. Supplies of goods and services that are subject to tax at this rate are known as standard-rated supplies. The legislation provides for various supplies to be excepted from tax at this rate, and those supplies are either zero-rated supplies or exempt supplies. Value added tax is a type of purchase tax which is intended to be borne by the final consumer.[13] Thus, where a business pays VAT on supplies made to it, and those supplies can be attributed to a standard-rated or zero-rated supply made by it, that VAT can be recovered by direct reclaim from HM Customs and Excise. Value added tax in these circumstances will therefore only represent a cash-flow cost to the business concerned. However, problems arise where the VAT is attributable to an exempt supply, because it is not possible to reclaim that VAT. Unfortunately, many supplies in the financial sector are exempt.

If a broking fee is payable, then this will be an exempt supply for VAT purposes. The company which pays the broking fee therefore will not incur a VAT cost, although the company which supplies the broking services, the originator, may incur some irrecoverable VAT on supplies made to it which are directly attributable to making the supply of broking services. On the other hand, if administration and management fees are payable, then these will be subject to VAT at the standard rate. As this VAT will be attributable to the supply of the loan finance in the form of the mortgages, which is exempt for VAT purposes, the VAT will prove to be irrecoverable.

Similarly, VAT that is charged on the supplies of legal and accountancy services, printing costs, rating agency fees and so on mentioned above will be irrecoverable and so will represent a further direct cost to the transaction.

If the maker and recipient of the supply are part of the same group for VAT purposes (which requires 51 per cent common ownership), then supplies which would normally attract VAT can be made free of VAT.[14]

12. S.167 of the Finance Act 1994.
13. See generally the Value Added Tax Act 1994.
14. S.43 of the Value Added Tax Act 1994.

Stamp duty is a documentary tax payable on transactions in the UK.[15] It is payable at various rates but most commonly at 1 or ½ per cent depending on the nature of the transaction. However, various transactions are subject to specific exemptions. Stamp duty on the transfer of mortgages was abolished in 1971.[16] In addition, any transfer of the financing bonds will generally fall within a specific exemption for the transfer of loan instruments.[17]

8.3 HP RECEIVABLES

Whereas the securitisation of domestic mortgages is well established in the UK, the securitisation of different types of receivables is a market which is less developed. In this section it is intended to look at the various tax issues which arise on the securitisation of a typical type of debt receivable, namely hire purchase receivables. Many of the issues that arise have already been considered in the previous section and only brief attention will be paid to them. However, there are also some different issues which arise and these will be considered in greater detail.

8.3.1 Withholding tax

Payments made by either individuals or corporates under HP contracts for the purpose of acquiring motor vehicles, plant and machinery and so on can be dissected into payments of capital and payments of hire charges or rent for the use of the asset.[18] Since the obligation to withhold basic rate tax only arises in relation to payments of interest by a corporate borrower and not to payments of rent, the problems discussed above connected with the securitisation of mortgages in the names of companies do not arise.

As before, it is possible to avoid the need to withhold tax from payments of interest on the bonds that are issued by making use of the quoted Eurobond exemption or by issuing paper at an original-issue discount.

8.3.2 Relief for funding and front-end costs

So far as funding and front-end costs are concerned, the relevant issues are again the trading/investment company distinction, the accruals/cash basis of taxation, where front-end costs should be borne, the deductibility of the incidental costs of obtaining the loan finance and the deductibility of the interest payable on the bonds. All these issues have been considered in the above section on mortgage securitisation.

15. See generally the Stamp Act 1891.
16. Section 64 of the Finance Act 1971.
17. Section 79 of the Finance Act 1986.
18. See *Darngavil Coal Co.* v. *Francis* (1913) 7 T.C. 1.

8.3.3 Profit extraction

The securitisation of HP receivables does not involve the MIRAS scheme nor any similar scheme for obtaining tax relief by reclaiming the amounts in question from the Inland Revenue. Therefore, it is possible to adopt the partial equitable assignment method of profit extraction. This method involves the assignment by the originator to the vehicle company of enough of the receivables to meet the funding and running costs of the vehicle company with the originator retaining beneficial ownership of the super-profit. This is sometimes achieved by placing the receivables in a trust under which the beneficial entitlements are split between the vehicle company and the originator as described above. The availability of this alternative method of profit extraction means that the problems discussed in the previous section regarding the deductibility of broking fees and the payment of deferred consideration by investment companies should not arise. Where the vehicle company is continuing to write its own HP contracts and has trading status, then the other methods of profit extraction can be considered.

8.3.4 Value added tax and stamp duty

The irrecoverability of VAT, again, presents an incremental cost to the securitisation of receivables. To the extent that VAT borne on supplies made to the vehicle company, such as legal and accountancy services, is directly attributable to exempt supplies made by the vehicle, then it will not be possible to recover that VAT. HP receivables by their nature require a higher level of administration, including in particular debt collection services; these services are therefore more expensive to perform. Where the partial assignment method is used then it may be possible to avoid the payment of VAT on management and administration fees by factoring these costs into the partial assignment mechanism. For a charge to VAT to arise, it must be in respect of a supply done for a consideration.[19] It is arguable, therefore, that there is no supply by the originator to the vehicle where the vehicle is merely purchasing part of a pre-administered receivables portfolio from the originator. It may, however, be a rating agency requirement that if it becomes necessary to appoint a third-party administrator for whatever reason at a later date then a fee will become payable on which VAT will be chargeable in the normal way.

The transfer of the underlying assets would be chargeable to VAT. It therefore may be preferable to transfer only the receivables contracts and not the underlying assets. The transfer of the receivables should be exempt for VAT purposes.[20] This will, however, have the effect of worsening the originator's liability to VAT, since it will increase the proportion of exempt supplies which

19. S.5(2)(a) of the Value Added Tax Act 1994.
20. Item 1, Group 5, Schedule 9, *ibid.*

the originator makes and will therefore reduce the proportion of unallocated expenses on which the originator can recover any VAT paid.[21]

Stamp duty would generally be payable at the rate of 1 per cent on any transfer of the underlying assets. It is sometimes possible to avoid this duty by effecting the transfer by delivery. Such delivery could be symbolic; for example, in the case of motor vehicles, through handing over the log books rather than through physical delivery of the vehicles themselves. However, as described above, for VAT reasons it may be advisable not to assign the underlying assets.

The assignment of the receivables would be subject to stamp duty at the rate of 1 per cent. However, this charge can be deferred by executing the assignment off-shore[22] and only bringing it into the UK if enforcement before a UK court is necessary.[23] Alternatively, the receivables can be transferred by a written offer to sell with acceptance by performance (for example, by payment) in order to avoid stamp duty (because stamp duty, as described above, is a tax on documents).

8.4 DEBT PARTICIPATION

Sub-participation in existing debt is conceptually similar to asset securitisation and is reasonably common in the UK. Again the issues that arise are often similar to those which arise on the securitisation of domestic mortgages. More attention will be paid in this section to those areas where there are differences.

8.4.1 Withholding tax

The identity of the debtor is of fundamental importance to the question of withholding tax. There is, as previously mentioned, an obligation on a corporate borrower to withhold basic-rate income tax on payments of interest.[24] There is no corresponding obligation where the debtor is an individual, who is thus able to make payments of interest gross. Therefore, unless the lender is a UK bank (in which case the withholding obligation does not apply), portfolios of loans made to corporate borrowers will not be suitable for sub-participation.

In a situation where loans made to corporates are assigned by one UK bank to another UK bank, then it is arguable that the exemption from withholding tax mentioned above would not apply to payments made to the assignee bank. This is because the payments would not, as the relevant section requires, be on an advance from a bank carrying on a bona fide banking business in the UK, since the original advance will have been made by a different bank.[25] However, it is understood that it is not Inland Revenue practice to adopt this approach and that therefore the withholding tax exemption will apply. Similarly, where the

21. S.26 *ibid.* and regulations 29 to 37 of the Value Added Tax (General) Regulations 1985.
22. S.15(3) of the Stamp Act 1891.
23. S.14(4) *ibid.*
24. S.349(2) of the Income and Corporation Taxes Act 1988.
25. S.349(3) *ibid.*

loan is assigned by a UK bank to a non-UK bank, it seems that the Inland Revenue will not contend that income tax should be deducted from subsequent payments of interest (at least so long as the borrower is unaware of the assignment).

If the sub-participator is an overseas bank operating through a London branch, then the question of withholding tax may again arise. A withholding obligation arises where payments are made to a person whose usual place of abode is outside the UK.[26] This may be considered to be the case where a non-UK bank, albeit operating through a UK branch, is involved in the sub-participation. However, it seems that the Inland Revenue do not seek to impose a withholding tax obligation in these circumstances; to do so would unfairly discriminate against non-UK banks and thus introduce a degree of distortion in the market. The profits of an overseas bank operating through a London branch will be within the charge to corporation tax in any event.[27]

In the banking sector, debt participations are more likely to be funded through the inter-bank market than through the issue of notes. The banking exemption will generally avoid the need to withhold tax from payments of interest on that funding. However, if paper is to be issued by a non-banking corporate to other non-banking entities, then the withholding tax obligation may be overcome by virtue of the quoted Eurobond exemption or the use of original-issue discount notes as above.

8.4.2 Relief for funding and front-end costs

Any sub-participation in debt receivables by banking concerns or finance houses will generally be part of their everyday trading activities. Thus, any front-end costs incurred for the purposes of the sub-participation should be deductible as a trading expense on an accruals basis.[28]

8.4.3 Profit extraction

The question of profit-extraction depends in the first instance on the basis of the sub-participation. If the reason for the sub-participation is the reduction of the original lender's risk, then the sub-participator will be entitled to the super-profit that arises from the intrinsic value of the debt. On the other hand, if the aim of the sub-participation is to free capacity on the original lender's balance sheet from a regulatory viewpoint, then the profit element may be for the account of the original lender with the sub-participator receiving a margin over its funding rate.

Once again, the MIRAS problem does not arise, which means that the partial assignment route may be considered appropriate. Alternatively, the profits can

26. S.349(2)(c) *ibid.*
27. S.11 *ibid.*
28. S.74(a) *ibid.*

be extracted by payment of deferred consideration over the life of the sub-participation equal to the true value of the loans (including the profit element). Management and/or administration fees can also be considered as a means of extracting profit. If management and administration fees are used, their size will need to be commercially justifiable. So long as the parties are acting in a bona fide manner at arm's length, any level of fee agreed between them should be commercially justifiable.

8.4.4 Value added tax and stamp duty

Once again, the irrecoverability of VAT on fees paid raises a problem. The ability of the payer (that is, the sub-participator) to recover any VAT paid on those fees is dependent on its partial recovery position for VAT purposes.[29] That position will depend upon the proportion which the standard-rated supplies made by the payer bears to the exempt supplies made by the payer. In the banking sector, the recovery of VAT is likely to be low.

The incidence of stamp duty depends on the nature of the debt which is being sub-participated. If the debt is in the form of commercial mortgages then there will be no stamp duty.[30] Similarly, if loan capital is being assigned then there will be no stamp duty.[31] If, however, loan receivables are being assigned, then stamp duty will be payable at the rate of 1 per cent of the consideration. In such a situation, execution off-shore may be advisable.[32]

STEPHEN M. EDGE
GRAHAM IVERSEN

29. S.26 of the Value Added Tax Act 1994 and regulations 29 to 37 of the Value Added Tax (General) Regulations 1985.
30. S.64 of the Finance Act 1971.
31. S.79 of the Finance Act 1986.
32. Section 15(3) of the Stamp Act 1891.

CHAPTER 9

ASSET SECURITIZATION IN FRANCE AND GERMANY

9.1 INTRODUCTION—FRANCE

The first eight sections of this chapter address the French legislation providing for the creation of securities representing interests in pools of financial assets such as consumer loans. The basic legislation, Law No. 88–1201 of December 23, 1988 ("Law No. 88–1201", and as amended, the "Act") has been supplemented by an implementing decree, Decree No. 89–158 of March 9, 1989 ("Decree No. 89–158" and as amended, the "Decree"). English translations of both the Act and the Decree are appended to this chapter.

In view of the slow development of securitization in France, partly attributed to overly complex regulation, Law No. 88–1201 has been substantially amended by Law No. 93–6 of January 4, 1993 and Law No. 93–1444 of December 31, 1993. Decree No. 89–158 was accordingly modified by Decree No. 93–589 of March 27, 1993.

These enactments have been supplemented by a series of further regulatory measures. Rules for approval of issuers and listing of their securities are set forth in a regulation and an implementing instruction of the French stock exchange commission, the Commission des opérations de bourse (the "COB").[1] The banking regulatory commission, the Comité de la réglementation bancaire (the "CRB"), has adopted regulations on accounting for dispositions of assets in connection with securitization[2] and on the treatment of securitization for capital adequacy purposes.[3] The tax administration has issued a release concerning the tax treatment of securitization transactions,[4] and the Ministry of the Economy has designated authorized rating agencies.[5]

1. COB Regulation No. 94–01 (the "COB Regulation") and the related Instruction (the "COB Instruction").

2. CRB Regulation No. 89–07, applicable to transactions accounted for before January 1, 1994, and CRB Regulation No. 93–06 of December 21, 1993, applicable to transactions accounted for on or after January 1, 1994 (together, the "Accounting Regulations").

3. CRB Regulation No. 93–07 of December 21, 1993, modifying CRB Regulation No. 90–02 (as amended, "CRB Regulation No. 90–02") and CRB Instruction No. 94–03 of March 14, 1994, modifying CRB Instruction No. 91–02 (as amended, the "CRB Instruction").

For footnotes 4 and 5, see page 186.

The purposes of the Act as they appear from the ample legislative history are, first, to permit banks to improve their capital ratios by disposing of certain assets and, second, to reduce the differential between interest rates on consumer credit and on other forms of credit by reducing the costs of intermediation between credit markets. The Act is intended to facilitate the development of a market in securities backed by various forms of loans, especially mortgage loans. Several provisions of French law have made this process of "securitization" difficult in the past. In particular, the Civil Code makes the transfer of consumer loans impractical, and French banking law restricts the ownership of loans to credit institutions which are subject to capital ratios.

The Act eliminates these and other obstacles for transactions that fall within its provisions. It does not rule out securitization by other means where that is feasible.

The sections which follow discuss the nature of the special-purpose issuing vehicle created under the Act, the assets eligible for securitization, the transfer and servicing of loans under the Act, the nature of the securities to be issued, certain regulatory considerations, and certain tax considerations.

9.2 THE FUND

The Act authorizes the creation of a limited-purpose investment vehicle called a *fonds commun de créances* (hereinafter, a "Fund"). The Fund is patterned on the *fonds commun de placement* ("FCP"), a form of investment vehicle that is in turn modelled on the unit investment trust. In the simplest terms, a Fund owns a pool of receivables (*créances*) and issues units (*parts*) to investors.

A Fund does not have legal personality, and accordingly it is not subject to companies law or insolvency laws. Instead Article 34, paragraph 1 of the Act describes a Fund as a "coproprietorship" (*copropriété*) among the holders of units; this term is borrowed from the legislation governing FCPs, but without many of the specific provisions that apply to FCPs. The precise meaning of the term under French law is not entirely clear, but the intention in adopting it was to ensure that holders of the units would have a direct claim on the underlying receivables and any collateral securing the receivables, rather than holding indebtedness of an entity that in turn owns receivables. For the most part, the rights of the unitholders are left to be defined by the charter (*règlement*) governing the Fund. With limited exceptions set forth in the Act, unitholders have none of the usual rights of either shareholders or bondholders under French law.

The purchase of receivables and the issuance of units constitute the exclusive

4. Instruction BOI 5–I–3–89 of the Direction Générale des Impôts of October 17, 1989 (the "1989 Tax Release"), Instruction BOI 5–I–2–90 of the Direction Générale des Impôts of April 3, 1990 (the "1990 Tax Release", and together with the 1989 Tax Release, the "Tax Releases") and Articles 79 and 81 of Law No. 93–1352 of December 30, 1993.

5. Arrêté of December 31, 1992, published in the *Journal officiel* dated January 6, 1993, p. 342.

purpose of a Fund. Article 34 of the Act sets forth a number of further restrictions on its operations, including the following:

- It may only issue units once.
- It may not sell its receivables, except that under Article 6 of the Decree it may sell them all (i) after the amount of the residual assets of the Fund falls below 10 per cent of the initial amount of the issue of units or (ii) if the Fund has been unable to acquire receivables after issuance of the units in accordance with its charter, and it is in the interests of unitholders to liquidate the Fund.
- It may not pledge its receivables.
- It may not borrow.

Before its amendment in 1993, Law No. 88–1201 imposed a prohibition on acquisitions of assets after the issuance of the units, which constituted a substantial restriction on the operation of the Fund. The Act now permits the Fund to acquire new assets after it has issued the units, provided that the receivables acquired after the issuance of the units are of the same nature as the initial receivables, and that the acquisition of new assets does not entail any deterioration in the level of security offered to unitholders (Decree, Article 8 *bis*). In particular, these new provisions will make it possible to securitize short-term receivables on a roll-over basis.

9.3 ELIGIBLE ASSETS

There are few limitations on the types of assets that may constitute the pool of receivables held by a Fund:

- They must be purchased from a French credit institution, a French insurance company or the Caisse des dépôts et consignations. Act Article 34, paragraph 1.
- They must not, at the time they are sold to the Fund, be classified as *immobilisées*, *douteuses* or *litigieuses* (Decree, Article 8); these terms designate categories in which French banks place problem loans.
- Payment of the principal amount of, and interest on, such receivables must be made in a single installment or in several installments payable periodically or upon fixed dates, in a fixed minimum amount. The conditions of reimbursement must be agreed in advance in writing. (Decree, Article 8)
- All the receivables in a given Fund must be "of the same nature" (Decree, Article 8). Commentary suggests that these terms refer to the activity financed by the relevant loans, such as, for example, automobile or housing loans.

The Fund mechanism is not limited to consumer loans; a Fund could also hold commercial loans. For commercial loans, however, simplified transfer procedures already existed under prior law, and some of the features of securitization may be achieved without resorting to the provisions of the Act.

As noted above, a Fund may acquire further receivables (*créances*) after its initial constitution, subject to certain limitations. A Fund is also authorized to invest limited amounts temporarily, pending their distribution, in specified categories of debt instruments: French treasury bills (*bons du Trésor*), certain mutual funds (SICAVs and FCPs), and debt instruments traded on a regulated exchange. (Act Article 34, paragraph 3; Decree Article 4.) The maximum amount of such investments is calculated each year according to rules set forth in an order by the Minister of the Economy, which differ according to whether the fund is permitted to acquire new assets after the issuance of the units or not. A Fund may enter into interest rate swap agreements and carry out transactions on regulated futures markets for the sole purpose of balancing its incoming financial flows against its undertakings to make payments, and provided, in the case of interest swap agreements, that such agreements are entered into with a French credit institution, a French insurance company or the Caisse des dépôts et consignations.

9.4 MANAGEMENT AND SERVICING

A Fund must be co-founded by a management company and a depositary. The management company must be a French company devoted solely to the management of Funds under the Act, with a capital at least equal to the greater of 1,500,000 French francs or 0.5 per cent of the total assets under its management, with a maximum of 5,000,000 French francs (subject to certain exceptions). Pursuant to Article 37 of the Act, the management company must be authorized by the COB. The COB may withdraw its authorization at any time but only for cause. The withdrawal of the COB's authorization results in the replacement of the concerned management company on the initiative of the depository and subject to the COB's approval. Concerning the management company's duties and powers, the Act only states that it is responsible for the management of the Fund and for its representation *vis-à-vis* third parties, including before the courts; any detail is left to be defined in the charter of the Fund. The legislation does not contemplate replacement of the management company except in the case of withdrawal of the COB's authorization, and it is not clear under what circumstances and in what manner that would be possible.

The depositary must be a French credit institution or another French entity authorized by the Ministry of the Economy, must hold the assets of the Fund (specifically including the receivables and the cash) and must monitor the activity of the management company. Otherwise its responsibilities, too, are left to be defined in the Fund's charter. Article 48 of the Act authorizes the depositary to petition a court for removal of the managers of the management company.

In case of public offering of units, the management company and the depositary must prepare an information memorandum (*note d'information*) relating to the Fund, that must be approved by the COB.

In addition to a management company and a depositary, each Fund must have a statutory auditor. The Act contains detailed provisions, and incorporates others by reference from French companies law, on the appointment, duties and removal of the statutory auditor.

Article 36 of the Act provides that the institution selling loans to the Fund will continue to "ensure [their] collection", under contract with the Fund's management company. This provision was designed to ensure that borrowers would continue to deal only with the originating institution, by requiring the latter to remain as the servicer. Before the amendment of Law No. 88–1201 in 1993, servicing responsibility could be transferred to a new institution only if the debtor consented in writing at the time of the transfer. The Act now provides that collection may be ensured by a credit institution other than the selling institution or by the Caisse des dépôts et consignations, provided that the debtor is notified by ordinary letter, and, for receivables arising after January 1, 1995, that the relevant loan agreement include a clause making reference to the possibility of a delegation of the collection.

The Act itself does not address whether the depositary, the management company and the seller of the receivables may be affiliated companies. Article 3 of the COB Regulation, however, limits the influence of the seller of the receivables over the management company: neither the seller, nor any entity controlling it, controlled by it or under common control with it, may own one-third or more of the shares of the management company. Under French company law this limitation prevents the seller from exercising significant power over the management company. On the other hand, the depositary may be an affiliate of either the management company or the seller.

9.5 TRANSFER OF LOANS TO THE FUND

General rules of French law provide several different methods for transfer of a receivable, each of which presents significant disadvantages of timing and cost in the context of securitization. As an exception to these general rules, Article 34 of the Act provides that the transfer of a loan to a Fund is made by means of a *bordereau* or assignment, which may cover a number of loans. This technique is adapted from the provisions that govern transfer of commercial loans under a 1981 law. The assignment is valid against third parties from the date affixed on the *bordereau* upon its delivery, and it results without any further formality in the transfer of any collateral securing the loan and the validity of such transfer against third parties. The Act also requires that the debtor be notified by ordinary mail, although it appears that this is not a condition to perfection of the transfer.

Because these simplified procedures do not require compliance with the rules that, under general French law, ensure notice to third parties, they could give rise to practical problems concerning competing claimants to a loan or to the collateral securing the loan. The applicable legal rules will depend on the legal nature of the specific receivables and collateral involved, but several different types of questions are likely to arise.

In the first place, although no case law exists on this issue, the Act arguably does not prevent claims arising prior to the transfer of receivables to the Fund, or indeed defenses valid against the lender, from being asserted against the Fund. Measures of "due diligence" will have to be devised to counter this possibility.

In the second place, although the Act provides that a transfer to the Fund is immediately valid against third parties as to a receivable and its collateral, the possibility that claims to the loan or the collateral could arise after they are transferred to the Fund will have to be studied for particular types of loans and collateral. Such risks can be avoided for some types if the depositary has custody of the documents that would be required to effect a subsequent transfer, but for other types (including real property mortgages or loans executed before a notary) this will not be possible. Thus the requirement of the legislation (Decree Article 3) that the depositary of the Fund's assets hold "titles to the receivables" transferred to the Fund is difficult to apply in practice. With respect to collateral, Article 2 of the Decree requires that the assignment contain an express undertaking of the seller to take any measures requested by the Fund for the recording, modification or enforcement of security. It may prove prudent, as to both receivables and collateral, for the depositary to take further measures from the outset to prevent competing claims of bona fide transferees from arising. In the specific case of real property mortgages, the question arises whether public filing is required to perfect the Fund's ownership. Before the amendment of Law No. 88–1201, the Act did not address the question, and commentary suggested that such filing was indeed required. The Act now provides that the transfer of collateral is valid *vis-à-vis* third parties "without the need for any other formality". Although not specifically expressed in that way, the next text was intended to avoid the requirement of public filing in the case of real estate mortgages.

9.6 THE UNITS

The legislation specifies little about the nature of the units and to our knowledge there has been no case law on this issue so far. The following points summarize features of the units that are specified by the legislation, or that can be inferred from the legislative history, the regulations adopted so far and other sources.

9.6.1 Legal characterization

Article 34 of the Law specifies that the units are securities (*valeurs mobilières*). Certain further features follow from this characterization: they are negotiable; they can be listed on a stock exchange; they must be issued in series.

In other respects, however, the legal nature of the units does not fit neatly into pre-existing categories under French law. For example, Article 1 of the Act itself contains a general definition of the term *valeurs mobilières* (heretofore undefined in French law), intended to be used in construing investment limitations on SICAVs and FCPs; the definition does not include the units issued by a Fund. Although it appears from the legislative history and other sources that this was not intended to limit investment in Fund units by SICAVs and FCPs, the confusion is symptomatic. Also, it is uncertain whether their form and transfer are governed by the provisions of French law requiring all securities to be in book-entry form unless they are issued outside France since such provisions only apply to securities issued by legal entities, and the Fund, as mentioned above, does not have legal personality. In addition, the French tax treatment of income paid in connection with units (see "Tax Matters" below) is generally based on the treatment of debt instruments, although in light of the legal character of the Fund itself (see "The Fund" above) the units are clearly not debt instruments. This kind of uncertainty may make it difficult to classify earnings and capital gains or losses for purposes of tax treaties and the tax legislation of other jurisdictions, and it may also make it difficult to classify the units for purposes of legal investment restrictions applicable to particular categories of non-French investors.

9.6.2 Basic financial characteristics

The Act provides few indications on the financial characteristics of the units. The legislative history of the Act and subsequent comments make it clear that the legislation is intended to permit the widest possible range of financial engineering. Unless more restrictive policies are developed in further administrative practice, it would appear in particular that:

- Units can be issued at a discount or a premium to their initial par value (principal amount).
- Principal can be subject to amortization, on a fixed schedule or depending on the performance of the pool of receivables. The units may not, however, provide for redemption at the option of the holder.
- Under Article 5 of the Decree, the "minimum amount" of a unit upon issuance may not be less than 5,000 French francs. This provision may present interpretive problems for some types of units (those issued at a discount or a premium, for example, or those representing interest only or principal only).
- Units can bear interest at fixed or floating rates, or not at all; the tax

provisions of the Act contemplate the possibility of "deep-discount" or "zero-coupon" units.

- The Act does not rule out units denominated in a currency other than French francs (or in ECU).
- Listing on a French stock exchange is required, under Article 23 of the COB Regulation, for units other than specific units (see "Credit enhancement" below) that are offered to the public and that have an initial par value of less than 1,000,000 French francs. (See "Approval, offering and placement in general" below.)

The legislation does not specify the relationship between the flow of interest and principal payments on the pool of receivables and the flow of payments to the holders of units. In view of the clear legislative intent to permit maximum flexibility, it is safe to assume that there are no particular requirements other than a case-by-case evaluation of the sufficiency of the aggregate cash flow from the receivables to service the units. Moreover, Article 34 of the Act specifies that the units of a single Fund may give rise to "different rights to principal and interest" in connection with the receivables. For example, a single Fund could:

(a) issue two or more classes of units, with principal to be repaid sequentially on each class ("fast-pay/slow-pay" units);

(b) issue a class of units whose holders receive only the amount (or some fraction) of the interest earned on the pool of underlying receivables, while the other class or classes receive the amount of principal repaid with respect to the pool ("stripped" units); or

(c) issue classes of units that are subordinated or preferred (see Decree, Article 9).

The cash flow from the receivables may also exceed that needed to service the units, so that the Fund builds up cash in what U.S. practice calls "reserve funds". In particular, Article 34 of the Act specifically envisions the existence of residual funds following liquidation (a *boni de liquidation*), and provides that the transfer agreement between the Fund and the selling institution may entitle the latter to receive them. It does not, however, specify whether this interest can be transferred or whether any other party may own it.

9.6.3 Credit enhancement

Under Article 37 of the Act, as implemented by Article 9 of the Decree, holders of units must be protected against the risk of default on the receivables in the pool by means of one or more of four specific measures:

- The Fund may obtain a guarantee from a French credit institution or insurance company or the Caisse des dépôts et consignations.
- The Fund may issue a subordinated class of units or "specific units" (*parts spécifiques*) that bears the risk of defaults. Such units may not, however, be held by individuals or by FCPs or SICAVs.
- The Fund may hold "an amount of receivables that exceeds the amount

of the units issued". The legislative history suggests that this provision should be read as giving ample leeway in the choice of the method of overcollateralization. It presumably includes the holding of receivables (a) whose principal amount exceeds the principal amount of the units or (b) whose cash flow exceeds the cash flow on the units. In such a situation, referred to as *surdimensionnement*, the value of receivables held by a Fund would presumably exceed the aggregate subscription price of its units. The balance (beyond any amount needed to provide for administration of the Fund) would constitute a liquidation interest (*boni de liquidation*).

- The Fund may obtain "adequate guarantees attaching to the acquired receivables".

In addition, as the prohibition on acquiring receivables after issuance of the units has been suppressed, it could be envisaged that the seller of the receivables undertake to replace loans that are in default or otherwise defective, although this credit enhancement technique would not fall within the scope of Article 9 of the Decree.

The institution selling receivables to the Fund will be an obvious candidate to provide credit enhancement, whether by means of overcollateralization, by retaining specific units, or by issuing a guarantee. The retention of risk by the selling institution raises the question whether the transfer of receivables to the Fund can be treated as a sale, or whether instead the seller must retain the assets on its balance sheet at least for purposes of bank regulatory accounting. In the latter case, the stated objective of permitting French credit institutions to dispose of assets in order to improve their capital ratios could only be achieved if outside providers of credit enhancement, such as pool insurers, could be found at economical prices. For accounting purposes, the Accounting Regulations address this problem by providing that any transfer of receivables to a Fund is treated as a sale, regardless of overcollateralization or the retention of a subordinated interest in the Fund. The Accounting Regulations also provide detailed rules regarding the accounting aspects of the various credit enhancement techniques referred to in Article 9 of the Decree. Retention of risk by the selling institution is however restricted by the recent amendment of capital adequacy rules (see below).

9.6.4 Treatment under capital adequacy rules

The European Union, of which France is a member, adopted capital adequacy regulations for credit institutions in all its member states based on the risk-based capital guidelines of the Basle Committee. In 1990 and 1991, the CRB issued regulations implementing the E.U. regulations. As a result, French credit institutions are required to maintain a solvency ratio of "own funds" to risk-adjusted assets and certain off-balance sheet items of at least 8 per cent. CRB Regulation No. 91–05 of January 15, 1991 ("CRB Regulation No.

91–05"), supplemented by the CRB Instruction, provides the rules for the computation of the solvency ratio. The numerator of the ratio consists of the own funds of the relevant credit institution, as defined by CRB Regulation No. 90–02. To compute the denominator of the ratio, the assets of the credit institution are assigned to broad categories of relative credit risk and the balance sheet value of each asset is multiplied by the percentage weight attributed to the relevant category. With respect to off-balance sheet items, their face value is first adjusted according to their risk classification, before application of the relevant percentage weight.

CRB Regulation No. 90–02, CRB Regulation No. 91–05 and the CRB Instruction specify the consequences of various aspects of securitization for purposes of capital adequacy regulations. Under the CRB Instruction, ordinary units held by a credit institution may be given the same risk weighting as the underlying receivables, provided that the credit institution can give some justification as to the nature of such receivables. As mentioned above, CRB Regulation No. 90–02 and the CRB Instruction were recently amended (see "Introduction"). These amendments, applicable to transactions accounted for as from July 1, 1994, have a great impact on the consequences of the retention of risk by the selling institution for capital adequacy purposes. Formerly, a guarantee issued by the selling institution to provide credit enhancement of a Fund was treated as an off-balance-sheet undertaking of such institution, taken into account in the denominator of the ratio, and subject to a 100 per cent percentage weight. Similarly, specific units retained by the selling institution were treated as assets of the selling institution subject to a 100 per cent percentage weight. Under the new rules, the amount of a guarantee from the selling institution, adjusted by application of the relevant percentage weight with respect to the underlying receivables, and net of any provisions, is deducted from the own funds of the credit institution, such deduction being subject to a maximum of 8 per cent of the risk-adjusted amount of the underlying receivables. According to indications by representatives of the Commission Bancaire, the regulatory authority for credit institutions, any form of retention of risk by the selling institution referred to in Article 9 of the Decree, including the subscription of specific units, would be considered a "guarantee" submitted to the new rules. The new rules reduce considerably the benefits of securitization for capital adequacy purposes in case of retention of risk by the selling institution.

9.7 APPROVAL, OFFERING AND REPORTING

9.7.1 Approval, offering and placement in general

The procedures for monitoring the creation of a Fund have been substantially simplified following the amendment of Law No. 88-1201 in 1993.

The creation or liquidation of a Fund and the terms of its charter no longer require approval of the COB. Instead, management companies must be authorized by the COB to exercise their activity and, where an information memorandum is prepared, such information memorandum must be approved by the COB according to a simplified procedure, known as *visa*. The COB is also specifically charged with approving the nomination of the statutory auditors of the Fund. In addition, the COB which generally oversees French securities markets and attends particularly to the protection of investors, plays an active role in the regulation of securitization.

Pursuant to Article 35 of the Act, a report on the units and the pool of receivables from a rating agency approved for this purpose by the Ministry of the Economy must be attached to the information memorandum and communicated to subscribers. The rating agencies approved to date have been Moody's France S.A. and Moody's Investor Service, Standard & Poor's Agence d'évaluation and Standard & Poor's Corporation, IBCA Notation and IBCA Notation Groupe. Article 35 of the Act and Article 7 of the Decree describe the scope of the rating agency's report in some detail.

The Act also imposes certain limitations on the placement of units, applicable to all Funds. In particular:

- *Démarchage* is not permitted in connection with units. The term *démarchage* (roughly translated as "solicitation") refers to a range of selling practices that involve the solicitation of prospective purchasers in their homes, in public, or in their places of employment.
- If a SICAV or FCP is related, in ways specified in Article 26 of the Act, to the seller of the receivables held by a Fund, the SICAV or FCP may not hold more than 5 per cent by value of the units issued by the Fund.

Otherwise, the only limitations on investors eligible to purchase units are those described below that apply to privately placed units.

9.7.2 Public offering and private placement

Part II of the COB Regulation ("Part II") sets forth rules regarding public offerings of units. Part II applies to Funds that have issued at least one category of units offered to the public.

Units are considered offered to the public if any of the following criteria is met:

- application has been filed for their listing;
- the number of offerees exceeds 300; or
- their placement relies on advertising methods of any kind.

Units that do not meet any of the above criteria are considered private and therefore not subject to Part II. Part II sets forth detailed rules as to the content of the information memorandum that the management company and the depositary must jointly prepare. The information memorandum may consist of a single document that must be filed with the COB at least 30 calendar days before the desired date of approval, or of two documents, a preliminary information memorandum and a transaction memorandum (*note d'opération*). In the latter case, the preliminary information memorandum must be filed with the COB at least 30 calendar days before the desired date of its approval, and the transaction memorandum must be filed with the COB within one month of the approval of the preliminary information memorandum, and at least two days before the desired date of its approval. Part II also provides a simplified "shelf registration" procedure for the marketing of a range of identical funds by the same management company and depositary. The COB Instruction also prescribes certain mechanics of closing the issuance of units. As mentioned above, ordinary units offered to the public must be listed on a French exchange, unless their initial par value is 1,000,000 French francs or more.

9.7.3 Information requirements

Part III of the COB Regulation and Chapter III of the COB Instruction specify the rules regarding disclosure of information by Funds that have issued at least one category of units offered to the public pursuant to the criteria set forth in Part II. Within four months following the end of each fiscal year, the management company must publish, for each Fund managed by it, and under the supervision of the depositary, an annual activity report verified by the statutory auditors of the relevant Fund, consisting of annual financial statements of the Fund certified by its statutory auditors (comprising the inventory of the Fund's assets and its annual accounts), a management report, and the indication of any amendment to the rating report or to the basic characteristics of the Fund as set forth in the information memorandum. The COB Instruction sets forth specific information that must be included in the management report. For example, the report must analyze the Fund's prepayment experience, default rates and weighted average life, and describe any events that may require the Fund to call on its credit enhancement.

Within three months of the close of the first half of each fiscal year, the management company must publish a report on the activity of the Fund during such period, containing in particular an inventory of the assets of the Fund, certain of the information required to be included in the annual management report, and the indication of any amendment to the rating report or to the basic characteristics of the Fund as set forth in the information memorandum.

The annual and semi-annual reports must be made available to holders of units on request and to the public at the premises of the management company and of any institution having received orders from subscribers to units and filed with the COB.

Before the entry into force of the COB Regulation in March 1994, the COB submitted privately placed Funds to certain information requirements, although less stringent than those applying to Funds offered to the public. By contrast, the COB Regulation does not impose any particular information requirements on Funds that have not issued at least one category of units offered to the public.

9.8 TAX MATTERS

9.8.1 The seller of receivables to the Fund

The gain or loss realized upon sale of receivables to a Fund is treated as ordinary income or loss. Where the seller provides credit enhancement by delivering receivables with a value in excess of the face amount of the units (*surdimensionnement*), it will generally receive proceeds worth less than the receivables, with the difference consisting of a liquidation interest in the Fund. Gain or loss on such a transaction for tax purposes will be determined taking account of the face amount of the liquidation interest, and the liquidation interest may not be depreciated for tax purposes until defaults on the Fund's receivables become likely. The seller will thus recognize, at the moment of transfer, any gains on the excess receivables transferred to the Fund. On the other hand, upon liquidation of the Fund, the seller would not be subject to tax on previously recognized gains.

Where the seller retains specific units, they are valued, for tax purposes, at their purchase price in accordance with ordinary rules concerning taxation of securities. The use of specific units would thus avoid the accelerated recognition of gain associated with *surdimensionnement*.

The Tax Releases are silent on the deductibility of provisions for possible losses created at the time the Fund is organized. It seems prudent to assume that these are not deductible until defaults become likely.

The sale of receivables is not subject to mandatory transfer tax. It is exempt from value added tax, and the parties may not opt for subjection to value added tax.

9.8.2 The Fund

The Fund itself is not subject to corporate income tax, and registration duties and value added tax do not apply to its transactions. In particular, the issuance of units is exempt from registration duty; the transfer of units is exempt from registration duty or stamp duty (*impôt de bourse*); and fees paid to the management company, the servicer and the depositary are exempt from value added tax. While the servicer may not opt for subjection to value added tax with respect to its fees, both the management company and the depositary may do so.

9.8.3 Holders of units

The Act and the 1989 Tax Release use the term "earnings from units" (*produits des parts*) without defining it. Presumably earnings from units include amounts characterized as interest or redemption premium and the recovery of any original-issue discount. The Act and the 1989 Tax Release appear to look to the way amounts are characterized with respect to the units, and not with respect to the underlying receivables. Thus amounts paid to investors as the repayment of principal on their units would not be taxed (subject to the rules on recovery of original-issue discount), and amounts paid as interest or premium would be taxed, regardless of the relative proportions of interest and principal received by the Fund in the same period on the underlying receivables. Earnings of the Fund are taxable only upon distribution to unitholders, except for entities subject to French corporate income tax. Entities subject to French corporate income tax are subject to tax at the standard rate (currently 33⅓ per cent) on the difference, calculated as of the date of the close of each fiscal year, between the mark-to-market value of the units held by them as of such date and the mark-to-market value of such units as of the first day of such fiscal year (or in case of a purchase during such fiscal year, the purchase price of such units).

Entities subject to French corporate income tax treat earnings from units, any gain on the distribution of a liquidation interest, and any capital gain on the disposal of units as ordinary income subject to the standard rate. For entities subject to French income tax (*impôt sur le revenu*) (as opposed to corporate income tax), capital gains on disposal of units held for two years or more may benefit from taxation at a reduced rate.

For individuals subject to French income tax, earnings on units are taxable as ordinary income, and may be included (under a system called the *abattement*) in a yearly amount of tax-free income from securities investments. The holder may also choose to be subject to withholding on earnings from units, which frees the payments from any further taxation. The rate of this withholding (called *prélèvement libératoire*) is 15 per cent plus various social contributions. Capital gains on the disposal of units with an original term to maturity not exceeding five years are also subject to French income tax at a fixed rate of 16 per cent plus various social contributions. Capital gains on the disposal of units with an original term to maturity in excess of five years are subject to tax only if the total amount of capital gains realized in any given year by the concerned unitholder with respect to securities generally exceeds a specified threshold (set at 336.700 French francs for 1994). In this case, the tax rate on such capital gains is a fixed rate of 16 per cent plus various social contributions. Capital losses on units sold in any given year (irrespective of the term to maturity of such units) may be offset exclusively against capital gains of the same nature realized during the same year or the five following years. For individuals, recovery of original-issue discount and capitalized interest income may be subject to special recognition rules if the original term to maturity is in excess of five years.

Earnings of non-resident holders are exempt from French tax, provided that the holder establishes to the satisfaction of the paying agent that it is not a resident of France or the French franc zone. Otherwise, earnings are subject to withholding (*prélèvement*) at a rate equal to 15 per cent. Holders that benefit from a tax treaty with France may also use treaty procedures (which are generally more cumbersome) to obtain a reduction or exemption from withholding. It will in principle be possible for an issue of units made outside of France to qualify for an exemption from withholding under the provisions applicable to eurobonds. Capital gains derived by non-resident holders not established in France would not be subject to any French tax.

9.9 INTRODUCTION—GERMANY

Asset securitization in the sense of transforming loans, receivables or other uncertificated financial assets into securities or similar instruments (such as participation certificates or preference shares) is still a novel financing technique in Germany. A few of the concepts that underlie the securitization of assets, however, are not new in Germany. For example, industrial and trading companies have, for quite some time, converted receivables and other financial assets into cash through factoring and similar arrangements. There have also been several repackaging transactions involving the transformation of loans into tradeable securities through the intermediation of a special purpose vehicle or a bank. Finally, the German mortgage bank system can be viewed as an efficient way of securitizing mortgage and public sector loans. Indeed, the German mortgage bond, or *Pfandbrief* as it is called in Germany, is a classic example of what one would call a "mortgage-backed bond" in the U.S. market.

Although there is no special legal framework for the securitization of assets in Germany, from a purely legal perspective, asset securitization is certainly feasible in Germany. The fundamental question is whether the benefits are worth the effort and cost that the development and implementation of a viable structure involves.

There have been several reports about private transactions involving the securitization of German assets in recent years. In 1990, Citibank Aktiengesellschaft, the German banking subsidiary of the Citibank group, completed what is believed to have been the first securitization of assets outside the mortgage and government loan area in Germany.[6] More recently, several German banks announced the creation of asset-backed commercial paper programs based, at least in part, on corporate receivables generated in Germany, and in the spring of 1995 a pool of mortgages was securitized through the issuance of DM-denominated bonds outside the framework of the German mortgage bank system.

6. See Asset Sales Report, January 14, 1991, p. 3; and *Financial Times*, December 18, 1990, "First German asset-backed deal emerges".

9.10 CONSIDERATIONS DRIVING SECURITIZATION IN GERMANY

Securitization as a financing technique may be chosen for a variety of reasons. The theory is quite simple: asset securitization should be considered if the sale of assets and the use of the proceeds to do new business generates a higher return than the financing of the new business with "on-balance sheet" debt or new equity capital. In practice, however, the matter is more complex. German banks and industrial companies generally do not know the exact costs of new equity capital in order to compare the relative economic benefits of retaining or selling the assets. Historically, the access to new equity capital has been comparatively easy in Germany. The funding pressures that have been the driving force of asset securitization in some other countries have simply not yet reached Germany. For banks, large balance sheets are often a matter of pride, perhaps partly due to international league tables that rank banks on this basis. Concerns about customer relationships or the complexity of the legal structure of asset securitization transactions may be further reasons for the reluctance of German parties to participate in such transactions.

Several recent developments, however, suggest that the prospects for asset securitization in Germany may improve. After a long period of relative abundance of capital, Germany may enter a phase in which capital is no longer available as easily or cheaply as it used to be. The increasing sophistication of market participants may also gradually overcome reservations about the complexity of the securitization process. Industrial or trading companies may opt for securitization to avoid the local German business tax that applies to interest payments on debt raised to refinance the assets "on-balance sheet". Most significantly, regulatory developments in the banking area may provide the strongest impetus. As a result of the implementation of the E.C. Solvency Ratio Directive, effective January 1, 1993, German banks are subject to more stringent capital ratio requirements. In the past, some German banks had been large purchasers of receivables and other financial assets from industrial and leasing companies, but more stringent capital ratios may discourage banks from buying such assets or at least force banks to offer less favorable terms to the sellers. Rather than buying the assets themselves, banks may find it more attractive to assist the seller in securitizing the assets.

9.11 STRUCTURE

In theory, there are at least three legal structures for securitizing financial assets in Germany: two domestic and one foreign. The two domestic structures would require the use of a German bank or a German special purpose vehicle as the purchaser of the assets and the issuer of the asset-backed securities. In the bank structure, a German bank would acquire the assets and issue the securities in a fiduciary capacity. The bank would either be the originator or would purchase the assets from the originator. This structure has apparently not yet been used for the securitization of assets in Germany, although there are precedents involving banks as issuers of non-recourse "pass-through" participation certificates or notes based on loans to third parties.

Each of these domestic structures may ultimately be feasible, but the bank structure raises several bank regulatory issues and the special purpose vehicle structure raises tax issues that would require discussions with the competent authorities. For these reasons, a foreign structure may be preferable. Such a structure is consistent with asset securitization transactions elsewhere in Europe and would therefore be familiar to potential investors and other market participants. In somewhat simplified terms, a foreign structure involves the sale of the assets by the originator, or by a bank acting as intermediary, to a foreign special purpose vehicle, which would assign the assets to a German or foreign trustee for the investors and issue debt securities (or other instruments) collateralized by the assets and serviced from their cash flow.

In order to avoid consolidation requirements under German law, the originator should not own or control the foreign issuing vehicle, as this could jeopardize the desired "off-balance sheet" treatment of the transaction. The shares of the vehicle could, for example, be held by a foreign trust company for the benefit of a charity (a structure frequently used in repackaging and asset securitization transactions in the Euromarkets). Alternatively, the originator could sell a sufficient amount of the share capital to independent third parties to avoid the need for consolidation. In any event, German tax residents should have no ownership interests in the vehicle to avoid the application of the tax attribution rules of the Act Against Tax Evasion (Außensteuergesetz). To minimize the risk of claims against the originator or the bank arranging the securitization, it may be desirable to avoid any affiliation of the issuer with the originator or the arranger and otherwise to clarify, through the name of the issuer and appropriate disclosure in the offering materials, that neither the originator nor the arranger supports the transaction from a credit perspective.

The formation and operation of the special purpose vehicle should be structured such that the vehicle can only engage in activities related to the asset securitization transaction ("bankruptcy remoteness"). All participants in the transaction should waive set-off and similar rights and undertake not to seek judicial enforcement of their claims against the vehicle and not to file an application for the opening of bankruptcy or similar proceedings.

9.12 THE ASSETS

9.12.1 Transfer

There are no legal considerations in Germany that would *per se* exclude from securitization any of the types of financial assets that have customarily been securitized in other countries. One of the basic requirements is the transferability of the assets. Loans (and other receivables) are generally freely assignable without the consent of the debtor, unless the loan or other documentation requires such consent or prohibits assignment altogether. It is therefore important to review the documentation (including applicable general business terms and conditions) for possible restrictions on assignment.[7] An assignment does not require notice to the debtor, but notice is necessary in order to eliminate the debtor's right to discharge its obligations by payment to the seller. Such notice would limit the debtor's right to offset its obligations against any counterclaim that it may have against the seller, although it would not be possible under German law to eliminate that right entirely.

If the seller continues to act as the servicer of the assets and, for customer relationship reasons, does not wish to give notice of the assignment to the debtors, the notice may be deferred until an event of default occurs. At that time, the purchaser of the assets (the special purpose vehicle) or the trustee could give such notice without requiring the seller's participation. Nonetheless, it may be useful to obtain an irrevocable power of attorney from the seller to give such notice on behalf of the seller in order to reduce possible inquiries from the debtors regarding the accuracy of the notice. Additional protection could result from the seller/servicer assigning or pledging the collection account to the trustee. The bank at which the account is maintained should waive all set-off and other rights with respect to the funds deposited in the account, whether arising by operation of law or under the bank's general business terms and conditions.

Appointment of the seller as servicer of the assets does not jeopardize the characterization of the transaction as a "true sale" from the perspective of the seller. There are no special rules in Germany setting forth when a sale of financial assets does not result in the transfer of the assets from an accounting or tax perspective. The general rule is that the sale is "true" unless the seller retains the credit risk of the assets. Warranties of the seller relating to the *legal* collectibility of the assets, such as the valid creation of the assets and the absence of counterclaims and other defenses of the debtor would not affect the characterization of the transfer as a "true" sale.

German law would permit additions to, and withdrawals from, the pool of assigned assets. New assets could be assigned in advance, provided that they could be sufficiently well defined to ensure that they would always be distinguishable from unassigned assets.

The securitization of receivables arising under certain types of executory contracts, such as leasing, service or maintenance agreements, raises special issues because the debtors may in certain circumstances, such as the bankruptcy of the seller, offset their outstanding payment obligations against claims for

7. Following a recent amendment to the Commercial Code, contractual prohibitions on the assignment of trade receivables are no longer permissible. This legislative development should provide greater opportunities for the securitization of trade receivables.

damages resulting from the non-performance by the seller of its obligations under the agreement.

9.12.2 Consumer Credit Act

The Consumer Credit Act of 1990 imposes strict formal requirements for the conclusion of loan and certain other financing arrangements for personal (as opposed to business) purposes with individuals. The borrower may, among other things, rescind a financing agreement if the lender fails to comply with certain disclosure and information requirements. In the case of a securitization of consumer loans and other consumer receivables, careful review of the documentation would be necessary to evaluate any such risk of rescission.

9.12.3 Collateralization

A range of technical issues arises with respect to the transfer of the collateral that secures the assets. In the case of automobile loans, the collateral generally consists of the transfer to the lender of title to the automobile. In this situation, the potential liabilities arising from the legal ownership of the car must be considered. For example, under German law the legal owner of a vehicle may be liable for certain repair costs and any person carrying out repairs could acquire a superior lien on the vehicle.

The creation of a security interest in the assets themselves should pose no special problems. Customarily, a security interest in a payment obligation, such as a loan or a receivable, is granted by assigning the obligation to the secured party. In an asset securitization transaction, this party would generally be the trustee acting for the benefit of the investors.

9.12.4 Prepayment risk

Prepayment questions must also be considered. Most German mortgage and consumer loans bear interest at a fixed rate. Until a recent amendment to the German Civil Code a few years ago, the borrower generally had the right to prepay any fixed-rate loan without penalty if the interest rate exceeded 6 per cent per annum. New legislation (Section 609a of the German Civil Code) now permits that right to be waived by contract, subject to certain conditions. Again, careful review of the documentation would be necessary to assess the prepayment risk. To the extent that prepayment occurs, no legal problem should arise with respect to reinvesting the prepaid amounts with a German or foreign financial institution until the next payment date on the asset-backed securities. In this case, however, there may be a yield risk.

9.12.5 Bankruptcy risk

A final issue with respect to the underlying assets is the need to insulate the issuer of the asset-backed securities and the assets themselves from the bankruptcy risk of the originator. Although German bankruptcy issues appear less complex than those in the United States and other jurisdictions, the risk of attacking the transfer of the assets under bankruptcy law must be minimized.[8] This situation could arise, for example, if the transfer occurred at a time when the seller was insolvent or had ceased to pay its debts generally. In the case of a securitization of receivables under executory contracts, consideration must be given to the rights of the debtors to offset their obligations against claims for damages resulting from a termination of the contracts in the event of the seller's bankruptcy.

9.13 DATA PROTECTION

A practical problem in regard to the assignment of financial assets could arise under German data protection laws and, if a bank is the seller of the assets, bank secrecy requirements, most of which are of a contractual nature. These rules restrict the disclosure of personal data (that is, data relating to individuals) to the assignee and other parties, such as rating agencies. Although the scope of the bank secrecy requirements is not entirely clear, the better view appears to be that banks which assign loans (or other financial assets) may disclose at least that information about the debtor which the assignee needs to enforce the loans. The basic principle of the German data protection legislation is that personal data may be disclosed to a third party only if such party has a legitimate interest in knowing the information. As under bank secrecy requirements, this should allow the disclosure to the assignee of such information as is necessary to enable the assignee to assert and enforce the assigned claims. It would probably not, however, permit disclosure of personal data relating to individual debtors to rating agencies for their evaluation of the pool of the assigned assets. The rating agencies should, however, be able to make such an evaluation without knowledge of individual personal information (for example, by receiving information on a coded basis).

9.14 REGULATORY ISSUES

9.14.1 Banking regulation

If the seller of the assets is a German bank, one of the most important regulatory issues is the treatment of the transaction for capital ratio and other bank regulatory purposes. Although the German banking authorities have not issued

8. In 1994, Germany adopted a new Insolvency Code which changes the insolvency and

any rules or guidelines on this issue, it is probably fair to assume that the desired "off-balance sheet" regulatory treatment for the seller of the assets would be achieved if

(i) the transaction qualified as a "true" sale by the selling bank for accounting purposes,
(ii) the issuer was not owned or controlled by the bank to an extent requiring consolidation under bank regulatory rules, and
(iii) the seller (or an entity controlled by the seller) did not retain any repurchase or indemnification obligations (other than obligations resulting from a warranty to the effect that the assigned obligation is valid and not subject to defenses and set-off rights).

The legal relationship between the selling bank and the issuer of the securities must be analyzed carefully to determine what risks remain with the seller.

Although as a legal matter the sale of financial assets by a German bank does not require the approval of the German banking authorities, the authorities have expressed a general concern about banks' securitizing "good" assets and retaining only "bad" assets.[9] For this reason, originators that are banks may wish to discuss a proposed securitization of bank loans and other bank assets with the Federal Banking Supervisory Authority in Berlin at an early stage of the structuring of the transaction.

A foreign (or a German) special purpose vehicle acting as issuer would not be subject to regulation by the German banking authorities because the *purchase* of loans or other financial assets does not constitute a banking activity subject to regulation by the Federal Banking Supervisory Authority. The German Banking Act makes clear that a banking license is required only for the *extension* of credits, not for the *purchase* of outstanding credits.

9.14.2 Securities regulation

There are no specific rules for the offer and sale of asset-backed securities in Germany. Such securities could be denominated in Deutsche Marks or a foreign currency; they could bear interest at a fixed or floating rate or could be issued as zero-coupon instruments. There are two regulatory issues, however, that deserve particular attention. First, under the German Prospectus Law of December 12, 1990, the issue of debt securities in Germany generally requires the preparation of a prospectus at the time of the launch of the offering, unless

(i) the issue is structured as a Euro-issue (which would require the use of an international syndicate),
(ii) the issue is privately placed with a limited number of investors in Germany, or

bankruptcy rules in several important respects. Most parts of the new Code will, however, not become effective until 1999 to give the bankruptcy courts time to adjust to the new rules.

9. It is difficult to understand this concern, as few assets are superior to the cash realized from securitization.

(iii) the minimum denomination (or the minimum purchase amount) of the securities is DM 80,000.

The second regulatory issue arises only if the securities are denominated in Deutsche Marks. The Bundesbank (the German Central Bank) issued guidelines for Deutsche Mark-denominated securities issues in July 1992. These guidelines require, among other things, that such securities be placed under the lead management of a German bank and that Deutsche-Mark denominated securities issued by foreign banks or other foreign issuers that engage in banking activities have a minimum maturity of two years. Because the foreign special purpose issuer of the asset-backed securities would not extend, but rather purchase, loans or receivables, it would not be deemed to engage in banking activities. The Bundesbank guidelines thus should not restrict the creation of an asset-backed Deutsche Mark commercial paper program. All issues of Deutsche Mark-denominated securities, however, would require certain notifications to the Bundesbank.

9.15 TAX ASPECTS

9.15.1 Taxation of the issuer

A foreign special purpose vehicle acting as the issuer of the asset-backed securities would not be subject to taxation in Germany unless it was managed from within Germany or had a permanent establishment, agent or representative in Germany. Such a vehicle should be located in a jurisdiction that imposes no or only negligible corporate income and other taxes and otherwise has a favorable regulatory climate. Jurisdictions that meet these criteria include the Cayman Islands, and, subject to certain qualifications, the Channel Islands (Jersey and Guernsey) and the Netherlands. There is a risk that the activities of the servicer could rise to the level of a permanent establishment of the issuer in Germany. The servicer's activities should be carefully structured in order to minimize this risk.

Use of a German company as the issuing vehicle raises several German tax issues that do not arise in the case of a foreign issuer. First, because a German company would be subject to German income tax, the transaction would have to be structured so as to avoid generating taxable income at the level of the company. Second, use of a German company as issuer in an asset-backed transaction would be feasible only if the business tax liability of the issuer could be avoided.[10] This could perhaps be accomplished by structuring the securities as non-recourse participation certificates (that is, by limiting the issuer's obligations under the securities to transferring to the investors those amounts which the issuer receives from the underlying assets). Such a non-recourse obligation would arguably not be a "debt" obligation for business tax purposes.

10. See footnote 7 *supra*.

Given the novelty of an asset-backed securities transaction in Germany, a tax ruling confirming this analysis should probably be obtained. This process could take several months.

9.15.2 Withholding tax

Payments in respect of the assets would not be subject to German withholding taxes, irrespective of the locations of the issuer of the securities and the trustee for the investors. Special rules would, however, apply to mortgage-backed securities and other securities secured on German real estate.

Interest payments on the asset-backed securities made in Germany to German investors, like interest payments on all debt securities, would be subject to the German interest withholding tax of 30 per cent. This tax applies irrespective of the location of the issuer and the currency of denomination of the securities.

9.15.3 Other tax considerations

A foreign trustee holding the assets (and any related collateral) for the benefit of the investors would not be subject to German taxation. No German VAT would be payable in respect of the assignment of the assets (and any related collateral) to the issuer and the trustee.

9.16 CREDIT ENHANCEMENT

The following approaches for credit enhancement could be considered:

(i) a partial guarantee may serve as a means of credit enhancement. Most German banks are active in the guarantee business. There are no legal restrictions on guarantees, but guarantees apply for capital ratio purposes and thus may be expensive. A limited guarantee by a foreign financial guarantee insurer or the seller of the assets would also be possible. In principle, the seller could guarantee a certain percentage of the assets or agree to repurchase delinquent assets, but such obligations could jeopardize the desired "off-balance-sheet" treatment of the assets.

(ii) the transaction could be structured as a multi-tranche issue involving a (rated) senior tranche and one or more (unrated) subordinated tranches. The repurchase of the subordinated tranche by the seller of the assets should not affect the characterization of the transaction as a "true" sale if structured properly.

(iii) back-up liquidity and other facilities could be used as a means of credit enhancement.

ROBERT BORDEAUX-GROULT
CHRISTOF VON DRYANDER

APPENDIX 1

LAW NO. 88–1201 OF 23 DECEMBER 1988 CONCERNING COLLECTIVE SECURITIES INVESTMENT VEHICLES AND CREATING FUNDS OF POOLED RECEIVABLES, AS AMENDED (EXCERPTS)

CHAPTER VI—COMMON PROVISIONS

Article 26

Units in funds of pooled receivables may not be held by the following organizations beyond a percentage fixed by decree:

— a *fonds commun de placement* whose management company is placed under the control (in the sense defined by Article 355–1 of Law no. 66–537 of July 24, 1966 mentioned above) of a credit institution which has transferred receivables to the fund;

— a SICAV whose corporate managers (*dirigeants sociaux*) and whose managers who have an employment contract are dependent on a credit institution which has transferred receivables to the fund.

CHAPTER VII—ON THE FUND OF POOLED RECEIVABLES

Article 34

The fund of pooled receivables shall be a coproprietorship (*copropriété*) whose sole purpose is the acquisition of receivables held by credit institutions, the Caisse des dépôts et consignations or insurance companies, and the issuance of units representing such receivables. The units of a fund of pooled receivables are issued in a single transaction.

The fund shall not have legal personality. The provisions of the Civil Code concerning certain jointly held property (*indivision*), as well as the provisions of Articles 1871 to 1873 of said Code, shall not apply to the fund.

The conditions under which the fund may acquire receivables after issuance of the units, and the rules governing the investment of monies which become temporarily available pending their allocation, shall be defined by decree. The fund may not borrow.

The units may give rise to different rights with respect to principal and interest.

The units shall be securities (*valeurs mobilières*). They cannot be redeemed by the fund at the request of the holders. The minimum amount of a unit issued by a fund of pooled receivables shall be established by decree.

The fund may not transfer the receivables that it acquires, except in the event of liquidation in accordance with conditions established by decree. It may not grant security interests in the receivables that it holds.

Transfer of the receivables shall be effected by the sole delivery of an assignment (*bordereau*), the terms of which shall be fixed by decree. The transfer shall take effect between the parties and be enforceable with respect to third parties as of the date affixed upon the assignment at the time of its delivery. Delivery of the assignment shall automatically entail transfer of the security interests guaranteeing each receivable, and the enforceability thereof with respect to third parties without the need for any other formality.

The debtor shall be informed by ordinary mail.

The transfer agreement may afford to the transferor rights on all or part of the surplus funds (*boni de liquidation*) after liquidation of the fund.

For all transctions carried out on behalf of the joint owners, the designation of the fund may validly be substituted for that of the joint owners.

Article 35

A document containing an assessment of the characteristics of the units which the fund is entitled to issue and the receivables which it proposes to acquire, and evaluating the risks that the latter present, shall be drafted by one of the entities listed by order of the Minister of the Economy, after consultation with the Commission des opérations de bourse. This document shall be annexed to the information memorandum and shall be communicated to the subscribers to the units.

Funds of pooled receivables may not be the subject of solicitation (*démarchage*).

Article 36

The transferring institution shall continue to ensure collection of the transferred receivables in accordance with the terms set forth in an agreement with the management company of the fund.

However, all or part of the collection may be delegated to a credit institution or the Caisse des dépôts et consignations, provided that the debtor shall be informed thereof by ordinary mail. For receivables arising after January 1, 1995, this option shall only exist on condition that the loan agreements include a clause which makes reference to the possibility of delegation of the collection.

Article 37

The fund of pooled receivables shall be established on the joint initiative of a company which shall be responsible for the fund's management, and a legal entity which shall be the depositary of the funds' assets.

The management company of the fund must be approved by the Commission des opérations de bourse, which may withdraw its approval pursuant to a reasoned decision.

The management company and the entity shall draft an information memorandum for the purpose of providing prior information to the subscribers about the transaction, in accordance with the terms of Articles 6 and 7 of Ordinance no. 67–833 of September 28, 1967 establishing a Commission des opérations de bourse and relating to information of securities holders and publicity for certain stock exchange transactions.

The nature and characteristics of the receivables which may be acquired by funds of pooled receivables and of the guarantees against risks of default on the part of the debtors in connection with such receivables shall be determined by decree.

[Article 38 omitted]

Article 39

Promoters of a fund of pooled receivables who shall have proceeded with placement of units in such fund without the consent of the management company of the fund or without the approval of the Commission des opérations de bourse shall be sanctioned by a fine of between FF. 100,000 and FF. 5 million, and between six months' and two years' imprisonment.

Article 40

I—[Deleted by Law No. 93–6, January 4, 1993, Article 32–IV]

II—The company referred to in Article 37 that is responsible for the management shall be a commercial company, the exclusive purpose of which shall be the management of funds of pooled receivables. It shall represent the fund *vis-à-vis* third parties and in all judicial proceedings whether as plaintiff or defendant.

III—The legal entity referred to in Article 37 that is the depository of the assets of the fund shall be a credit institution or any other entity approved by the Minister of the Economy. It must have its principal place of business in France. It shall be the depository of the receivables acquired by the fund and of [its] cash. It shall ensure the regularity of the decisions of the management company.

IV—The holders of the units shall be liable for the debts of the fund only to the extent of the fund's assets and in amounts proportional to their holdings.

V—The charter of the fund shall set forth the length of the fiscal year, which may not exceed 12 months. The first fiscal year, however, may have a longer duration, not exceeding 18 months.

Within six weeks following the end of each half fiscal year, the management company must take, for each of the funds that it manages, an inventory of the assets under the control of the depository.

VI—The statutory auditor (*commissaire aux comptes*) of the fund shall be appointed for a term of six fiscal years by the board of directors, manager or executive board of the management company after the approval of the Commission des opérations de bourse.

The provisions of Articles 218 to 222, 230, 231, 233, second and third paragraphs, 234 and 235 of Law No. 66–537 of July 24, 1966 cited above shall be applicable to the statutory auditor.

The statutory auditor shall inform the management of the management company, as well as the Commission des opérations de bourse, of any irregularity or inaccuracy that he discovers during the course of his duties.

Holders of units of the fund shall have the rights granted to shareholders by Articles 225 and 227 of Law No. 66–537 of July 24, 1966 cited above.

Article 41

Within six months following the extinguishment of the last receivable, the management company shall proceed to liquidate the fund.

[Article 42 omitted]

APPENDIX 2

DECREE NO. 89–158 OF 9 MARCH 1989 IMPLEMENTING ARTICLES 26 AND 34 TO 42 OF LAW NO. 88–1201 OF 23 DECEMBER 1988 AND CONCERNING FUNDS OF POOLED RECEIVABLES, AS AMENDED

Article 1

The percentage envisaged by Article 26 of the above-cited law [Law No. 88–1201 of December 23, 1988] shall be 5 per cent of the value of the units issued by the fund, as indicated in the last semi-annual report described in paragraph V of Article 40 of the above-cited law.

Within three weeks of the end of each semi-annual period, SICAVs and management companies of *fonds communs de placement* shall inform the management company of the fund of pooled receivables of the amount of units they hold.

The management company of the fund of pooled receivables shall disclose the percentage of units held by collective securities investment vehicles in the semi-annual report described in paragraph V of Article 40 of the above-cited law.

Article 2

The assignment (*bordereau*) envisaged by Article 34 of the above-cited law shall contain the following indications:

(1) the title "Transfer of Receivables";
(2) a statement that the transfer is subject to the provisions of Law No. 88–1201 of 23 December 1988 concerning collective securities investment vehicles and creating funds of pooled receivables;
(3) the name of the transferee;
(4) the name and characteristics of the transferred receivables, the identity of the debtors, the amount of the receivables, their date of final maturity or conditions of reimbursement in the event that such date is not set. If the transfer of the receivables is made by a computer procedure permitting their identification, the assignment may indicate only, in addition to the elements mentioned in (1), (2) and (3) above, the method by which the receivables are identified, their number and aggregate amount;
(5) a statement that the transfer entails the obligation for the transferor to take at the request of the transferee, all actions necessary for the preservation, possible modification, enforcement, release or foreclosure of the collateral security interests.

Article 3

The depositary is responsible for the safekeeping of the titles to the receivables transferred to the fund.

Article 4

The sums mentioned in the third paragraph of Article 34 of the above-cited law may be invested in:

- Treasury bills
- shares of SICAVs or units of *fonds communs de placement*, except *fonds communs de placement* governed by Articles 22 and 23 of the above-cited law;
- securities admitted to transactions on a regulated market, except units of funds of pooled receivables and securities giving direct or indirect access to a company's share capital.

The amount of these sums shall be limited in accordance with the conditions set by an order issued by the Minister of the Economy.

The charter of the fund shall specifically include rules governing the use of such sums.

Article 4 bis

For the sole purpose of balancing its incoming financial flows against its undertakings to make payments, the fund of pooled receivables may conclude interest rate exchange contracts with a credit institution, a company governed by the French Insurance Code or the Caisse des dépôts et consignations, or it may carry out purchase or sale transactions on regulated futures markets.

The charter of the fund shall make express mention of the rules governing such hedging transactions.

Article 5

The minimum amount of a unit of funds of pooled receivables upon issuance shall be FF 5,000.

Article 6

The receivables held by a fund of pooled receivables may be transferred, in whole and in a single transaction, if the amount of the residual assets of a fund falls below 10 per cent of the initial amount of the issue or if the fund has been unable to acquire receivables after issuance of the units in accordance with the provisions of the charter of the fund, and it is in the interest of the holders of the units to proceed with liquidation of the fund. The transfer is made in accordance with the terms set forth in Article 2 of this decree.

Article 7

The document described in Article 35 of the above-cited law shall be prepared prior to the issuance of units by the fund of pooled receivables. This document is required regardless of the nature or the characteristics of the receivables transferred. It shall indicate in particular the characteristics of the receivables transferred and of the units issued. It shall also indicate the nature and the scope of the guarantee attached to the issued units.

In the event that the charter of the fund provides for the acquisition of receivables after issuance of the units, this document should indicate that fact.

The entity which has drawn up the above-mentioned document shall monitor the level of security offered by the issued units. The results of such monitoring must be made public on a regular basis.

Article 8

The fund of pooled receivables may acquire only receivables of the same nature which are not *immobilisées*, *douteuses* or *litigieuses*. Payment of the principal amount of, and interest on, such receivables must be made in a single installment, or in several installments payable periodically or upon fixed dates, in a fixed minimum amount. These conditions for reimbursement must be agreed in advance in writing.

Article 8 bis

The charter of the fund shall make express mention of the rules governing acquisitions of receivables.

Receivables acquired by the fund of pooled receivables after issuance of the units must be of the same nature as those receivables initially acquired. The acquisition of receivables after issuance of the units must not entail any deterioration in the level of security offered to the holders of units.

The management company of the fund shall be responsible for ensuring that these conditions are adhered to.

Article 9

Risks of default of debtors in connection with receivables acquired by the fund of pooled receivables may be covered by:

— the obtention of a guarantee from a credit institution, a company governed by the French Insurance Code or the Caisse des dépôts et consignations, which may not defer payment of sums due to the fund;
— the issuance of specific units bearing the risk of default of debtors in connection with the receivables. These units may not be subscribed by collective securities investment vehicles or by individuals;
— the transfer to the fund of an amount of receivables which exceeds the amount of the issued units;
— the existence of adequate guarantees attaching to the acquired receivables.

The charter of the fund shall make express mention of the means of coverage against the risk of default by debtors in connection with transferred receivables.

Article 10

The information referred to in Article 45 of the above-mentioned law shall be communicated to the Banque de France by the management company of the fund of pooled receivables.

The management company must also communicate to the entity which drafted the document provided for in Article 35 of the above-mentioned law the documents which are necessary for monitoring the fund as mentioned under Article 7 of this decree.

Article 11

The Minister of Economy, Finance and Budget shall be responsible for the implementation of this decree, which shall be published in the *Journal officiel* of the French Republic.

CHAPTER 10

ACCOUNTING FOR ASSET SECURITIZATIONS

10.1 INTRODUCTION

Over the past several years there has been an incredible growth in the use of asset securitizations to raise capital for asset sales and financings. The securitization process changes the nature of assets into marketable securities that can be traded in the capital markets. Much of the popularity relates to the fact that these structures can produce a means to increase the gain on a sale, improve liquidity or lower the cost of financing. Additionally, a properly structured asset securitization can result in either sale or financing treatment for financial reporting purposes.

10.2 EXISTING GUIDANCE

The primary accounting guidance for asset securitizations is found in Statement of Financial Accounting Standards No. 77 (SFAS No. 77) *Reporting by Transferors for Transfers of Receivables with Recourse* and Financial Accounting Standard Board Technical Bulletin No. 85–2 (FTB 85–2) *Accounting for Collateralized Mortgage Obligations* (CMOs). This guidance provides the criteria to determine the proper accounting for asset securitizations under different structures. There is additional guidance presented by the Emerging Issues Task Force (EITF), which relates to specific application questions related to particular types of assets, such as credit card and other types of receivables.

The legal structure of a securitization transaction can result in different accounting treatments. Transactions that purport to be a sale look to SFAS No. 77 for accounting guidance. Transactions structured as financings are accounted for in accordance with FTB 85–2. It is imperative to properly structure the transaction at the beginning, in order to achieve the desired accounting treatment.

10.2.1 SFAS No. 77

SFAS No. 77 states that a transferor ordinarily should report a sale of receivables with recourse transaction as a sale if (a) the transferor surrenders its control of the future economic benefits relating to the receivables, (b) the transferor can reasonably estimate its obligation under the recourse provisions, and (c) the transferee cannot return the receivables to the transferor except pursuant to the recourse provisions. If those conditions do not exist, the amount of proceeds from the transfer should be reported as a liability.

SFAS No. 77 relates to transfers of receivables with recourse that *purport* to be sales of receivables. It also relates to participation agreements that provide for recourse, factoring agreements that provide for recourse, and sales or assignments with recourse of leases or property subject to leases that were accounted for as direct financing leases.

Under SFAS No. 77, receivables are removed from the balance sheet and the related gain or loss on the sales transaction is recognized in the income statement if all of the following criteria are met (SFAS No. 77, ¶5):

(a) *The transferor surrenders control of the future economic benefits embodied in the receivables.* Control has not been surrendered if the transferor has an option to repurchase the receivables at a later date.

(b) *The transferor's obligation under the recourse provisions can be reasonably estimated.* Lack of experience with receivables with characteristics similar to those being transferred or other factors that affect a determination at the transfer date of the collectibility of the receivables may impair the ability to make a reasonable estimate of the probable bad debt losses and related costs of collections and repossessions. A transfer of receivables shall not be recognized as a sale if collectibility of the receivables and related costs of collection and repossession are not subject to reasonable estimation.

(c) *The transferee cannot require the transferor to repurchase the receivables except pursuant to the recourse provisions.* If a transfer of a receivable qualifies for sale treatment, then the effect of all probable adjustments in connection with the recourse provisions must be estimated and recognized at the date of the transfer. *Per* SFAS No. 77 the gain or loss to be recognized is calculated as follows:

> "the difference between (a) the sales price (adjusted for the accrual for probable adjustments) and (b) the net receivables shall be recognized as a gain or loss on the sale of receivables. If receivables are sold with servicing retained and the stated servicing fee rate differs materially from a current (normal) servicing fee rate or no servicing fee is specified, the sale price shall be adjusted to provide for a normal servicing fee in each subsequent servicing period, which shall not be less than the estimated servicing costs."

If any of the above criteria are not met, then the assets shall not be removed from the balance sheet and the amount of proceeds received from the securitization shall be recorded as liability in the financial statements.

10.2.2 FTB 85–2

FTB 85–2 specifically addresses the accounting for bonds secured by mortgage loans as collateral, commonly referred to as Collateralized Mortgage Obligations (CMOs). FTB 85–2 states that "CMOs should be presumed to be borrowings that are reported as liabilities in the financial statements of the issuer unless all but a nominal portion of the future economic benefits inherent in the associated collateral have been irrevocably passed to the investor and no affiliate of the issuer can be required to make future payments with respect to the obligation". The FASB staff has indicated that FTB 85–2 should also be applied to other types of receivable transactions by analogy.

The bonds are typically issued by a minimally capitalized special purpose entity (issuer) established by the sponsoring parent entity. The mortgage collateral is acquired by the issuer and then pledged to an independent trustee until all obligations to the investor are met. The investor can look only to the assets in the trust (the mortgage loans) and insurers for repayment of the bonds. Accordingly, the sponsor has no continuing interest in the collateral, except that it may provide servicing of the loans for the investors.

The technical bulletin provides criteria that, if met, require sale treatment for financial reporting purposes. Sale treatment results in the elimination of the collateral and related liabilities from the balance sheet and recognition of a gain or loss in the income statement. *Per* FTB 85–2 the criteria are as follows:

(a) The issuer and its affiliates surrender the future economic benefits embodied in the collateral securing the obligation.

- (1) Neither the issuer nor its affiliates have the right or obligation to substitute collateral or obtain it by calling the obligation.
- (2) The expected residual interest, if any, in the collateral is nominal. In practice, the nominal amount of residual interest is considered to be in the range of 1% to 3% of the collateral amount.

(b) No affiliate of the issuer can be required to make any future payments with respect to the obligation.

- (1) The investor can look only to the issuer's assets or third parties (such as insurers or guarantors) for repayment of both principal and interest on the obligation and neither the sponsor of the issuer nor its other affiliates are secondarily liable.
- (2) Neither the issuer nor its affiliates can be required to redeem the obligation prior to its stated maturity other than through the normal pay-through of collections from the collateral.

FTB 85–2 goes on to say

"if the associated collateral is eliminated from the financial statements because all of the above conditions are met, any expected residual interest in the collateral should not be recognized as an asset. Rather, such residual interest should be recorded as it accrues to the benefit of the issuer or its affiliates. If servicing rights are retained by an affiliate of the issuer and the stated servicing fee rate is less than a current (normal) servicing fee rate, the CMO proceeds should be adjusted to provide for a normal servicing fee in each subsequent servicing period.

Additionally, "because a majority-owned entity formed to issue the CMO is merely a conduit for the sponsor, the financial statements of that entity should be consolidated with those of the sponsor".

The FTB also notes that it is not proper to offset the collateral amount against the amount of the bonds in the balance sheet of the issuer.

10.2.3 Special purpose entities

As noted above, many securitization transactions are carried out through bankruptcy remote special purpose entities (SPE). Historically, these SPEs have had little or no tangible equity. If the SPE is owned by the sponsor, the SPE should be consolidated.

In other cases the SPE may not be owned directly by the sponsor but by a not-for-profit entity or an employee of the investment banking firm handling the securitization. The Securities and Exchange Commission has indicated that to achieve non-consolidation and sale treatment of the assets to the SPE, the majority owners of the SPE must:

(a) be an independent third party.
(b) have made a substantive capital investment in the SPE, with substantive being at least 3% of the SPE's assets.
(c) have control of the SPE, and have the substantive risk and rewards of ownership of the assets of the SPE.

10.3 PROPOSED GUIDANCE

As a part of its financial instruments project, the Financial Accounting Standards Board (FASB) is currently addressing the subject of securitizations and other transfers of financial assets. The objective of the securitization project is to determine when financial assets should be considered sold and removed from the balance sheet and when the related revenues and expenses should be recognized.

The FASB is considering two basic approaches, the predominate-characteristics paradigm and the financial-components paradigm. The FASB has not reached a decision on which approach to adopt, although the FASB is currently focusing on the financial-components paradigm.

Under the predominate-characteristics paradigm, the objective is to determine what are the predominate characteristics of the transaction. The test is whether the transaction more resembles a financing or a sale and the accounting treatment follows, as entirely a sale or entirely a financing.

Under the financial-components paradigm, the objective is to determine the nature of the financial components of the transaction and to account for them individually. This approach requires that securitizations and other transfers of financial assets be treated as sales by the transferor and to record each remaining interest held in the transferred assets as its fair value, if the transferor has relinquished control over the beneficial rights to the assets. If the beneficial rights to the assets have not been relinquished, the transaction is recorded as a collateralized borrowing.

There are three criteria to be considered when determining whether a transaction should be recorded as a sale or a collateralized borrowing. These criteria are the transfer of control, continuing involvement by the seller and reliable measure of what is retained.

Control is deemed to have been relinquished if the assets have been *isolated* from the transferor. Isolation means that (a) neither the transferor nor its creditors have any ownership or security interest in the transferred assets (except for beneficial interests retained by the transferor) even if the transferor becomes bankrupt and the transferred assets are not part of the bankrupt estate and (b) the transferees have the unrestricted right to exchange or hold to maturity their beneficial interests in the transferred assets.

Continuing involvement includes holding beneficial interest in or incurring an obligation (e.g., recourse) with respect to the transferred assets. If there is no continuing involvement, the transferred assets are removed from the balance sheet of the transferor and the difference between the proceeds from the sale and the carrying amount of the assets is recognized in income.

If the transferor holds an interest in or incurs an obligation related to the transferred assets, that is, has continuing involvement, the transferor must next determine how to measure and record the continuing involvement. If the involvement cannot be reliably measured, two alternatives are being considered. One is to record a sale and to recognize the proceeds using the cost recovery method. The other alternative would recognize the transfer as a collateralized borrowing.

If the involvement can be reliably measured, then the FASB is considering three methods for recognizing the retained interest or obligation. The first, which is favored by the staff, would be to record the retained interest or obligation at its fair value and establish a new cost basis of accounting. The second method is to allocate the carrying value of the transferor's assets before the transfer between those interest and obligations sold and those held based on their relative fair value, consistent with historical cost accounting. The third alternative is to allocate the carrying value to assets held by the transferor based on the relative fair value and to measure obligations held by the transferor at fair value, consistent with historical cost accounting for assets.

The timing for this project is uncertain and the FASB has not projected a date for any Exposure Draft. If the FASB continues to support this project and the financial-components paradigm, it is probably safe to say that securitizations will survive as a financial technique but they will be much more difficult to analyze and the accounting for securitizations will be more complex and subjective than it is today.

10.4 UK GAAP

The Accounting Standards Board (ASB) has concluded deliberations regarding asset securitizations and has produced a paper setting forth their proposals. The paper requires that when an originator retains significant benefit or risk related to securitized assets, the assets should remain on the balance sheet and treated as a financing. Further, the ASB required that when the originator's benefit and risk is limited, a "linked presentation" should be utilized; whereby, the securitized assets would be shown on the face of the balance sheet, with the off-setting liabilities immediately underneath, to arrive at a net amount.

The "linked presentation" would only be used when the following criteria are met:

(a) the liabilities must finance a specific portfolio of mortgages (or other assets) and are secured by such assets;
(b) to the extent that the liabilities are to be shown deducted from the assets on the face of the balance sheet, both the investors and the issuers must have no recourse, either explicit or implicit, to the orignator for losses;
(c) the directors of the originator must state explicitly in each set of accounts where a linked presentation is used that it is not required to support any losses, nor does it intend to do so;
(d) the investors and the issuer must have agreed in writing that they will seek repayment of the liabilities only to the extent that sufficient funds are generated by the assets (or by an external credit enhancement) and they will not seek recourse to the originator in any form, such agreement being noted in each set of accounts where a linked presentation is used;
(e) if funds generated by the assets are insufficient to pay off the investors or any other of the issuer's creditors, this does not constitute an event of default for the originator;
(f) there is no provision, either in the securitization itself or otherwise, whereby the originator has either a right or an obligation to keep the securities assets upon repayment of the liabilities or to re-acquire them at any time.

10.4.1 Special purpose entities

Under UK GAAP, consolidation of an SPE would be evaluated based on the guidelines established to account for subsidiary undertakings (the Companies Act 1985 and Financial Reporting Standard No. 2 *Accounting for Subsidiary*

Undertakings). This guidance provides that subsidiary undertakings should be consolidated with its parent, except in certain scenarios. An undertaking is defined as a body corporate or partnership; or an un-incorporated association carrying on a trade or business with or without a view to profit.

A subsidiary undertaking is defined as a subsidiary undertaking of the parent undertaking, if the parent:

(a) holds a majority of the voting rights in the undertaking; or
(b) is a member of the undertaking and has the right to appoint/remove board members with the majority of votes at board meetings; or
(c) has the right to exercise a dominant influence over the undertaking by virtue of provisions contained in the undertaking's memorandum or articles or a written control contract (regardless of whether any shares are held); or
(d) is a member of the undertaking and controls, pursuant to an agreement with other members a majority of the voting rights in the undertaking; or
(e) has a participating interest in the undertaking and

    (i) either actually exercises a dominant influence over it, or
    (ii) the two undertakings are managed on a unified basis.

The Companies Act 1985 notes exceptions to preparing consolidated accounts when the company:

(a) is a subsidiary undertaking of another undertaking established under the law of a Member State of the European Community (subject to satisfaction of various regulatory requirements); or
(b) heads a small or medium-sized group (as defined) which contains no public company, banking or insurance company, or any company authorized under the Financial Services Act.

Additionally, the Companies Act 1985 contains a list of circumstances under which it is considered appropriate not to consolidate particular subsidiaries. Subsidiary undertakings are permitted to be excluded from the group accounts where:

(a) significant long-term restrictions substantially hinder the exercise of the rights of the reporting company over the assets or management of the undertaking. The rights referred to are those by reason of which the company would not be the parent company;
(b) the undertaking is held exclusively for resale and has not previously been consolidated; or
(c) the information necessary for the preparation of group accounts cannot be obtained without disproportionate expense or undue delay; or

(d) the activities of the undertaking are so different from those of the other undertakings in the group that its inclusion in the consolidation would be incompatible with the overriding requirement to give a true and fair view.

JAMES ROUNDTREE

CHAPTER 11

U.S. FEDERAL INCOME TAXATION OF MORTGAGE-BACKED SECURITIES[1]

11.1 DISTINGUISHING CHARACTERISTICS OF MORTGAGE-BACKED SECURITIES

The subject of this chapter is the U.S. federal income taxation of mortgage-backed securities. The enactment of the Tax Reform Act of 1986 (TRA 1986) was a watershed event in this area. TRA 1986 gave birth to a new scheme for taxing pools of mortgages that qualify as real estate mortgage investment conduits or REMICS and the holders of REMIC securities. The legislation also changed the treatment of discount on non-REMIC mortgage-backed securities to take account of the unusual payment characteristics of those securities. The REMIC rules have had the effect of increasing greatly the variety of mortgage-backed securities that are routinely issued to include many that would have been considered fanciful in 1986.

This chapter is concerned primarily with mortgage-backed securities that are supported exclusively (or almost so) by (1) payments made on a fixed pool of mortgages, or (2) payments made on a fixed pool of mortgages together with earnings from the reinvestment of those payments over a short period (generally not more than six months). Typically, these securities have two payment features that distinguish them economically from conventional publicly held debt obligations: their principal amount (if any) is payable in installments and they are subject to mandatory calls to the extent the mortgages that fund them are prepaid.

Some mortgage-backed securities are further distinguishable from conventional, callable bonds by the fact that their value is attributable largely or entirely to rights to a fixed or variable share of the interest on mortgages. These securities are issued at a very high premium over their principal amount (which may be zero). Because the unamortized premium is forfeited if the securities are prepaid, holders of such securities may experience a zero or negative rate of return, even in the absence of defaults. The highly contingent nature of these securities poses a problem for any system that seeks to measure periodic income and loss.

1. See n.28.

In terms of tax attributes, mortgage-backed securities may differ from conventional debt instruments in two other respects. First, in the hands of institutional investors, mortgage-backed securities may qualify for certain tax benefits associated with investments in real property mortgages. Second, certain types of mortgage-backed securities are treated for tax purposes as ownership interests in the underlying mortgages rather than as equity or debt of the issuing entity. This "look-through" feature raises a host of tax issues.

The federal income tax questions peculiar to mortgage-backed securities relate primarily to the features described above, the legal structures that are used in transforming whole mortgages into non-REMIC mortgage-backed securities and the REMIC rules.

This chapter addresses only federal tax issues. Readers are cautioned that while the state or local income or franchise tax consequences of issuing, investing in or sponsoring mortgage-backed securities often mirror the federal consequences, there can be material differences.[2]

11.2 TYPES OF MORTGAGE-BACKED SECURITIES

11.2.1 Introduction

The principal types of mortgage-backed securities currently available are pass-through certificates, pay-through bonds, equity interests in issuers of pay-through bonds, and REMIC interests. REMIC interests are either regular interests (which from a tax perspective resemble pay-through bonds) or residual interests (which from a tax perspective resemble equity interests in issuers of pay-through bonds that are taxed as partnerships).

These securities have two common features: first, they can be used, alone or in combination, to repackage whole mortgages in a manner that increases their attractiveness as investments, and second, the issuers of the securities generally are not subject to tax on the income from the underlying mortgages as it passes through their hands to investors.

It would not be economical to issue a mortgage-backed security unless it were possible to eliminate all material incremental taxes on the issuer. Thus, it is not ordinarily feasible to issue mortgage-backed securities in the form of stock of a corporation. The income from mortgages held by the corporation would bear the full weight of the corporate income tax because no offsetting deductions would be allowed in computing the corporation's taxable income for dividends paid on the stock.

The various types of mortgage-backed securities that are currently available address the problem of issuer level taxes in different ways. Pass-through

2. Many states have adopted whole or partial tax exemptions for entities that qualify as REMICs under federal law. A list of these exemptions may be found in J. Peaslee & D. Nirenberg, *Federal Income Taxation of Mortgage-Backed Securities* (rev. ed. 1994, Probus Publishing) (hereinafter "Peaslee & Nirenberg"), Appendix B.

certificates are generally issued by a grantor trust, which is not considered to be a taxable entity; indeed, for almost all federal income tax purposes, the trust is simply ignored. Issuers of pay-through bonds, or the owners of such issuers, are generally subject to income tax on the taxable income from the mortgages supporting the bonds (which is gross income less deductions), but the burden of that tax typically is small because of the interest deductions allowed for interest on the bonds. A REMIC is exempt from tax by statute (except for certain penalty taxes).

The ability of a non-REMIC issuer of pay-through bonds to avoid an issuer-level income tax changed dramatically at the beginning of 1992, when special tax rules governing taxable mortgage pools or TMPs became effective. These rules automatically classify as a corporation any trust, partnership, or other entity if at least 80 per cent of its assets are debt obligations, more than half of those obligations are real estate mortgages, and the entity issues two or more classes of pay-through bonds with different maturities. A TMP is, with limited exceptions, subject to corporate tax on its taxable income and cannot join in a consolidated return with other corporations. In most, although not all, cases, it would be economically unfeasible for an entity to issue pay-through bonds if it would as a result become a TMP. The TMP rules were enacted as an adjunct to the 1986 REMIC legislation to ensure that, after a five-year transition period, REMICs (which are subject to certain tax avoidance rules) would be the exclusive means of issuing multiple class mortgage-backed securities without an issuer level tax.[3]

Sections 11.2.2 through 11.2.5 describe more fully pass-through certificates, pay-through bonds, equity interests in issuers of pay-through bonds, and REMIC interests. Although REMIC interests may take the form of pass-through certificates, pay-through bonds, or equity interests, except where otherwise indicated, these terms will be used in this chapter to refer only to securities not subject to the REMIC rules.

Ordinarily, the mortgages underlying mortgage-backed securities are not in default when the securities are issued, and either are expected to produce only modest default losses or are guaranteed or insured against loss by third parties. The discussion in Sections 11.2.2 through 11.2.5 below relates only to securities of this type.[4]

Most of the mortgage-backed securities that are issued today take the form of pass-through certificates or REMIC interests. Nonetheless, a discussion of pay-through bonds, and equity interests in issuers of such bonds, continues to be relevant for three principal reasons. First, REMICs were patterned after (and designed to improve on) pre-1992 owner trusts that issued pay-through bonds. Some knowledge of these predecessor securities is helpful in understanding the REMIC rules. Second, entities holding mortgages and issuing pay-through

3. TMPs are more fully discussed in Peaslee & Nirenberg, *supra*, n.2, Chapter 3, part D.

4. Issues arising in the securitization of financially troubled mortgages are discussed in Peaslee & Nirenberg, *supra*, n.2.

bonds may not be TMPs, either because they issue only a single class of debt, or because the mortgages are financially troubled. (The TMP rules contain an exception for entities formed to liquidate distressed loans.) Last, techniques developed in the mortgage area are being used to finance automobile loans and other non-mortgage receivables. While issuers without real property mortgages cannot take advantage of the REMIC rules, they also are not TMPs.[5]

Section 11.2.6 considers another type of trust security that takes the form of a pass-through certificate but has the economic characteristics of debt of the issuing trust. These securities will be referred to as "pass-through debt certificates". They have been issued almost exclusively by trusts holding automobile loans or credit card or other non-mortgage receivables, but in special cases the structure could have applications for mortgages. Moreover, the tax analysis of the certificates provides an interesting contrast to the analysis of more conventional types of asset-backed securities.

11.2.2 Pass-through certificates

General

In their most common form, pass-through certificates are issued by a trust or custodial arrangement that holds a fixed pool of mortgages. The mortgages may bear interest at a fixed or adjustable rate. The arrangement is created by a sponsor that transfers the mortgages to the trust against receipt of the certificates and then, typically, sells all or a portion of the certificates to investors. The certificates evidence ownership by the holders of specified interests in the assets of the trust.

To avoid an entity level tax, the trust must be classified as a trust for tax purposes and not as an association taxable as a corporation. Trust classification can be achieved only if the trust has, with a limited exception, a single class of ownership interests, and the power under the trust agreement to change the composition of the mortgage pool or otherwise to reinvest mortgage payments is severely restricted. (The exception to the single-class-of-ownership requirement allows stripped certificates and senior and subordinated certificates, as described below.)[6]

Given these tax constraints, pass-through certificates are generally issued in a single class, with each holder having a pro rata interest in the mortgage pool.

5. A bill was introduced in Congress in 1993 that would create a new vehicle for issuing securities backed by non-mortgage receivables. See H.R. 2065 (introduced May 11, 1993) (providing for the creation of Financial Asset Securitization Investment Trusts, or FASITs). See also American Bar Association, Tax Section, Committee on Financial Transactions, "Legislative Proposal to Expand the REMIC Provisions of the Code to Include Nonmortgage Assets", 46 *Tax Law Review* 299 (Spring 1991). Further, certain municipal bond dealers have proposed the establishment of a new vehicle, a Tax Exempt Municipal Investment Conduit (TEMIC). See "Draft of TEMIC Legislation Available", 94 *Tax Notes Today* 4–64 (January 6, 1994).

6. For a more detailed discussion of the requirements for classification of a trust as a grantor trust,

Thus, if 1,000 such certificates are issued, each would represent a right to 1/1,000 of each payment of principal and interest on each mortgage in the pool. Mortgage payments received by the trustee are passed through to certificate holders, generally monthly in parallel with the receipt of mortgage payments by the trust. The distributions are reduced by fees for mortgage servicing, pool administration, and any applicable guarantees or pool insurance. These fees generally are fixed in advance over the life of the pool so that certificate holders can be guaranteed a specified "pass-through rate" of interest on the principal balance of the certificates, representing the earnings on the mortgages after deduction of such fees. Depending on the mortgages in the pool and the fees charged, the pass-through rate may be fixed or variable.

A trust that issues pass-through certificates and is classified as a trust is taxed under the grantor trust rules set forth in section 671. (Unless otherwise specified, references herein to sections are to the Internal Revenue Code of 1986 (Code)). Consequently, for federal income tax purposes, the trust is effectively ignored and certificate holders are recognized as the owners of the mortgages held by the trust.

One consequence of disregarding the separate existence of a pass-through trust is that certificate holders who report taxable income under a cash method of accounting (which is true of virtually all holders who are individuals) must report income for tax purposes based on the timing of receipts of mortgage payments by the trust, *not* on the timing of distributions made to them by the trust. The trustee is viewed as an agent collecting mortgage payments on the certificate holders' behalf. While certificate holders are obliged to include in income the gross amount of interest on the mortgages, they are allowed deductions (subject to special limitations in the case of individuals) for mortgage servicing and other expenses paid out of such interest, again on the theory that those amounts are paid on their behalf. An individual certificate holder's deductions for servicing and other expenses may be limited under section 67, which provides that an individual is allowed certain miscellaneous itemized deductions (including deductions for investment expenses) only to the extent that the aggregate amount of such deductions exceeds 2 per cent of the individual's adjusted gross income. In addition, an individual is subject to an alternative minimum tax (AMT) at graduated rates up to 28 per cent of alternative minimum taxable income (AMTI) if such tax exceeds the individual's regular federal income tax liability. No deduction is allowed for investment expenses in computing an individual's AMTI.

Because pass-through certificate holders are treated as owning the assets of the issuing trust, certain special rules that apply to loans to individuals and real estate loans held by certain institutional investors would apply to the certificates.

---

see Peaslee & Nirenberg, *supra*, n.2, Chapter 3. The Treasury regulations that prevent multiple class trusts from being classified as trusts are known colloquially as the "Sears regulations".

Stripped pass-through certificates

Pass-through certificates may also represent, instead of a pro rata share of all payments on the underlying mortgages, a right to a fixed percentage of the principal payments and a different fixed percentage of the interest payments.[7] Such pass-through certificates are often referred to as "stripped mortgage-backed securities or stripped pass-through certificates". They are generally sold when there is a divergence of views regarding anticipated prepayment rates. The principal component of a mortgage, viewed in isolation without interest, is more valuable the earlier it is repaid. On the other hand, interest ceases when principal is repaid, so that the interest component of a mortgage, standing alone without principal, is more valuable the later the date on which principal is repaid. Thus, by varying the mix between principal and interest, the effect of prepayments on a class of pass-through certificates can be changed.

The earliest stripped pass-through certificates that were publicly available *reduced* the effect on investors of changes in prepayment speeds by transforming discount or premium mortgages into par securities. To illustrate this type of transaction, suppose that a thrift institution holds a pool of mortgages bearing interest at a rate of 10 per cent (net of servicing) at a time when the current market rate of interest for pass-through certificates is 8 per cent. If the thrift believes that investors will assume a higher prepayment rate, and thus would be willing to pay a smaller premium for a pro rata interest in the mortgages than the thrift thinks is appropriate, the thrift could keep the premium, and insulate investors from the risk of a reduction in yield resulting from prepayments, by retaining a right to ⅕ of each interest payment on the mortgages and selling pass-through certificates at par with an 8 per cent pass-through rate.

Sometimes, rather than retaining a portion of interest on the loans, the sponsor charges a fee for servicing the mortgage loans (an "excess servicing" fee) that has the same effect. Excess servicing is typically characterized as an ownership interest in the mortgages for federal income tax purposes.

Similarly, if the thrift held discount mortgages and wished to sell pass-through certificates at par based on those mortgages, it could accomplish its objective by allocating to the certificates all of the interest payments but only a fraction of the principal payments.

Stripped pass-through certificates have also been created that *increase* the effect on *all* investors of variations in prepayment speeds by creating greater discounts and premiums than are inherent in the underlying mortgages. At the extreme, there is a complete separation in the ownership of rights to interest and principal. In a typical transaction, mortgages are transferred to a trust in exchange for two classes of certificates. One class (referred to as "PO Strips") represents the right to receive 100 per cent of each principal payment on the

7. In general, these percentages must be set at the time of issuance of the certificates and may not be changed subsequently. Otherwise, the trust issuing the certificates would be considered an association taxable as a corporation and would be subject to an entity-level tax.

mortgages. The other class ("IO Strips") represents the right to receive 100 per cent of each interest payment. PO Strips, which are similar to zero coupon bonds payable in installments, are issued at a substantial discount and are purchased by investors who expect a high rate of prepayments compared with the market as a whole, or who wish to hedge against a risk of loss from declining interest rates. (Declining interest rates generally increase prepayments and thus increase the value of PO Strips.) IO Strips, which are issued with what amounts to an infinite premium, are purchased by investors who expect a low rate of prepayments or who wish to hedge against a risk of loss from rising interest rates.

Senior/subordinated pass-through certificates

Pass-through certificates typically provide for some type of credit support that protects investors from defaults or delinquencies in payments on the underlying mortgages. The credit support may take the form of a guarantee, insurance policy, or other agreement by the sponsor or a third party to replace defaulted or delinquent payments or purchase defaulted or delinquent loans. Credit support can also be provided in whole or in part by creating senior and subordinated classes of pass-through certificates. Mortgage defaults or delinquencies are charged first against distributions that otherwise would be made on the subordinated class until they are exhausted, thereby protecting the senior class. Additional credit support may be provided through a reserve fund that is funded initially either with cash provided by the sponsor or with monies diverted from the subordinated class during the early years of the pool. It is common practice to require that any reserve fund be held outside of the trust as security for a limited recourse guarantee of the mortgages, to avoid possible classification of the trust as an association taxable as a corporation. For the same reason, it was also common practice before 1992 to restrict the transfer of subordinated certificates by the trust sponsor. This concern was eliminated by an IRS ruling.

11.2.3 Pay-through bonds

Unlike pass-through certificates, which represent an ownership interest in mortgages, a pay-through bond is a debt obligation of a legal entity that is collateralized by mortgages (or interests in mortgages). A holder is considered to own the bond, but not an interest in the underlying mortgages, in the same way that the holder of a public utility bond, for example, would be considered the owner of the bond but not of the power generating station that secures it. Although the payment terms of a pay-through bond and of the underlying mortgage collateral are not identical, the relationship between them may be quite close. In most cases, the mortgages, and earnings from the reinvestment of mortgage payments over a short period, are expected to be the sole funding source for payments on the bonds, and mortgage prepayments are "paid through", in whole or in part, to bondholders in the form of mandatory calls on the bonds.

A collateralized mortgage obligation (CMO) is a type of pay-through bond which is divided into classes. As described further below, these classes typically have different maturities and payment priorities. Most often, CMOs are issued by a special purpose entity organized by a sponsor. The entity is typically an owner trust or corporation, although a partnership or possibly even a limited liability company could be used. As further described below, owner trusts and other non-corporate issuers of pay-through bonds may be classified as corporations for tax purposes under the TMP rules if they issue bonds after 1991.

Where the issuer is an owner trust, the trust is established pursuant to a trust agreement between the sponsor and an independent trustee, acting as owner trustee. The owner trustee is usually a commercial bank. In most transactions, the sponsor initially transfers a nominal amount of cash to the owner trustee against the receipt of certificates representing the equity or ownership interest in the owner trust. When the CMOs are issued, the mortgage collateral is transferred to the owner trustee in exchange for the net proceeds of the CMOs plus any additional cash equity contribution that may be made to the owner trust, either by the sponsor or by other investors in exchange for new ownership certificates. The sponsor may retain its certificates or sell all or a portion of them to others. The owner trustee pledges the mortgage collateral to another commercial bank acting as bond trustee on behalf of the holders of the CMOs under a bond indenture. Over the life of the CMOs, the bond trustee collects payments on the collateral, reinvests those payments over a short period, makes payments on the CMOs, pays expenses, and remits any excess to the owner trustee, which distributes such excess (after paying or providing for expenses) to the owners of the equity of the owner trust. Equity interests in issuers of pay-through bonds are discussed further below.

If the issuer of CMOs is not an owner trust, the structure is substantially the same, with the issuer and the owners of its equity replacing the owner trustee and the beneficiaries of the trust. The federal income tax treatment of the holders of CMOs is not generally affected by whether the issuer is classified as a corporation, trust or partnership.

CMOs are a more recent innovation than pass-through certificates. They are similar to pass-through certificates in that they are funded primarily out of payments received on a fixed pool of mortgages or interests in mortgages and, as a group, closely resemble those mortgages or interests in terms of the timing and amounts of payments. Unlike pass-through certificates, however, CMOs are typically divided into classes that have different maturities and different priorities for the receipt of principal, and, in some cases, interest. Most often, there are "fast-pay" and "slow-pay" classes. Thus, all principal payments (including prepayments) may be made first to the class having the earliest stated maturity date until it is retired, then to the class with the next earliest maturity date until it is retired, and so on. Alternatively, principal payments may be allocated among classes to ensure to the extent possible that designated classes receive principal payments according to a fixed schedule. Under that arrangement, the greater stability in the timing of payments on the designated classes (often called "planned amortization class" or "PAC bonds") would be balanced by greater variability in the timing of payments on the remaining classes (often called "support classes"). Payment priorities may also change (either temporarily or permanently) based on the occurrence of some triggering event (such as interest rates reaching a certain level). Classes of this type are known colloquially as "nonsticky jump classes" (where changes in priorities are temporary) and "sticky jump classes" (where changes are permanent). Another common feature of CMOs is an interest accrual or compound interest class that receives no interest or principal payments until all prior classes have been fully retired. Until that time, the interest that accrues on an interest accrual class is added to its principal balance and a corresponding amount is paid as additional principal on prior classes. When CMOs were first issued, there was typically only one interest accrual class which was the class with the latest stated maturity date. It supported all prior classes. Because the different classes of CMOs were typically denominated by letters indicating payment priority, accrual bonds became known as "Z bonds". More recently, issues of CMOs have included classes of Z bonds that are inserted between other classes of bonds with shorter and longer terms, and accrual classes that support (colloquially, are local to) only certain designated prior classes.

Three other differences between CMOs and pass-through certificates are worth noting. First, CMOs may bear interest at a floating rate (a rate that varies directly, or in some cases inversely, with an index or market rates of interest, such as LIBOR), even though interest is paid on the mortgage collateral at a fixed rate. Second, CMOs generally provide for quarterly payments, with the issuer being responsible for reinvesting monthly receipts on the mortgages until the next CMO payment date. Finally, CMOs are usually callable at the option of the issuer at a time when a material amount of CMOs remain outstanding, so that the issuer can potentially benefit from increases in the value of the collateral by selling the collateral and retiring the CMOs.

Tax considerations dictated the original choice of pay-through bonds over pass-through certificates as the vehicle for creating mortgage-backed securities with different maturities or a floating interest rate not related to the mortgage collateral. If a typical non-REMIC pass-through trust issued multiple classes of pass-through certificates (that is, ownership interests in the trust) having either of these features, then it is likely that the trust would be classified as an association taxable as a corporation and the certificates would be treated as stock. As a result, the trust would be subject to corporate income tax on the gross income from the mortgages it holds with no deduction for "dividends" paid to certificate holders. An issuer of pay-through bonds, or its owners, may also be subject to corporate income tax on the taxable income of the issuer.

However, because pay-through bonds are recognized for tax purposes to be debt of the issuer, deductions are allowed for interest on the bonds.

The status of pay-through bonds as debt obligations of the issuer rather than ownership interests in the underlying mortgages has other tax consequences. For example, holders are taxed based on the payments they are entitled to receive on the bonds rather than on the payments received by the issuer on the underlying mortgages.

11.2.4 Equity interests in issuers of pay-through bonds

It will be helpful to consider separately the economic and tax-related features of equity interests in issuers of pay-through bonds.

Economic features

Where an issuer of debt has assets that produce uncertain cash flows and debt with a fixed payment schedule, substantial equity is needed to fill in the gap and provide assurance to creditors that they will be paid. By contrast, virtually no equity would be needed by an issuer of pay-through bonds to protect bond holders if the bonds provided for payments matching in the aggregate the payments (including prepayments) to be made on the underlying mortgages, and that collateral was essentially risk free from a credit standpoint (for example, because it benefits from a GNMA, FNMA, or FHLMC guarantee). A dollar-for-dollar matching of payments on assets and liabilities could be achieved without giving the bonds "equity features" since the underlying assets are themselves debt instruments.

Unfortunately, the most efficient economic result is not generally achievable for tax reasons. An issuer that was a pure conduit would run a material risk of losing deductions for interest it pays on its bonds, on the ground that the bonds should be recharacterized for tax purposes as disguised ownership interests in the issuer or in a separate corporation holding the collateral.

Although there are no hard and fast rules and opinions differ, most tax counsel would consider the following combination of factors sufficient to conclude that a typical issue of CMOs backed by GNMA, FNMA, or FHLMC pass-through certificates will be recognized to be debt for tax purposes:

(1) the regular interval between payments on the bonds is not less than three months and monthly mortgage payments are reinvested until needed to make payments on the bonds in money market instruments earning interest at a current market rate at the time they are purchased,

(2) the issuer has a right to call the bonds at a price of 100 per cent of their principal amount when the total outstanding principal amount of bonds has been reduced to approximately 20 per cent of the original aggregate principal amount of all bonds, and

(3) the cash payments available to be distributed to the equity owners, determined based on reasonable assumptions as to reinvestment rates, expenses, and mortgage prepayments, have a present value at the time of issuance of the bonds, calculated using as the discount rate the highest initial yield of any class of bonds, of between one and two per cent of the aggregate issue price of all of the bonds.

If these tests are met, tax counsel typically would not insist on any minimum initial balance sheet equity or rights to substitute mortgage collateral.

An issuer that has these features will produce some surplus cash that is available for distribution on the equity interests. The cash would be attributable to the spreads between the rates of interest on the mortgages and on one or more classes of bonds, reinvestment income that exceeds the amounts assumed in sizing the issue of bonds, gain resulting from the exercise of rights to call the bonds, and any excess of budgeted over actual administrative expenses.

Tax features

The taxes imposed with respect to an equity interest in an issuer of pay-through bonds will depend on the amount and timing of the issuer's taxable income, the tax classification of the issuer (whether it is a corporation, partnership or trust) and the circumstances of the equity owners.

Any equity interest can be expected to generate taxable income equaling the economic income from the investment based on the actual or anticipated cash distributions thereon. Issuers of pay-through bonds may also produce taxable income that is non-economic in the sense that it will always be reversed through subsequent losses. Such income, which is commonly referred to as "phantom income", generally arises when pay-through bonds are divided into different classes with staggered maturities, and the longer-term classes have higher yields than the shorter-term classes. Phantom income is discussed in greater detail in 11.4.5 below.

If the issuer of an equity interest is classified for tax purposes as a partnership or trust, then it is not itself subject to tax; instead, its taxable income is allocated among the equity owners in accordance with their respective interests. Such income is taxable to them regardless of the cash distributions they receive. The ultimate tax burden depends on the circumstances of the owners (e.g., whether they have offsetting losses or tax credits).

The result is quite different where an issuer is a corporation (or classified as a corporation). A corporation is subject to the corporate income tax on its taxable income. Unless a corporation is a member of an affiliated group of corporations filing a consolidated return, losses or credits of shareholders cannot be used to reduce the corporation's tax bill. A corporation can join in a federal consolidated return with other corporations only if other group members own at least 80 per cent of its stock, measured by voting power and value (but disregarding certain non-voting, non-participating preferred stock). However,

TMPs must file separate returns. In the absence of tax consolidation, earnings of a corporation are potentially subject to a second layer of taxation when they are distributed to shareholders. The additional shareholder taxes would be reduced by the dividends received deduction in the case of distributions made to corporations. They may also be reduced by tax losses of credits available to the shareholders.

11.2.5 REMICs

As the prior discussion indicates, a grantor trust cannot issue pass-through certificates that are divided into multiple classes with staggered maturities. Also, pay-through bonds cannot be created that provide for payments, in the aggregate, that precisely mirror the payments on a fixed pool of mortgage collateral. Thus, certain securities that are attractive economically cannot be issued as either pass-through certificates or pay-through bonds, because they have a class structure inconsistent with the grantor trust rules and match the underlying mortgages too closely to be recognized for tax purposes as debt. Moreover, even if a security could be issued as a pay-through bond, compared with an ownership interest in mortgages, debt often has financial accounting disadvantages (the need to show the debt on someone's balance sheet) and tax disadvantages for certain institutional investors (the debt is not considered a real property loan). Finally, holders of equity interests in issuers of pay-through bonds may realize phantom income.

To address some of these concerns, TRA 1986 enacted the REMIC rules (sections 860A through 860G). These rules treat a pool of mortgages that meets certain requirements (relating to, among other things, the composition of its assets and the payment terms of the securities issued) as a REMIC if an appropriate election is made, and state how the REMIC and the holders of interests therein will be taxed.[8]

The REMIC rules are applied to a pool of mortgages and related securities based on their functional characteristics, without regard to legal form. Thus, a REMIC may be a state law trust, corporation, or partnership, or simply a segregated pool of mortgages that is not a separate legal entity. Similarly, REMIC interests may be evidenced by ownership certificates, debt instruments, stock, partnership interests, or a contractual right to receive payments. The functional approach of the REMIC rules allows the state law legal form of a REMIC and the interests therein to be structured to best achieve financial accounting and other non-tax objectives.

By statute, a REMIC is not subject to an entity level tax (except for certain penalty taxes). Instead, the income from its assets is allocated among the holders of REMIC interests. All of the interests in a REMIC must be either regular interests or residual interests, as those terms are defined in the REMIC rules.

8. The discussion below in the text provides only a brief overview of the REMIC rules, which are described in detail in Peaslee & Nirenberg, *supra*, n.2, Chapters 4–5.

There is no required number of classes of regular interests. By contrast, a REMIC must have one (and only one) class of residual interests. In general, regular interests resemble conventional debt in that they must have a specified principal amount and interest thereon (if any) must be based on a fixed or floating rate. A regular interest may also entitle the holder to a non-varying "specified portion" of the interest payments on underlying mortgages, with or without some additional claim to principal. There are no similar limitations on the economic characteristics of residual interests. Credit losses may be allocated in any way that is desired among different classes of REMIC interests. Further, a REMIC can hold assets in a credit or expense reserve fund.

The income of a REMIC is allocated among the different classes of interests as follows. The income of holders of each class of regular interests is determined as if those interests were debt of the REMIC. The holders of the residual interest are allocated all income of the REMIC, determined as if it were a taxable entity but reduced by the interest deductions that would be allowed to the REMIC if the regular interests were debt.

The allocation of income among REMIC interests is similar to the allocation that would be made if the REMIC were an owner trust taxed as a partnership and the regular interests and residual interests were pay-through bonds and equity interests in the trust, respectively. However, there are important differences between REMICs and owner trusts. First, as previously noted, there is no requirement that a REMIC or REMIC interests take any particular legal form. Second, the characterization of regular interests as debt of a REMIC follows directly from the statute, and there is no requirement that a REMIC have any minimum equity value or that the payments on regular interests and the underlying mortgages be mismatched. In addition, for purposes of determining the taxation of the sponsor of a REMIC and the status of regular interests as real property loans in the hands of institutional holders, regular interests are treated as ownership interests in the underlying mortgages rather than as debt.

While the REMIC rules represent a significant step forward in the tax law governing mortgage-backed securities, they are not the answer to every prayer. The REMIC rules were created primarily to permit the issuance of multiple class pass-through certificates. They achieve that goal, but do little more. The REMIC rules do not, for example, offer much relief from the restrictions on management powers that apply to grantor trusts. The permitted activities of a REMIC are limited, in much the same manner as a grantor trust, to holding a fixed pool of mortgages and distributing payments currently to investors. Indeed, in some respects (particularly in disposing of assets), a REMIC has even less freedom of action than a grantor trust. Another significant problem with the taxation of non-REMIC mortgage-backed securities—the phantom income that is recognized by issuers, or the owners of issuers, of certain pay-through bonds—also is not resolved by the REMIC rules. Indeed, they make it worse. Where a REMIC issues multiple classes of regular interests with staggered maturities, phantom income is realized by residual interest holders in much the same manner as if they held equity interests in an owner trust and the regular interests were pay-through bonds. However, the REMIC residual holders must contend with certain anti-tax avoidance rules that do not apply to owner trusts. As explained in 11.2.1, the TMP rules were adopted largely to prevent taxpayers from choosing owner trusts over REMICs in order to achieve more favorable treatment of holders of equity interests.

11.2.6 Pass-through certificates taxable as debt

Description of structure

Ordinarily, non-REMIC trusts issue one of two types of interests: pass-through certificates that are treated for tax purposes as ownership interests in the assets of the trust, or debt instruments that are recognized for those purposes to be debt of the trust. Trusts formed to hold automobile, credit card, and other non-mortgage receivables have issued to investors a third type of interest that takes the *form* of a pass-through certificate but represents *economically* debt of the issuing trust. These certificates are referred to here as "pass-through debt certificates". Pass-through debt certificates are cast as ownership interests notwithstanding their economic similarity to debt so the sponsor can characterize the sale of the certificates as a sale of trust assets rather than a borrowing for financial accounting or other non-tax purposes.

In a typical transaction, the payments due on pass-through debt certificates are not tied directly to payments made on any identified fixed pool of receivables,[9] and the trust is not fully protected against the risk of delinquencies and defaults on the receivables it holds. Sometimes, floating rate pass-through certificates are issued that are backed by fixed rate receivables. The trust is able to make required payments on the certificates despite the mismatching of receipts and payments and delinquency or default losses because the amount of certificates it issues is significantly smaller than the amount of trust assets. In other words, there is, to use a debt term, substantial overcollateralization. The residual interest in the trust (that is, the right to all assets remaining after making payments on the certificates) is retained by the trust sponsor.

Tax analysis

The federal income tax analysis of pass-through debt certificates is somewhat complex. In most transactions, it is very clear that the certificates are debt (either of the issuing trust or of the sponsor) except in name. Where that is true, the certificates should be taxed as debt (and not as ownership interests in the trust), at least if the certificates are consistently treated as debt for tax purposes by the

9. To bridge gaps between the timing of receipts and payments, the trust may have a right to reinvest payments until they are needed to make payments on the certificates. In addition, the trust sponsor may have the right to add new receivables to the trust or to substitute new receivables for old ones.

trust and the holders of interests in the trust. Nonetheless, in some cases this conclusion is open to potential challenge by the Internal Revenue Service ("the Service") on the ground that the parties to a transaction should be bound by their choice of form.

If in a particular case pass-through debt certificates were characterized for tax purposes as ownership interests in the issuing trust, the trust would not be classified as a trust (because it would have multiple ownership classes). Instead, it would be classified either as an association taxable as a corporation or as a partnership, depending on the terms of the trust and its interests. In the transactions where issuers are not able to conclude with a high degree of confidence that the debt characterization of the pass-through debt certificates will withstand challenge, steps are taken to ensure that if the debt argument fails, the trust will be classified as a partnership.

As a partnership, the trust itself would not be subject to tax. Instead, the sponsor and certificate holders would be treated as partners and would be required to include in income their distributive shares of the income of the trust. It is likely that each certificate holder's share would approximately equal the interest income such holder would have reported had the certificates been classified as debt. As a result, most U.S. investors would not be significantly affected if pass-through debt certificates were characterized as partnership interests. However, because of the special rules that apply to such investors, certificate holders that are non-U.S. persons, pension plans, or other tax-exempt organizations, and possibly certain financial institutions, may have a strong desire to avoid such a characterization.

Application to mortgages

Except as described in the next paragraph, the tax structure described above has not been widely used by trusts that hold real property mortgages (as opposed to automobile or credit card receivables), for several reasons. First, since the beginning of 1987, such a trust potentially could qualify as a REMIC. If the REMIC rules applied, the pass-through debt certificates would be considered regular interests in the REMIC. Thus, the principal tax objectives of sponsors of pass-through debt certificates (avoidance of a tax on the issuing trust and treatment of the certificates as debt) would be achieved with certainty under the REMIC rules. Second, if the REMIC rules did not apply, the risks that a sponsor would be required to assume (in terms of a mismatching between payments on the mortgages and on the certificates) in order to establish that pass-through debt certificates are economically debt of the issuing trust are likely to be more significant for mortgages than for other consumer receivables, because mortgages have longer maturities and, ordinarily, less predictable payment patterns. Third, the steps required to make available a partnership backup argument could represent an additional economic cost. Finally, the availability of a partnership backup argument would be constrained by the TMP rules, which can be applied under an anti-avoidance rule to an entity that does not borrow but has outstanding equity classes resembling debt.

Despite these considerations, mortgage-backed securities resembling pass-through debt certificates have been issued in so-called "kitchen sink" transactions. These transactions are unusual in that neither the REMIC rules nor the TMP rules apply. Typically, a trust acquires existing agency-backed interest-only and principal-only pass-through certificates or REMIC regular interests. The trust issues two classes of beneficial ownership certificates, a senior floating rate class (F) that bears interest at a spread over an interest rate index (generally LIBOR), and a residual class (R). All cash is distributed on the F class until it is retired, after which distributions are made on the R class. Because of contingencies affecting payments of principal, the F class may not meet the definition of a REMIC regular interest. For that reason, the trust does not make a REMIC election. The trust is structured, in much the same way as a trust issuing pass-through debt certificates, so that it is classified as a partnership rather than an association taxable as a corporation. The trust is not a TMP because it does not have debt classes with multiple maturities.

From an economic standpoint, the F class bears a strong resemblance to debt of the trust. Nonetheless, the argument for overcoming the form of the F class as an ownership interest is somewhat weaker here than in typical transactions where pass-through debt certificates are issued, because the trust assets consist of a fixed pool of mortgage-backed securities, the timing of payments on the F class is tied to the timing of receipts on those assets, and the F class is subject to some risk of non-payment because of factors other than mortgagor defaults. For that reason, the F certificates are typically sold on the basis that they will be characterized as partnership interests for tax purposes, but with disclosure that they may be recharacterized as debt.

11.3 TAXATION OF HOLDERS OF MORTGAGE-BACKED SECURITIES TAXABLE AS DEBT

11.3.1 Introduction

As Part 11.2 indicates, from the perspective of investors, mortgage-backed securities can be divided into three groups: those taxable as debt; REMIC residual interests and equity interests in owner trusts that are not TMPs, which generally are taxed based on the net income of the REMIC or trust, respectively; and equity interests in TMPs which are treated as stock in a corporation. This Part 11.3 discusses the taxation of holders of mortgage-backed securities taxable as debt.

The following categories of mortgage-backed securities are taxable as debt:

- REMIC regular interests, which the Code deems to be debt obligations of the issuing REMIC, regardless of their legal form,

- pass-through certificates, which are considered ownership interests in the underlying mortgages,
- CMOs and other pay-through bonds, which are debt obligations of the entity that issues them, as well as pass-through debt certificates that are recognized to be debt of the issuing trust.

References in this Part to mortgage-backed securities should be understood to be references to one of these three types of securities. Also, except where otherwise indicated, references to debt instruments or obligations, or bonds, include REMIC regular interests.

In applying the tax rules for debt instruments to a pass-through certificate, it should be kept in mind that such a certificate is not generally considered a single security for tax purposes, but instead represents an ownership interest in each of the mortgages held by the issuing trust. Technically, the holder of a pass-through certificate should calculate income or loss for each mortgage separately by allocating among the mortgages, in proportion to their respective fair market values, the price paid for the certificate and the price received on resale. Such an allocation is rarely necessary in practice, however, because, in most instances, the tax results obtained by viewing the mortgages alternatively in isolation or as a single aggregated debt instrument would be the same. For convenience, and except where otherwise noted, the discussion in this Section 11.3 of mortgage-backed securities assumes the security is in all cases a debt obligation of one debtor (either an interest in a single mortgage or a single pay-through bond).

The mortgage-backed securities considered in this Part generally are subject to the Code rules governing conventional debt instruments. Thus, for example, stated interest on such a security generally is taxable as ordinary income as such interest accrues, for an accrual method taxpayer, or when it is received, for a cash method taxpayer. Assuming the security is purchased at its principal amount, principal payments represent a non-taxable return of the investor's capital regardless of when principal is paid. Upon sale of the security, gain or loss is recognized in an amount equal to the difference between the net proceeds of such sale and the seller's adjusted basis in the security (generally, the seller's cost for the security, increased by amounts included in income and reduced by losses and payments received). With limited exceptions, any such gains or losses are treated as capital gains or losses if the security is held as a capital asset, which generally would be the case unless the holder is a dealer in securities. Capital gain is long term if the security has been held at the time of sale for more than one year. A preferential tax rate applies to long-term capital gain income earned by high-income individuals (although not to capital gains of corporations). An amount paid as accrued interest upon sale of a mortgage-backed security between interest payment dates is treated by the seller as an interest payment and may be used by the purchaser to offset the interest received on the next interest payment date.[10]

10. Two exceptions to these rules apply to REMIC regular interests, but they are likely to have

The tax treatment of a mortgage-backed security is more complex if the security was purchased at a price different from its principal amount, that is, at a discount or a premium. If a mortgage-backed security is purchased at a discount and the full principal amount is eventually paid, the excess of the principal amount over the cost of the security represents additional income. A question then arises as to the proper timing of recognition of that income and its character as ordinary income or capital gain. The purchase of a security at a premium raises similar concerns. These questions are addressed in the remainder of this Part.

11.3.2 Overview of taxation of discount and premium

The traditional approach to the tax treatment of a debt instrument deals separately with three sources of income—stated or coupon interest, original issue discount and market discount—and one item of expense (or offset to interest)—bond premium. Stated interest was discussed above; discount and premium are considered here.

In general, original issue discount (or OID) is discount at which a debt obligation was sold to investors in connection with its original issuance, and market discount is discount that arises from decreases in the market value of a debt obligation following its issuance. The technical definition of OID is somewhat complicated, and includes not only discount at which an obligation is issued below its principal amount but also stated interest that is not paid currently over the life of the obligation. The most important difference, in terms of tax consequences, between OID and market discount is that, in general, OID is includible in income by the holder of a discount obligation as the discount accrues under a constant yield method, whereas (absent certain taxpayer elections) market discount is taxable only when principal payments are received or the obligation sold. In January of 1994, the Service issued extensive final regulations interpreting the OID rules of the Code, which will sometimes be referred to as the "OID regulations".

---

little, if any, practical significance for most investors. First, income from REMIC regular interests must always be reported under an accrual method even if the holder is otherwise a cash method taxpayer. Second, gain recognized by an investor on a sale of a REMIC regular interest that otherwise would be capital gain will be treated as ordinary income to the extent such gain does not exceed the excess of (1) the income that would have been reported by the investor if it had reported income as it accrued based on a yield to the investor equal to 110% of the "applicable Federal rate" (generally, an average yield of U.S. Treasury obligations of different ranges of maturities published monthly by the Service) in effect for the month in which the interest was acquired by the investor, over (2) the ordinary income previously reported by the investor. The legislative history of the 110% rule indicates that it was intended to prevent the underaccrual of original issue discount because of the failure to take account of mortgage prepayments. Another special rule of minor significance relates to regular interests in "single-class REMICs" (a defined term which includes certain multiple-class REMICs) held by individuals and certain pass-through entities. Such holders are required to include in income, and are treated as paying, an allocable share of the REMICs investment expenses.

There is a fundamental difference between REMIC regular interests and pay-through bonds, on the one hand, and pass-through certificates, on the other hand, which affects the status of discount as OID. Regular interests and pay-through bonds are considered obligations in their own right for tax purposes, so that any discount at which they are issued is generally OID (even if such discount can be traced to market discount on underlying mortgages). By contrast, pass-through certificates are treated as ownership interests in, rather than debt of, the issuing trust. As a result, OID will exist for those certificates only if the mortgages held by the trust have OID (which is rare for residential mortgages) or the bond stripping rules discussed below apply.

Although (absent a holder election) the Code does not require market discount on a debt instrument to be included in income by the holder as it accrues, it nonetheless provides a number of special rules governing market discount. Gain on the sale of a debt instrument is treated as ordinary income (which is interest income for most purposes) to the extent that it does not exceed the market discount that has accrued thereon and not yet been included in income. In the case of debt instruments that have some OID, accruals of market discount are generally proportionate to accruals of OID. A principal payment on a debt instrument generally must be included in income by the holder, as a payment of accrued market discount, to the extent it does not exceed the portion of the market discount on the entire instrument that has accrued during the period the holder owned the instrument and not yet been included in income. As a result, where the holder of a debt instrument receives principal payments at least annually that equal or exceed accruals of market discount, such discount effectively will be included in income as it accrues. Deductions for interest on debt incurred (or continued) to finance market discount bonds are deferred to prevent the generation of losses attributable to the current deductibility of interest and the deferral of market discount income.

Prior to 1986, there was considerable uncertainty as to how mortgage prepayments should be taken into account in accruing OID. TRA 1986 addressed the point by enacting section 1272(a)(6). This section requires OID to be accrued on REMIC regular interests and pay-through bonds based on changes in the present value of the instrument. Present values are calculated (1) by taking account of actual mortgage prepayments that have already occurred and projecting the rate at which future prepayments will occur using an assumed prepayment rate, and (2) using the original yield to maturity as the discount rate. This accrual method (which we refer to as the PAC method for reasons explained below) does not by its terms apply to pass-through certificates except when they are held by a REMIC.

The distinction between OID and market discount is blurred by the "bond stripping" rules of section 1286. These rules apply when rights to principal and interest on a debt obligation are held separately or in different proportions and play a significant role in the taxation of certain pass-through certificates. If rights to payments on a debt obligation qualify as stripped bonds, then, with certain exceptions, all income from the holding of those rights (both stated interest and discount) is subject to taxation under the OID rules.

The special Code rules governing OID and market discount do not apply to *de minimis* amounts of discount on a debt instrument. In general, such discount is recognized by the holder ratably as principal payments are received, and is characterized as gain from the retirement of the instrument.

With respect to *de minimis* discount, or discount on a pass-through certificate or other obligation that is not subject to the PAC method, a further distinction in determining the tax treatment of discount is whether the debtor is an individual, corporation, or other legal entity. Gain realized upon the receipt of a payment of principal on the obligation of an individual that is treated as gain from retirement of the obligation (and not as OID or accrued market discount) is *always* ordinary income, whereas gain from the retirement of an obligation of a corporation or other legal entity may be capital gain if the obligation is held as a capital asset.

Unlike discount, all premium on a given debt instrument is treated alike. Premium on a debt instrument that is held for investment can be amortized if an election is made by the holder under section 171. Amortized premium will offset interest income to the extent thereof and otherwise will be allowed as a deduction. Premium is amortized under a constant yield method that is similar to the method used in calculating accruals of OID.

The discussion of discount in this Part assumes that the mortgage-backed securities in question have an original term to maturity of more than one year. A different tax regime, which is of little relevance in the mortgage area, applies to discount on short-term obligations.

11.3.3 Original issue discount

This Section explains how the OID rules apply to REMIC regular interests and pay-through bonds. Specifically, the discussion will define OID, describe how accruals of OID are calculated under the PAC method, illustrate the method with an example, and describe special rules for debt instruments with variable or contingent interest. Unless otherwise stated, it is assumed that interest on a debt obligation accrues at a fixed rate. Pass-through certificates are addressed in 11.3.4.

OID defined

Original issue discount is defined as the excess of the stated redemption price at maturity of an obligation over its issue price. However, if the amount of discount as so defined is less than a *de minimis* amount (generally ¼ of one per cent of the stated redemption price at maturity times the number of completed years to maturity), then the amount of OID is considered to be zero. The stated redemption price at maturity is not limited to the principal amount, but also includes all payments of stated interest other than qualified stated interest payments. A qualified stated interest payment is any one of a series of payments equal to the product of the outstanding principal balance and a single fixed rate (appropriately adjusted for the length of time between payments) and is payable unconditionally at least annually during the entire term of the obligation (variable rates are discussed below). Thus, interest is not qualified stated interest (and is includible in OID) to the extent it is payable during any year at a rate higher than the lowest rate at which interest is payable during any year over the life of the instrument. For example, all interest on an interest accrual or compound interest bond (which provides for the complete deferral of interest for at least one year) is includible in OID. A portion of the interest on a bond with a payment lag (that is, a lag between the end of the period over which interest accrues and the date on which such interest is paid) may be includible in OID if the bond has more than *de minimis* OID.

Under the OID regulations, the issue price of each debt instrument in an issue issued for money is the first price at which a substantial amount of the debt instruments is sold to investors.

Accrued interest with which a debt instrument is issued is generally included in both the issue price and stated redemption price at maturity of the instrument. However, if the first interest payment is made within one year of the issue date and at least equals the amount of pre-issuance accrued interest, then such interest may be directly offset against such accrued interest (with the result that both amounts may be disregarded in OID calculations).

OID accruals under the PAC method

An investor who purchases a pay-through bond having OID at a yield to maturity not less than the yield to maturity at which it was initially offered must include in income, for each taxable year in which the investor holds the bond, the portion of the OID that is considered to accrue in such year (regardless of whether the investor otherwise reports income under a cash or accrual method of tax accounting). As explained in more detail below, the portion of the OID on a bond that is considered to accrue in any period generally equals the amount by which the value of the bond would increase during such period if it continued at all times to have a yield to maturity equal to its yield to maturity at the time of issuance, calculated based on its issue price. This method of accruing OID is known as the constant yield, compound interest, or scientific method. It gives effect to the compounding of interest by including accrued but unpaid OID in the base to which the yield to maturity of the bond is applied in calculating future accruals of such discount.

The yield to an investor of a debt obligation purchased at a discount below its principal amount is greater the shorter the life of the obligation. In the case of most pay-through bonds, it is highly probable that principal will be prepaid to some degree. The possibility of prepayments raises two related issues: first, whether OID should be accrued based on a yield that is calculated assuming that prepayments will occur at some reasonable rate; and second, how income is to be adjusted to account for differences between the assumed prepayment rate (a zero rate or a reasonable estimate) and the actual prepayment rate. Prior to the enactment of TRA 1986, there were no certain answers to these questions. TRA 1986 clarified that, in the case of a pay-through bond issued after December 31, 1986,

(1) the yield that is used in calculating accruals of OID will be determined based on a reasonable assumption ("prepayment assumption") as to the rate at which the underlying mortgages will be prepaid and, if earnings on temporary investments would affect the timing of payments on the bond, the rate of those earnings;
(2) income will be adjusted in each taxable year (whether or not principal payments are made on the bond in that year) to reflect the economic gain or loss for that year (calculated based on changes in present values assuming a constant yield) resulting from past and present differences between actual prepayment experience and the prepayment assumption, but assuming that future prepayments on remaining mortgages will conform to the prepayment assumption; and
(3) in general, those adjustments will increase or decrease interest income and not be treated as capital gain or loss. The method for calculating accruals of OID introduced by TRA 1986 will be referred to as the prepayment assumption catch-up method, or "PAC method" for short.

In general, the prepayment assumption for any issue of bonds corresponds to the prepayment rate assumed in pricing the initial offering of the bonds and is stated in the offering materials for the bonds. Once determined, the prepayment assumption will not change to reflect changes in prepayment rates occurring after the issuance of the bonds. The prepayment assumption relates to a pool of mortgages and not to classes of bonds. Accordingly, for any pool of mortgages, the same assumption must be used with respect to each class of bonds that is affected by the performance of that pool. Once determined, the prepayment assumption will not change to reflect changes in expectations of future prepayment rates. However, the PAC method does not take actual prepayment experience into account.

A bondholder is required to include in gross income in each taxable year the sum of the daily portions of OID for each day during the taxable year on which it holds the bond. For an investor who purchased the bond in the initial offering at the issue price, two steps are needed to determine the daily portions of OID. First, a calculation is made of the portion of the OID that is allocable to each accrual period during the term of the bond. For a bond that provides for payments at fixed intervals over its life except for a short initial or final period, the accrual periods are generally the periods that end on each payment date and begin on the day after the immediate preceding payment date (or in the case of the first such period, begin on the issue date). Second, the portion of the OID attributed to each accrual period is allocated ratably to each day during the period to determine the daily portion of OID for that day.

Under the PAC method, the amount of OID on a bond that is attributed to each accrual period is the *excess* of:

- the sum of the present value, as of the end of the accrual period, of all of the payments, if any, to be made on the bond in future periods and the amount of any payments made on the bond during the accrual period that are includible in its stated redemption price at maturity, *over*
- the adjusted issue price of the bond at the beginning of such period.

The present value of the future payments on the bond would be calculated for this purpose (1) assuming that the mortgages underlying the bond will be prepaid in future periods in accordance with the prepayment assumption (but taking account of the actual prepayments that have occurred to date) and (2) using a discount rate equal to the yield to maturity of the bond.

The yield to maturity of the bond is the discount rate, assuming compounding at the end of each accrual period, that causes the present value of all future payments on the bond to equal its issue price on the issue date, calculated assuming that the bond will be prepaid in all periods in accordance with the prepayment assumption. The adjusted issue price of a bond at the beginning of an accrual period equals its issue price, increased by the aggregate amount of OID on the bond attributed to all prior accrual periods, if any, and decreased by the amount of any payaments made on the bond in prior periods that were includible in its stated redemption price at maturity. Thus, the adjusted issue price represents an initial purchaser's remaining capital investment in the bond, adjusted for the amount of OID that has been earned and included in income for tax purposes but not yet paid. Special rules apply to initial short accrual periods.

The method of calculating daily accruals of OID outlined above applies to any investor that purchases a pay-through bond at a price equal to or less than its adjusted issue price at the time of purchase. Where the purchase price exceeds the adjusted issue price, the holder is allowed to offset that excess amount ("acquisition premium") against the daily portions of OID. In particular, each daily portion is reduced by a fixed fraction. The numerator of the fraction is the acquisition premium and the denominator is the sum of the daily portions (determined without regard to any acquisition premium adjustment) for all days on or after the purchase date through the maturity date of the bond. Thus, the acquisition premium for any bondholder represents 25 per cent of the aggregate amount of OID that remains to be accrued after the purchase date, the amount of OID that would otherwise be required to be included in the holder's income for any day would be reduced by 25 per cent. An investor that buys an OID bond at a premium (i.e., a price exceeding its remaining stated redemption price at maturity) is not required to include any OID in income.

If prepayments on mortgages backing a discount bond are slower than assumed, it may be possible for the PAC formula to produce an amount for an accrual period that is negative. The TRA 1986 legislative history states that, in such an event, the amount of OID allocable to the period would be treated as zero and the computation of OID for the next accrual period (and presumably for successive periods until the formula produced a positive amount of OID) would be made by treating the first accrual period and the later ones as a single accrual period. Although the language is not entirely clear, it appears to mean only that no deduction for negative amounts of OID will be allowed, and the adjusted issue price at the beginning of each accrual period (determined under normal rules) will be increased by any negative amounts of OID for prior periods for which no deduction was allowed.[11]

Example It will help in explaining the PAC method to apply it to a concrete example. For the sake of simplicity, the example assumes an obligation that pays interest currently at a fixed rate and provides for a single payment of principal. The extension of the method to obligations that provide for payments of principal in installments is straightforward, although the computations can rapidly become burdensome. We will begin by assuming no anticipated or actual prepayments.

Consider a pay-through bond having a principal amount of $1,000 that was issued at a price of $770.60 on April 1, 1994, bears interest at an annual rate of 8 per cent, payable on April 1 and October 1, and matures on April 1, 2004. Principal is required to be paid prior to maturity out of principal prepayments on the mortgage collateral. The bond has OID of $229.40. Suppose initially that the prepayment assumption is that no morgage will be prepaid, and that, under that assumption, the entire $1,000 will be paid at maturity. Given that assumption, the semi-annual yield to maturity of the bond, based on compounding at the end of each accrual period, is 6 per cent.[12] The OID allocable to the first accrual period ending October 1, 1994 is $6.24. This represents the *excess* of:

- the sum of (1) the present value as of October 1, 1994 of the future payments to be made on the bond, calculated using a discount rate equal to the yield to maturity of the bond and assuming, in accordance with the prepayment assumption, no future prepayments ($776.84), and (2) the principal payments made on the bond in the accrual period, which are the only payments includible in its stated redemption price at maturity ($0), *over*
- the adjusted issue price at the beginning of the accrual period, which for the first accrual period equals the issue price of $770.60.

11. For a discussion of negative accruals of OID in the context of prepayment losses on interest only (or other high coupon) REMIC regular interests, see Peaslee & Nirenberg, *supra*, n.2, Chapter 6, Part G.1.

12. In other words, the present value of all interest and principal payments on the bond, calculated using a discount rate for each semi-annual period of 6%, equals the $770.60 purchase price.

The corresponding amount for the second accrual period ending April 1, 1995 is $6.61 [($783.45 + $0) – $776.84]. If the initial holder of the bond reports income based on the calendar year, the holder would include in income for 1994 the sum of all daily portions for the first accrual period ending October 1, 1994 ($6.24) and the sum of the daily portions for the days in the second accrual period which are on or prior to December 31, 1994. Using a 30-days-per-month/360-days-per-year convention, the second accrual period consists of 180 days, of which 90 are on or prior to December 31, 1994. Thus, the sum of the daily portions of OID for the days in the second accrual period that are on or prior to December 31, 1994 is 90/180 times $6.61, or (rounding up) $3.31. The total amount of OID includible in income by such holder in 1994 is therefore $9.55 ($6.24 + $3.31).

It has been assumed, so far, that the pay-through bond is not expected to be, and is not in fact, prepaid. However, the PAC method accommodates both expected and actual prepayments. Expected prepayments are taken into account by assuming that the mortgages underlying the bond will prepay according to the prepayment assumption, both initially in calculating the yield to maturity and over time in determining the present value of future payments. Actual prepayment experience affects the amount and timing of the current payments and expected future payments that enter into the PAC formula.

To illustrate the consequences of different prepayment expectations, suppose that the prepayment assumption is changed and that, under the new assumption the entire $1,000 principal amount of the bond will be paid four years prior to maturity on April 1, 2000. Given that assumption, the semi-annual yield of the bond would increase from 6 per cent to 6.87 per cent. Using that yield in the formula set forth earlier,[13] and assuming that prepayments occur in accordance with the prepayment assumption, the amounts of OID allocable to the first two accrual periods would increase from $6.24 and $6.61, calculated above, to $12.92 [($783.52 + $0) – $770.60] and $13.82 [($797.34 + $0) – $783.52].

To illustrate the case where prepayments are received at a faster than expected pace, suppose that prepayments on the bond described in the immediately preceding paragraph conform to the prepayment assumption until October 1, 1997, but because of greater than expected prepayments between October 2, 1997 and April 1, 1998, the bond is fully retired on April 1, 1998. In that event, the adjusted issue price on October 1, 1997 would equal $881.99, the present value at that time of all future payments on the bond, calculated assuming a $1,000 payment of principal on April 1, 2000. Under the PAC formula, the amount of OID allocable to the accrual period ending April 1, 1998 would equal $118.01, which is the excess of the payments received during the accrual period that are includible in the stated redemption price at maturity, or $1,000, plus the

13. The OID regulations require yield, when expressed as a percentage, to be calculated with at least two decimal place accuracy. A greater number of significant digits was used in the example, with the results being rounded to the nearest cent.

present value of all future payments ($0, because the bond is fully retired at the end of the period) over $881.99. Thus, the OID that otherwise would be included in income over two years and six months (October 1, 1997 through April 1, 2000) is allocated instead to the accrual period ending April 1, 1998 because of the earlier than expected prepayments.

The PAC method also takes account of changes in the expected timing of future payments determined by applying the prepayment assumption to actual mortgages in the second preceding paragraph. If prepayments follow the prepayment assumption until October 1, 1996, the adjusted issue price of the bond at that time would be $844.73, the present value of the future payments on the bond based on a $1,000 payment of principal on April 1, 2000. If mortgage prepayments continued to track the prepayment assumption throughout the next accrual period ending April 1, 1997, the amount of OID that would be allocated to that period would be $18.01. However, suppose instead that during that accrual period, mortgage prepayments are, alternatively, faster or slower than anticipated. As a result, it is determined (by applying the prepayment assumption to the mortgages held by the issuer at the end of the accrual period) that the $1,000 principal amount will be paid six months earlier, in the case of the faster prepayments, or six months later, in the case of the slower prepayments, than originally anticipated. Moving the expected retirement date forward (or back) increases (or decreases) the present value of the future payments on the bond as of April 1, 1997 from $862.74 to $881.99 (or $844.73), and thus increases (or decreases) the amount of OID allocated under the PAC method to the accrual period ending April 1, 1997 to $37.26 (or $0), respectively.

The examples just discussed involve a bond that provides for only a single payment of principal. In most cases, however, pay-through bonds provide for payments of principal in installments. The only difference that this change would cause in applying the PAC method is that the amount included in the formula for payments that are included in the stated redemption price at maturity would be positive for each accrual period during which some principal amount is paid.

Variable rates

REMIC regular interests are allowed to pay interest at a variable rate, to the extent provided in regulations. The REMIC regulations allow a wide range of variable rates based on interest rate indices or a weighted average of the rates on the underlying mortgages. Combinations of different indexed, weighted average, or fixed rates are also allowed. Further, a REMIC regular interest can pay interest equal to a specified portion of the interest payments on one or more qualified mortgages bearing interest at a variable rate.

The OID regulations divide variable rate debt instruments into two groups: variable rate debt instruments or VRDIs and contingent payment debt instruments. Different substantive rules apply to each type of obligation. The definition of VRDI is tailored to the needs of the OID rules and is not the same as the definition of permitted variable rate regular interests. The VRDI definition is both narrower and broader in some respects. Under current law, many variable rate regular interests would fall into the contingent payment category.

The OID rules are applied to a VRDI by converting the variable interest payments into equivalent fixed interest payments, and then applying the general OID rules to the resulting fixed rate instrument. Qualified stated interest or OID allocable to an accrual period is adjusted if the actual interest for the period differs from the assumed fixed interest amount. The adjustment increases or decreases qualified stated interest if the fixed interest for the period is qualified stated interest and the adjustment is reflected in the amount actually paid during the period. Otherwise, the adjustment increases or decreases OID for the accrual period.

As of this writing, the tax rules governing contingent payment debt instruments are in a state of flux. In practice, the principles of the VRDI rules are applied to all types of variable rate REMIC regular interests, and also generally to variable rate non-REMIC pay-through bonds if the variation in rates is based on changes in market interest rates, even where those rules do not technically apply.

One major payment contingency affecting most mortgage-backed securities is, of course, uncertainty as to the timing of mortgage prepayments. The PAC method takes a direct aim at this problem, and accordingly will most likely be considered to pre-empt any more general contingent payment rules that may be adopted as a means of dealing with prepayments. The PAC method can easily be combined with the principles of the VRDI rules. Those rules account for OID as if it were earned with respect to a hypothetical fixed-rate debt instrument, and income on that instrument can be calculated under the PAC method in the normal way.

A REMIC regular interest can bear interest at a rate equal to a weighted average of the interest rates on qualified mortgages held by the REMIC (provided those mortgages themselves bear interest at a fixed or variable rate permitted under the REMIC rules). In a case where mortgages bear interest at different fixed rates, then the rate payable in each period will depend on the relative principal balances of the mortgages taken into account in the average. The prepayment assumption can be used to predict the relative balances of individual mortgages in future periods and hence the average rate. Once uncertainty as to future payments has been eliminated, the PAC method can be applied. If the loans included in the weighted average include one or more variable rate loans, then the principles of the VRDI rules could be applied to address the variable rate contingency.

11.3.4 Pass-through certificates

The degree to which the OID rules will influence the taxation of a pass-through certificate depends primarily on whether the stripped bond rules of section 1286 apply. If they do, then the OID rules will play a central role. On the other hand, OID is unlikely to be present in pass-through certificates that do not fall within that section, except in cases in which the underlying mortgages provide for negative amortization, or have teaser rates (initial below market rates) that reflect unusually large discounts below market rates. The two types of pass-through ceritificates are considered next, beginning with those subject to the stripped bond rules.

Pass-through certificates subject to the stripped bond rules

Definition of stripped bond or coupon Section 1286 contains special rules governing the taxation of stripped bonds and stripped coupons. A stripped bond is a bond isued with coupons (which, for this purpose, includes any rights to receive stated interest), where there is a separation in ownership between the bond and any coupons that have not yet come due. A stripped coupon is a coupon relating to a stripped bond. The tax treatment of stripped bonds and stripped coupons is generally the same, and the term stripped bond will be used in this discussion to refer to both.

The classic example of a bond-stripping transaction is a sale by the owner of a whole bond of unmatured interest coupons to one investor and rights to principal to a second investor. (Alternatively, the seller could sell only the coupons or the rights to principal and retain the remaining interests in the bond.) IO and PO strips represent the extension of this transaction pattern to mortgage-backed securities.

Subject to two important exceptions described in the next paragraph, the bond-stripping rules also extend to situations in which there is some but not complete separation in the ownership of rights to principal and interest. One common example is the transaction described above in which a mortgage originator holding discount or premium mortgages creates pass-through certificates that can be sold at par by retaining a share of interest payments (in the case of the premium mortgages) or a share of principal payments (in the case of the discount mortgages). Where mortgages have a range of interest rates, rights to interest payments exceeding the lowest common rate may also be retained in order to provide a single pass-through rate for investors. The retention of a partial ownership interest in mortgage interest payments is often achieved mechanically by charging excess servicing. The IRS has ruled that excess servicing (defined as a right to payments for servicing that exceed compensation at a market rate) is treated for tax purposes as an ownership interest in mortgage interest payments.

Section 1286 does not apply to investors purchasing an interest in a stripped mortgage (one from which some interest coupons have been removed) in two cases:

(1) where the stripped mortgage would be considered to have no OID under the general OID *de minimis* rule if, *immediately after* the separation in ownership of the interest strip, the stripped mortgage was newly issued at an issue price equal to the price at which it is sold to investors, and

(2) where the amount of interest that has been stripped from the mortgage (including excess servicing but not including reasonable servicing compensation) does not exceed 100 basis points per annum (without regard to whether the stripped mortgage would have OID if it were newly issued).

Whether these exceptions apply to a stripped mortgage in the hands of any investor depends on the nature of the original stripping transaction and not on the price paid for the stripped mortgage by the investor. The first of the two rules has the practical effect of nullifying section 1286 for investors purchasing pass-through certificates from which some interest has been stripped, if those certificates were not sold immediately following the stripping transaction at a discount below their principal amount that exceeded ¼ of 1 per cent of the aggregate principal amount of the mortgages multiplied by their remaining weighted average life (calculated assuming no prepayments and by rounding partial years to zero).

The consequences of recombining all of the stripped interests in a single debt instrument are not clear. It appears, however, that section 1286 would continue to apply to those interests in the hands of any person who has held any of them as a stripped bond, but would not apply to a new investor who purchases all of the stripped interests together.

Treatment of stripped bonds Subject to the exceptions described in the last section, section 1286 generally transforms the discount at which a stripped bond is purchased into OID. Specifically, section 1286(a) provides that if a person purchases a stripped bond, then, for purposes of applying the OID rules of the Code, the stripped bond will be treated, while held by that person, as a bond originally issued on the purchase date having OID equal to the excess of the stated redemption price at maturity of the stripped bond over its purchase price. However, no amount is treated as OID if that excess amount is less than a *de minimis* amount (determined by applying the general OID definition as if the stripped bond were a newly issued debt obligation with an issue price equal to the purchase price). Where a stripped bond is considered to be purchased with more than a *de minimis* amount of OID, then under the OID rules of the Code, the holder will be required to include such OID in income in each taxable year as it accrues. In calculating accruals of OID, all payments on a debt instrument of a single borrower should be aggregated and treated as a single stripped bond with a single yield to maturity. It is not clear if rights to stated interest payments included in a stripped bond would be treated as qualified stated interest where they would be so treated if the stripped bond were a newly issued bond, or whether they would, instead, be included automatically in OID, but this issue does not have much practical significance.

A significant issue that arises in calculating accruals of OID with respect to pass-through certificates that are stripped bonds is whether the PAC method applies (and, if so, what prepayment assumption is used). As a technical matter, the PAC method does not apply, because a pass-through certificate (other than one held by a REMIC) is not the type of security to which the method applies. Nevertheless, many issuers for purposes of information reporting, and many investors, calculate income as if that method did apply, generally based on a prepayment assumption determined at the time of issuance of the certificates. Alternatively, an investor might be able to use a prepayment assumption based on expectations as of the date on which it purchased its certificates. Because the PAC method is based on the prepayment experience of a pool of mortgages, it would make sense if that method is applied to treat all mortgages underlying a pass-through certificate as a single debt instrument with a single yield.

If the PAC method does not apply to pass-through certificates that are stripped bonds, then income should be computed under a method that is similar to the PAC method except that the Prepayment Assumption used in calculating the yield to maturity and present values would be an assumption that no future mortgage prepayments will occur, and income or loss that results when a mortgage is prepaid (calculated, generally, in a manner similar to the PAC method by comparing the amount received, if any, as a result of the prepayment with the present value of the payments that would have been received if the mortgage loan had not been prepaid) and would be income or loss from retirement of the mortgage loan and not an adjustment to OID. Any such income or loss would be ordinary income or loss if the mortgage loans are obligations of individuals, and generally would be capital gain or loss if they are obligations of corporations, partnerships, or other legal entities and the pass-through certificates are held as capital assets. Deductions for losses would not be curbed by the PAC method limitation on deductions for negative OID.

Pass-through certificates that are not stripped bonds

OID is not likely to be encountered in a pass-through certificate to which the stripped bond rules do not apply unless, as discussed below, interest payments on the underlying mortgages are scheduled to increase over time. The exchange of such pass-through certificates for mortgages is not treated as the creation of a new debt security for tax purposes. Accordingly, the existence or lack of OID is not affected by the price at which the certificates were originally sold. Rather, it is necessary to apply the OID definition to the original loan between the mortgagor and the mortgage originator, giving effect to the price at which the loan was originated.

In the case of a fixed rate residential mortgage originated after March 1, 1984, some portion of the stated interest payments may be includible in OID if the amount unconditionally payable as interest in each year, expressed as a percentage of the outstanding principal balance of the loan, is stepped up or down over the term of the loan. For example, such a mortgage generally will be considered to have OID, even if it was originated at par, if it provides for negative amortization of principal or, subject to a special *de minimis* rule for interest holidays and teaser rates, bears interest payable at fixed rates that are scheduled to increase over the life of the loan. The general effect of applying the OID rules to loans with these features will be to require holders (1) of a negative amortization loan to include stated interest in income as it accrues, and (2) of a loan that bears interest at increasing rates to include interest in income as it accrues based on the yield to maturity of the loan (that is, a yield representing a blend of the stated interest rates).

An adjustable rate residential mortgage typically would be a VRDI. Accordingly, the OID rules generally should be applied by treating the mortgage as if it provided for fixed interest payments equal to the interest that would be paid if the applicable interest rate index were frozen at its value on the date of origination of the mortgage, with adjustments then being made in each month for differences between the assumed and actual interest rates. Under that approach, subject to the special *de minimis* rule for interest holidays and teaser rates, stated interest would included in whole or in part in OID if the mortgage provides for a scheduled increase in interest payments not dependent on a change in the index. Also, if over the life of an adjustable rate mortgage, the index increases and accrued interest is not paid currently because of a payment cap, the unpaid interest would be includible in income as it accrues under the VRDI rules.

If a mortgage is considered to have been issued with OID, an investor's interest therein most likely would be taxable under a method similar to the PAC method, except that the prepayment assumption used in calculating yield and present values would be an assumption that no prepayments will occur, and any gain from a prepayment would be treated as gain from retirement of the mortgage loan, not as an adjustment to OID.

11.3.5 Market discount

Overview

Any discount at which an obligation is purchased below its principal amount (if the obligation has no OID), or below its adjusted issue price (if the instrument does have OID), is considered to be market discount. The treatment of market discount was significantly altered by the Tax Reform Act of 1984 ("TRA 1984") and TRA 1986.

Prior to the enactment of TRA 1984, market discount on a mortgage-backed security was generally allocated among all principal payments in proportion to their amounts, regardless of when they were due. The discount was included in income as principal payments were received or when the security was sold.

Thus, if a obligation having an outstanding principal amount of $1,000 was purchased by an investor for $750, the investor would report 25 per cent of each principal payment as income when the payment was received while it held the obligation. Such income was ordinary income (although not interest income) if the obligation was the debt of an individual; otherwise, it was generally capital gain, assuming the obligation was held as a capital asset. Given the same assumption, gain realized upon sale of the obligation was always capital gain. Such gain would reflect any market discount allocated to the principal of the obligation that remained unpaid at the time of the sale, because the seller's adjusted basis for purposes of computing gain would equal the portion of the initial purchase price, reflecting the market discount, that was allocated to such unpaid principal.

TRA 1984 and TRA 1986 did not change the rule of prior law that permits market discount on an obligation to be deferred until the obligation is disposed of or principal thereon is paid. However, TRA 1986 introduced a rule for allocating discount among principal payments that can significantly increase the amount of market discount income that is recognized when a principal payment is made. For an obligation that provides for partial principal payments in each accrual period, which describes many mortgage-backed securities, this change can have the effect of substantially eliminating the difference between OID and market discount in terms of the timing of the inclusion of such discount in income.

As a result of TRA 1984, market discount income reported by the holder of an obligation is treated as ordinary interest income for most tax purposes to the extent of the portion of the discount that accrued while the holder held the obligation. TRA 1984 also provided rules to ensure that accrued market discount will not be exempted from tax under certain non-recognition provisions in the Code. Finally, another TRA 1984 amendment defers deductions for all or a portion of the tax losses that otherwise might be generated by borrowing at market rates to finance low-coupon market discount obligations, claiming current deductions for interest expense on the borrowing and deferring the inclusion in income of the market discount until the obligation is disposed of or repaid. These special market discount rules do not apply to a obligation that has a fixed maturity date not exceeding one year from issuance.[14]

Detailed discussion

TRA 1984 added to the Code section 1276, which provides that gain from a sale or other disposition of an obligation acquired with market discount[15] will be treated as ordinary income (generally as interest income) to the extent the gain

14. TRA 1984 also offers investors an election, in section 1278(b), to treat market discount as OID. Market discount obligations affected by the election are not subject to the income conversion and loss deferral rules described in the text.

15. Market discount is defined in section 1278(a)(2) as the excess of the stated redemption price at maturity of an obligation over its basis immediately after its acquisition by the taxpayer. However,

does not exceed the portion of the market discount that is considered to have accrued from the acquisition date to the time of the sale or other disposition. Subject to certain exceptions, such income is recognized notwithstanding other non-recognition rules in the Code. Similarly, the stripping of a market discount obligation is considered a disposition that triggers the recognition of accrued market discount.

Discount that otherwise would be market discount is not treated as market discount for purposes of sections 1276 through 1278 if it is less than a *de minimis* amount. Any such *de minimis* discount is included in income ratably as principal payments are received, and is characterized as gain from retirement of the debt instrument.

TRA 1986 introduced a new rule for determining the amount of market discount income that is recognized when a partial principal payment is made. The rule, found in section 1276(a)(3), states that a partial principal payment on an obligation will be included in gross income as ordinary income to the extent of the accrued market discount on the obligation. In other words, the market discount that must be included in income when a principal payment is received is not, as under prior law, simply the portion of the remaining market discount that is allocable to the principal paid (for example, half of such discount if half of the principal balance is paid), but instead is generally the lesser of the amount of the payment and the amount of market discount that has accrued (but not yet been included in income) on the obligation as a whole. As discussed below, special rules govern the treatment of prepayments. If principal payments are made in each year at least equal to the market discount that accrues in that year, then the new rule effectively requires market discount to be included in income as it accrues.

For a non-REMIC pass-through certificate, it appears that the rule for partial principal payments would be applied separately to each of the underlying mortgages rather than to the certificates as a whole, so that principal payments received on one mortgage would not result in the recognition of accrued market discount on other mortgages. On the other hand, a REMIC regular interest would be treated as a single obligation for this purpose, even if it takes the form of a pass-through certificate.

Subject to the discussion in the next paragraph, market discount is considered to accrue on an obligation under a straight-line method unless the holder elects, on an obligation-by-obligation basis, to use a constant yield method. If the election is made, accrued market discount for any period equals the portion of such discount that would have been included in the holder's income during that period as accrued OID if the obligation had been issued on the date on which it was purchased by the holder and the market discount had been OID. Sophisticated investors are likely to make a constant yield election for all of their

---

for an obligation having OID, the stated redemption price at maturity is replaced by the adjusted issue price.

market discount bonds, because the election slows the rate at which market discount accrues.

TRA 1986 authorized the Treasury to issue regulations to determine the amount of accrued market discount with respect to an obligation on which principal is payable in installments. The legislative history states that until these regulations are issued, holders of such obligations may elect to accrue market discount either in the same manner as OID or (1) in the case of debt obligations that have OID, in proportion to the accrual of OID, or (2) for debt obligations that have no OID, in proportion to payments of stated interest. For an obligation that would be subject to the PAC method for accruing OID if the instrument had such discount (which would include any pay-through bond issued after December 31, 1986), the same prepayment assumption that would be used in accruing OID will be used in accruing market discount, regardless of which of the foregoing methods is used. Issuers of obligations subject to the PAC method are required to report information necessary to calculate accruals of market discount.

If accruals of market discount are calculated under a method similar to the PAC method, then actual prepayments would be reflected automatically in the calculation of accrued discount. The treatment of prepayments on a debt instrument is less clear where the PAC method does not apply (for example, in the case of pass-through certificates that are not stripped bonds). In such a case, the rate of accrual of market discount should be calculated disregarding the possibility of optional prepayments. If and when a loan is prepaid *in full*, the holder would recognize gain from retirement of the instrument. That gain would be treated as ordinary income to the extent it does not exceed the accrued market discount on the instrument that has not previously been included in income. Any remaining gain would have the same character as if the special market discount rules did not apply (see above).

Where a debt instrument is prepaid *in part*, it is necessary to address three questions: First, is the amount of prepaid principal that is treated as a payment of accrued market discount limited to the accrued market discount attributable to the portion of the instrument that is prepaid? Second, is the holder required to recognize any portion of the unaccrued market discount on the obligation? Finally, if accrued and unaccrued market discount are included in income only to the extent they are allocated to the portion of the instrument that is prepaid, how is that allocation to be made?

The treatment of partial prepayments in the OID regulations gives some indication of the current views of the Service on these points. The OID regulations contain a payment ordering rule that generally treats a payment on a debt instrument first, as a payment of accrued OID and, second, as a payment of principal. This rule does not apply, however, to a pro rata prepayment (defined as a prepayment that results in a substantially pro rata reduction of each payment remaining to be paid on the instrument). A pro rata prepayment is treated instead as a payment in retirement of a portion of the instrument, resulting in the same amount of gain or loss as if the retired portion of the instrument were a separate instrument that was retired in full. All tax attributes of the instrument (adjusted issue price, the holder's basis, and accrued but unpaid OID), determined immediately before the prepayment, are allocated between the retired and remaining portions of the instrument based on their principal amounts.

While the OID regulations make no mention of section 1276, presumably the same principles would apply in determining the effect of a prepayment on market discount. Thus, in the case of a pro rata prepayment of a market discount bond, the holder would allocate its tax basis, adjusted issue price and accrued market discount pro rata between the retired and remaining portions of the bond, and treat the prepayment as if it were a prepayment in full of the retired portion of the bond. Any other prepayment would be treated in the same manner as a scheduled payment (first, as a payment of accrued OID, second, as a payment of accrued market discount, in each case on the obligation as a whole, third, as a return of basis that reduces the adjusted issue price dollar-for-dollar but not below zero, and fourth, as gain from retirement of the debt instrument). Thus, the prepayment would not trigger the recognition of any unaccrued market discount except to the extent basis has been reduced to zero. Although a non-pro rata prepayment would increase the instrument's yield (calculated based on the adjusted issue price and future payments), there is no rule that adjusts the yield used in calculating future accruals of market discount under the constant yield method (where it applies). In general, holders of residential mortgages would prefer the rule for non-pro rata prepayments over the rule for pro rata prepayments. Remaining market discount on those mortgages is more likely to be unaccrued than accrued because accrued market discount must be included in income as scheduled principal payments are received.

The preamble to the OID regulations states that partial retirement treatment is restricted to pro rata prepayments because that type of prepayment is common and the extension of the rule to non-pro rata prepayments would be unduly complex. These statements were apparently made without the mortgage markets in mind. Almost invariably, partial prepayments on residential mortgages are not pro rata prepayments but are credited against the last payments due. As a result, under the principles of the OID regulations, full and partial prepayment in the same amount will have different consequences for investors. Information necessary to distinguish the two types of prepayments is not ordinarily reported to holders of pass-through certificates, however, so that even a well meaning investor would be unable to treat the two differently. Under these circumstances holders are likely to make the simplifying assumption that all prepayments are prepayments in full.

TRA 1984 also added section 1277 to the Code, which requires the deferral of tax losses that otherwise would result from financing an investment in market discount obligations with debt that bears interest at a current market rate.

Section 1277 states that "net direct interest expense" with respect to a market discount obligation shall be allowed as a deduction in any taxable year only to the extent such expense exceeds the market discount that accrues during the days in such year on which the taxpayer held the obligation. The rate of accrual of market discount is determined under the rules of section 1276 described earlier (including the election to use a constant yield method). Net direct interest expense is the excess of the interest paid or accrued during the taxable year on debt incurred, or continued, to purchase, or carry, the market discount obligation over the aggregate amount of interest on the obligation (including OID) includible in gross income for the taxable year by the holder. The "incurred or continued to purchase or carry" standard used to link a borrowing with an investment in market discount obligations is amorphous and yet familiar, having been used for many years under section 265 in determining whether investments in tax-exempt bonds are debt financed. A special interest expense allocation rule applies to banks and thrifts.

The deductions for net direct interest expense on a market discount obligation that are disallowed under section 1277 are allowed (subject to other limitations that may apply to deductions for interest expense) (1) when the market discount obligation is disposed of in a taxable transaction, or (2) if the taxpayer so elects, prior to such a disposition to the extent necessary to offset any net interest income on the obligation (the excess of the interest income over interest expense on related borrowings) recognized in years subsequent to a year in which the deductions were disallowed.

The policy underlying section 1277 is that deductions for apparent losses resulting from a leveraged investment in a market discount obligation should be deferred, if and to the extent the losses are offset economically by the accrual of market discount, until the accrued market discount is included in income. Thus, if an investor borrows at 12 per cent to finance the purchase of an 8 per cent mortgage that has a yield, taking account of market discount, of 11 per cent, the investor's economic loss is only 1 per cent, the amount by which the rate of interest paid on the borrowing exceeds the yield on the mortgage. Obviously, income and expense would be mismatched if a deduction were allowed for the apparent additional 3-percentage-point loss before the corresponding amount of accrued market discount income is recognized.

11.3.6 Premium

Section 171 generally allows the holder of a debt instrument purchased at a premium (unless the holder is a dealer in securities) to elect to amortize such premium over the period from the date of purchase to the maturity date of the instrument (or, if it results in less rapid amortization of the premium, over the period to an earlier call date). For this purpose, premium is determined with reference to the basis of a debt instrument and the "amount payable on maturity" or, if it results in smaller amortizable bond premium for the period to an earlier call date, the "amount payable on earlier call date". Amortized premium is allocated among the interest payments on a debt instrument and, to the extent so allocated, is applied against and reduces those payments. Any amount not so allocated is allowed as a deduction.

Section 171 was significantly amended by TRA 1986, effective for debt instruments issued after September 27, 1985. Under the amended section, premium is amortized under a constant yield method. In applying that method, prepayments should be accounted for under a method similar to the PAC method, at least in the case of a debt instrument issued after December 31, 1986 to which the PAC method would apply if such instrument had been issued at a discount.[16]

Premium on a debt instrument that is not amortized under section 171 is allocated among the principal payments to be made on the instrument and is allowed as a loss deduction when those payments are made. Such a loss would be an ordinary loss for an obligation of an individual (or a partnership or trust if the obligation was issued prior to July 2, 1982) and otherwise would be a capital loss, provided the obligation is held as a capital asset.

11.4 TAXATION OF HOLDERS OF EQUITY INTERESTS IN OWNER TRUSTS AND REMIC RESIDUAL INTERESTS

11.4.1 Introduction

This Part 11.4 discusses the federal income taxation of holders of (1) equity interests in owner trusts that are not TMPs and (2) REMIC residual interests. The tax characteristics that are common to both types of securities are considered first, followed by a review of special considerations applicable to owner trusts and special considerations applicable to REMIC residual interests. The section concludes with a discussion of phantom income. Except as otherwise indicated, in this Part 11.4, the term "owner trust" means an owner trust that is not a TMP, the term "conduit issuer" means an owner trust or a REMIC, the term "equity interest" means an equity interest in a conduit issuer, and the terms "bond" and "CMO" include REMIC regular interests. Because, absent special circumstances, it is unlikely that a mortgage-backed security will be intentionally structured as an equity interest in a TMP, the taxation of TMPs, and holders of equity interests in TMPs, is not addressed.[17]

16. For a debt instrument issued on or before September 27, 1985, an investor may elect to amortize premium under section 171 only if the instrument was issued by a corporation or a government or political subdivision thereof. If the election is made, premium is amortized under the method of amortizing bond premium that the holder regularly employs, provided such method is reasonable, and otherwise under a straight-line method.

In determining whether premium may be amortized on a pass-through certificate evidencing an interest in mortgages, the date of origination of the mortgages would determine whether the new or old version of section 171 applies. Thus, an election could be made under section 171 to amortize premium on a pass-through certificate backed by residential mortgages that are obligations of individuals only to the extent the mortgages were originated after September 27, 1985.

17. For a discussion, see Peaslee & Nirenberg, *supra*, n.2, Chapter 8.

11.4.2 Common tax characteristics

Conduit issuers are generally not subject to tax. Instead, each holder of an equity interest is required to include in income its share of the taxable income (or loss) of the related conduit issuer allocable to that holder without regard to the distributions made by the issuer. In computing taxable income, the conduit issuer would have income from the mortgage collateral, the reinvestment of mortgage payments, and any reserve fund investments, and would be allowed deductions for interest (including OID) and retirement premiums on the bonds it issues, and operating expenses. In any period, the deductions allowed for bond interest (net of any premium received by the issuer) generally would equal the income that would be reported by original holders of the bonds if they bought the bonds on the issue date at the issue price (for bond issues having more than one class, computed on a class-by-class basis), except that the OID *de minimis* rule would be ignored. A conduit issuer that retires a bond for an amount less than its adjusted issue price generally would have ordinary cancellation of indebtedness income equal to the difference. It may be possible to offset that income against the basis of assets or other tax attributes if the issuer is insolvent.

11.4.3 Special considerations applicable to owner trusts

As discussed above, an owner trust may be classified either as a grantor trust or as a partnership. A major difference between grantor trusts and partnerships is that a grantor trust is essentially ignored for federal income tax purposes, whereas a partnership is recognized as an entity for some tax purposes. Thus, if an owner trust is classified as a grantor trust, each holder of an equity interest therein would be treated as if the holder purchased and owned directly a share of the assets of the trust, subject to its share of the indebtedness of the trust. Accordingly, each holder would have an initial tax basis in its share of the trust's assets equal to the cost of its equity interest plus its share of the aggregate adjusted issue price of the bonds at the time of purchase of the equity interest. In addition, the holder's income would be computed under its own method of accounting, and the holder would make any applicable tax elections, for example, to amortize bond premium on the mortgage collateral. If the holder sold an interest in the owner trust, it would be considered to have sold an interest in the underlying mortgages. Accordingly, as discussed further below, if the holder was a thrift institution or bank, any resulting gain or loss would be ordinary income or loss. Cash distributions from a grantor trust are not taxable.

By contrast, if an owner trust is classified as a partnership, taxable income would be computed, and in general elections made, at the partnership (or owner trust) level, using the partnership's accounting method (which almost always would be an accrual method). Each holder of an equity interest would report its share of the partnership's taxable income in the holder's taxable year in which the taxable year of the partnership ends. In most cases, the taxable year of the partnership would be the calendar year. Each partner would be considered to own an interest in the partnership (as contrasted with a direct interest in partnership assets). The partnership interest would have an initial basis in the hands of the partner equal to its original cost (the cash purchase price, or the basis of property exchanged for such interest in a tax-free exchange), plus the partner's share of partnership liabilities. Over time, such basis would be increased by the partner's share of partnership income and contributions, and decreased by the partner's share of losses and distributions (treating as distributions any reductions in the partnership's liabilities). The amount of the partnership's liabilities in respect of the bonds would equal the bonds' aggregate adjusted issue price, as described above.

Unlike a grantor trust, a partnership is considered to have its own basis in its assets (inside basis). While initially the inside basis of an owner trust that is classified as a partnership would equal the sum of the holders' bases in their equity interests (outside basis), a discrepancy could develop if (1) equity interests were sold at a gain or loss and (2) the sale did not result in (and is not followed by) a termination of the partnership under section 708. Under section 708, a partnership is considered to be terminated and reformed if 50 per cent or more of the total interest in partnership income and capital is sold or exchanged within a 12-month period. Any discrepancy between inside and outside bases following a sale of a partnership interest at a gain (or loss) could result in overtaxation (or undertaxation) of the purchasing partner. The partnership could eliminate or mitigate the problem by making an election under section 754 to adjust the basis of its assets for purposes of computing the taxable income of the purchasing partner.

If an owner trust is classified as a partnership, then gain or loss from the sale of an equity interest may be capital gain or loss, even though, in the case of a thrift institution or bank, a sale of a direct ownership interest in the mortgages held by the trust automatically would be ordinary income or loss. Such gain or loss would be computed by comparing the seller's adjusted basis in its partnership interest with the amount realized in the sale (which would include the seller's share of the trust's liabilities). Distributions of cash by a partnership to a partner are not taxable unless they exceed the partner's basis in its partnership interest, in which case the excess is treated as gain from sale of that interest. Gain from this source would be rare in the case of an owner trust because an equity owner's basis in its equity interest would include its share of the trust's liability for the bonds.

A pension plan, charity, individual retirement account, or other tax-exempt organization that is subject to tax on its unrelated business taxable income (UBTI) under section 512 will be taxable on substantially all of its income from an equity interest in an owner trust, regardless of whether the trust is classified as a grantor trust or partnership.

11.4.4 Special considerations applicable to REMICs

From a tax perspective, a REMIC resembles a partnership more than a grantor trust. Income or loss is computed at the level of the REMIC and is then allocated among the holders of residual interests as ordinary income or loss. Specifically, taxable income or loss of the REMIC is computed for each calendar quarter and each holder of a residual interest is considered to earn, on each day it holds such interest, that day's ratable share of the REMIC's taxable income or loss for the quarter. Neither the Code nor the legislative history indicates how a REMIC should allocate its taxable income for a year among different calendar quarters. Hopefully, some flexibility will be allowed in choosing an allocation method.

In general, the taxable income of a REMIC is determined in the same manner as in the case of an individual. However, there are five statutory exceptions to this rule. First, a REMIC must use an accrual method of accounting. Second, regular interests, if not otherwise debt instruments, are treated as indebtedness of the REMIC, so that, among other consequences, interest thereon is deductible. Third, market discount on any qualified mortgage or other debt instrument held by the REMIC is includible in income as if such discount were OID (and the obligation was issued on the date on which it is acquired by the REMIC). Fourth, items of income, gain, loss or deduction allocable to a prohibited transaction are disregarded. Finally, deductions for net operating loss carryovers or carrybacks are not allowed. Certain other minor adjustments are also found in the REMIC regulations. They treat all gain or loss from the disposition of an asset as ordinary, and allow deductions for ordinary and necessary operating expenses, interest and bad debts without regard to certain limitations that apply to individual taxpayers.

The deductions allowed to a REMIC for interest or other income on a regular interest should match inclusions in income by an original holder who acquires the interest at its issue price. Thus, the discussion above of the timing of income recognition by holders of regular interests is also relevant in determining the taxable income of a REMIC. Indeed these issues may be more significant for the REMIC than for regular interest holders because of the special anti-tax avoidance rules (discussed in 11.4.5) applicable to residual interests. There is no counterpart to these rules for regular interests. One timing issue that is particularly significant in determining a REMIC's taxable income is whether deductions are allowed to holders (and there is a corresponding inclusion in income by the REMIC) for negative amounts determined under the PAC method with respect to high-coupon regular interests.

A REMIC does not recognize gain or loss on the issuance of regular or residual interests in exchange for cash or other property. If a REMIC distributes property in kind with respect to a regular or residual interest, gain is recognized by the REMIC in the same manner as if it had sold such property to the distributee at its fair market value, and the basis of the property to the distributee is that same amount.

In order to calculate the taxable income of a REMIC, it is necessary to determine the REMIC's basis in its assets. In general terms, the REMIC's aggregate basis in its assets at the time it is formed equals the aggregate issue price of all REMIC interests (both regular interests and residual interests). Although there is no clear guidance on the point, that aggregate basis presumably would be allocated first to cash and cash equivalents held by the REMIC, and then among the other assets of the REMIC in proportion to their fair market values.

The most significant assets of a REMIC are the qualified mortgages that it holds. Income from holding those mortgages is determined under the rules discussed above, except that a REMIC must include discount in income as it accrues under the PAC method, in the same manner as if the mortgages had been issued on the date on which they were acquired by the REMIC with an issue price equal to their initial basis to the REMIC. A REMIC that sells or disposes of qualified mortgages recognizes gain or loss determined under general tax principles.

No Code provision permits or requires adjustments to be made to a REMIC's basis in its assets to reflect subsequent purchases of residual interests at a price greater or less than the seller's adjusted basis. The legislative history of TRA 1986 indicates that it "may be appropriate" to make such adjustments, but leaves the issue unresolved. The REMIC regulations do not address the point.

Under section 67, an individual is allowed to deduct investment expenses (other than interest) only to the extent they exceed two per cent of his adjusted gross income. Also, investment expenses are not deductible in calculating AMTI, the tax base for the alternative minimum tax. In the case of investment expenses of a REMIC, these rules are applied at the investor rather than REMIC level. Specifically, a REMIC must allocate its investment expenses among certain holders of REMIC interests (referred to as "pass-through interest holders"). Pass-through interest holders are required to include the amount of allocated expenses in income and are allowed an offsetting deduction if and only if the deduction would have been allowed had they incurred the expenses directly (in other words, for individuals, the two per cent limitation applies and the expenses are not deductible in calculating AMTI). A pass-through interest holder is defined generally as an individual (other than certain non-resident aliens), trust or estate, or certain pass-through entities, including another REMIC, but not including a REIT or pension plan. Beneficial rather than record ownership is taken into account in determining whether an interest is held by a pass-through interest holder.

Ordinarily, a REMIC's investment expenses are allocated pro rata among all residual interests (although only pass-through interest holders are required to take the allocated amount into account in determining their tax liability). However, in the case of a single-class REMIC, a portion of the REMIC's investment expenses must also be allocated to each class of regular interests. In particular, a single-class REMIC must allocate its investment expenses for any calendar quarter ratably to the days in the quarter and then among the regular and residual interests outstanding on any day in proportion to the income accruing on those interests for that day. A single-class REMIC is defined as any REMIC that would be classified as a grantor trust in the absence of a REMIC election, including any multiple-class trust that falls within the exceptions in the Sears regulations for trusts with stripped, or senior and subordinated, pass-through certificates. Because of the requirement to allocate investment expenses, it will be necessary for a REMIC to determine whether any "excess servicing" with respect to the mortgages it holds (or in which it owns an interest) is truly servicing (and thus an investment expense of the REMIC) or is instead an ownership interest in the mortgages retained by the servicer (and thus not such an investment expense). Similarly, where a REMIC's qualified mortgages are pass-through certificates, the REMIC will need to determine whether any excess servicing charged with respect to the mortgages underlying the certificates is truly servicing or an ownership interest in the mortgages.

In the case of a REMIC that is not a single-class REMIC, as indicated above, all investment expenses are allocated pro rata among individual holders of the residual interest. Because the value of the residual typically is small compared with the REMIC's assets and expenses, the requirement to include those expenses in income without a full offsetting deduction (or any deduction in calculating AMTI) can produce seriously adverse consequences for individual holders that are out of all proportion to the value of their investments.

Special rules apply to the portion of the income from a residual interest that is an excess inclusion. With limited exceptions, excess inclusions are *always* subject to tax, even in the hands of tax-exempt investors. The excess inclusion rules were adopted primarily to ensure taxation of phantom income and are discussed further in that context below. Income from residual interests that is not an excess inclusion should be exempt from tax in the hands of pension plans and other tax-exempt entities that are taxable only on UBTI to the same extent as, for example, income from a partial ownership interest in mortgages (that is, residual interests should not be considered debt-financed merely because the regular interests are considered debt obligations of the REMIC for some tax purposes).

A REMIC will have a net loss for any calendar quarter in which its deductions exceed its gross income. Such a loss may not be carried over or back to other periods by the REMIC, but instead is allocated among the current holders of the residual interest in the same manner as taxable income. However, the portion of net loss that is allocable to the holder of a residual interest will not be deductible by the holder to the extent it exceeds the holder's adjusted basis in such interest at the end of the quarter (or at the time of disposition of such interest, if earlier), determined before taking account of such loss.

Such adjusted basis would generally equal the cost of the interest to the holder, increased by any amount the holder has previously reported as income from such interest, and decreased (but not below zero) by any losses it has deducted and any distributions it has received. The holder's basis does not include any amount on account of the REMIC's liabilities. Any loss that is not currently deductible by reason of the basis limitation may be carried forward indefinitely and deducted from the holder's share of the REMIC's taxable income in later periods, but otherwise cannot be used.

If a residual interest is sold, the seller will recognize gain or (except as described below) loss equal to the difference between its adjusted basis in such interest and the amount realized in the sale. Such gain or loss generally will be capital gain or loss if the residual interest is held as a capital asset, except that if the holder is a bank or thrift, the gain or loss will always be ordinary. If the seller acquires (or enters into a contract or option to acquire) any residual interest in a REMIC, any equity interest in an owner trust or any interest in a taxable mortgage pool that is comparable to a residual interest in a REMIC, during the period beginning six months before, and ending six months after, the date of the sale, then the sale will be treated as a "wash sale" subject to section 1091. Any loss realized in a wash sale is not currently deductible, but instead increases the seller's adjusted basis in the newly acquired interest.

Distributions on a REMIC residual interest are treated as a non-taxable return of capital to the extent of the holder's basis in its interest. Distributions in excess of basis are treated as gain from the sale of the residual interest.

11.4.5 Phantom income

General

If a conduit issuer purchased a pool of mortgages and financed the purchase entirely with borrowed funds, and the debt service on the borrowings exactly matched the payments received on the mortgages, then the issuer would have no economic gain or loss from the transaction (assuming the mortgages are held to maturity and all payments are used to repay the borrowings). Given the lack of *economic* profit or loss, it might be expected that the interest or discount income on the assets and deductions in respect of the borrowings would exactly match for tax purposes as well, resulting in no taxable income or loss for the issuer. While that result would hold true over the entire life of the transaction, it may not be true in any particular year. The issuer may be required to report positive amounts of taxable income in some taxable years that are offset by matching losses in other periods. Non-economic taxable income and losses of this type are generally referred to as "phantom income" and "phantom losses".

In a typical offering of multiple-class sequential-pay bonds by a conduit issuer, some phantom income will be realized in the early years after the issuance of the bonds, followed by a corresponding amount of phantom losses in subsequent years. The cause is a difference in the distribution over time of the yields that are used in calculating mortgage income and bond deductions. In particular, interest deductions are calculated separately for each class of bonds, based on the yield to maturity of that class. Thus, the aggregate deductions allowed in any year will be determined by reference to the weighted average yield to maturity of all classes of bonds outstanding in that year. With a rising yield curve, the yield to maturity is lower for shorter-maturity classes of bonds than for longer dated classes. As a result, the weighted average yield to maturity of outstanding bonds increases over time as bonds are retired. By contrast, the yield to maturity of the mortgages remains constant, because they are not divided into sequential-pay classes. The combination of income based on a fixed yield and deductions based on an escalating yield produces the pattern of phantom income and losses previously described.

Where REMIC securities are issued using two tiers of REMICs, phantom income resulting from yield curve effects is realized only by the upper-tier REMIC (and is allocated to the residual interest in that REMIC).[18] The reason is that, in determining the taxable income of the two REMICs, the lower-tier regular interests held by the upper-tier REMIC are aggregated and treated as a single class of debt obligations with a single yield.

Phantom income can be illustrated with a simplified example. Consider a conduit issuer that purchases at par a mortgage that bears interest at a rate of 10 per cent, payable annually, and provides for two principal payments of $500 each, due one year and two years after the date of purchase, respectively. At the time of such purchase, the conduit issuer issues two bonds, each of which provides for a single principal payment of $500 at maturity. The first bond is issued at par, matures at the end of one year, and bears 8 per cent interest, payable at maturity. The second bond bears 10 per cent interest, payable annually, matures at the end of two years, and is issued at a price of $491.44 to yield 11 per cent. For simplicity, bond issuance and administrative costs are ignored. The conduit issuer is required to invest $8.56 of equity to finance the purchase of the mortgage and in exchange receives a cash distribution of $10 at the end of the first year and nothing thereafter, as shown in Table 11.4.1.

Table 11.4.1 Mortgage and bond payments

	Years from bond issuance		
	0	1	2
Mortgage payments	($1,000.00)	$600	$550
Bond 1 payments	500.00	(540)	—
Bond 2 payments	491.44	(50)	(550)
Funds available to conduit issuer	(8.56)	10	—

The taxable income, economic income, and phantom income and loss realized by the conduit issuer in each of the two years that the bonds are outstanding are shown in Table 11.4.2. The equity has received its entire economic return at the end of the first year. The loss of $4.50 in the second year is a phantom loss that offsets the same amount of phantom income in the first year.

18. For a discussion of two-tier REMICs, see Peaslee & Nirenberg, *supra*, n.2, Chapter 4, Part C.7.

Table 11.4.2 Income and loss of the conduit issuer

	First bond year	Second bond year
Mortgage income (10% of principal balance)	$100.000	$50.00
Deduction on Bond 1 (8% of principal balance)	(40.00)	—
Deduction on Bond 2 ($50 plus original issue discount of $4.06 in first year and $4.50 in second year)	(54.06)	(54.50)
Taxable income (loss) (mortgage income minus bond deductions)	5.94	(4.50)
Economic income ($10 minus $8.56)	1.44	—
Phantom income (loss) (taxable income minus economic income)	4.50	(4.50)

Another way to describe the phantom income problem is that the owner of an equity interest is not permitted to amortize the cost of its interest directly against the cash distributions the owner expects to receive, as would be possible, for example, if the right to those distributions were treated for tax purposes as a debt obligation of the conduit issuer. Instead, the owner must recover its investment over the life of the underlying mortgages. Thus, as shown in Table 11.4.2, although the equity interest in the conduit issuer becomes worthless following the distribution of the $10 payment at the end of the first year, the equity investor is permitted to treat as a return of capital in that year only $4.06 (the excess of the $10 distribution over taxable income of $5.94) rather than the full $8.56 cost of the equity interest.

Another less significant source of phantom income for non-REMIC issuers that does not relate to the sequential-pay nature of bonds arises from the rule that requires holders of pass-through certificates to report income based on the timing of receipt of payments on the underlying mortgages rather than the timing of distributions on the certificates (which lags the receipt of mortgage payments). Even where there is a close matching between the payments and aggregates income on pass-through certificates and the payments and deductions on bonds, there can be an acceleration of income and subsequent loss because the period over which income is reported on the certificates (from the date of acquisition of the certificates until mortgage principal is received) is shorter than the period for accruing deductions on the bonds.

It is not clear whether the same result arises when a REMIC holds a pass-through certificate. A REMIC is required to report market discount income on qualified mortgages (including pass-through certificates) under the PAC method as such discount accrues. Under the PAC method, discount accrues based on a prepayment assumption that is applied to the entire underlying pool. Because individual mortgages lose their tax identity under this approach, many REMICs calculate income from pass-through certificates based on the distributions made on the certificates, as if they were pay-through bonds.

Acceleration of net remaining phantom losses through sales of equity interests

When an equity interest is sold, the seller generally recognizes gain or loss equal to the difference between the amount realized in the sale and its adjusted basis in the interest. If the seller has recognized a net amount of phantom income, that amount would have increased the adjusted basis of the interest but not its value. As a result, the gain that otherwise would be realized from the sale would be decreased, or the loss would be increased, by the net amount of phantom income. Stated differently, the corresponding amount of future phantom losses that otherwise would be recognized over time generally would be accelerated into the taxable year of the sale. However, if the sale produces a net loss, this tax advantage may not be achieved for two reasons. First, for most investors other than banks, thrifts, and securities dealers, loss from the sale of an equity interest would be a capital loss that can be offset only against capital gain. Second, loss from the sale of a REMIC residual interest may be deferred under the special REMIC "wash sale" rule discussed in 11.4.4, above.

Special rules for REMICs; excess inclusions and negative value residual interests

Overview Phantom income realized by a REMIC is taxable to the holders of the residual interest. However, unlike equity interests in owner trusts, there is no tax requirement that a REMIC residual interest have any minimum economic value. In addition, because phantom income is not economic income, a residual interest could produce substantial phantom income without having any economic value. Accordingly, absent special rules, the tax on phantom income associated with residual interests could be avoided easily by reducing the economic value of those interests to a nominal sum and transferring them (and the related tax liability) to investors that are tax-exempt, or are not currently paying federal income tax (for example, because they have unrelated losses).

To frustrate such tax avoidance, a portion of the income from a residual interest, referred to as an excess inclusion, is, with an exception discussed below for certain thrift institutions, subject to federal income taxation in all events. Thus, an excess inclusion with respect to a residual interest:

(1) may not except as described below, be offset by any related losses or loss carryovers of the owner of such interest;

(2) will be treated as UBTI if the owner is a pension plan or other organization that is subject to tax only on its UBTI;
(3) is not eligible for any exemption from, or reduction in the rate of, withholding tax if the owner is a foreign investor; and
(4) may not be offset with an increased deduction for variable contract reserves if the owner is a life insurance company.

Any tax resulting from these rules can, however, be offset with otherwise available credits.

The rule that prevents the use of unrelated losses to offset excess inclusion income does not prevent the holder of a residual interest from using losses from a disposition of the residual interest to offset excess inclusion income, provided the holder's taxable income from other sources is at least as great as its excess inclusion income. For example, if, in a given taxable year, the holder has excess inclusion income of $100 and also realizes a loss of $100 from sale of the residual interest which (apart from the excess inclusion rules) is currently deductible, then the holder's taxable income would not increase because of ownership of the residual interest, provided the holder's taxable income, disregarding the residual interest, is at least $100. In a case where a residual interest is held by a partnership or S corporation, the prohibition on offsetting losses might apply at both the entity and owner level, although there seems to be no authority addressing the point.

If the holder of a residual interest is a corporation that is part of a group of corporations that files a consolidated federal income tax return, the entire group is ordinarily treated as one taxpayer in applying the excess inclusion rules. However, thrifts are subject to a special regime (discussed below).

The tax on excess inclusion income could potentially be avoided by transferring residual interests to holders that do not pay taxes because they are governmental entities, have no assets, or are located outside of the United States. Special measures exist to prevent the avoidance of tax through transfers of this type.

The text below addresses various topics relating to excess inclusions: the definition of the term; the exemption for thrifts from the limitation on the use of losses; special rules for REITSs, RICs, and other pass-through entities; surrogate taxes that are imposed in lieu of taxes on governmental holders of residual interests; rules disregarding tax motivated transfers of residual interests; and flaws in the existing excess inclusion rules (which have the effect of overstating phantom income).

The effectiveness of the battery of rules aimed at ensuring taxation of excess inclusion income is evidenced by the fact that residual interests are often economic liabilities (i.e., have negative value), because the tax burden on the holder exceeds the value of any right to receive distributions.[19]

19. For a discussion of certain issues raised by negative value residuals, see Peaslee & Nirenberg, *supra*, n.2, Chapter 7, Part E.4.h.

Definition of excess inclusion In general terms, the excess inclusion with respect to a residual interest equals the excess of the income from the holding of the interest over the income that would have accrued on the interest if it had earned income at all times from its issuance at a constant, compounded rate equal to 120 per cent of a long-term U.S. Treasury borrowing rate. More precisely, in any calendar quarter, the excess inclusion is the excess, if any, of (1) the taxable income of the REMIC allocated to the holder, over (2) the sum of the daily accruals for all days during the quarter on which the holder owns the residual interest. The daily accruals are determined by allocating to each day in the calendar quarter its ratable portion of the product of the adjusted issue price (defined below) of the residual interest at the beginning of the calendar quarter and 120 per cent of the federal long-term rate (defined below) in effect at the time the residual interest was issued. The adjusted issue price at the beginning of any calendar quarter equals the issue price of the residual interest, increased by the sum of the daily accruals for all prior quarters and the amount of any contributions made to the REMIC with respect to the residual interest after the start-up day, and decreased (but not below zero) by the aggregate amount of payments made on the residual interest in all prior quarters. The federal long-term rate is an average of current yields on Treasury obligations with a remaining term greater than nine years, computed and published monthly by the Service.

As an exception to the general rule just described, the Treasury has authority to issue regulations treating *all* income from the holding of a REMIC residual interest as an excess inclusion if the interest does not have significant value. The legislative history of TRA 1986 indicates that these regulations may be retroactive in "appropriate cases", but in any event will not apply where the value of the residual interest is at least two per cent of the combined value of all REMIC interests. The current REMIC regulations do not implement the significant value rule. Whether it is ever implemented is likely to be of limited importance because the formula for calculating excess inclusions already is linked (through the definition of daily accruals) to the issue price of a residual interest. Thus, if a residual interest has a nominal value, the daily accruals would be close to zero, and virtually all of the income from the interest would be an excess inclusion without regard to the significant value rule.

Thrift exception Certain thrift institutions are exempt from the rule (discussed above) prohibiting excess inclusions from being offset with unrelated losses. The exemption applies, however, only to residual interests that have significant value. A residual interest meets this test if (1) the aggregate issue price of the residual interests in the REMIC is at least two per cent of the aggregate issue price of all regular and residual interests in the REMIC, and (2) the anticipated weighted average life of the residual interest is at least 20 per cent of the anticipated weighted average life of the REMIC. The second part of the test prevents the two per cent test from being met during only a short initial period, after which capital invested in the residual interest is withdrawn.

As indicated above, if a group of corporations files a consolidated return, the group generally is treated as one taxpayer for purposes of applying the excess inclusion rules. However, the thrift exception is applied separately to each thrift that is a member of such a group. As a result, losses of a thrift generally cannot be offset against excess inclusions realized by other group members (including other thrifts) in a consolidated return. Similarly, losses of other group members generally cannot offset any excess inclusions of a thrift that exceed the losses of that thrift (determined without regard to the excess inclusions). The only exception to this rule is that a thrift and a qualified subsidiary are combined and treated as a single thrift (so that losses of one can offset excess inclusions of the other). A corporation is a qualified subsidiary for this purpose if (1) all of its stock, and substantially all of its indebtedness, is held directly by the thrift, and (2) it is organized and operated exclusively in connection with the organization and operation of one or more REMICs. Thus, a qualified subsidiary apparently cannot issue non-REMIC pay-through bonds or purchase interests in REMICs in the secondary market.

Pass-through entities Normally, the taxable income of an entity that holds residual interests cannot be less than the excess inclusions that it realizes from those interests. How does this rule apply to real estate investment trusts (REITs) and regulated investment companies (RICs)? These two types of entities are generally subject to a corporate tax on their taxable income, but they are allowed deductions in determining such income for dividends paid to shareholders. Can excess inclusion income be offset with a dividends paid deduction?

The answer is "yes", REITs and RICs are taxable on "real estate investment trust taxable income" (defined in section 857(b)(2)) and "investment company taxable income" (defined in section 852(b)(2)), respectively. These special brands of income are calculated by making adjustments to the "taxable income" of the REIT or RIC. One of these adjustments is the dividends paid deduction. Thus, a requirement that "taxable income" not be less than the amount of excess inclusions would not prevent the use of that deduction to eliminate the tax base of a REIT or RIC.

On the other hand, the fact that a REIT or RIC can avoid tax on its excess inclusion income does not import that the tainted character of such income disappears. Instead, the taint is shifted to the shareholders of the REIT or RIC. In the case of REITs, section 860E(d) authorizes regulations to be issued that would (1) allocate among the shareholders of a REIT the excess of the REIT's aggregate excess inclusions over REIT taxable income (as defined in section 857(b)(2), excluding any net capital gain), and (2) treat any amount so allocated to a shareholder as if it were an excess inclusion from a residual interest held by such shareholder. Similar rules apply to RICs, bank common trust funds, and certain cooperative organizations that are taxed under part 1 of subchapter T of the Code. No regulations have been issued under this grant of authority. Although pass-through entities generally can escape tax on excess inclusion income allocated to investors, as described in the next section, a pass-through entity in which interests are owned by certain governmental entities may be taxed on excess inclusions allocated to those entities.

Surrogate taxes on excess inclusions allocable to certain governmental entities Although every effort has been made to ensure that excess inclusions will be subject to tax under the Code, certain organizations that are exempt from all taxes under the Code could potentially hold residual interests without paying tax on excess inclusions. The REMIC rules refer to such a holder as a "disqualified organization". The principal example of a disqualified organization is a governmental entity.

A number of measures have been adopted to prevent tax on excess inclusions from being avoided through the ownership of residual interests by disqualified organizations. An entity cannot qualify as a REMIC unless it adopts reasonable arrangements designed to ensure that residual interests are not held by such organizations. In addition, if a disqualified organization (1) holds a residual interest despite such arrangements, or (2) becomes an indirect owner of such an interest through a pass-through entity, then a tax is imposed on someone else as a substitute for the tax on excess inclusions that would have been paid by the disqualified organization if it had been a taxpayer. In the first of these two situations, the "surrogate tax" is imposed on the person that transferred the residual interest to the disqualified organization. In the second, the pass-through entity is taxed. The sections which follow describe in more detail the operation of the surrogate taxes on transfers and pass-through entities.

Transfer tax A tax is imposed on transfers of REMIC residual interests to disqualified organizations. The tax is generally imposed on the transferor. However, if the transfer is made through an agent for a disqualified organization (for example, a securities firm buying as a broker for a disqualified organization), then the tax is imposed on the agent rather than on the transferor, apparently even if the transferor is aware of the transferee's identity.

A transferor or agent can protect itself from any possible liability for the tax by obtaining a statement from the transferee stating under penalties of perjury that the transferee is not a disqualified organization. Although section 860E(e)(4) refers to an "affidavit", a formal, notarized document is not required; a statement indicating that it is made under penalties of perjury will suffice. Further, because disqualified organizations do not have social security numbers (as distinguished from employer identification numbers), in the case of a transfer to an individual, the transferee's statement may simply provide a social security number and recite under penalties of perjury that the number is that of the transferee. The affidavit will not be effective, however, if the transferor or agent, as the case may be, has actual knowledge, as of the time of the transfer, that the affidavit is false. Transferors of residual interests and persons buying such interests on behalf of others often obtain such affidavits as a matter of course.

If the tax applies to a transfer of a residual interest, it is calculated by multiplying the highest marginal federal corporate income tax rate by an amount equal to the present value of the total anticipated excess inclusions on such interest for periods after the transfer. Anticipated excess inclusions are determined using the same prepayment assumption that applies in accruing OID under the PAC method, and present values are computed using the applicable federal rate as the discount rate. Where a tax is imposed on a transfer of a residual interest to a disqualified organization, the issuing REMIC is required, within 60 days after request, to provide the information necessary for computing the tax to the person required to pay the tax and to the Service. The REMIC may charge the taxpayer (but not the Service) a reasonable fee for providing the information.

The Service has authority to waive the tax on any transfer of a residual interest if, within a reasonable time after discovery that the transfer was subject to tax, steps are taken so that the interest is no longer held by the disqualified organization, and the Service is paid a surrogate tax equal to the product of the highest marginal corporate tax rate and the amount of excess inclusions that accrued on the residual interest while it was held by the disqualified organization.

Tax on pass-through entities A tax is imposed on any pass-through entity (as defined below) if a disqualified organization is the record holder of an interest in the entity. A pass-through entity may rely on a statement from a record holder made under penalties of perjury to establish that it is not a disqualified organization if the entity does not know that the statement is false. The tax equals the highest marginal federal corporate income tax rate multiplied by the amount of excess inclusions allocable to the interest in the entity held of record by the disqualified organization. No tax is imposed on a pass-through entity if interests in the entity are owned beneficially by a disqualified organization, provided the disqualified organization is not the record holder. In these circumstances, the nominee is treated as the pass-through entity (as described in the next paragraph) and is subject to the tax.

A pass-through entity is defined as any RIC, REIT, bank, common trust fund, partnership, trust or estate. The term also includes cooperative organizations taxed under part 1 of subchapter T of the Code. The definition does not include corporations taxed under subchapter S, presumbly because the definition of an S corporation would not allow a disqualified organization to be a stockholder. Except as provided in regulations, a person holding an interest in a pass-through entity as a nominee for another person is treated with respect to that interest as a pass-through entity (and the other person is treated as a record holder of an interest in the deemed pass-through entity represented by the nominee arrangement).

To illustrate how the tax operates, suppose that a REIT holds a REMIC residual interest and a broker holds stock in the REIT as a nominee for a disqualified person. In that event, the broker and not the REIT would be subject to tax on the portion of the excess inclusions of the REIT that is allocable to the interests in the REIT held for the disqualified organization through the broker.

Any tax imposed on a pass-through entity is deductible from the entity's ordinary gross income. Further, a REIT or a RIC is permitted to charge against dividends paid to a disqualified organization the tax expense arising out of its ownership of stock without causing dividends paid by the REIT or RIC to be preferential within the meaning of section 562(c) (which disallows the dividends paid deduction for preferential dividends). A REIT should be able to prohibit record ownership of its stock by a disqualified organization without running afoul of the tax requirement that it have transferable shares.

Certain tax-motivated transfers disregarded The panoply of measures described above for ensuring the payment of tax on excess inclusion income has two potential gaps: first, a residual interest could be transferred to a U.S. person that is subject to U.S. taxes but has no assets or otherwise does not intend to pay taxes that are due. Second, a residual interest could be transferred to a foreign person that, as a practical matter, will not pay U.S. taxes unless the taxes are withheld, in circumstances where the distributions on the residual interest from which tax may be withheld are less than the current tax liability.

The REMIC regulations fill in these gaps by disregarding certain transfers of residual interests where the collection of tax from the transferee is doubtful. The effect of disregarding a transfer of a residual interest is that the transferor continues to be liable for the tax on income, including excess inclusions, from the interest. Where a residual interest is newly issued to a person other than the REMIC sponsor, the REMIC sponsor is treated as the transferor.

As described below, different standards apply in disregarding transfers depending on whether the transferee is a U.S. or non-U.S. person.

Transfers to U.S. persons The regulations disregard the transfer of any "noneconomic" residual interest (described below) to a U.S. person if a significant purpose of the transfer is to impede the assessment or collection of tax. Such a purpose exists if the transferor either knew or should have known (had "improper knowledge") that the transferee would be unwilling or unable to pay the taxes due on its share of the taxable income of the REMIC.

Under a safe harbor rule, a taxpayer is presumed not to have improper knowledge if:

- the transferor conducts, *at the time of the transfer*, a reasonable investigation of the financial condition of the transferee and, as a result of the investigation, finds that the transferee historically paid its debts as they came due and found no significant evidence to indicate that the transferee will not continue to do so, and

- the transferee represents to the transferor that it understands that, as a holder of the residual interest, it may incur tax liabilities in excess of any cash flows on the residual interest and that the transferee intends to pay taxes associated with holding the residual interest as they become due.

It is not clear why the rule is only a presumption. If there are factors indicating that the transferee will not pay taxes that become due, those factors should be taken into account in determining whether the transferor made a reasonable investigation and the proper findings, and not prevent the safe harbor from applying if its terms are met. Otherwise, the rule would be worthless.

The regulations do not explain how extensive an investigation must be in order to be reasonable. Only a fairly cursory investigation should be required where the transferee is known to conduct substantial activities other than holding residual interests, and there are no obvious signs of financial distress. Needless to say, conducting an investigation will be more difficult for transferees that are privately held companies than for an SEC reporting company.

A residual interest is considered to be non-economic for this purpose unless *at the time of the transfer*:

- the present value of the expected future distributions thereon at least equals the product of the present value of anticipated excess inclusions and the highest marginal corporate income tax rate for the year of the transfer, and
- the transferor reasonably expects that, for each anticipated excess inclusion, the transferee will receive distributions from the REMIC at or after the time taxes accrue on the anticipated excess inclusion in an amount sufficient to satisfy the accrued taxes.

A non-economic residual interest includes not only interests that have a nominal fair market value at the time of the transfer, but also interests that have substantial values but may receive distributions in advance of realizing excess inclusion income. There is no requirement that distributions sufficient to pay taxes on excess inclusions be made within any particular period following the accrual of such income, although delays in the timing of distributions will reduce their present value. Because the determination of whether a residual interest is non-economic is made at the time of transfer, a residual interest that is economic for part of its life can become non-economic (and thus have restricted transferability) at a later time.

Transfer to foreign investors As further discussed below, a foreign investor holding a residual interest generally is subject to a 30 per cent withholding tax on excess inclusion income. Under current law, the tax is imposed on excess inclusions not as the income accrues, but only when distributions are made on the residual interests. The REMIC regulations prevent this rule from being abused by disregarding any transfer to a foreign person of a residual interest that has "tax avoidance potential". A "foreign person" should include anyone who may be subject to U.S. withholding tax. A residual interest has tax avoidance potential unless, *at the time of the transfer*, the transferor reasonably expects that, for each excess inclusion the REMIC will distribute to the transferee residual interest holder an amount that will equal at least 30 per cent of the excess inclusion, and such amount will be distributed at or after the time at which the excess inclusion accrues and not later than the close of the calendar year following the calendar year of accrual.

If a residual interest is transferred to a foreign person, a transfer of the residual interest by that person to a U.S. person will be disregarded (so that taxes will continue to be withheld on distributions) if the effect of the transfer would be to allow the transferor to avoid the withholding taxes on excess inclusions. Thus, it is not possible to avoid the taxes on excess inclusions by having a foreign person hold a residual interest while excess inclusions accrue and then transferring it to a U.S. person before the related cash distributions are made.

Negative value residual interests Residual interests often have negative fair market values, because the tax cost of the associated phantom income exceeds the value of any right to receive distributions. In such a case, an owner would need to pay another party to take over its ownership position.

Although there are no authorities addressing the point, the party receiving such a payment should be required to include in it income as an ordinary item.[20]

11.5 SPECIAL RULES FOR NON-U.S. INVESTORS

A principal tax objective of non-U.S. investors purchasing mortgage-backed securities issued in the United States is to avoid the U.S. 30 per cent withholding tax on interest income. A second goal may be to hold such securities in bearer (as distinguished from registered) form. Section 11.5.1 discusses the TEFRA registration requirements that limit the issuance of debt instruments in bearer form. (The TEFRA registration requirements are tax related and distinct from any need to register securities with the Securities and Exchange Commission or state agencies under U.S. securities laws.) The withholding tax is the subject of 11.5.2. The part concludes with a brief comment in 11.5.3 on the implications for mortgage-backed securities of the Foreign Investment in Real Property Tax Act of 1980 (FIRPTA).

20. For a more complete discussion of this point, see Peaslee & Nirenberg, *supra*, n.2, Chapter 7, Part E.4.h.

11.5.1 TEFRA registration requirements

Overview

With a view to increasing taxpayer compliance, TEFRA amended the Code to prohibit, with limited exceptions, the issuance or holding of debt obligations in the United States in bearer form. More particularly, the TEFRA rules require all registration-required obligations (as defined below) to be in registered form. An obligation is in registered form for these purposes if

(1) it is registered as to both principal and interest with the issuer or its agent, and can be transferred only by the surrender of the old obligation to the registrar and either its reissuance, or the issuance of a new obligation, to the new owner;
(2) principal and interest may be transferred only through a book entry system maintained by the issuer or its agent; or
(3) the obligation can be transferred only through either of the methods described in (1) or (2).

Any obligation that is not in registered form is considered to be in bearer form. An obligation which is convertible into bearer form is in bearer form.

The issuance of a registration-required obligation in bearer form can result in severe sanctions for the issuer. Any U.S. taxpayer who holds such an obligation in bearer form in violation of the TEFRA rules is also subject to certain tax penalties.

A registration-required obligation is generally defined in section 163(f)(2) as any obligation other than an obligation that

(1) is issued by an individual,
(2) is not of a type offered to the public, or
(3) has a maturity at issue of not more than one year.

Thus, the TEFRA registration requirements do not apply directly to home mortgages and other consumer loans that are obligations of individuals. In fact, such obligations are almost never issued or held in registered form. Although most tax practitioners have concluded that conventional commercial mortgages are not of a type offered to the public, the emergence of a market for single class pass-through certificates backed by a single conventional commercial mortgage may, over time, cause a rethinking of that conclusion.

In addition, for purposes of applying the issuer sanctions only, an obligation is not registration-required if it is issued under the so-called "Eurobond exception", which allows bearer paper to be offered outside of the United States to non-U.S. investors. In general, an obligation qualifies for the Eurobond exception if

(1) the obligation is "targeted" to non-U.S. investors upon its original issuance,

(2) the obligation provides for interest to be payable only outside the United States, and

(3) for any period during which the obligation is held other than in temporary global form, the obligation and each coupon contains a TEFRA legend (a statement to the effect that any United States person who holds the obligation will be subject to the TEFRA holder sanctions).

The Eurobond exception, however, never applies to U.S. Government, or U.S. Government-backed, securities. For this purpose, a U.S. Government security is any security issued or guaranteed by the U.S. or any U.S. owned or sponsored agency, including, for example, GNMA, FNMA and FHLMC. A security is U.S. Government-backed if more than 50 per cent of the income or collateral supporting it (whether as an asset underlying a pass-through certificate or as collateral for a debt obligation) consists of income, or principal, of a U.S. Government security. Thus, any pass-through certificates guaranteed by the U.S. or a U.S. sponsored agency, and pay-through bonds more than 50 per cent collateralized by such certificates, are ineligible for the Eurobond exception.

Although an obligation issued or backed by the U.S. Government may not be held in bearer form, it can be held in targeted registered form if it was targeted to foreign investors upon its original issuance. A targeted registered obligation generally must comply with the regulations implementing the Eurobond exception. Targeted registered obligations are considered to be in registered form for purposes of the TEFRA requirements and accordingly may be resold freely to U.S. investors. As discussed in 11.5.2, the certification requirements that must be met by a foreign investor to receive interest on a registered obligation free of U.S. withholding tax under the portfolio interest exemption are more lenient for a targeted than a non-targeted, registered obligation.

Mortgage-backed securities

The TEFRA rules apply in a straightforward way to pay-through bonds and REMIC regular interests. They are registration-required obligations and must be issued in registered form unless the Eurobond exception applies. Although REMIC residual interests are probably not "obligations" for TEFRA purposes, they cannot be issued in bearer form without jeopardizing the issuer's status as a REMIC.

The treatment of pass-through certificates under the TEFRA rules is more complex. As described in Parts II. B. and II. D., for substantive tax purposes pass-through certificates are not recognized to be debt of the issuing trust; instead, they merely evidence ownership of trust assets by certificate holders. If this analysis were followed in applying the TEFRA rules, then pass-through certificates would not themselves be "obligations" that could be "registration-required". Further, registration of the certificates could not be mandated on the ground that they represent ownership interests in registration-required obligations if the underlying obligations are obligations of individuals or loans not of a type offered to the public. However, it would make little sense to exclude pass-through certificates from the reach of the TEFRA rules. They are generally liquid securities similar to traded debt instruments. In addition, if the status of a pass-through certificate under the TEFRA rules depended solely on the status of the underlying obligations, it would not be possible to issue bearer certificates under the Eurobond exception if the trust assets included any registration-required obligations.

These unsettling results are avoided under regulations issued in 1985 that effectively treat pass-through certificates as defined in the regulations as obligations of the issuing trust for TEFRA purposes. Thus, the nature of the underlying obligations is irrelevant in applying the TEFRA rules to such certificates. The certificates must be in registered form unless the Eurobond exception applies based on an offering of the certificates (as distinguished from the obligations held by the trust) outside of the United States.

The regulations define a "pass-through certificate" as a "pass-through or participation certificate evidencing an interest in a pool of mortgage loans" (emphasis added) to which the grantor trust rules apply, or a "similar evidence of interest in a similar pooled fund or pooled trust treated as a grantor trust". An example in the regulations concludes that certificates of interest in a trust that holds 1,000 residential mortgages that are obligations of unrelated individuals are "pass-through certificates". Thus, the 1,000 mortgages are considered a "pool".

The regulations also grant the Service broad authority to characterize pass-through securities "in accordance with the substance of the arrangement they represent" and to impose issuer sanctions accordingly. The regulations indicate that this authority might be used to prevent a domestically offered bond from being issued indirectly in bearer form by issuing the bond in registered form to a trust that issues bearer pass-through securities that are not within the Eurobond exception.

Apart from the example of a trust holding 1,000 residential mortgages, the regulations offer no guidance on the distinction between an interest in a "pool" of loans and pass-through securities that are subject to characterization "in accordance with the substance of the arrangement they represent". Nonetheless, applying the regulations to pass-through securities representing interests in residential mortgages should be straightforward. The regulations were apparently written with these securities in mind, and any group of home mortgages large enough to be grouped and used to support a pass-through security should qualify as a pool, even if the number of loans is significantly below 1,000. On the other hand, suppose that a trust holds five commercial mortgage loans, each of which has a principal balance in excess of $5 million. It is much less obvious that those loans would be considered a pool.

Some guidance about the factors that may be relevant in determining whether a pool exists can be gleaned from an examination of typical residential mortgage pass-through securities, if they are taken as the clearest example of a pass-through certificate within the meaning of the regulations. Home mortgages have a number of characteristics that make them unattractive as direct investments. First, the creditworthiness of individual borrowers is unknown. Second, because of the possibility of prepayment, the cash flow from a single loan is unpredictable. Finally, any one loan is too small to make it divisible into units suitable for public trading. A pass-through arrangement addresses these problems by combining many home mortgages in a trust, adding insurance, a guarantee or other credit support, and creating trust interests in relatively small denominations. The aggregation of many mortgages evens out cash flows and credit risk from the perspective of any one investor; the credit support further simplifies the credit analysis; and the size of the pool enables the pass-through securities to trade actively in public markets. Thus, an analysis of these securities suggests that a group of loans held by a trust should be considered a pool (and interests in the trust should be treated as pass-through certificates within the meaning of the regulations) if individual interests in the trust are qualitatively different from the underlying loans by virtue of differences in predictability of payments, credit risk, and liquidity.

11.5.2 Withholding tax

Overview

In general, a non-U.S. investor who has no connection with the United States other than the holding of the mortgage-backed security under discussion (and in particular does not hold the security in connection with a U.S. trade or business) and who receives from U.S. sources "fixed or determinable annual or periodical income" (FDAP income) is subject to a 30 per cent tax on the gross amount of such income, unless a statutory exemption applies, or the tax is reduced or eliminated under an income tax treaty between the U.S. and the country of residence of the investor. The tax is required to be collected and paid over to the Service by any withholding agent in the chain of payment (generally, any person who pays the income to a non-U.S. person), but is due whether or not it is collected by withholding. A withholding agent may not withhold, or may withhold at a reduced rate, in reliance on a treaty only if the agent receives an IRS Form 1001 from the foreign investor stating that the investor is eligible for the treaty benefit.

The two types of income that are likely to be earned by an investor in mortgage-backed securities are interest and gain from the sale or exchange of the securities. Interest is FDAP income, and gain from the sale or exchange of securities is not. Thus, the discussion herein of the withholding tax concentrates on interest income. Certain other types of income that may be earned from mortgage-backed securities are discussed below.

In general, interest income is subject to the withholding tax if it is derived from U.S. sources, unless the exemption for portfolio interest described below applies, or the rate is reduced or eliminated under a treaty. Certain special rules apply to original issue discount.[21]

The source of interest income depends on the status of the borrower. Interest is generally U.S. source if the borrower is organized or resident in the U.S. Thus, interest on pass-through certificates representing an ownership interest in home mortgages that are obligations of U.S. resident individuals, and interest on pay-through bonds issued by a U.S. corporation or owner trust, typically would be sourced in the United States. Although there is no explicit source rule for REMIC interests, it is highly likely that income from both regular and residual interests would be sourced in the United States if the issuing REMIC is organized and operated in the U.S. and the underlying mortgages are obligations of U.S. borrowers. Apart from the source question, the withholding tax applies to REMIC regular interests in the same way that it applies to conventional debt obligations.

Income on a REMIC residual interest representing a share of the REMIC's taxable income is treated as interest for withholding tax purposes. No exemption from such tax or reduction in rate applies to the portion of the income from a residual interest that is an excess inclusion. In the unusual case where income from a REMIC residual interest is considered to be derived from sources outside of the U.S., however, such income should not be subject to U.S. withholding tax, even if it is an excess inclusion. The withholding tax generally is imposed on income from a residual interest when such income is paid or distributed (or when the interest is disposed of). Such income may have to be taken into account earlier, under regulations, if the residual interest does not have significant value, but to date no such regulations have been issued. Instead, the REMIC regulations address the issue by providing that a purported transfer of a residual interest to a foreign investor is ignored for tax purposes—with the hapless transferor retaining ownership of the interest for tax purposes—unless the residual interest is reasonably expected to produce cash distributions sufficient to pay withholding tax liabilities no later than the close of the calendar year following the year in which the related income accrues.

For withholding tax purposes, the holder of an equity interest in a non-TMP owner trust, whether taxable as a grantor trust or as a partnership, is treated

21. With an exception for obligations with an original term of 183 days or less, accrued OID earned by a non-U.S. investor is generally subject to the 30% tax in the same manner as other interest income. However, the tax is imposed on the OID on an obligation only when (1) a payment on the obligation is made, in an amount not exceeding the lesser of (a) the total amount of tax on the accrued portion of such discount not previously taken into account and (b) the amount of the payment (net of any withholding tax otherwise imposed on the payment) or (2) the obligation is sold or exchanged, in an amount equal to the total amount of tax on the accrued portion of such discount not previously taken into account. For this purpose, accruals of OID are calculated in the same manner as for domestic taxpayers with an exception for short-term obligations. Until regulations are adopted, only the issuer of an obligation and its agents are required to withhold the tax on accrued OID from the proceeds of a sale or exchange of the obligation under section 1441 or 1442. See Revenue Ruling 68–333, 1968–1 C.B. 390. Regulations imposing a broader withholding requirement have been proposed but not adopted.

essentially as if it owned directly the underlying mortgages and other trust assets. Thus, the 30 per cent tax, to the extent it applies, is based on the gross amount of interest received by the trust (that is, without a deduction for interest payments made on the related bonds). For that reason, it is unlikely that a foreign investor would purchase an equity interest in such a trust unless the investor is certain that all interest received by the trust will be exempt from withholding tax, either as portfolio interest or under a tax treaty.

The discussion above assumes that interest income is not effectively connected with a U.S. trade or business engaged in by the investor. Effectively connected income is not subject to the 30 per cent withholding tax. Instead such income, net of deductions for expenses and other items, is subject to tax at the regular rates applicable to U.S. taxpayers. A foreign investor owning equity in a partnership (including an owner trust classified as a partnership) that is engaged in a U.S. trade or business must treat its share of the partnership's business income as effectively connected income. Moreover, the partnership would be required to pay estimated taxes on the investor's behalf.

It is unlikely that a typical partnership or owner trust that holds a fixed portfolio consisting largely of performing loans and borrows funds would be considered to be engaged in a trade or business. The risk of finding business activity would be greater for an entity formed to work out financially distressed mortgage loans, particularly if it acquires and manages a number of properties securing the loans.

The treatment of income earned on a pass-through debt certificate will depend on whether it is characterized as debt for tax purposes or as a partnership interest and, if classified as a partnership interest, whether the partnership is considered to be engaged in a trade or business and whether the amounts paid are treated as guaranteed payments. (Arguably the revolving nature of the assets backing an issue of pass-through debt certificates increases the likelihood that the issuing trust, if treated as a partnership, would be considered to be engaged in a trade or business.)

Portfolio interest exemption

Under sections 871(h) and 881(c), enacted by TRA 1984, interest on obligations issued after July 18, 1984 (the date of enactment of TRA 1984) is exempt from withholding tax if such interest qualifies as portfolio interest. With limited exceptions, most significantly for payments to related parties,[22] interest on an obligation (including OID) is portfolio interest if (1) the obligation is in bearer form, and was issued in compliance with the Eurobond exception to the TEFRA

22. Portfolio interest does not include (1) any interest paid by a corporation to a 10% shareholder (measured by voting power) or by a partnership to a 10% partner (measured by the higher of the capital or profits interest), or interest paid to a controlled foreign corporation related to the payor, or (2) except in the case of interest paid on an obligation of the United States, interest paid to a bank on an extension of credit pursuant to a loan agreement entered into in the ordinary course of its trade or business. See sections 871(h)(3) and 881(c)(3).

registration requirements described in 11.5.1, or (2) the obligation is in registered form, and the beneficial owner provides the withholding agent with a statement, signed under penalties of perjury, giving the owner's name and address and certifying that the owner is not a United States person. In the case of an obligation issued in "targeted registered" form, a more lenient certification procedure applies if the obligation is held through an appropriate foreign financial institution. In such a case, the financial institution need only certify that the beneficial owner of the obligation is not a United States person, without disclosing the beneficial owner's identity.

The portfolio interest exemption applies in different ways to pass-through certificates, pay-through bonds and REMIC regular interests, equity interests in owner trusts, and REMIC residual interests.

Prior to the issuance in 1985 of regulations applying the TEFRA registration requirements to pass-through certificates, it was unclear whether interest paid to non-U.S. investors on residential mortgage pass-through certificates could qualify as portfolio interest. Home mortgages are typically held in bearer form. Interest on a bearer obligation can qualify as portfolio interest only if the obligation was issued under the Eurobond exception, which would not be true for such mortgages. Thus, interest on residential mortgages, and apparently therefore interest on pass-through certificates representing ownership interests in those mortgages, could not be portfolio interest.

The 1985 regulations solved this problem by treating pass-through certificates as separate obligations of the issuing trust for purposes of the TEFRA rules. Under the regulations, interest on a pass-through certificate can qualify as portfolio interest if (1) the certificate itself is in bearer form and was issued under the Eurobond exception, or (2) the certificate is in registered form and the appropriate investor certification is received, in each case without regard to the status of the underlying obligations. However, a pass-through certificate continues to be treated as an ownership interest in trust assets for other tax purposes, including application of the effective date of the portfolio interest rules. Accordingly, interest on a pass-through certificate can be exempt from withholding tax as portfolio interest only to the extent that the mortgages backing the certificate were originated after July 18, 1984.

Pay-through bonds and REMIC regular interests are considered debt instruments in their own right and thus can qualify for the portfolio interest exemption (assuming, in the case of pay-through bonds, an issue date after July 18, 1984) regardless of the date of origination of the underlying mortgages or mortgage-backed securities.[23]

23. As described in n.22, *supra*, the portfolio interest exemption does not apply to interest paid by a corporation or partnership to a 10% owner. Thus, the exemption would not apply to interest on pay-through bond issued by a corporation or by an owner trust classified as a partnership if the payee is a 10% owner of the issuer. Further, if an owner trust is classified as a grantor trust, the exemption may not apply to interest paid by the trust that is allocable (as an expense) to any corporate or partnership beneficiary of the trust if the payee is a 10% owner of the beneficiary. It is not clear how the 10% owner limitation would be applied to a REMIC regular interest. Because a REMIC is not

In the case of an owner trust which is taxed as a partnership or trust, interest earned by the trust that is allocable to an equity interest held by a foreign investor should be eligible for the portfolio interest exemption to the same extent as if such interest were received directly by the foreign investor. Thus, assuming that the investor provides appropriate certifications to the owner trustee or possibly other withholding agents, such interest should be tax free to the extent it is earned on mortgages or other debt obligations issued after July 18, 1984 (with the possible exception of interest on certain short-term obligations in bearer form).[24] (Dividends paid on amounts invested in money market mutual fund, although similar to interest would not qualify as profits less interest.) A similar look-through approach applies to REMIC residual interests. However, income that is an excess inclusion can never benefit from the portfolio interest exemption.

Recent amendments to the Code exclude from the definition of portfolio interest any interest that, with certain exceptions, is contingent on the profits or cash flow of the debtor (including related parties), the value of its property, or distributions on its equity.[25] Thus, such interest will generally be subject to the

---

treated as a corporation or partnership for tax purposes (section 860A(a)), the limitation should not be based on ownership of a 10% or greater interest in the REMIC. If the rule is applicable at all, it would seem to make sense to apply it based on the relationship between the holder of the regular interest, on the one hand, and the obligors on the loans held by the REMIC, or possibly the holders of residual interests, on the other hand.

24. Typically, the mortgage-backed securities owned by an owner trust and the equity interests in the trust are held in registered form. Thus, in determining whether interest earned on those securities is portfolio interest, problems raised by the existence of bearer obligations do not arise. However, an owner trust may also earn interest on short-term obligations that is not portfolio interest because the obligations are held in bearer form and were not issued under the Eurobond exception. (As indicated in the text above, short-term obligations are not registration-required. Although the bearer or registered status of the obligations held by an owner trust would be irrelevant if the trust were classified as a grantor trust and the equity interests in the trust were treated as pass-through certificates within the meaning of the 1985 TEFRA regulations (see the text accompanying n.16), neither result can be assumed.) Interest on short-term obligations may be exempt from withholding tax on other grounds. For example, there is an exemption for original issue discount on obligations with an original maturity of 183 days or less (section 871(g)(1)(B)(i)) and for interest on bank deposits (sections 871(i)(2)(A) and 881(d)).

25. Sections 871(h)(4) and 881(c)(4), as added by RRA 1993. The amendments apply to interest received on or after January 1, 1994, with an exception for interest on fixed-term debt issued on or before (or under a binding contract in existence on or before) April 7, 1993. The new rules do not apply to interest on a debt solely on account of (1) a contingency as to the timing of any interest or principal payment, (2) the debt being non-recourse or limited recourse, (3) the interest being determined by reference to interest that itself is not contingent (or by reference to the principal amount of debt that does not bear contingent interest), (4) the debtor entering into a hedging transaction to reduce interest rate or currency risk, or (5) the interest being determined with reference to (a) changes in the value of publicly traded property, including stock, but not including U.S. real property interests, (b) changes in the yield of such property (other than contingent interest debt, or stock or other property that represents a beneficial interest in the debtor), or (c) changes in an index of such value or yield. In the case of a debt instrument that pays both contingent and non-contingent interest, only the contingent interest fails to qualify as portfolio interest. H.R. Rep. No. 111, 103rd Cong., 1st Sess. (RRA 1993 House Report) at 288. If a debt instrument provides for a minimum rate of non-contingent interest, the minimum interest is treated as non-contingent, notwithstanding any overlap with interest computed under a contingent interest formula. H.R. Rep. No. 312, 103rd Cong., 1st Sess. (RRA 1993 Conference Report) at 183–184.

30 per cent withholding tax unless a treaty exemption or reduction applies.[26]

This change in law is unlikely to have much significance for mortgage-backed securities. Interest on pay-through bonds and REMIC regular interests might be thought to be contingent in that it is generally payable only out of (and to the extent of) the issuer's cash flow or interest income. Also, any such instrument that is issued at a discount or premium would have a value that depends significantly on the timing of prepayments on the underlying mortgages. Nonetheless, the legislation was not aimed at securities that merely carve up cash flows on mortgages that do not themselves pay contingent interest. The statutory exceptions to the definition of contingent interest cover the features of typical mortgage-backed securities that are likely to raise questions.

Section 2105(b)(3) effectively exempts debt obligations from the U.S. estate tax applicable to non-resident alien individuals if interest thereon would be eligible for the portfolio interest exemption if received by the decedent at the time of his death (without regard to any certification requirement). This exemption should apply to any mortgage-backed security to the extent income thereon is portfolio interest, although admittedly the question is a much closer one for equity interests in owner trusts that are classified as partnerships and REMIC residual interests than for pay-through bonds, REMIC regular interests, or interests in grantor trusts.

Income from swaps and rents

Two other categories of FDAP income that may be realized by holders of mortgage-backed securities are income from swaps and income from the rental of real property. These types of income are discussed in the next two sections.

Swaps Recently, securities have been issued that represent ownership interests in a trust holding both (1) a REMIC regular interest or pass-through certificate and (2) a notional principal contract, such as an interest rate swap, cap or floor agreement. The trust may be classified for tax purposes as a grantor trust or partnership. The withholding tax treatment of regular interests and pass-through certificates is discussed above and would not change because the securities are held through a trust.

The income from payments received on the notional principal contract would generally be FDAP income. Thus, the income would be subject to U.S. withholding tax unless the tax is eliminated or reduced under a tax treaty, or the

---

The RRA 1993 House Report at 288–289 states that the new rules will not apply to REMIC regular interests merely because, for example (1) the period they remain outstanding is contingent on mortgage prepayments, earnings on REMIC assets, or expenses, (2) interest equals a percentage of non-contingent interest on qualified mortgages, or (3) interest varies inversely with interest on qualified mortgages.

26. The legislation would not override treaties. See RRA 1993 House Report at 286, 290. Contingent interest that is not treated as interest under general U.S. tax principles would, of course, generally not be considered to be interest for treaty purposes.

source of the income is outside of the U.S. (The portfolio interest exemption would not apply, because swap income is not interest.) In fact, the withholding tax rarely applies to income from a notional principal contract, because such income is, in general, sourced based on the residence of the taxpayer receiving the payments, not the residence of the payor. A non-U.S. investor that owns an interest in a notional principal contract through a grantor trust would clearly benefit from this source rule. The trust would be ignored. On the other hand, if the owning trust is classified as a partnership, and is organized under U.S. law, the taxpayer receiving the payments would arguably be the domestic partnership, raising the specter of a withholding tax where a treaty exemption does not apply.

Rental income Rental income from real property located in the U.S. generally is considered U.S. source FDAP income. There is no withholding tax exemption for such income comparable to the one for portfolio interest. Thus, where a non-U.S. investor holds pass-through certificates, or equity interests in owner trusts that are taxed as a trust or partnerships, and the issuer acquires U.S. real property in connection with a default or anticipated default on a mortgage, the withholding tax generally would apply to the investor's share of any rents received on the property. Interesting allocation issues arise where pass-through certificates are divided into junior and senior classes. On the other hand, income earned on an instrument that is taxed as debt of the issuer, such as a pay-through bond or REMIC regular interest, continues to be interest even if it is derived from rental income. Although uncertain, it appears that all income on a REMIC residual interest would be treated as interest income for withholding tax purposes regardless of the REMIC's sources of income.

11.5.3 FIRPTA

FIRPTA enacted section 897, which subjects non-U.S. investors to U.S. tax on gain from sales of certain U.S. real property interests (including equity interests in "United States real property holding corporations") in the same manner as if such gain were effectively connected with a U.S. trade or business. Section 1445 imposes a related requirement to withhold tax from the proceeds of sales. The FIRPTA rules do not apply to interests in real property that are solely creditor interests with no participation in the income, revenues, or appreciation of the property. Thus, a foreign investor holding a mortgage-backed security will not be affected by this legislation if the mortgages underlying the security lack such participation features and the issuer does not acquire the underlying real property.

Where a non-U.S. investor holds a pass-through certificate, or an equity interest in an owner trust that is taxed as a grantor trust or partnership, and the issuer acquires a real property interest in connection with a mortgage default, the investor will generally be treated for purposes of FIRPTA as owning a non-creditor interest in such property. Any gain attributable to such property that is allocable to the investor will potentially be taxed under FIRPTA either when the owning entity disposes of the real property, or when the investor disposes of its interest in the entity. A creditor acquiring real property collateral generally would have a basis in the acquired real property equal to its fair market value at the time of acquisition, so that any gain would be limited to increases in the property's value during the period it is held by the entity.

If any class of interests in the entity are regularly traded on an established securities market (including certain over-the-counter markets), then gain from disposition of interests in the entity (whether or not of the traded class) generally would not be subject to tax.[27] This rule does not affect the taxation of gain realized upon a disposition of real property by the entity. The definition of "regularly traded on an established securities market" is highly technical. For example, under current regulations, a class of interests is not "regularly traded" if 100 or fewer persons own 50 per cent or more of the class, or if the market is outside the U.S. and the interests are not in registered form.

The section 1445 withholding tax does not currently apply to dispositions of interests in partnerships or trust, unless, among other requirements, at least 50 per cent of the gross assets of the entity consist of U.S. real property interests. A domestic trust or partnership that disposes of interests in real property is, however, required to withhold tax on a non-U.S. investor's share of any gain.

A REMIC regular interest should be treated as a creditor interest that is not subject to the FIRPTA tax without regard to any holdings of real property by the issuing REMIC. The tax treatment of residual interests is less clear.

11.6 TAXATION OF SPONSORS

Previous parts of this chapter concentrated on the taxation of issuers and investors. This part looks at sponsors. For any issue of securities backed by a pool of mortgages, the term "sponsor" is used here broadly to refer to any person who (1) owned an interest in those mortgages before the securities were issued and (2) immediately after issuance of the securities, holds (at least temporarily) some or all of the securities or another interest in the securities'

27. Treasury Regulation §1.897–1(c)(2)(iv). This regulation states that if any class of interests in a partnership or trust is regularly traded on an established securities market ("regularly traded"), then interests in the entity are taxed as if the partnership or trust were a corporation. As a result, gain on disposition of interests in the entity by an investor would be taxed only if (1) the entity cannot establish that at all times during a five-year period the U.S. real property it owned was less than 50% of its holdings of real property and other trade or business assets (this parallels the definition of United States real property holding corporation), and (2) the investor owned interests exceeding a 5% threshold (see Treasury Regulation §§1.897–1(c)(2)(iii)(A) and 1.897–9T(b)). The rule counting personal property only if it is a trade or business asset is intended to prevent the "stuffing" of an operating company with passive assets. A trust or partnership issuing mortgage-backed securities that is not engaged in any trade or business nonetheless should be able to treat mortgages as "trade or business assets" for purposes of the 50% assets test, with the result that the test rarely would be met by a trust, holding a pool of mortgages because of real property acquired in connection with defaults. See Treasury Regulation §1.897–1(f)(3)(ii).

issuer. The tax treatment of a sponsor may be affected by many factors. Therefore, the discussion in this Part 11.6, is intended only as a general summary of the most likely tax results in a number of common situations.

The tax consequences to a sponsor of the issuance and sale of mortgage-backed securities depend primarily on (1) whether the transaction is treated for tax purposes as a financing or sale, and (2) if it is a sale, the proportion of the property held by the sponsor that is considered to be sold. Pledging an asset as security for a loan is not ordinarily considered a taxable disposition of the asset. On the other hand, if the asset (or an interest therein) is sold, the seller recognizes gain or loss equal to the difference between the amount realized in the sale and its adjusted basis in the property sold.

As the discussion below explains, these basic tax principles apply in different ways to sponsors of pass-through certificates, pay-through bonds, and REMIC interests.

Before turning to the different types of mortgage-backed securities, it is worth taking note of special considerations that apply to a sponsor that is also a servicer and receives excess servicing (a servicing fee in excess of reasonable compensation for the services performed). In 1991, the Service issued a ruling holding that excess servicing must be treated as an ownership interest in the related mortgages (or, more technically, as a stripped coupon within the meaning of section 1286). As a result, such a sponsor must allocate some part of its basis in the mortgages it sells to excess servicing, thereby increasing its gain (or reducing its loss) from the sale. References in this section to ownership interests in mortgages, or pass-through certificates evidencing such ownership interests, should be understood to include excess servicing.

11.6.1 Pass-through certificates

The tax treatment of sponsors of pass-through certificates is for the most part straightforward. The exchange of mortgages for *all* of the pass-through certificates issued by a grantor trust is not a taxable event. When the sponsor sells some or all of those certificates, however, it is treated as selling an interest in the underlying mortgages and recognizes gain or loss accordingly. The gain or loss equals the difference between the amount realized in the sale and the portion of its aggregate adjusted basis in the mortgages that is allocated to the certificates sold (which would be a pro rata portion if there is only one class of ownership interests in the trust).

11.6.2 Pay-through bonds

Two steps may be involved in issuing pay-through bonds: (1) the issuance of the bonds for cash and (2) the transfer of all or a portion of the mortgage collateral by a sponsor to the issuer in exchange for cash and/or other consideration. The issuance of the bonds is not considered a sale of the collateral and is not otherwise a taxable event. The tax treatment of the transfer of the mortgages to the issuer is quite complex and would depend on at least three factors, the first two of which are related:

(1) whether for tax purposes the transfer is treated as a sale, or is instead viewed as an exchange of mortgages for an equity interest in the issuer,
(2) the extent to which equity interests in the issuer are owned by the sponsor rather than unrelated investors, and
(3) whether the issuer is, for tax purposes, a grantor trust, partnership, or corporation.

In very general terms, if the issuer is an owner trust that is classified as a grantor trust, then the sponsor would recognize gain or loss as a result of the transfer of mortgages to the issuer only if equity interests in the issuer are owned by persons other than the sponsor, and then only to the extent that the sponsor would recognize gain or loss if it transferred directly to those other persons an interest in the mortgages corresponding to the equity interest they own.

If the issuer is classified as a partnership, gain from a sale of the mortgages to the partnership would be recognized, but loss would not be recognized if the sponsor owns more than 50 per cent of the equity interests in the issuer. No gain or loss would be recognized upon an exchange of mortgages for an equity interest.

Finally, if the issuer is a corporation, gain or loss from a sale of mortgages to the issuer by the sponsor generally would be recognized. However, if the sponsor is a corporation that files a consolidated federal income tax return with the issuer, then any such gain or loss would be deferred. Moreover, even if the sponsor and the issuer do not file a consolidated return, loss would be deferred, or in some cases shifted to the issuer, if the sponsor and the issuer are part of the same "controlled group" (a group of corporations tied together through more than 50 per cent stock ownership links). If the mortgages are exchanged for stock (or stock and cash) upon formation of the issuer, loss would not be recognized in the exchange. Gain may be recognized, in an amount not exceeding the amount of cash received, but any such gain would be deferred to the same extent as gain from a sale. The transferor may also recognize interest income up to the amount of accrued market discount on the mortgages not previously included in income.

Regardless of the tax status of the issuer or whether gain or loss was recognized upon transfer of the mortgages to the issuer, if the sponsor sells some or all of its equity interest in the issuer to unrelated investors, it will recognize gain or loss in that sale equal to the difference between the amount realized and its adjusted basis in the portion of the equity interest that is sold.

11.6.3 REMICs

With a limited exception, a sponsor that transfers mortgages to a REMIC in exchange for regular and residual interests, either directly or through intermediaries, does not recognize gain or loss in the exchange. The aggregate adjusted basis of the property transferred (increased by the REMIC's organizational expenses) is allocated among the REMIC interests received in proportion to their respective fair market values on the pricing date or, if none, the start-up day. Each time the sponsor sells an interest in the REMIC (whether a regular interest or a residual interest), it recognizes gain or loss equal to the excess of the amount realized (net of syndication expenses) over its basis in that interest. The tax consequences to the sponsor would be the same if the REMIC, instead of issuing regular and residual interests to the sponsor in exchange for mortgages, issued those interests to the sponsor or unrelated investors for cash and used that cash to purchase the mortgages from the sponsor. The alternative transaction would be characterized for tax purposes as a contribution of the mortgages by the sponsor to the REMIC in exchange for all interests in the REMIC, followed by a sale by the sponsor for cash of those interests which it does not retain.

As this discussion suggests, the major difference in tax consequences for a sponsor of pay-through bonds of making or not making a REMIC election relates to the portion of the sponsor's overall economic gain or loss (represented by the difference between the sum of the fair market values of the bonds and equity interests in the issuer and the sponsor's basis in the mortgages) that is recognized at the time of the bond offering and upon sale of equity interests in the issuer. If no election is made, the sponsor would not recognize any portion of such gain or loss at the time of the bond sale, but would recognize a portion of such gain or loss each time an equity interest is sold, corresponding to the portion of the equity interest that is sold. By contrast, if a REMIC election is made, the sponsor would recognize a portion of such gain or loss equal to the portion of *all* interests in the issuer (equity and bonds) that is sold, as those interests are sold. Thus, for example, if the bonds represent 95 per cent of the value of all REMIC interests, 95 per cent of such gain or loss would be recognized when the bonds are sold. Of course, the recognition of gain or loss is only one of a number of factors influencing the decision whether to make a REMIC election.

The tax consequences for a sponsor of the creation and sale of pass-through certificates would be substantially the same whether or not a REMIC election is made.

A REMIC interest that is issued in exchange for mortgages or other property generally is taxed as if it had been issued at a price equal to its initial fair market value. Under section 860F(b)(1), the income of the sponsor from holding any REMIC interest is adjusted to take account of any difference between its issue price and initial basis in the hands of the sponsor. In particular, that difference is required to be included in income if the issue price is higher, or is allowed as a deduction if the issue price is lower, (1) in the case of a regular interest, as if that difference were original issue discount or bond premium, respectively, or (2) in the case of a residual interest, ratably over the anticipated weighted average life of the REMIC.

JAMES M. PEASLEE
DAVID Z. NIRENBERG[28]

28. James M. Peaslee, Partner, Cleary, Gottlieb, Steen & Hamilton and David Z. Nirenberg, Partner, Orrick, Herrington & Sutcliffe, 1995. The discussion in this chapter is current through June 1, 1995 and is, of course, subject to change through subsequent legislation, administrative actions, or judicial decisions. A more complete discussion of the topic, complete with citations to, and reprints of, primary source materials may be found in J. Peaslee & D. Nirenberg, *Federal Income Taxation of Mortgage-Backed Securities* (rev. ed. 1994, Probus Publishing) ("Peaslee & Nirenberg"). This book includes a more complete description of questions raised in structuring issuances of mortgage-backed securities.

CHAPTER 12

CURRENT STATUS AND PERSPECTIVES OF DEVELOPMENT OF SECURITIZATION IN ARGENTINA

12.1 INTRODUCTION

Having left hyperinflation five years behind and intending to become something more than an attractive emerging market in today's global economy, Argentina has been undergoing lately a process of structural reforms to have its legal system adopt the institutions needed to make securitization a workable financial scheme. My intention is to describe the efforts of the Argentine Government to establish a legal environment in which securitization transactions can not only be securely entered into, but also be given adequate incentive.

Securitization, in its most basic form, is the repackaging of asset cash flows into securities.[1] It can also be described as the financial mechanism by which a portfolio of analogous or homogeneous credits generated by one or more originators is transferred to a Special Purpose Vehicle (SPV) that will obtain the necessary funds for its acquisition in the market through the issuance and placing of negotiable instruments backed mainly by the aforesaid portfolio of transferred credits. From an economic perspective, securitization is a financial technique that allows companies to raise funds through the pooling of cash-generating financial assets. The distinction between the originator of the cash generating financial assets and the investors is essential to the mechanism. By resorting to securitization, a company can originate assets without having to invest its own funds in them. The raising of funds is done on the basis of the credit quality of their debtors. In the past six years the issue of asset-backed securities in Latin America has grown significantly, there being a market of five billion U.S. Dollars originated in the region. Argentina, currently with one digit inflation rate per annum, appears to be an excellent candidate for the rapid development of securitization. In fact, Citibank International has recently made a three-year offshore issue of 50 million U.S. Dollars in the Eurobond market, and in the United States under Rule 144A of the Securities and Exchange

1. Conf. Chammah, Walid A., "An Overview of Securitization" in *Asset Securitization: International Financial and Legal Perspectives*, edited by Joseph Norton and Paul Spellman, Centre for Commercial Law Studies, Queen Mary and Westfield College, University of London (London: Blackwell Finance, 1991), at p. 2.

Commission, backed by the receivables of its Argentina-sourced car loans. That asset-backed transaction has been characterized as a reflection of the impressive boom the local automobile industry is experiencing.

The Argentine Comisión Nacional de Valores (CNV) has under study the only concrete securitization project for the local market. It is the application for the authorization to function of a close-ended common fund ("*Fondo Común Cerrado de Crédito*"—FCCC) called Unicar 1994–1 Fondo Común Cerrado de Crédito formed by the local bank UNB, who would act as custodian entity, having Unifund S.A. as the managing entity of the close-ended common fund. The initiative is still awaiting the green light to take off. It is a 30 million U.S. Dollar FCCC, established for a two-and-a-half-year term, with a proposed pass-through yield of 9 per cent per annum, rated as AA by two local credit-rating agencies. The backing assets are 625 chattel mortgages over new buses financed by the UNB Bank.[2] Such application has not been approved yet, most probably waiting for the coming into force of many indispensable reforms in the applicable laws.

Though much has been written and discussed about securitization in Argentina in the past two years, it will be seen that there still are important legal obstacles in the Argentine legal system that hinder the development of the mechanism. In this chapter the current legal reform effort will be described and analyzed inasmuch as it is applicable to securitization.

Thus, the traditional manner of seeing the local or foreign sourced bank direct lending as the most important means of procuring credit has been gradually replaced by the practice of Argentine companies of issuing negotiable obligations ("*Obligaciones Negociables*") in the local, New York and London capital markets. Further, some Argentine companies are seeking listings in major financial centers and, in some cases are even floating stock issues in those centers. It would appear that another step in the financial evolution of Argentina would be the widespread adoption of securitization.

12.2 EXISTING RULES REGARDING SECURITIZATION

12.2.1 The common investment funds ("*Fondos Comunes de Inversión*—FCIs) have existed in Argentina for some decades; the basic law which governs their licensing, functioning and operations has recently been reformed by Law No. 24.083 (published on June 18, 1992) and its enacting Decree No. 174 dated February 8, 1993. The Law No. 24.083 contemplates close-ended FCIs where the maximum number of certificates remains fixed upon creation of the FCI and certificate holders have to await dissolution of the fund and consummation of the investment plan described in its "*Reglamento de Gestión*" before their certificates are finally redeemed. Article 15 of Decree No. 174, in turn,

2. Conf. "Un proyecto local en la CNV. Banco UNB: en la línea de largada", *Ambito Financiero*, June 26, 1994, Suplemento Económico, at p. 14.

prescribes that when organizers of a close-ended FCI apply to CNV for the license to operate as such they must also apply for a license allowing the FCI certificates to be eligible for public offering. The idea behind this latter provision is to have the FCI certificates listed in a stock exchange in order to assure liquidity to investors who, during the life of the FCI, will enjoy no rights of redemption.

The FCI is a fund authorized to operate as such by the CNV which acts as an investment vehicle for holding a diversified portfolio of securities, precious metals, foreign currencies, options, futures, bonds and other debt instruments. An FCI is not an independent juridical person *per se*.

The ownership of the assets held therein is represented by certificates of participation, which are property of the investors, who are their holders. Each certificate represents an undivided percentage right over the entire portfolio of assets held in the FCI and can be traded in the market. The assets of an FCI are required to be kept on deposit with a custodian entity duly authorized by the CNV ("*Sociedad Depositaria*") and management and investment decisions are undertaken either by a financial institution or by a company also specially authorized by the CNV ("*Sociedad Gerente*"). Managers of the FCI operate under a so-called management regulation ("*Reglamento de Gestión*") which stipulates in detail the objectives, limits and guidelines of investment decisions.

The aggregate number of certificates issued by a typical FCI is variable and open-ended because, on the one hand, holders of certificates are entitled to have the FCI repurchase them at any time and, on the other, additional certificates are issued to any new investors contributing fresh funds to the FCI.

Resolution 237 of August 26, 1993 chose the close-ended FCIs as the vehicle to allow "pass-through" securitization in Argentina.[3] This Resolution expressly allows for the organization of *Fondos Comunes Cerrados de Crédito* ("FCCC").

The characteristics of an FCCC are:

(1) It is formed exclusively of financial assets or creditor rights belonging to a determined category ("*conjuntos homogéneos o análogos de activos o derechos creditorios*");
(2) A financial entity authorized to operate as such by the Argentine Central Bank has to be the transferor of the assets or creditor-rights eligible to be held by an authorized FCCC;
(3) The assets or creditor rights held by the FCCC will not be able to be sold unless otherwise required by the management reglament. The proceeds can only be applied to service payments due to holders of the FCCC certificates, after deducting fees, costs and expenses;
(4) At least two local credit-rating agencies have to rate the FCCC certificates; and

3. Resolución General No. 237—Fondos Comunes Cerrados de Crédito—published in the Official Bulletin of September 3, 1993.

(5) FCCC certificates will be listed in a local stock exchange. Therefore, FCCC certificates have to meet the requirements of CNV for eligibility for public offerings.

On October 7, 1993 Resolution 238 was issued. It said CNV establishes the minimum contents of prospectuses to be utilized in public offerings of the certificates to be issued by the FCCC.

When the CNV issued the Resolution No. 237 it explained the context within which was laying out the new rules of the game:

> The current stage of development of the international capital market has seen the appearance of new instruments, born—as in the case of traditional shares and bonds—from the need of the demand of funds' actors to offer to the most widespread base of investors the possibility to participate in already existing or to be developed business by such issuers of instruments, within the framework of a process which has come to be known as "*titulización*" or—following the name prevailing in the Anglo-Saxon world—"securitization"... (It) is convenient that the regulation of the Argentine capital market foresee the ways to channel this process of "*titulización*" or "securitization", in any of its forms: with instruments backed by assets ("asset-backed securities"), or with participations in portfolios of assets.

Further, that

> The common investment funds, with the prolonged life of its juridical regime, the formation of an undivided and separate patrimony, and the consequent trust created among the investors, have represented the principle of dispersion in the ownership of portfolios, which places them as extremely apt vehicles for the development of securitization mechanisms, particularly those close-ended funds foreseen in article 21 of Law 24.283 and article 15 of its enacting regulatory decree...

Pursuant to its intention to facilitate securitization in Argentina, the CNV Resolution No. 237 added Article 20 *bis* to its regulations governing negotiable obligations licensing applications. Aforesaid resolution allows issuers to collateralize service payments to holders of the negotiable obligations with a security interest granted "... over fixed or variable portfolios of creditor rights... or other fixed or variable pools of assets which are analogous or homogeneous".

Article 20 *bis* also provides that in negotiable obligations issues including such a special guarantee, it may consist of a security interest granted "... over creditor rights secured by mortgages on real estate". "... to this end, the issuer must assign such creditor rights as are secured by a mortgage in favour of a trustee in terms of Article 2662 of the Civil Code".

The basic legislation governing negotiable obligations is Law No. 23.576 of July 27, 1988. Article 3 of this law provides that negotiable obligations may either be unsecured or issued with collateral consisting of floating, special or fixed guarantees on assets of the issuer.

The CNV has to authorize the issuance of negotiable obligations or any portion thereof if the issuer intends to place it by public offerings in Argentina. To this end a special application must be made with the CNV fulfilling the requirements for eligibility of the public offerings ("Régimen de Oferta Pública"). Approved negotiable obligations for public offerings enjoy an important tax benefit which consists of an exemption from income tax withholding amounting to the 12 per cent on interest payments which otherwise applies generally to all foreign sourced credits to Argentine borrowers other than those applied to the financing of imported capital goods.

The FCCC, following the French experience with the "*Fonds Commun de Créances*", formed pursuant to Law No. 88–1201 (December 23, 1988), and enacting regulatory Decree No. 89–158 (March 9, 1989), were enacted to eliminate many of the obstacles existing in that country for securitization transactions.[4]

12.2.2 Central Bank Circular No. 2156

On October 29, 1993 the Argentine Central Bank issued Circular "A" 2156 which authorizes financial institutions to assign loan portfolios to third parties without recourse, including the transfer in favour of FCCCs; to repurchase such loan obligations under certain terms and conditions; and to act as trustees in respect of portfolios of loan-obligations for other financial institutions or FCCCs.

The benefits of securitization of loan portfolios are clearly visible. Securitized transactions are often of a better quality than that of the originator. Thus, the originator can have access to funding at a lower financial cost. In many instances, companies rated below acceptable investment grades have higher incentives to securitize, precisely because of the possibility of obtaining funding at a lower cost. Therefore, the strict monitoring of the system by the CNV and the fact that any FCCC must count with the pertinent favourable rating of two credit-rating agencies adds transparency and security to the market. For banks securitization implies the possibility of improving loan-deposit ratios, fund-matching gaps, liquidity ratios and lending capacity. In general terms, securitization is a source of expansion of bank credit and resources at a lower cost of funds. From the investor's angle securitization provides an alternative form of investment where factors as risk evaluation and liquidity are facilitated.

12.2.3 Decree No. 2088

Acting also on an initiative of CNV, the National Executive Branch of Government on October 13, 1993, that is to say, shortly after CNV Resolution 237, issued Decree No. 2088. This Decree is addressed to all public real estate registries organized by the Federal Government whose functions are to register

4. Bordeaux-Groult, Robert, "Securitization of Financial Assets under French Law" in *Asset Securitization: International Financial and Legal Perspectives*, footnote 1 *supra*, at p. 341.

property rights. The Decree in question specifically allows the registration of fiduciary property titles based on Article 2662 of the Civil Code. Article 2 of the Decree goes further to establish that property rights may also be recorded in the name of an FCI, in which case such circumstance should be registered expressly.

12.3 STATUS OF FIDUCIARY PROPERTY UNDER ARGENTINE LAW: LAW FOR THE FINANCING OF HOUSING AND CONSTRUCTION

12.3.1 Article 2662 of the Argentine Civil Code is the only existing provision of Argentine substantive law which is addressed to regulate the notion of fiduciary property and is generally cited as the legal basis for establishing fiduciary relationships. It states:

> Fiduciary property is that which is acquired by a singular trust ("*fideicomiso singular*"), which is intended to last only until a condition for its termination is met, or up to the elapse of a term established for its termination, for the purpose of restoring the property to a third party.

It is worth mentioning that Article 2662 of the Civil Code is the only provision existing under Argentine law regarding the regulation of trusts, there being no other regulations clarifying the way to resolve the complex bundle of relationships created by the establishment of a contractual trust.

Based on the above transcribed succinct prescriptions of Article 2662 of the Argentine Civil Code certain Argentine prestigious authors have encouraged the effective utilization of the institution by clarifying the different rights and obligations stemming therefrom to the parties involved.[5] Even though the fiduciary property concept established in Article 2662 of the Civil Code has been lately utilized in some complex financial transactions governed by Argentine Law (some of them even involving the Argentine Government in privatization matters), there is no established case law regarding its interpretation and enforceability. It can be affirmed that the fiduciary property institution is widely ignored by the business and legal community of the country, this being true even among the banking and financial operators in general. The lack of a valid counterpart to the Anglo-Saxon notion of trust has been a major obstacle for the establishment of low-cost, high-efficiency complex contractual structures under Argentine contract law.

12.3.2 In this context, the Argentine Government decided to implement the badly needed reforms in several areas of its legal system to make it more certain. Reacting to an open request from the business community in general, the government has been trying to provide the minimum juridical security that a nation has to grant to promote the undertaking of securitization transactions,

5. Carregal, Mario, *El Fideicomiso. Regulación Jurídica y Posibilidades Prácticas*, Editorial Universidad, Buenos Aires, 1982; and Kiper, Claudio Marcelo, *Régimen Jurídico del Dominio Fiduciario*, Editorial La Ley, Buenos Aires.

with the idea of stimulating economic growth of the country as a whole.[6] Curiously enough, this very important across-the-board legal reform has not been presented as such to the Argentine Congress by the Executive Branch. The Executive Branch presented its reform proposal in a draft bill for the restructuring of the housing and construction industries of the country, realizing how important the availability of modern financial tools is for the level of economic activity within the country. The bill is named "Law for the Financing of Housing and Construction" ("the Law").[7] The Executive Branch asserts that by adopting the Law the Argentine government would be fulfilling not only a main objective of its administration, but also the constitutional mandate to assure all inhabitants of this nation the conditions to avail themselves of a dignified house.

To said end the Law regulates in detail the fiduciary property or trust ("*Fideicomiso*"), the leasing contract, and the real estate common investment funds ("*Fondos Comunes de Inversión Inmobiliaria*"—FCII). The Law also regulates in detail the creation of a mortgage note ("*letra hipotecaria*"), which is a negotiable instrument to facilitate the execution of real estate transactions backed by mortgages, and the creation of trusts and mortgage-backed common funds to issue securities under the public offering regime, thus channelling the community's savings to long-term mortgage-backed lending. The Law further goes onto amending profoundly the Code of Civil Procedure eliminating the need of judicial foreclosure proceedings in order to collect unpaid mortgage-backed notes, and limits severely the right of real estate brokers to collect commissions from both parties involved in a real estate transaction. Further, it eliminates grave doubts regarding the tax treatment to be given to securitization transactions by also amending the pertinent value added tax law and the income tax law provisions. Finally, it introduces new criminal conducts, and consequent sanctions, in the Argentine Penal Code. In essence, what the Law is aiming at is the reduction of the transaction costs[8] to enter into this sort of transaction in Argentina, thus reducing the country risk, commonly denominated by Argentine politicians and economists as the "Argentine cost".

12.3.3 Fiduciary property

The Law was patterned in this respect after two prior regulatory intents of the institution made in the Projects of Amendment of the Civil Code of 1986 and of

6. North, Douglas C., *Structure and Change in Economic History*, W.W. Norton & Company, New York, London, 1981.

7. Just before publication of this paper the Argentine Congress sanctioned the bill submitted to it by the Executive Branch under the name of "Law for the Financing of Housing and Construction"—"Ley de Financiamiento de la Vivienda y la Construcción", Law No. 24.441, sanctioned on December 22, 1994, promulgated on January 9, 1995, and published in the Official Gazzette on January 16, 1995.

8. Alchian, Armen and William, Allen, *Exchange and Production: Competition, Coordination and Control*, 2nd edition, Wadsworth Publishing Company, 1977, at p. 247.

1992. Its sources could be traced in the Commercial Code of Colombia, the General Law of Negotiable Instruments and Credit Transactions of Mexico, the law No. 17/1941 of Panama, the Civil Code of Quebec, Canada, sanctioned on December 18, 1991, as well as the law No. 19301 of Chile.

The Law, in its Article 71 substitutes completely Article 2662 of the Civil Code, reading now as follows:

> Fiduciary property is that acquired on account of a trust ("*fideicomiso*") established by contract or by will, and is to last only until the end of the trust, to the effect of delivering the good to whom it may correspond according to contract, will or the Law.
>
> The beneficiary may not exist at the moment of granting of the contract, but the data that allow for his future identification must be included therein. If the trust is granted with the purpose of issuing negotiable instruments or guaranteeing them, the nominees of said negotiable instruments will be considered the beneficiaries thereof.

The Law then regulates the functioning of this new institution in 26 Articles—seven chapters:

(i) The Trust;
(ii) The Trustee;
(iii) Effects of the Trust;
(iv) The Financial Trust;
(v) The Participation Certificates and Debt Instruments;
(vi) Of the Insufficiency of the Entrusted Patrimony in the Financial Trust;
(vii) Termination of the Trust.

The Law in its Article 1 stipulates that:

> There will be a trust when a person (settlor—"*fiduciante*") transfers the fiduciary ownership over determined goods to another (trustee—"*fiduciario*"), who obligates to exercise (the ownership) in the benefit of whom is designated in the contract (beneficiary—"*beneficiario*"), and to transfer it upon the elapse of a term or the happening of a condition to the settlor, to the beneficiary or to a third party ("*fideicomisario*").

The term or condition imposed on the transferred property will not be able to survive beyond 30 years counted as from the date of granting (Article 4). Any natural or juridical person can be a trustee, but the services of trustees can only be offered to the public in general if said trustees are duly licensed by the Argentine Central Bank as financial entities, or companies authorized by the Executive Branch to function as such (Article 5). The trustee will not be waived from its obligation to render accounts, nor of the negligence or dolus that he or the employees might incur in the performance of his duty. The trustee is prohibited from purchasing definitively for himself the goods under trust (Article 7). The rendering of accounts has to take place periodically in the agreed upon periods, but never beyond one year each time. Regarding the effects of the granting of a trust, the Law establishes that the goods placed under trust are regulated by Title VII of Book III of the Civil Code, as modified in the new text of Article 2662 and its 26 Articles. Article 14 of the Law stipulates very clearly that the goods placed under trust constitute a separate patrimony to that of the settlor and the one of the trustee. Further, the said goods are exempt from the singular or collective actions of the creditors of the trustee. As a manner to preserve the patrimony of the trustee—thus encouraging the entrance of new participants into the market—it has been established in Article 16 that the patrimony of the trustee will not be liable for the obligations assumed by the trustee in the due performance of the trust. Said obligations will rest exclusively with the patrimony under trust which, as stipulated by Article 1261 of the Civil Code of Quebec taken as a source, is a patrimony with specific purpose ("*patrimonio de afectación*"). If said goods under trust are insufficient, the "*patrimonio de afectación*" is not declared bankrupt, but liquidated by the trustee, being responsible to pay to the creditors according to the ranking of privileges set by the Argentine Bankruptcy Law ("BL"). The trustee is considered to have ample powers to perform his duty, being able to sell or encumber the goods under trust without the consent of the settlor or of the beneficiary, unless otherwise stipulated.

12.3.4 The Financial Trust ("*Fideicomiso Financiero*") is, according to Article 19 of the Law, a trust that meets the definition set in Article 2662 of the Civil Code, in which the trustee is a financial entity duly licensed by the Argentine Central Bank or a company specifically authorized to function as a financial trustee by the Executive Branch, and the beneficiary is formed by the holders of participation certificates ("*Certificados de Participación*") in the fiduciary property, or by the holders of debt negotiable instruments backed with the assets so transferred. The participation certificates and the negotiable debt instruments could be publicly offered in the market.

12.3.5 The trustee will be the issuing entity of the participation certificates. The negotiable debt instruments could be issued by the trustee or by a third party. Both the participation certificates and the negotiable debt instruments can be nominative or bearer, endorseable or not, or recorded in the issuer's books in the name of the holder ("*escriturales*"). The participation certificates can be issued as global certificates for their registration in CEDEL or EUROCLEAR. Said certificates will be considered to be definitive, divisible and negotiable.

The Law foresees that there can be different classes of participation certificates granting different rights. Within each class the participation certificates have to grant equal rights. The issues can be divided in series. The fact that participation certificates can be issued in different classes granting different rights is coupled with another very important reform of the Civil Code. By Article 74 of the Law, a new paragraph is added to article 3876 of the Civil Code, providing that: "It can be agreed the subordination of the rights of the creditor until the total or partial payment of other present or future debts of the debtor."

The above transcribed is another important legal reform for the functioning of securitization, by expressly allowing the establishment of senior/subordinated debt as another means of credit enhancement, something which had not been clearly stated before under Argentine Law.

12.3.6 The Law establishes special rules for the case of bankruptcy of the financial trustee. In such a case it is clearly prescribed that the (one or more) "*patrimonio(s) de afectación*" that the financial trustee might have had under trust will be sold separately from its patrimony. There are rules therein established in detail as to how and when the Meeting of Participation Certificates or Negotiable Debt Instruments Holders will assemble and vote the pertinent rules of management and liquidation of the "*patrimonio(s) de afectación*".

The emphasis given in the Law to the separation of patrimonies is very important, since the existing uncertain legal status of the goods placed under trust in case of bankruptcy of the settlor and/or of the trustee under Argentine Law has given cause to a myriad of different considerations on account of the risks posed to bona fide participation certificates of negotiable debt instruments holders.[9] As in the case of the United States, the key issue in this respect is making the SPV "bankruptcy remote", to which end there must be a "true sale" of the goods under trust.[10] This is because Article 122 of BL stipulates that the following transactions carried out by the debtor which is in the "stopping of payments" ("*cesación de pagos*") status will not be able to be opposed to creditors of the insolvent originator ("*ineficaces respecto de los acreedores*"). The transactions sanctioned in this manner are:

(a) gratuitous transactions,
(b) opional prepayment of debts to be matured normally at a date on or after the date of bankruptcy,
(c) payments in kind, and
(d) the granting of guarantees such as chattel mortgages ("*prenda*") or mortgages ("*hipoteca*") for already existing obligations not originally incurred with that sort of collateral, thus improperly "enhancing" the credit to the detriment of the mass of unsecured creditors.

A bona fide securitization transaction should not fall in any of the above cases, since under existing Argentine Law there must be an onerous assignment of the transferred goods placed under trust from the originator to the trustee, namely that there be a price bargained at arm's-length between the parties involved that reflects the true discount value, and that there has to be a valid, defendable price paid to the originator and accounted for in the originator's books.

Article 123 of BL brings another potential threat to securitization. It states: "All other transactions carried out during the period of suspicion may be

9. In this respect, a very interesting comment can be seen in Badessich, Juan Andrés, "Algunas Reflexiones Sobre las Consecuencias de la Quiebra en la Securitización" in 257 *Información Empresaria, Revista de la Cámara Argentina de Sociedades Anónimas*, Buenos Aires, July 1994, at p. 12.

10. Schwarcz, Steven L., "Structuring and Legal Issues of Asset Securitization in the United States" in *Asset Securitization: International Financial and Legal Perpectives*, footnote 1 *supra*, at p. 17.

declared as not being opposable to third parties when evidence is produced that the third party had knowledge of the status of cessation of payments of the debtor."

Thus, it is very important that the trustee not have actual knowledge of the status of "*cesación de pagos*" the originator might hold. A debtor who is in "*cesación de pagos*" status is obligated by the BL to seek one of the courses of action provided therein. These steps that can be taken in such a situation are either (a) to request the Courts for the formation of creditors' meeting proceedings, called the "*concurso preventivo*"; or (b) if the debtor is not in a situation to meet the stringent requirements for the acceptance by the intervening Court of a "*concurso preventivo*" established by the BL,[11] to petition for its own bankruptcy judicial declaration.

Thus, the notion of cessation of payments is one that can bring a cloud to transfers of goods into trust by originators that are in such a critical financial situation. This is because acts that imply the transfer of property in favour of third parties carried out by a debtor which is in cessation of payments will be liable to be analyzed by the court's receiver and the court itself, to establish whether there existed actual knowledge by the originator's counterpart. Further, the exact date when a debtor that has petitioned for the formation of its creditors' meeting proceeding or is in bankruptcy incurred in "*cesación de pagos*" is to be determined by the intervening judge, the BL only giving a time-limit cap. The risk is posed because the period running between the date of "*cesación de pagos*" and the date the actual bankruptcy is declared by the intervening judge is considered by the BL as the "suspicion period" ("*período de sospecha*").

The effects of having a given transaction falling into any of the above cases based on Articles 122 and 123 of the BL is the revocation of such transactions entered into after "*cesación de pagos*", was determined. That implies that, should the revocation action prosper, the trustee would have to return to the originator's patrimony the transferred goods placed under trust or what replaced them and file a claim against the bankruptcy for restitution of the price paid. The fact that the originator in a "pass-through" securitization becomes insolvent, placing at risk the participation certificates or negotiable debt instruments holders to return the goods placed under trust to the bankrupt patrimony of the originator and file a claim in that bankruptcy to recover the price paid, with very little chance of recovering anything, has been taken care of in the Law by establishing that the goods placed under trust constitute a "*patrimonio de afectación*" that is beyond the reach of the creditors of the originator and of the trustee, except fraud.

Thus, bona fide securitization transactions will have the necessary legal certainty. It has to be borne in mind that this sort of transaction will normally

11. Established in Article 11, Law No. 19.551.

occur between an originator and a duly authorized trustee, under the scrutiny of the CNV and there being the positive rating of two mandatory credit-rating agencies. There has definitely been an effort to shield investors, protecting the market from the above described risks. Furthermore, concurring with the drive to make the Argentine legal system more workable from a business perspective, the Executive Branch has also sent to Congress a bill to reform the BL, overhauling completely the existing system, making it more flexible for corporate reorganizations. The bill sent has been taken from the U.S. Chapter 11, plus the German, English, Japanese, French and Italian models, also considering the examples of Hong Kong, Singapore, Canada, Australia, Chile, Mexico and Eastern Europe. The main emphasis of the new legislation is to separate the patrimony of the debtor under "*cesación de pagos*" from debtor as a shareholder, thus allowing more room for negotiated solution.[12] It has to be borne in mind that however "bankruptcy remote" the SPV is made through legal provisions and/or contractual techniques, the insolvency of the originator will no doubt have a detrimental market effect on the value of the securities involved. The example of the DAF Leyland transaction closed in December 1992, rated as a AAA note issue, later affected by the collapse of the DAF parent company, should not be forgotten by the CNV and local credit-rating agencies when analyzing these sort of transactions before being authorized.

12.3.7 The Trust will end by the fulfilment of the term or condition to which it had been subjected, or the expiration of the 30-year maximum term allowed by the Law. It can also terminate in case of revocation by the settlor, if he kept for himself such a capacity. Lastly, it can terminate if a special cause stipulated in the contract has occurred.

12.4 SOME OTHER MATTERS RESOLVED BY THE LAW FOR THE FINANCING OF HOUSING AND CONSTRUCTION

The drafters of the Law had a clear understanding that other areas of Argentine Law had to be amended in order to give the minimum legal certainty to securitization development in Argentina. Therefore, other very important reforms are contained in the Law, to wit:

12.4.1 Tax treatment

As until recently securitization was unknown to Argentine business and legal practice, the unfavourable tax treatment given by the value added tax and income tax laws made a specialized author conclude that:

12. Hoberman, Jeffrey and García Conejero, María Laura, "Nueva Ley de Concursos y Quiebras" in 257 *Información Empresaria, Revista de la Cámara Argentina de Sociedades Anónimas*, footnote 9 *supra*, at p. 27.

> After a quick overview of the regulations that are in principle applicable to a securitization process utilizing a common close-ended fund or a common investment fund, we believe it is not an exaggeration what stated at the beginning of this comment when we said that, being before a concrete business possibility that could be implemented in Argentina, the tax obstacles are really frustrating...[13]

The Law, in order to give incentive to the execution of asset-backed securitization transactions, assimilated the tax treatment given to this sort of transaction to the one given to negotiable obligations above described. To said end, the financial transactions related to and the contractual obligations related to the issuance, underwriting, placing, transfer, payment of principal and of interest and cancellation of negotiable debt instruments issued by trustees with respect to trusts formed for the securitization of assets are exempt from Value Added Tax. The results deriving from the purchase and sale, exchange, barter, conversion and disposal of said negotiable debt instruments issued by trustees with respect to trusts formed for the securitization of assets, as well as their interests, and adjustments of capital are exempt from income tax law, except for some particular cases. Further, when the goods placed under trust are credits, the transfers to the trust will not be considered as contractual obligations or financial transactions taxable under the value added tax law.[14] In order that the above described tax treatment be applicable, the negotiable debt instruments will have to be publicly listed.

12.4.2 Assignment of rights

Other than the strict formal requirements established by the Civil Code for assignment of rights contracts not effected through endorsements, Article 1474 of the Civil Code provides that a debtor, even after having accepted the assignment and without requiring any reservations, is entitled to raise against the assignee all defenses which he may have against the assignor, excluding only the right of setoff. This can be an important obstacle to securitization transactions.

One solution is given by the Law in its Article 40, that prescribes that the mortgage-backed notes ("*letras hipotecarias*") will be transferable by nominative endorsement, further stating it is not necessary that the original debtor-issuer be notified of the transfers made, and that said original debtor-issuer will not be able to oppose to the bearer or endorsee the defenses that he might have against prior endorsees or bearers of the note, except in case of change of domicile of payment. The endorsement is without recourse to the endorser.

13. García Cozzi, José María, "Securitización. Aspectos Impositivos" in 257 *Información Empresaria, Revista de la Cámara Argentina de Sociedades Anónimas*, footnote 9 *supra*, at p. 19.

14. To comprehend how complex the tax treatment of securitization can be, see Peaslee, James M. and Nirenberg, David, "U.S. Federal Income Tax Treatment of Mortgage-Backed Securities", and Edge, Stephen M. and Murphy, Michael, "U.K. Tax Considerations", in *Asset Securitization: International Financial and Legal Perspectives*, footnote 1 *supra*.

Further, by Article 71 of the Law, Article 1459 of the Civil Code is substituted by the following text:

The assignment has effects against third parties as from moment of notification made to the assigned debtor or by the acceptance of the assignment by aforesaid assigned debtor, except that the credit be registered with a registry, in which case the effects will start as from date of registration. With respect to the debtor the assignment will have effects disregarding the notification in the case it is stipulated that payments made by the debtor will be valid in a determined domicile.

Also, by Article 71 of the Law, Article 1484 *bis* is added to the Civil Code. It allows the assignment of credits in one global deed, detailing each credit's characteristics, stating the amount, terms, interests and guarantees. In this case said assignments should be made for:

(a) collateralizing the issuance of negotiable instruments through public listing;
(b) form the patrimony of a company, with the object that said company issue publicly offered negotiable instruments, and that the payments of principal and interest thereof be backed by said asset(s);
(c) form the patrimony of an FCCC.

Article 72 of the Law, in its turn, adds Article 1484 *ter* to the Civil Code, which clarifies that in the cases foreseen in Article 1484 *bis*, the following rules will be applicable:

(a) The assignment produces effects as from the moment the instrument in which it is made acquires certainty as to its date of celebration;
(b) Will only be able to be opposed against the assignee the defense based on the invalidity of the debtor-creditor relationship, or documented payment made before the date of celebration of the assignment;
(c) In its case, the assignments will be registered with the pertinent registries;
(d) The documentary evidence of the assigned right, should it exist, will be delivered to the assignee or to the trustee or, in its case, to a custodian, or to the custodian of the FCCC.

So, it can be appreciated that the main obstacles have been taken care of properly. Any other problems in this respect should be taken care of by a special waiver included in the text of the pertaining assignment agreement.

12.4.3 Mortgage-backed notes

The law establishes that in first degree mortgage deeds where the parties have agreed that mortgage-backed notes be issued, said notes will be considered negotiable instruments. The issuance of said notes implies the novation of the original obligation, thus cancelling it. The issuance of the notes does not hinder the right of the owner to sell the mortgaged property, being the new owner liable for payment of the mortgaged property. Article 39 of the Law establishes strict issuance and content requirements since the notes will be able to be used by trustees and administrators of CFIs to issue participation certificates backed by the same, or to form FCCCs with them, according to the regulations to be enacted.

These mortgage-backed notes, as well as other mortgage agreements that adhere to the system established in the Law, could be collected in out-of-court proceedings, in a procedure established in Title IV of the Law that really implies a conceptual revolution for Argentine rules of civil procedure.

12.5 CONCLUSION

Securitization has not really started yet in Argentina as it should, according to what are the expectations of the market and the Government officials that view it as an ideal tool for the reactivation of vast sectors of the economy. We have seen in this chapter how the Government has been trying to overcome the regulatory, legal and tax obstacles with a piecemeal approach. In this respect it is worth mentioning that the first legislative measure (CNV Resolution No. 237) dates only from August 1993. There was another effort to complement aforesaid Resolution with other measures in October of 1993 (CNV Resolution No 238, Decree No. 2883). The just sanctioned law No. 24.441, almost a year after, seems to address adequately the issues that had not been resolved which, as previously explained, were many and substantial. The Law No. 24.441 will be a major step towards a more secure and friendly environment for securitization, solving the majority of the existing problems. It is a sound legislative effort that attacks not only substantive law matters, but also those of procedure, always with the idea of reducing transaction costs, which from a law and economics perspective is the avenue to experiment.[15] Argentina is going in the right direction. The rest depends on the international and local business and legal communities' creativity.

DIEGO CESAR BUNGE

15. Posner, Richard A. *Economic Analysis of Law*, 2nd edition, Little Brown and Company, Boston, 1977.

CHAPTER 13

SECURITIZATION OF AUTO LOANS IN JAPAN

13.1 OVERVIEW

13.1.1 Preface—Definition of securitization of assets

Securitization of assets occurs when a company or financial institution, in order to obtain financing, packages certain of its assets, sells those assets and issues securities based on those assets. The securitization of assets differs from the traditional method of financing through the issuance of securities in the way that the risk is handled. In a traditional issuance of securities the credit of the issue depends mainly upon the credit of the issuer. However, in the securitization of assets, the credit of the issue depends on the credit of the assets themselves and the cash flow which will be generated by those assets. As a consequence the structuring of the securitization is crucial to its success.

13.1.2 Assets in Japan which can be used for securitization

Our analysis will deal with the securitization of consumer-related assets because they often consist of a large number of identical assets which makes them suitable for securitization.

13.1.2.1 At present, consumer-related assets which are potentially suitable for securitization are (i) credit cards loans, (ii) housing loans and (iii) automobile loans. Figure 13.1 and Tables 13.1 and 13.2 below show the change in volume in recent years of each of these types of loans.

The figure and tables reveal that the volume of these loans in Japan is sufficient to allow for them to be used as the basis for securitization. In addition to the types of loans described above, there are various types of receivables and lease claims which theoretically could be used for securitization. However, such receivables and most leases are not consumer-related and usually do not consist of a large number of identical loans. Therefore, securitization of such assets is usually not practical and accordingly they will not be dealt with in this article.

Table 13.1 Credit card loans

Item	*1983*	*1984*	*1985*	*1986*	*1987*	*1988*	*1989*	*1990*	*1991*	*1992*
Number of credit cards issued (19,000)	7,381	8,683	9,705	11,036	12,101	14,447	16,612	18,696	20,300	21,452
Total amount purchased with credit cards (¥100 million)	38,186	41,999	50,902	57,520	65,924	78,606	94,624	115,287	124,936	131,003

Note: The numbers of credit cards issued as of the end of each fiscal year.

Figure 13.1 Changes in total amount of housing loans outstanding

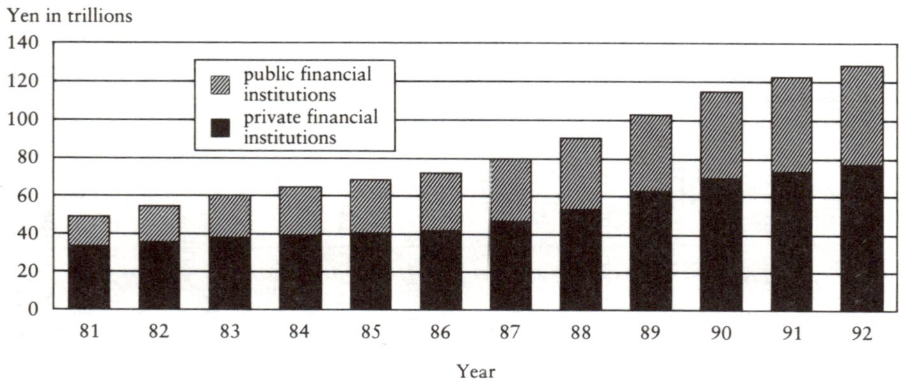

Table 13.2 Consumer credit offered by car dealers (as of 1992)

Creditors	*Types*	*Amount Newly Granted*		*Balance*	
		(¥100 million)	Previous Year comparison (%)	(¥100 million)	Previous year comparison (%)
Car dealers	Installment sales (Purchase of account receivable by installment contract paper)	4,523	11.5	2,629	29.2
	Credit card	15	16.7	9	55.0
	Non-installment sales (Purchase of account receivable by installment contract paper)	2,871	1.7	294	44.1
	Sales by personal loans of finance institutions	30	14.3	6	14.3
Total amount		7,439	5.8	2,938	31.2

Source: Consumer Credit Statistics in Japan by Japan Consumer Credit Industry Association

13.1.2.2 Since loans to car rental companies have a different structure than loans to ordinary consumers and generally do not exist in huge volumes, they also will not be dealt with in this article.

13.1.2.3 Recently non-life insurance companies have begun entering into the guaranty business using their comparatively higher credit rating. Such guaranties can also be used in the structuring of securitizations.

13.1.3 Applicable regulations

The regulations which are relevant to securitization are (1) Securities Exchange Law, (2) Claimable Rights Law and (3) Lending Business Law. Also, in certain circumstances, the Investment Law may also apply.

13.1.3.1 Securities Exchange Law

In Japan, the definition of securities is rather narrow and is limited to those items which are specified in Article 2 of the Securities Exchange Law. Recently there was some discussion regarding changing this definition to include a "wider range of securities"; however, the final result was that no wide-sweeping changes were made. Instead, the changes were limited to the addition of a few items to the existing definition. There is also a provision which allows for adding new items to the definition but this must be done by Cabinet Order, which, judging by past experience, is not easily done.

We have set forth below the definition of securities under the current Securities Exchange Law. As you will see, the range is rather narrow compared with the definition of securities under U.S. law.

ARTICLE 2

(i) The term "Securities" in this Law shall mean the following:

(1) National government bonds;
(2) Local government bonds;
(3) Bonds issued by juridical persons in accordance with special laws;
(4) Debentures issued by corporations;
(5) Investment certificates issued by juridical persons established under special laws;
(6) Share certificates (including certificates of fractional shares and any reference hereinafter to share certificates shall include certificates of fractional shares), or certificates representing subscription rights for new shares;
(7) Beneficiary certificates for securities investment trusts or loans trusts;
(8) Such promissory notes as shall be determined by ordinance of the Ministry of Finance from those which are issued by juridical persons to raise funds necessary for their operations;
(9) Securities or certificates issued by foreign countries or foreign juridical persons, which are of the same nature as those mentioned in the preceding items;
(10) Such securities or certificates as shall be prescribed by ordinance of the Ministry of Finance from those issued by a foreign juridical person representing

beneficiary rights or other similar rights of a trust in which the claimable rights for loans of a person who engages in the banking business or otherwise engages in the business of money lending are entrusted; and

(11) In addition to those items mentioned in the preceding paragraphs, such other securities and certificates as shall be prescribed by Cabinet Order as being necessary to protect the public interest or investors, in view of their negotiability or other conditions;

(ii) The rights which are represented by the Securities mentioned in any of the items in the preceding paragraph shall be deemed to be Securities even though the relevant Securities are not actually issued. The rights set forth below shall also be deemed to be Securities even though such rights are rights which are not represented by securities or certificates, and this Law shall apply to all of these rights:

(1) such beneficiary rights of trust loans as shall be prescribed by Cabinet Order among beneficiary rights of a trust in which the claimable rights for loans of a bank, trust company, or other financial institution as may be designated by Cabinet Order, or a person who engages as a business in the lending of long-term funds necessary to acquire houses (including land for residential use and property rights incidental thereto) are entrusted;

(2) Rights against a foreign juridical person, the substance of which is similar to that mentioned in the preceding item; and

(3) In addition to those rights mentioned in the preceding two items, monetary claimable rights whose circumstances of distribution are determined by Cabinet Order to be equivalent to those of the Securities in the preceding paragraph and for which it has been determined by Cabinet Order as being necessary and appropriate for the protection of the public interest or investors in view of their being of the economic substance, or having the same characteristics, as the Securities set forth in the preceding paragraph or other conditions.

Items which fall within the definition of securities under the Securities Exchange Law, such as bonds or shares, will be treated as securities under the Securities Exchange Law and will be subject to the provisions thereof. However, if an item does not fall within this definition, it is presently unclear who can sell or transfer it, in what manner it can be sold or transferred and who may act as an intermediary in a sale or transfer. The degree to which disclosure must be made to investors is also unclear. For these reasons, it may be difficult to arrange for wide distribution of such items.

13.1.3.2 Claimable Rights Law

In June of 1993, the Law relating to the Regulation of Business Concerning Specified Claimable Rights ("Claimable Rights Law") became effective. This law applies to certain lease receivables including credit card receivables and receivables arising from instalment sales of specified goods.

The receivables governed by this law are not included in the definition of securities found in the Securities Exchange Law. The main advantage provided by this law is that when specified types of receivables are transferred through designated types of structures, the Japanese Civil Code's requirement of consent by, or notice, with a confirmation date endorsed thereon to, a debtor in respect of such assignment does not apply and instead, is replaced by a requirement for a general public notice. However, since the object of the Claimable Rights Law is limited, it is mainly only Japanese non-bank financial institutions which can take advantage of it. Thus, unfortunately, though this law shows some progress in the field of securitization, its range of application is quite limited.

13.1.3.3 Others

The Investment Law, Lending Business Law and other related regulations may also be applicable to certain types of securitization. Under the Investment Law (Shusshi-hō), it is unlawful to accept an amount as an investment and at the same time promise to return an amount which is the same as, or more than, the invested amount. In addition, this law prohibits engaging in the business of receiving deposits unless such business is permitted under another law. Therefore, any promise to return the principal amount of an investment would constitute a breach of this law.

The Investment Law also provides that an entity which is in the business of lending money is prohibited from issuing bonds, notes or commercial paper. However, if the investment comes within the definition of securities as provided in the Securities Exchange Law, the Investment Law is not applicable. Therefore, if a special purpose company (SPC) issues securities which come within that definition, as part of a securitization, the Investment Law will not apply.

The Lending Business Law (Kashikin-gyō-hō) provides that a license must be obtained in order to engage in the business of lending money to the general public. In addition, if a company which is engaged in the money-lending business ("lending business company") wants to transfer loans to a third party, the Lending Business Law provides that:

(1) The transferor must give notice to the transferee of certain matters specified therein.
(2) The prohibition on using unfair acts to collect loans which applies to a transferor is also applicable to the transferee (§24-2).
(3) Upon the transfer of the loans, the transferee must send notice to the borrower of certain matters specified therein (§24-2, 17).

Thus, where the transferor of the loans is a lending business company, these provisions of the Lending Business Law greatly increase the administrative workload of the transferee. However, it must be noted that, since the aim of these regulations is to make certain that the transferee does not use unfair methods to collect loans, an argument can be made that where the transferor continues to be the collection agent, these regulations should not apply.

In summary we note that, as shown above, the current legal framework is not favorable to the securitization of assets; however, there is not any provision in the law which expressly prohibits securitization.

13.1.4 Legal or practical impediments

Generally speaking, assets which are suitable for securitization have the following characteristics:

(a) obligations are standardized;
(b) obligors are diverse (credit risk is diversified);
(c) cash flow of the assets is foreseeable;
(d) life of the assets is long enough to absorb the cost of securitization; and
(e) regulation is minimal.

Having regard to these characteristics we would like to discuss certain legal and practical impediments to the securitization of those types of assets described in 13.1.2 above.

13.1.4.1 Credit cards loans

Though, as we discussed, the volume of such loans is increasing, the main problem is that, in Japan, these loans are generally repaid in a single payment and the balance of such loans does not revolve. Therefore, the term of the loan is usually rather short and is not suitable for securitization.

13.1.4.2 House loans

In Japan, the default rate on house loans is very low and the term of such loans is usually very long and fixed. Therefore, Japanese banks want to retain them for their own portfolios. In addition, though a fixed interest rate is preferable for securitization, the interest rates for such loans are usually floating.

13.1.4.3 Others types of assets

As discussed above, because lease claims are not consumer-related they are not included in this analysis. However, from a practical point of view, since the benefits in leasing are, generally speaking, found in tax advantages, which would be lost in a securitization, leases are usually not suitable for securitization.

13.1.4.4 Automobile loans

The following is generally true of automobile loans:

(1) detailed data is available, including the rate of default on previous auto loans;
(2) low rate of default;
(3) identical financial asset;
(4) clear repayment patterns and clear cash flow;
(5) average maturity is usually more than one (1) year; and

(6) borrowers are diversified (diversification of credit risk).

From the above it would seem that automobile loans would be ideal for securitization. Is this true? To make this determination we would like to examine such loans in more detail.

13.2 AUTO LOANS

13.2.1 Structure of auto loans

Figure 13.2 shows an example of the structure which is normally used in financing the purchase of an automobile in Japan (Appendix). The details of this structure are examined below. (We note that automobile purchase financings which consist of loans to car purchasers by financial institutions, which are guaranteed by finance companies connected to dealers, while common in other countries, are not popular in Japan.)

13.2.1.1 Master agreement

A master agreement is entered into between a finance company, which is an affiliate of the automobile manufacturer ("finance company"), and an automobile sales company ("auto sales company"). This master agreement includes, among other provisions, the terms under which financing will be provided for the purchase by consumers ("purchasers") of cars supplied by the auto sales company to its dealers, which are affiliates of an automobile manufacturing company ("dealers"). The agreement states that (1) the loans proceeds will be paid by the finance company directly to the dealer and (2) the repayment of the loan will be made directly by the purchaser to the finance company. The master agreement generally is applicable to the sale by the dealers of all cars supplied by the auto sales company.

13.2.1.2 Dealer agreement

A dealer agreement is concluded between each dealer and the finance company. This agreement covers financing for the sale of all cars obtained by that dealer from the auto sales company. It usually provides that the dealer (1) consents to the terms of the financing and (2) retains ownership of any car sold, as security on behalf of the finance company, until the purchaser repays the loan in full.

13.2.1.3 Loan agreement

The purchaser buys a car from a dealer with the sale price to be paid by the finance company. A non-bank financial institution (the "guarantor") which is not an affiliate of the auto manufacturing company, is commissioned by the purchaser to guaranty the payment made by the finance company. The details of those aspects of the transaction are included in a single loan agreement which is signed by the purchaser, the dealer, the finance company and the guarantor.

An extract and summary of a sample loan agreement is provided below.

Translation

SAMPLE AUTO LOAN AGREEMENT

(Summary and Extract)

A (hereinafter referred to as "Purchaser"), D (hereinafter referred to as "Dealer"), X Finance Corp. (hereinafter referred to as "Finance Corp") and Y Company (hereinafter referred to as "Guarantor") hereby agree as follows with respect to the Sales Contract, the Advance Commission Contract and the Guarantee Commission Contract.

[THE ADVANCE COMMISSION CONTRACT]

Article 1 (Contents of the Sales Contract and the Advance Commission Contract)

(1) The Dealer shall sell the Automobile (hereinafter referred to as the "Product") to the Purchaser and the Purchaser shall purchase the Product from the Dealer (hereinafter referred to as the "Sales Contract").

(2) The Purchaser shall commission the Finance Corp. to pay to the Dealer, on behalf of the Purchaser, an advance, in the manner prescribed by the Finance Corp. and in an amount equal to the total purchase price of the Product under the Sales Contract less the amount paid as a down payment on the Product (hereinafter referred to as the "Unpaid Portion of the Product Proceeds"). The Finance Corp. shall agree to this commission (hereinafter referred to as the "Advance Commission Contract").

Article 2 (Effective Date of the Contracts)

(1) The Advance Commission Contract between the Purchaser and the Finance Corp. shall become effective when the Finance Corp. notifies the Dealer that the Finance Corp. has approved the Advance Commission Contract and the Guarantor has notified the Dealer, pursuant to Article 9, of its agreement to guarantee, jointly and severally, the advance obligations of the Purchaser to the Finance Corp. under the Advance Commission Contract. Upon receipt of such notification, the Dealer shall notify the Purchaser. Any amounts paid to the Dealer upon application for the Advance Commission Contract shall be applied to the down payment on the Product upon the Advance Commission Contact becoming effective.

(2) The Sales Contract between the Purchaser and the Dealer shall be deemed to be effective when the Dealer applies to the Finance Corp. for the Advance Commission Contract on behalf of the Purchaser; provided, however, that the Sales Contract shall not become effective until such time as the Advance Commission Contract becomes effective. If the Advance Commission Contract does not become effective, the Sales Contract shall be deemed not to have been entered into by the parties and the application form for the Advance Commission Contract, together with any amounts paid in respect of the application shall be promptly returned to the Purchaser by the Dealer.

Article 3 (Method of Payment of Installments)

The Purchaser shall pay to the Finance Corp. through the Guarantor, acting as collection agent for the Finance Corp., an amount equal to the Unpaid Portion of the Product Proceeds plus the stated installment fee (hereinafter referred to as "Total Installments") in such time and in such manner as is provided for in the payment terms and conditions of the Advance Commission Contract.

Article 4 (Commissioning of Collection, etc.)

(1) The Finance Corp. shall commission the Guarantor to perform, on its behalf, all actions necessary for the collection, receipt, and transmission of payment notices in respect of each payment of the Total Installments. The Purchaser shall consent to such commission.

(2) The Purchaser shall pay each payment of the Total Installments no later than the applicable payment date by way of bank account transfer pursuant to a transfer request contract to be separately agreed between the Purchaser and the Finance Corp.; provided, however, that upon receipt of a notice from the Guarantor, the Purchaser shall make repayment in accordance with such other method as may be specified by the Guarantor in the notice.

Article 5 (Delivery of Product)

The Product shall be delivered to the Purchaser by the Dealer after the Advance Commission Contract becomes effective but in any event no later than the agreed date of delivery.

Article 6 (Events of Default)

(1) If any of the following events occur with respect to the Purchaser, any obligations of the Purchaser under the Advance Commission Contract shall become due and payable and the Purchaser shall pay any such obligations forthwith:

(i) the Purchaser defaults in payment of any of the payments when due and fails to remedy such default within such time period as may be specified in a demand notice delivered pursuant to Article 4(1); provided that such time period shall not be less than twenty (20) days;

(ii) any note or cheque issued by the Purchaser is dishonored, or the Purchaser suspends payment in general;

(iii) an application or petition is submitted for attachment, provisional attachment, preservative attachment or injunction, or any action is taken to secure the collection of taxes, with respect to the Purchaser;

(iv) an application or petition is submitted for bankruptcy, composition, company arrangement, special liquidation or corporation reorganization against the Purchaser, or the Purchaser files any application in connection with any such matter;

(v) the purchase of the Product under the Sales Contract is considered a commercial act of the Purchaser, and the Purchaser delays even one of its payments of the Total Installments; or

(vi) the Purchaser commits any act which constitutes a disposition of all or a part of the ownership of the Product including, but not limited to, a pledge, transfer or least of the Product.

(2) If any of the following events occur with respect to the Purchaser, any obligations of the Purchaser under the Advance Commission Contract shall become due and payable upon request by the Guarantor pursuant to Article 4(1) and the Purchaser shall pay any such obligations forthwith:

(i) the Purchaser commits a material violation of the contract; or
(ii) the creditworthiness of the Purchaser significantly deteriorates.

Article 7 (Default Interest for Delay)

Article 8 (Special Arrangement in case of Early Repayment)

In the event the Purchaser makes all payments in respect of the Total Installments as specified in the Sales Contract, or prepays the Total Installments in a single lump-sum payment, prior to the expiration of the stated payment period, the Purchaser may claim against the Finance Corp. for the reimbursement of a pro rata portion of installment fees as calculated by the Finance Corp.; provided, however, that any application therefor shall be made to the Guarantor pursuant to Article 4(1).

[GUARANTEE COMMISSION CONTRACT]

Article 9 (Time of Conclusion of the Contract)

(1) The Purchaser shall commission the Guarantor to guarantee, jointly and severally, its obligations to the Finance Corp. under the Advance Commission Contract (hereinafter referred to as the "Guarantee Commission Contract").

(2) The Guarantee Commission Contract shall become effective when the Guarantor consents to be the guarantor and the Guarantor notifies the Finance Corp. of its consent.

Article 10 (Performance of Guarantee Obligations)

Upon the occurrence of any of the events of default set forth in Article 6 or in the event the Purchaser defaults in payment of any payment of the Total Installments, the Guarantor shall perform such obligation of the Purchaser without notice to the Purchaser.

Article 11 (Execution of Compensation Obligations)

In the event that the Guarantor performs any obligation on behalf of the Purchaser pursuant to Article 10, the Purchaser shall pay to the Guarantor the amount set forth below together with all expenses incurred in connection with such performance:

(1) In the event of a default in payment of any part of the Total Installments, the amount paid by the Guarantor in respect of such default; and
(2) in the event of the occurrence of any of the events of default set forth in Article 6, the total amount paid by the Guarantor in respect of such event of default.

Article 12 (Right to Recourse)

Upon the occurrence of any of the events of default set forth in Article 6, the Purchaser shall comply with any request (1) to perform any obligations arising with respect to any default in payment of any portion of the Total Installments and (2) for payment of default interest for any delay in payment as provided for in Article 13(2) notwithstanding that the guarantee obligations of the Guarantor to the Finance Corp. have not been fulfilled.

Article 13 (Default Interest for Delay in Payment)

[COMMON PROVISIONS]

Article 14 (Cancellation of the Sales Contract or other contract due to Discrepancy between the Sample or Catalogue item and the Product Delivered)

Article 15 (Responsibility in Case of Loss or Damage of the Product)

(1) In the event that the Product is destroyed or damaged due to fire, wind, flood, theft, or any other reason, before the completion of its obligations under the Advance Commission Contract, the Purchaser shall promptly notify the Finance Corp. of such destruction or damage; provided however, that the Purchaser shall not be relieved of any of its obligations under the Advance Commission Contract or otherwise as a result of the destruction or damage.

(2) Notwithstanding the provisions of the preceding paragraph, if any of the events set forth in the preceding paragraph (1) occur after the Guarantor performs all of its obligations pursuant to Article 10, the Purchaser shall immediately upon the happening of such event, pay to the Guarator all outstanding obligations pursuant to Article 11.

Article 16 (Special Agreement in Relation to Reservation of Ownership)

(1) The ownership of the Product shall be transferred to the Finance Corp. when the Advance Commission Contract between the Purchaser and the Finance Corp. becomes effective and shall be held by the Finance Corp. until the obligations of the Purchaser to the Finance Corp. under the Advance Commission Contract have been paid in full or otherwise cease to exist; provided, however, that the Purchaser shall not object to the Product being registered in the name of the Dealer on behalf of the Finance Corp.

(2) In the event that the Guarantor performs, on behalf of the Purchaser, any of its obligations pursuant to Article 10 hereof, the ownership of the Product shall be transferred from the Finance Corp. to the Guarantor and shall be held by the Guarantor until all obligations of the Purchaser to the Guarantor in connection therewith have been fulfilled. In such event, the Purchaser shall not object to the transfer from the Dealer to the Guarantor of ownership of the Product.

(3) As long as the ownership is held by the Finance Corp. or the Guarantor, the Purchaser shall provide such care for the Product as would be provided by any good manager and shall in no case commit any act which would constitute a disposition of all or a part of the ownership of the Product including, but not limited to, any pledge, transfer or lease of the Product.

(4) In the event of the occurrence of a threat to ownership of the Product by any third party, the Purchaser shall promptly, upon becoming aware of such threat, notify the Finance Corp. or the Guarantor of such threat and shall forthwith endeavor to eliminate such threat by asserting and verifying, in any manner that may be necessary, that the Product is under the ownership of the Finance Corp. or the Guarantor.

(5) The Purchaser shall in no event change the original condition of the Product either by alteration or damage or otherwise.

Article 17 (Taking the Product into Custody and Evaluation/Appropriation)

(1) Upon the occurrence of any of the events of default set forth in Article 6, the Finance Corp. may take the Product into custody based on its reservation of ownership.

(2) In the event the Guarantor performs, on behalf of the Purchaser, its obligations pursuant to Article 10, the Guarantor may take the Product into custody based on its reservation of ownership pursuant to Article 16(2).

(3) In the event the Finance Corp. or the Guarantor takes the Product into custody pursuant to paragraphs (1) or (2) above, as the case may be, and sells the Product for an amount to be determined by a valuation by [ ] or any other qualified entity, the Purchaser agrees that the sale proceeds shall be applied first to cover the expenses of collection and disposal of the Product and second to repay the outstanding obligations of the Purchaser to the Finance Corp. or the Guarantor, as the case may be; provided however, that if the said amount is not sufficient to cover such expenses and outstanding obligations, the Purchaser shall immediately pay any deficiency.

(4) In the event the Finance Corp. or the Guarantor takes the Product into custody from the Purchaser pursuant to paragraphs (1) or (2) above, the Finance Corp. or the Guarantor, as the case may be, shall be entitled to retain the Product together with any items attached thereto and the Purchaser shall have no claim against the Finance Corp. or the Guarantor, as the case may be, for refund or compensation or otherwise with respect to the loss of such items.

Article 18 (Burden of Costs, etc.)

Article 19 (Burden of Taxes, etc.)

Article 20 (Defense of Suspension of Payment)

(1) If any of the following events occur, the Purchaser may suspend payment for the Product until such event is remedied:

(i) the Product is not delivered;
(ii) the Product when delivered is damaged, defaced, broken or has any other defect; or
(iii) any other event occurs in respect of the Product which would, at law, entitle the Purchaser to suspend payment for the Product.

(2) The Purchaser shall notify the Finance Corp. or the Guarantor of any suspension of payment pursuant to paragraph (1) above and the Finance Corp. or the Guarantor, as the case may be, shall immediately take all the necessary procedures to remedy such event.

(3) Prior to providing notification pursuant to paragraph (2), the Purchaser shall first endeavor to negotiate with the Dealer to remedy the event giving rise to the need to notify.

(4) In providing notification pursuant to paragraph (2), the Purchaser shall endeavor to promptly submit a written notice together with all relevant materials, if any, to the Finance Corp. or the Guarantor setting forth the details of the relevant event. Furthermore, if the Finance Corp. or the Guarantor determines it necessary to investigate any event referred to above, the Purchaser shall cooperate in such investigation.

(5) Notwithstanding the provisions of paragraph (1), in the event of any of the following, the Purchaser may not suspend payment:

(i) the Sales Contract is deemed to be a commercial act of the Purchaser;
(ii) the aggregate amount left to be paid in respect of the Product is less than forty thousand yen (¥40,000); or

(iii) the suspension of payment by the Purchaser is deemed not to be made in good faith.

Article 21 (Joint Guarantor)

Article 22 (Notice of Change of Address and Name, etc.)

Article 23 (Notarial Deed)

The Purchaser and the Guarantor shall execute a notarial deed at the expense of the Purchaser with respect to the Guarantee Commission Contract approving such methods of enforcement as the Guarantor deems to be necessary and agreeing to submit any necessary documents to the Guarantor.

Article 24 (Transfer of Rights)

The Purchaser and the Guarantor shall agree that the Finance Corp. may transfer, whenever it deems it necessary, its rights under the Advance Commission Contract to any financial institution with which the Finance Corp. or the Guarantor has business relations.

Article 25 (Consent to Registration under or Scrutiny by Information Investigation Agency)

Article 26 (Agreed Jurisdiction)

13.2.1.4 Servicing agreement

The finance company and the guarantor enter into a servicing agreement pursuant to which the guarantor agrees to (1) guarantee the payments under the loan and (2) act as a collector of the installment payments to be made by the purchaser to the finance company.

13.2.2 Legal problems

For the purposes of this analysis, we have set forth in Figure 13.3 (Appendix) an example of a structure used in a securitization. This is a simple form of securitization in which a SPC would purchase automobile loans from a finance company and issue securities such as bonds or commercial paper to investors. This structure and the problems associated with it are examined below.

13.2.2.1 The purchasers

When structuring and pricing a securitization it is possible to make legitimate assumptions regarding the potential default risk of the purchasers under the subject automobile loans because the past default rate of automobile loans is well documented. In addition, the fact that the purchasers' obligations will be fulfilled by the guarantor in case of default can also be taken into consideration. Therefore, adjustments for potential loan defaults can be made when the loans are purchased from the finance company.

13.2.2.2 The finance company

The automobile loans are sold by the finance company to the SPC which then issues the securities which will be sold to the investors. It is imperative that the transaction be clearly structured as a sale because, under Japanese law, if it is unclear whether the transaction is actually a sale, then it is possible that, in the event of the finance company becoming bankrupt or undergoing insolvency reorganization, the transaction will be treated as a secured loan. This is not as serious in a bankruptcy because under the Bankruptcy Law such loans can be dealt with outside of the bankruptcy proceedings and are actually given a priority in payment (Bankruptcy Law §92 and §95). However, under the Reorganization Law the loans must be repaid in the reorganization procedure. This would cause serious difficulties under the terms of the securitization.

To avoid the possibility of either the Finance Company assigning the loan to another entity or some other entity attaching the loan, the SPC would need to perfect the assignment. The Japanese Civil Code provides for perfection as follows:

ARTICLE 467

1. The assignment of a nominative claim cannot be set up against the obligor or any other third person, unless the assignor has given notice thereof to the obligor or the obligor has consented thereto.

2. The notice or consent mentioned in the preceding paragraph cannot be set up against a third person other than the obligor, unless it is put in a writing under a notarial act (*kakutei-hizuke*).

In addition, it is important to notice the provisions of the Bankruptcy Law §74 and the Reorganization Law §80. According to these provisions, an entity is protected if it has perfected its right (even after the filing of a petition for bankruptcy or reorganization) not more than 15 calendar days after the assignment. If it perfects its right after the filing of a petition for bankruptcy or reorganization and more than 15 calendar days have elapsed between the date of the assignment and the date of perfection, such assignment can be avoided by the trustee in the bankruptcy or reorganization proceedings.

A more serious problem arises in dealing with the requirement for notice with certified date. In Japan, to obtain a certified date, certified content letters (*Naiyoshoumei*) must be sent. However, because they have serious financial implications for the purchasers, a business decision is often made not to send such certified content letters until the seller's (finance company's) financial condition significantly deteriorates. However, practical problems arise in waiting until that point because letters then must be sent in respect of thousands of loans and unfortunately, because of the post office's lack of capacity, it takes several days to send that number of certified content letters.

In the event of the bankruptcy of the finance company, the servicing agreement, which is in the legal form of a mandate (*Inin*), would terminate and the obligations of the guarantor under the servicing agreement to act as collection agent would not be enforceable. However, despite the termination, the guarantee obligations would still exist and consequently, the guarantor would have an interest in continuing to serve as collection agent.

13.2.2.3 Collection agent

The main concern in respect of the collection agent is the effect the insolvency of the collection agent would have on the securitization. The money received by the collection agent belongs to the collection agent because of the nature of money, i.e. the ownership of money is vested in the person who actually possesses it. The servicing agreement is, as noted above, terminated upon the issuance of the bankruptcy order, however, it does not automatically terminate upon the filing of a petition for bankruptcy or reorganization. Therefore, the provisions of the servicing agreement should provide for its termination in the event of the filing of a petition for bankruptcy or reorganization. In the event such termination requires prior notice, the time limits involved in giving notice may cause problems where the delay results in a loss of money. In addition, if the servicing agreement provides for a gap between the receipt of money and payment by the collection agent, the SPC will be treated as an unsecured creditor with respect to such monies.

13.2.2.4 Dealer

The dealer retains ownership of the cars as security. However, such ownership is held on behalf of the finance company (after the assignment, SPC), and consequently, the cars do not form part of the assets of the dealer. Therefore, the finance company (after the assignment, SPC) is protected as an owner even in the event of the dealer's bankruptcy or reorganization.

13.2.2.5 SPC

2.5.1 (1) The SPC's only assets should be the auto loans because it is intended to be a bankruptcy-remote entity, i.e. a company not likely to become the subject of bankruptcy proceedings.

(2) Under Japanese law, the corporate veil can be disregarded when it is determined that (1) the corporation exists solely to avoid the application of certain regulations, or (2) there is only one shareholder and the corporation is, in reality, merely a shell. Since evidence that the shareholder and the corporation are, in reality, one and the same entity (such as the commingling of the assets of

the corporation and the shareholder) could allow for the piercing of the corporation veil, it is important that the assets and activities of the SPC be kept as separate and distict as possible from those of the other participants in the securitization.

At the very least, the SPC should have:

(a) a separate office;
(b) separate and independent directors (especially from the directors of the transferor of the loans);
(c) separate books;
(d) separate administration of funds obtained from the issuance of the securities;
(e) sufficient of its own capital to operate its business; and
(f) the intent to obtain a profit in any business in which it engages with related companies.

(3) In Japan, under the Commercial Code, there was, until recently, a limit on the total volume of bonds or notes which could be issued by a corporation. Though such provision was recently abolished, it is still necessary to provide initial capital in the amount of ten million yen (¥10,000,000) to establish a company in Japan. In addition, an ordinance of the Ministry of Finance establishes specific criteria which must be met by a company in order to issue bonds. For example, in order to issue straight public bonds, a company must be rated BBB or higher. The details of such criteria should be examined before attempting to implement a securitization plan. These provisions make it more difficult to establish a SPC in Japan and for a SPC to issue securities in Japan.

(4) In order to issue securities outside Japan, the loans would have to be transferred outside of Japan. However, under the Foreign Exchange and Foreign Trade Control Law, a transfer of loans from Japan to a jurisdiction outside of Japan needs the approval of the Ministry of Finance (§21,1,1). This provision is also applicable even if the Tokyo branch of the SPC was simply transferring loans to the head office of the SPC outside of Japan. One possible way around such a problem is for the SPC to provide such loans in Japan as security for the securities of the SPC's head office.

13.2.3 Conclusion

From our brief explanation of auto loan securitization in Japan, it can be seen that, while it is not easy to effect securitization in Japan, from a legal point of view, it is not prohibited. However, the reality is that companies in Japan are not eager to engage in securitization, although they have studied the possibilities. One reason why Japanese companies are not eager to engage in securitization is that companies which have sufficient assets to engage in securitization can usually obtain funds from banks at a low cost. Therefore, they cannot see the need to implement securitization which would usually require a greater initial outlay of money at the time of the structuring of the transaction.

Therefore, until such time as (1) it becomes more difficult for Japanese companies to obtain funds from banks, and (2) Japanese companies realize securitization can be, in the long term, cost saving because the management of the SPC is very stable and restricted (when compared with the management of ordinary companies), securitization will not grow in popularity in Japan.

HIROSHI MAEDA
KAYOKO NAITO
LAWRENCE WILDE

APPENDIX

FIGURE 13.2

(1) CASH FLOW

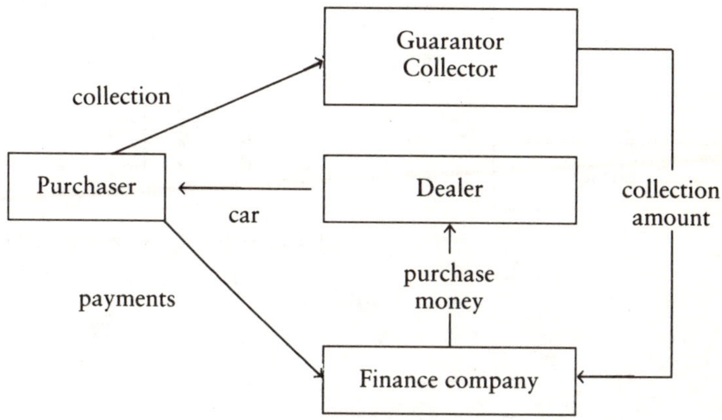

(2) AGREEMENTS

(Note: - - - - loan agreement)

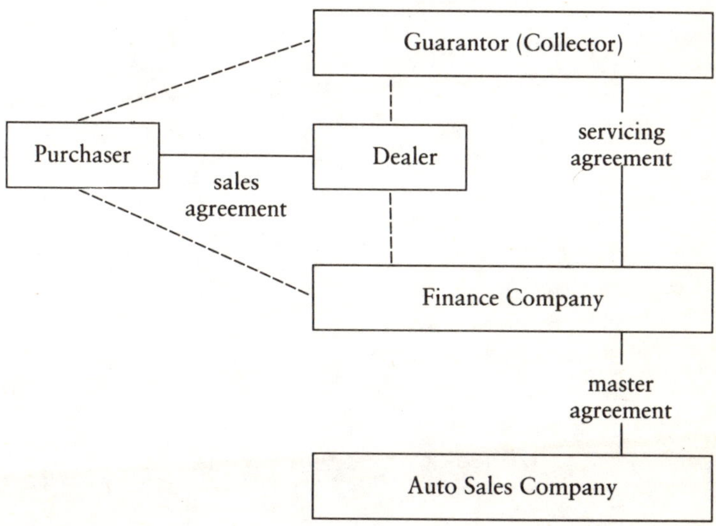

FIGURE 13.3

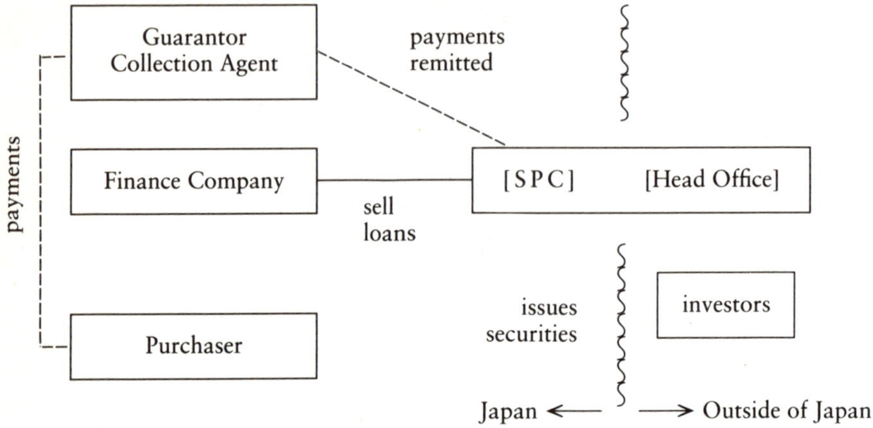
Guarantor
Collection Agent
payments
remitted
payments
Finance Company
sell
loans
[SPC]
[Head Office]
issues
securities
investors
Purchaser
Japan
Outside of Japan

CHAPTER 14

ASSET SECURITISATION IN SWITZERLAND

14.1 INTRODUCTORY SUMMARY

The Swiss market for asset-backed financings is a very recent development and though there are several projects in the pipeline, only one has come to the market at the time of writing. The reason for the slow development is not the legal and accounting environment, which does not pose major problems. The regulatory framework, however, imposes some restrictions on financial institutions wishing to participate in securitisation transactions and an unfavourable tax regime will also in the future prevent originators from issuing asset-backed securities using a Swiss SPV. Capital is still rather cheap and larger entities tend to have easy access to credit. As a consequence, costs of funds will normally be less important as a reason for securitising assets than it might be in other jurisdictions. Securitisation is currently most attractive for the following three groups of potential originators:

(i) originators in distress;
(ii) originators which have no access to the international capital markets because they are either not rated or too small;
(iii) originators which profit from tax advantages.

Costs of a securitisation are still very high in Switzerland because there is no standard documentation and much education of the parties involved is still necessary. High transaction costs require big transaction amounts, which limit the number of standalone SPVs. It is, therefore, expected that international multi-seller vehicles will be the driving market force in the years to come. Currently, not only US, UK and German but also two Swiss banks operate such vehicles. It may also be expected that Swiss originators will use the technique more and more but because of the tax regime, the debt issues backed by Swiss receivables will be made and placed outside Switzerland.

The first section of this chapter reviews the structures available for securitisations under Swiss law. The second section focuses on legal and tax issues related to non-financial institutions. A third section looks at the regulatory environment affecting financial institutions.

14.2 STRUCTURES AVAILABLE UNDER SWISS LAW

14.2.1 Pass-through structures

Pass-through securities represent ownership of an undivided interest in a pool of assets. Interest and principal payments are passed through to the owners of the securities on a pro-rata basis by the servicer or the trustee of the pool. The only structure available in Switzerland for pass-through instruments is an investment fund under the new Investment Fund Act which came into force on January 1, 1995. Given the strong opposition of the Federal Banking Commission to the use of investment funds for mortgage securitisation, it will not be easy to use an investment fund as a vehicle for the securitisation of assets. It is expected that the supervisory body will also oppose the use of investment funds as vehicles for the securitisation of non-mortgage assets unless a high level of credit enhancement protects the investors. Although credit enhancement is currently unknown to Swiss investment funds, there should be no legal objection to providing credit enhancement to protect the value of a fund (by insulating it against losses up to a maximum agreed amount) because economically there is no difference between credit enhancement and buying portfolio insurance such as, e.g., the purchase of a covered put option.[1]

14.2.2 Pay-through structures

Pay-through securities are general obligation bonds of the issuer (SPV), the cash flow of which is linked to the cash flow of the underlying collateral. Although in theory, various forms of companies are available to form an SPV under Swiss law, only a company limited by shares is a real alternative. The debt instrument issued by the company does not give the investors title to the pool of assets held by the company. The investor has a mere claim against the SPV which would be secured by a security interest over the assets sold by the originator to the SPV. Depending on the way the pay-through SPV is refinanced, the SPV may fall within the province of the Swiss Banking Act, thus making a full banking licence necessary. Under the revised Banking Act which came into force on February 1, 1995, an SPV issuing bonds and acquiring debts of indiscriminate third parties will no longer be considered a bank.[2]

14.2.3 Multi-seller programmes

Two of the big three Swiss Banks operate multi-seller vehicles but none of these vehicles is located in Switzerland. The banks have only started their marketing efforts in Switzerland recently and market participants know of just two

1. Federal Banking Commission, Circular 18 on investment funds, dated 3 October, 1988.

2. Markus Kroll, "Securitisation—Arbitrage in der Unternehmensfinanzierung", *Der Schweizer Treuhänder* (October 1993), p. 763.

planned or carried on transactions involving Swiss originators at the time of writing. Activity is expected to increase, however, over the next few years.

14.3 ASSET SECURITISATION BY NON-FINANCIAL INSTITUTIONS

Thus far, only asset-backed financings in the non-financial sector have taken place. This is probably due to the fact that the regulatory environment of the banking sector makes securitisations for financial institutions much more complex than for non-financial institutions.

14.3.1 Assignability of assets and notification under Swiss law

All kinds of claims are freely assignable in full or in part under Swiss law provided that

(i) there is no express statutory prohibition against the assignment,
(ii) there is no clause in the underlying contract prohibiting the assignment, and
(iii) the nature of the claim is not irreconcilable with the assignment.[3]

Notification is not necessary to make title pass or to prevent further assignments.[4]

14.3.2 Insolvency aspects

14.3.2.1 Insolvency of the originator

The SPV can to a large extent be insulated from the bankruptcy of the originator. Swiss law does not recognise the doctrine of substantive consolidation, which means that as long as the originator is not a shareholder in the SPV, creditors of the originator cannot lay claim to or attach the assets of the SPV in order to satisfy liabilities due from the originator. Complete insulation from the insolvency of the originator is not possible if over-collateralisation is used as a means of credit enhancement because the discounted purchase price of the assets might constitute a transaction at an undervalue, if done within the six months prior to the initiation of the liquidation and a discount rate clearly below market rates.[5] The transaction would, however, not be void; the SPV would only have to reimburse the difference between the market price and the price actually paid for the assets.[6]

3. Swiss Code of Obligations, Art. 164.
4. Gauch/Schluep, *Schweizerisches Obligationenrecht Allgemeiner Teil*, 5. Auflage (Zurich 1991), N3603.
5. Art. 286 Abs. 2 Ziff. 1 SchKG.
6. Federal Supreme Court decision 115 III 141.

14.3.2.2 Insolvency of the servicer

The bankruptcy of the servicer/administrator is no threat to the SPV as long as there is no commingling of funds in the servicer's collection account. If for business reasons no separate account can be used[7] for the collection on behalf of the SPV of receivables sold to it by the originator, only a timely notification may prevent the SPV from having to prove in the liquidation of the servicer (or originator) as an unsecured creditor.[8] This is the case because Swiss law does not recognise the trust concept.

14.3.2.3 Insolvency of the SPV

Only the shareholders, and not the directors, of a Swiss company (SPV) have the right to file a voluntary bankruptcy petition or to liquidate the company. It is therefore important that the originator is not a (major) shareholder of the SPV. Creditors may not force an SPV into involuntary liquidation unless the SPV is not paying its debts as they become due. Limiting the business, in which the SPV can engage in, is the obvious solution to this risk. Investment funds can be structured in such a way that the SPV can only be dissolved with the consent of the investors in the fund.

14.3.3 Data protection

The first Swiss Data Protection Act[9] came into force on July 1, 1993. The impact of the Act on securitisations and similar transactions such as factoring is not completely clear as the law gives only general guidance and there is no case law yet. The compilation of data on the customers of the originator qualifies probably as data collection as defined in the Act and when passed on to third parties abroad (such as the servicer and the agent/trustee of the transaction) such transfer probably requires notification to the relevant authorities in Switzerland. No consent of the persons affected by the data will, usually, be required prior to its being provided to third parties such as the SPV, any third party servicer or a trustee.

14.3.4 Consumer Credit Act

The Consumer Credit Act[10] which came into force on April 1, 1994 has probably only a limited impact on securitisations: its scope is limited to unsecured loans to individuals for consumer purposes and to amounts of less than SFr 40,000 (approx. $30,000) with a payment period in excess of usually three months. This means that credit card receivables will normally not fall under the Act. A debt arising under a regulated consumer credit agreement is not

7. A separate collection account would not fall in the liquidation estate (BGE 102 II 301).
8. Swiss Code of Obligations, Art. 167 para. 1.
9. SR 235.1.
10. SR 221.214.1.

severable from the underlying purchase contract between the seller or provider of servicers and his customer. If the seller does not fully discharge his obligations under the sales contract, the consumer is not obliged to fulfill his obligations under the credit agreement. The consumer/borrower has the right to repay the loan early and he has the right to veto the assignment of the loan.[11] For these and other reasons, consumer credits are quite difficult to securitise.

14.3.5 Taxes

Switzerland's tax regime is not very attractive for securitisations. A securitisation structure based either on a Swiss company limited by shares or on a Swiss investment fund would lead to additional tax liabilities as compared to a direct loan financing.

14.3.5.1 SPV as a company limited by shares in Switzerland (pay-through structure)

If the SPV is a company limited by shares with its (legal or factual) seat or a permanent establishment in Switzerland, it will be subject to rather high Swiss income and capital tax.[12] Further, there is a stamp duty on the issue of share capital and debt instruments[13] and there are thin capitalization rules that would prevent the use of the typical, highly-geared SPV structure.

Value added tax will probably not be payable on the underlying receivable but will have to be paid on the administration commission.[14] A hefty withholding tax of 35 per cent would apply, however, to all payments to investors exceeding the amount they initially paid in or which exceeds nominal share capital.[15]

14.3.5.2 SPV as a Swiss investment fund (pass-through structure)

Income or net assets of investment funds in Switzerland are not subject to tax. Following changes to the Stamp Duty Act in 1993, the issue of certificates is free of stamp taxes. There is, however, still a withholding tax of 35 per cent on all disbursements constituting income of the fund.[16] As long as there is a withholding tax, the certificates cannot be placed with investors abroad. There is, however, a parliamentary initiative pending that will eventually improve the situation.[17]

11. Arts. 12 and 13, Consumer Credit Act.

12. Art. 57 ff., Federal Income Tax Act ("FITA") and Art. 24 ff., Tax Harmonisation Act; Art. 73 ff., FITA and Art. 29 ff., Tax Harmonisation Act.

13. Arts. 5 and 9a, Stamp Duty Act.

14. At the time of writing, the Swiss VAT was not in force yet. It is therefore not possible to refer to case law to confirm the author's understanding of the law.

15. Art. 4, Withholding Tax Act.

16. Art. 9, Withholding Tax Act.

17. Motion der Mehrheit für Rechtsfragen des Nationalrates vom 26. Oktober 1993 (93.3528).

14.3.5.3 SPV as a company limited by shares with its seat outside Switzerland

As long as the foreign SPV has no place of business in Switzerland, there is no income or capital tax due in Switzerland. A Swiss withholding tax would, however, be levied on interest payments made by the SPV to investors. The reason for this "extraterritorial" taxation is that Swiss tax authorities view the sale of the assets of a Swiss company to the SPV in order to enable the latter to issue bonds as an economic guarantee. It is a well established practice that interest on debt instruments issued by a "subsidiary" abroad with a guarantee of the Swiss parent company with the issue proceeds flowing into Switzerland is subject to Swiss withholding tax.[18] The tax authorities have not yet established clear guidelines with respect to securitisation. There are, however, structures which supposedly are not subject to Swiss withholding tax.

14.3.6 Accounting issues

Swiss accounting rules are much less detailed than US or UK GAAP or IAS, which are more and more used by Swiss multinationals. Under Swiss rules, there is much more reliance on general principles which favour a very "cautious and prudent" approach. It is, therefore, rather easy to derecognise an asset even if some benefit remains with the seller of the asset. If risk associated with the sold asset remains with the originator, such risk has, however, to be accounted for though not necessarily in the full amount of the assets sold. Accounting is, thus, no obstacle to securitisations.[19]

14.4 ASSET SECURITISATION BY FINANCIAL INSTITUTIONS

So far, there have been no securitisations by financial institutions in Switzerland. An attempt by a cantonal bank to securitise mortgages, act as servicer, use its state guarantee as credit enhancement and to underwrite the issue was not a structure acceptable to the Federal Banking Commission as a disposal of the assets for capital adequacy purposes. As a consequence, the transaction was aborted.

In addition to the general legal and tax aspects outlined in the section above, there are regulations that apply to financial institutions only, as described below.

18. Swiss Bankers' Association, Circular No. 6746, dated 29 June, 1993.
19. See also: Markus Kroll, "Securitisation—Arbitrage in der Unternehmensfinanzierung", footnote 2 *supra*, p. 761 ff.

14.4.1 Banking secrecy

Unlike in many common law countries, Switzerland's banking secrecy is a statutory obligation of the banks, making even a negligent breach a criminal offence.[20] There are circumstances that allow a bank to breach the banking secrecy, e.g. when assigning claims against customers to a bank or a finance company in order to refinance the bank.[21] Most securitisation transactions could probably not rely on this exemption. Disclosure of customer information by a bank to the acquirer of bank assets would thus in many cases constitute a breach of the banking secrecy obligation, unless the customer consents, e.g. in advance when signing the initial contract with the bank.

14.4.2 Regulatory environment

The Federal Banking Commission ("FBC") has not yet made public a policy with regard to securitisation.[22] The FBC would take, however, an approach in line with the Basle Committee on Banking Supervision. The FBC has raised concerns with regard to the following:

14.4.2.1 Banks as originators

In order to derecognise an asset for capital adequacy purposes, the FBC employs a more stringent definition of "true sale" than the one used for accounting or legal purposes. In particular, if loans to individuals are sold to a special purpose vehicle, it must be made clear that neither the holder of the securities (investor) nor the original customer of the bank can rely on the pity or generosity of the bank in times of hardship (moral risk). This seems to imply that the customer must be notified about the assignment of his debt.

The FBC would also look at the impact the sale of assets has on the remaining balance sheet. It would require more than the minimum capital if the average quality of the remaining assets deteriorated significantly.

14.4.2.2 Banks as administrators

If banks are the originator and act as servicers/administrators, moral risk becomes an issue. Although the FBC would not as, a matter of principle, prevent a bank from taking on such a dual role, it would, again, require the bank to tell its customers that they cannot look to the bank for support if they default on their loans. A bank acting as independent administrator does not give raise to particular concerns.

20. Art. 47, Banking Act.

21. Bodmer/Kleiner/Lutz, *Kommentar zum schweizerischen Bankengesetz* (Zürich, looseleaf), Art. 47 N93.

22. Christopher McHale, "Bankenaufsichtsrechtliche Aspekte der Sekuritisierung", Presentation given at the Seminar "Securitization: Ein Finanzierungsmodell für Schweizer Banken und Unternehmen?" Mimeo, 22 June, 1994.

14.4.2.3 Banks as credit enhancers and liquidity providers

In terms of strict legal commitment, credit enhancement supports usually only a portion of the SPV's portfolio. Economically, it encompasses, however, total expected losses in a highly condensed form. Currently the Swiss banking supervisors are considering the appropriate amount of capital required to support credit enhancement activities. It is expected that in future more capital will be required to support credit enhancement facilities than is currently necessary for banks undertaking such commitments. Although Switzerland can at best be seen as an emerging securitisation market, any changes in the Swiss regulatory treatment of credit enhancement will be important as the big Swiss banks are, owing to their excellent rating, major credit enhancers in structured finance transactions.

Liquidity support will probably not be affected by more stringent capital adequacy requirements as long as there is no element of credit enhancement in it.

14.4.2.4 Consolidation of the SPV

The Banking Act applies a test of materiality for the definition of a subsidiary.[23] As long as the SPV is legally and economically remote from the bank and the transaction is a true sale also with regard to moral risk, no consolidation will be necessary.

14.4.2.5 Consolidation of multi-seller vehicles

Banks which sponsor multi-seller vehicles usually perform several functions within the structure of the vehicle. As long as there is no implicit guarantee given by the bank nor would support, for whatever reasons, have to be provided ("support-test") and the vehicle cannot be considered to be economically a part of the bank ("economic entity-test"), and as long as the vehicle can, as a matter of fact, act as an independent third party ("control-test"), no consolidation is necessary.[24]

14.5 MORTGAGE SECURITISATION[25]

Mortgage securitisation has been widely discussed in Switzerland especially during the years of rising interest rates (1989–1991). The general view in Switzerland seems to be that mortgage securitisation is desirable but that there are too many obstacles for the time being to the creation of a viable market for mortgage-backed securities. A first attempt to overcome these hurdles is

23. Art. 13, draft Banking Ordinance.
24. Art. 13, draft Banking Ordinance.
25. See for more details: Markus Kroll, "Will the new investment fund bill kick-start mortgage securitisation in Switzerland?", *International Securitisation Report* (November 1993), pp. 61–64.

the revised Investment Fund Act ("IFA") which expressly provides for mortgage investment funds and which came into force on January 1, 1995.

14.5.1 Huge mortgage market

The Swiss mortgage market is significant with roughly SFr450 bn outstanding, which is over 30 per cent more than the GNP of Switzerland.[26]

14.5.2 Typical mortgage instrument

Until 1981, mortgage loans were almost exclusively floating rate instruments. Fixed-interest-rate mortgage loans then became more popular and mortgage loans were introduced that postponed part of the interest payments on the mortgage loans to a later stage. It was common practice that there be no direct link between the instruments that refinanced the mortgage loans and the mortgage loans themselves. Since 1989, when interest rates rose sharply, fixed-rate mortgage loans have become less attractive to the banks, which are looking for instruments that more directly match the characteristics of the refinancing tools in terms of basis risk and maturity. Today, a first security-interest mortgage loan is typically a floating rate and, for tax reasons, non-amortizing instrument without a fixed term that can be terminated usually on six months' notice. A long-term refinancing of these instruments is, obviously, very risky from the banks' points of view as the mortgagor has the option to swap into another instrument whenever he sees an arbitrage opportunity. Only about 25 to 30 per cent of the first ranking mortgages are fixed-rate, fixed-term loans.

14.5.3 Inefficient and segmented mortgage market

Securitisation of mortgages is and will remain intricate for years to come as mortgage loans usually are not standarised either with regard to size, loan-to-value ratios or documentation. Mortgage market regulations vary depending on the canton, as each canton has the legal right to restrict the term of mortgages and to impose taxes on the creation of mortgages and the transfer of mortgage instruments other than promissory notes constituting bearer negotiable instruments. This leads to a highly segmented market with many regional and local specialities. More important than government regulations is, however, the political pressure on the market: rental payments are linked to the cost of mortgage loans. An increase in interest rates on mortgage loans can be (partially) rolled over to the tenants even if the house-owner has no debt outstanding. This

26. All figures and data on the mortgage market and interest rates are data taken from publications of the Swiss National Bank.

matters because the Swiss people are typically tenants and not house-owners. The link between the costs of mortgage loans and the setting of rental levels has two consequences. The first is that because as a matter of law the full interest costs of a mortgage cannot be passed on to the tenants, there is permanent over-demand in the rental market as incentives to build new houses are lacking. The second consequence is that when towards the end of the economic cycle prices and interest rates rise and tenants would prefer to cut down their expenses, rental rates increase. The resulting social impact of mortgage rate increases leads to political pressure which, without any formal state intervention, leads to such pressure on the banking sector that it subsidises mortgage lending itself by "voluntarily" putting a cap on the mortgage rates. Obviously, the problem only exists with floating-rate mortgages. The size of market distortion is enormous: the spread differential between the variable mortgage rate and six-month LIBOR varied between almost plus *and minus* 300 bp over the last 10 years. The higher LIBOR, the further away are the mortgage rates from LIBOR and the lower LIBOR, the higher the margin. It is obvious that in times of negative margins (if cheap deposits cannot be used), those banks whose core business is domestic mortgage lending come under immense pressure. The development of a secondary market for the most important assets of the smaller savings and loans institutions, that is mortgage loans, is becoming a question of survival especially since many investors moved money from the smaller banks to larger ones after the failure of Spar & Leihkasse Thun. Securitisation would offer such a secondary market.

House-owners have, historically, not paid directly for the cap on the mortgage rates, a fact that is slowly changing now. So far banks have been covering their costs of the cap in two ways: margins have been increased once interest rates have started to go down, that is, there is a subsidy across time. Somewhat counterproductively, interest groups representing tenants have been exerting political pressure on the banks to reflect immediately decreasing interest rates in the mortgage rates. As a result, banks have started to bring more and more instruments to the mortgage lending market that make the cap explicit and make the mortgagor pay for it by, for example, offering collared mortgage loans at rates which reflect market prices for the cap and the floor.

The second way to pay for the political cap on mortgage rates was to keep saving rates artificially low when interest rates started to rise. The margin between an open market rate such as LIBOR and deposit rates as published by the Swiss National Bank reflects exactly the level of the interest rate: rises in wholesale market interest rates have not been passed on to savers. Obviously, savers are less and less willing to subsidise home-owners and are moving their funds to higher yielding instruments, thus forcing the banks to pay rates close to market rates on saving accounts, which in turn makes the cap on mortgage rates even less sustainable in economic terms. Investors have become much more sensitive to interest rate changes as they have now easy access to higher yielding instruments such as money market funds which are not riskier than saving accounts. It will, thus, be just a matter of time before mortgage rates track market rates very closely.

14.5.4 Mortgage bonds as indirect securitisation

Roughly SFr25 bn (US $18 bn) of the Swiss mortgage market is refinanced by mortgage-backed bonds (*Pfandbriefe*) which are, and this may explain their lack of a wider acceptance with investors, an indirect form of refinancing: two special institutions issue bonds and lend the proceeds with a margin of roughly 10 per cent to mortgage banks which have, of course, their indebtedness and the mortgage loans on the balance sheet. The investors purchase, however, a very secure instrument as the banks which receive a loan from such a bond issuer have to pledge their mortgage interests to it. The mortgaged houses of the ultimate debtors serve thus as collateral in addition to the banks' duty to repay the loan and the issuing institution's balance sheet. For the so called "regional banks" and the cantonal banks these bonds are quite important as they provide 15 per cent and 9.2 per cent respectively of the refinancing of their mortgage loans. The very successful German version of the *Pfandbriefe* is much more attractive because the banks can issue the bonds directly, which saves cost and adds flexibility.

14.5.5 Attempted solution: revised Investment Fund Act

Many countries have introduced special legislation to make securitisation possible. Only the securitisation of mortgages presents a real problem under Swiss law and it is therefore not surprising that Switzerland intended to introduce a law facilitating mortgage securitisation. Instead of preparing a special bill, the revision of the Investment Fund Act was used to provide for the creation of a special type of funds, mortgage investment funds. The Act, which came into force on January 1, 1995, gives, however, only a very general framework. It was expected that the more important secondary legislation would give more guidance, but that is not the case. One might speculate that it is the lack of experience within the government department in charge of the secondary legislation coupled with the rigid opposition of the Federal Banking Commission to this type of investment that has delayed the clarification of the ordinance.

If, however, very stringent secondary legislation is not introduced, investors remain highly exposed: they will bear the whole risk of default on the mortgage pool because there is no compulsory credit enhancement and mortgage insurance is virtually unknown in Switzerland. All defaults on the mortgages would have an immediate effect on the performance of the pool, which directly determines the value of the individual investments. If a default occurs, the mortgagor's house, which ultimately is the collateral of the pool, must be sold. Liquidation by forced sale can take (depending on the canton) between one and two years after a default has occurred. Regulations will be necessary for the case where an investor sells his certificates after a default has occurred on underlying mortgage loans, and the fund receives the proceeds of the sale of collateral only some time after he sold his investment. Should the original investor be credited because the default on the mortgage payment occurred while he was the holder of an investment certificate, or should the next investor benefit? No solutions to this problem have been discussed so far.

The Act is piercing one of the key principles of Swiss investment fund legislation, namely the investors' right to redeem their certificates at any time. Instead of a right to redeem, the Act requires that the certificates be quoted on a stock exchange or the fund management organisation or the depository bank be under an obligation to repurchase the certificates.[27] This requirement creates, however, valuation problems. As floating-rate mortgages form the bulk of the market, they should probably also constitute the assets of the mortgage funds. Although valuation models of variable-rate mortgages with prepayment options exist, the valuation depends heavily on the underlying assumptions of the model. Valuation is, however, crucial to the existence and maintenance of an orderly secondary market for the certificates. As the mortgage loans are not standardised, even the most sophisticated investors will not be in the position to value a mortgage fund including floating-rate and defaulting mortgage loans in a consistent or reliable way. A solution to this dilemma is obvious: different classes of securities may be issued on the strength of a single pool of mortgages, some of which instruments will have a predictable cash flow, thus creating collateralised mortgage obligations.

14.5.6 Additional tax considerations

In addition to the tax considerations made above, a special tax may be imposed on the SPVs located outside Switzerland: the new Federal Income Tax Act, which came into force on January 1, 1995, includes a withholding tax on interest payments made abroad if they are secured with a security interest over Swiss real estate.[28] Cantons have or are about to introduce similar tax laws.[29]

14.5.7 Reaction to the revised IFA

The general response to the proposal was mixed. The Federal Banking Commission is against this kind of investment fund because all risks are passed to investors, which is contrary to the stated scope of the bill, namely, investor protection.[30] Other critics were more positive but still do not expect the structure to succeed in the market place because of the lack of transparency in

27. Art. 24, revised Investment Fund Act.
28. Art. 5, para 1, lit. c and Art. 51, para 1, lit. d, FITA.
29. Art. 35, para 1, lit. e, Tax Harmonisation Act.
30. Bundesgesetz über Anlagefonds, Bericht über die Vernehmlassungsergebnisse (July 1992), p. 15.

such funds. Experience gained in other jurisdictions might help to adapt the mortgage fund to a pass-through vehicle which, combined with credit enhancement, can offer investors a first-class low-risk investment opportunity. Without any protective measures for the benefit of investors, the mortgage fund proposal will in any event most probably not be accepted in the market, irrespective of the concerns of legislators to provide investor protection.

MARKUS J. KROLL

INDEX